FABRICS &
WALLPAPERS

FOR HISTORIC BUILDINGS

JANE C. NYLANDER

RICHARD C. NYLANDER

WILEY

JOHN WILEY & SONS, INC.

Library of Congress Cataloging-in-Publication Data:

Nylander, Jane C., 1938-
    Fabrics and wallpapers for historic buildings / by Jane C. Nylander and Richard C. Nylander.
        p. cm.
    Includes bibliographical references and index.
    ISBN 0-471-70655-8 (cloth : alk. Paper)
    1. Textile fabrics–Reproduction–Catalogs. 2. Wallpaper–Reproduction–Catalogs. 3.
    Historic buildings–Conservation and restoration. I. Nylander, Richard C. II. Title.

    TS1767.N93 2005
    747′.5–dc22
                                              2004043116

Printed in the United States of America

10 9 8 7 6 5 4 3 2 1

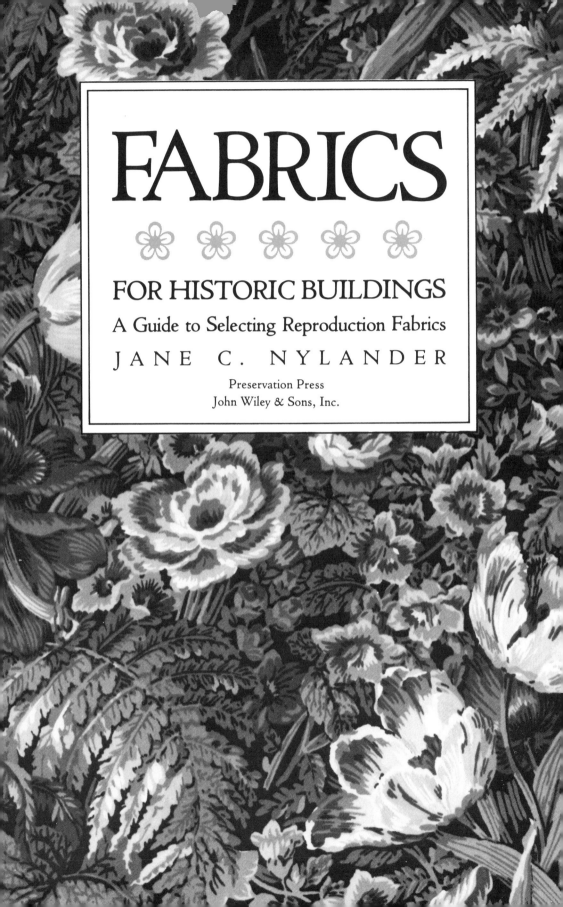

FABRICS

FOR HISTORIC BUILDINGS

A Guide to Selecting Reproduction Fabrics

JANE C. NYLANDER

Preservation Press
John Wiley & Sons, Inc.

Fourth edition

Printed in the United States of America
6 5 4 3

Library of Congress Cataloging in Publication Data

Nylander, Jane C., 1938–
    Fabrics for Historic Buildings: a guide to selecting reproduction
fabrics / Jane C. Nylander. — Rev. ed.
        p. cm.
    Includes bibliographical references.
    ISBN 0-471-14379-0
    1. Textile fabrics — Reproduction. 2. Historic buildings — Con-
servation and restoration I. Title
TS1767.N94 1990
747'.5 — dc20   90-44185

Cover and title page: FERNDALE, c. 1850. Schumacher. (See p. 143.)

Endleaves: LES SPHINX MEDAILLONS, c. 1810–20. Brunschwig & Fils.
(See p. 80.)

Pages 16–17: COMPAGNIE DES INDES, late 18th century. Clarence House.
(See p. 83.)

CONTENTS

CATALOG OF
REPRODUCTION
FABRICS

APPENDIX

INTRODUCTION

Fabric furnishings — window curtains and roller blinds, furniture upholstery and slipcovers, bed curtains and coverings, table coverings and other incidental ornamental fabrics — are a fundamental part of the restoration or period interpretation of any historic interior. The visual impact of a room is largely dependent on the design and color of the textiles used within it, and the impression of a particular historical period depends on the accuracy with which these textiles are selected and installed. Because textiles are highly perishable and because they are changed more frequently than architectural details, few original installations of furnishing fabrics are available for study. The fragility of antique textiles and their often faded condition render them unsuitable for restoration use. Carefully selected modern reproductions offer both greater durability and the intensity of color that once characterized the original fabrics. If such fabrics are used correctly, they contribute a great deal to the success of a restored interior.

This book is intended to help people with limited fabric experience select and order documentary reproduction fabrics as well as other kinds of fabrics that are suitable for furnishing historic properties. While the book addresses basic historical, curatorial and practical considerations, it is not intended as a substitute for the careful study of period documents, secondary sources and both original and reproduction fabrics themselves.

The catalog sections of this book list reproductions of fabrics used in the United States between 1650 and 1955. They are organized by period and fabric type. Brief discussions of the characteristic fabric furnishing styles of each period are provided as a general guide to the evolution of

An example of restoration work in which currently available fabrics (Brunschwig & Fils's "Bird and Thistle" and "Coralito") were selected to approximate the visual effect, color and date of the original documented set of bed hangings. (The John Brown House, Providence, R.I.)

7

fabric design, changes in textile technology and popular styles of drapery and upholstery. These discussions should be supplemented by study of books cited in the bibliography and by specific research related to the restoration or furnishings problem at hand. A glossary is included to provide information about specific textile terminology and guide the reader to illustrations that may be useful if no collection of historic fabrics is available for study.

The catalog entries provide specific information for selecting and ordering commercial reproduction fabrics. Where it was not possible to illustrate designs, references to illustrations in other published sources have been given. The companies listed are highly regarded for the quality of their products. Fabric companies change their offerings as often as once or twice a year, introducing new designs, retaining successful patterns and discontinuing those that do not sell well or present production difficulties. As a result, the reader should keep in mind that some fabrics listed in this book may be discontinued and that new and appropriate but unlisted patterns may be introduced. Fortunately, some manufacturers keep the printing screens and weaving patterns of discontinued styles, and in such cases it may be possible to obtain a discontinued design through special order.

The fabrics reproduced commercially today are more an indication of their present popularity than a reflection of their popularity in their original period. The years following 1900 saw an increasing use of 18th-century silk damask and brocade designs in traditional interiors; in less formal rooms, reproductions of copperplate-printed textiles called "toiles" were popular, and the bold two-color resist prints had an especially strong appeal in the 1950s and 1960s. Period rooms in museums as well as traditional interiors in private homes made abundant use of these types of fabric. Many accurate reproductions of period textiles were commissioned for specific restoration projects, but the fact that they have remained commercially viable reflects their present popularity. As a result, some fabrics that were rare in 18th-century America, such as woven silks and resist prints, are now reproduced and used in great quantities, while the more commonly used woolen textiles are seldom reproduced.

This situation is changing to reflect new trends in historic house restoration and popular taste. The new interest in accurate and well-documented interior restoration has resulted in the careful reproduction of more of the common period textiles. A much greater variety of reproductions of 18th-century wools can now be found, and more are being planned. Also, the last five years have seen an abundance of the boldly patterned floral chintzes popular in the mid-Victorian period. Many newly reproduced designs reflect the growing interest in late 19th- and early 20th-century design. Fabrics must be chosen carefully, however. Today's ready availability of designs by William Morris and the Viennese designers of the early 20th century and the appeal of these designs to the late 20th-century eye do not necessarily mean that they were the first choice of average late 19th-century Americans, any more than rich silk damasks were found in the houses of average Americans during the colonial period. The range of fabric designs available in any period responds to the demands of the marketplace. Although reproduction fabrics are a strong component of the modern market, they are not all used in restoration work. The simple availability of a handsome design does not necessarily mean that it is right for restoration work; detailed research must govern fabric selection.

WHY USE REPRODUCTIONS?

Why should fabric reproductions be considered for use if original fabric is available? Period designs usually call for so much yardage that the use of antique textiles would be impossible. In those rare cases where original curtains or ample original yardage has survived, preservation of the original materials should be the primary goal. In most cases these original fabrics have survived only because they have been carefully protected from light, dirt and insects; exposure would only hasten their destruction. Virtually no circumstances justify the damage caused to original textiles by exposure to light and dust for long periods.

Displaying certain antique textile items such as quilts or other bed coverings may be acceptable on a short-term basis, provided the light in the room can be controlled and other damaging factors eliminated. No antique quilt should be displayed on a bed where guests are encouraged to pile their coats during a party or animals are permitted to sleep. If original textiles cannot be protected and rotated regularly, reproductions should be substituted for everyday display. In no case should original textiles be left out for long periods of time.

The practice of cutting up original bed curtains, bedspreads, quilts, coverlets and other historic textiles for curtains, table covers, upholstery or clothing also should be avoided. Such uses are historically inaccurate as well as destructive. Even cutting up old linen sheets or homespun blankets for use as curtains or as a ground for embroideries is unacceptable. This practice is also impractical: the weakened antique fibers will not survive long, and the new work will soon be lost as well.

The use of reproduction fabrics, therefore, allows the preservation of original documents while re-creating authentic period effects. An additional benefit of using reproductions is that the fabrics can be cleaned by modern commercial methods and can be replaced when necessary to maintain the freshness of the colors and appearance.

What Is a Reproduction Fabric?

A documentary reproduction fabric is a modern textile that copies as accurately as possible a historic original, or document. The fibers, width and repeat, and every detail of the design have been exactly copied. Some companies, notably Scalamandré, further define as a "historic representation" a fabric in which even one of these components has been altered. All agree that when even more elements have been changed, the product is an "adaptation." In an adaptation the fibers, colors or scale may have been altered or the design simplified somehow. In the catalog sections of this book, these terms are used carefully and changes from original documents noted whenever possible.

In some cases fabrics that are not specifically termed documentary reproductions are also suitable for restoration work. One should consider carefully the use of adaptations or historic interpretations in which the fiber content has been changed from expensive 100 percent silk to cotton or synthetic fibers, for example, or the scale of a design has been altered slightly to fit power looms. Many such fabrics are listed in the catalog sections, with detailed information about the changes that have been made from the original documents. They may not be perfect, but they are often the best available option.

Some mid- or late 19th-century and some 20th-century designs have never been discontinued. In addition, plain-woven fabrics of pure fibers, such as silk taffeta, cotton organdy or mohair velvet, which have changed little over time, are still available from a variety of commercial sources. Machine technology has produced some alterations in width and texture, but by and large these changes are acceptable in restoration work. Some specific examples and sources of nondocumentary fabrics appropriate for historic buildings are cited in chapter 7, but these are only suggestions.

DOCUMENTARY RESEARCH BEFORE FABRIC SELECTION

A common mistake in the restoration of historic interiors is to neglect preliminary documentary research and instead arbitrarily select a date for restoration (often the date of original construction of the building) and then look for beautiful designs and materials appropriate to that date. Some of the interiors created by this procedure would probably astonish the original owners, who might never have dreamed of having silk draperies made from designs published in Paris the year they were married.

Few projects will have the documentary evidence and surviving material to ensure accurate restoration to a single early date. The selection of a broad time frame, on the other hand, opens up a considerable range of choices. For example, what style of curtain is appropriate for an 18th-century house in which most of the furniture dates from the mid-19th century and which was inhabited by the same family from the time it was built to the early 1900s? Or what does one do with an otherwise Federal-style interior if original curtains survive from the 1870s? What if the room's function has changed? The choice of appropriate furnishings grows out of a comprehensive understanding of the property and its occupants, one that expands rather than limits the impression of the whole.

The first task in selecting fabrics for use in historic interiors is to establish the purpose of the restoration or rehabilitation and the extent and quality of existing documentation. The adequacy of documentary evidence may, in fact, determine whether the restoration is to emphasize an exact date or a broad historical period. If samples of original textile material (or written descriptions of colors and fabrics, early photographs or even drawings) have survived, then consider whether it is desirable to re-create a specific moment in the history of a particular room or building. If so, the search for commercially available reproductions that approximate the surviving documents can begin. Now is the time also to consider ordering custom reproductions of surviving fabric documents.

If, on the other hand, no evidence exists about the use of earlier furnishing textiles, what does one do? The first step is to undertake research in primary sources specifically related to the house and to similar houses in the same geographic area. These sources include inventories, diaries, letters, account books, photographs, paintings, newspapers, design books, advice books and magazines. It is important to know as much as possible about the interior before making any decisions. Ask these kinds of questions: How old is the building? Who built it? What purpose did it serve? How was each room used? If the building is a house, how many people lived there? How old were they? Were they married? If so, when? How many children did they have? How long did their descendants live there? Was this their first house? When was it remodeled and why? What was the owners' economic status within the community? Did they purchase furnishings locally? If not, did they order them from a commercial supplier? Did they have servants? If so, how many and what were their tasks? Did they travel? If so, where? What types of furnishings and architecture might they have seen? In other words, what sources of fabric and design were available to the owners within their known geographic and economic limitations? The answers to such questions will guide the researcher in gathering information and making decisions.

With the intent of the restoration determined and the historical research carefully done, decisions can then be made about the period to be represented. Because the furnishing fabrics will be a major factor in re-creating a period effect, the importance of selecting the fabrics and using them in proper context cannot be overemphasized. If possible, study original textiles from the selected period before choosing a reproduction fabric. Becoming familiar with the appearance of original textiles also provides a better basis for judging the accuracy of reproduction work. Many major art museums and historical societies maintain textile study collections that can be viewed by appointment. A good source for locating collections in a particular geographic area or with a given specialty is Cecil Lubell's three-volume guide *Textile Collections of the World.*

Some fabric manufacturers maintain archival collections of historic texiles as well as of their own productions through the years. Both the antique and the reproduction textiles in these archives serve as inspiration for contemporary designers within the firm and as touchstones of detail when an accurate reproduction is sought. For research in the history of 20th-century fabrics, these archives are an invaluable source, documenting the changing tides of taste and the patterns of historical revival and survival. As fabric companies reach significant anniversaries, several of them have reviewed their archives, sponsored exhibitions and published catalogs. Among the most helpful in this respect have been Schumacher, Scalamandré and Lee Jofa in New York and Warners, G.P.& J. Baker, Ltd., and Sandersons in London. The catalogs of these anniversary exhibitions are cited in the bibliography.

If it is not possible to examine original textiles firsthand in a museum or archive, one should study at least the details of design and printing illustrated in published sources. Probably the most helpful books are Florence Montgomery's *Printed Textiles* and *Textiles in America,* Clouzot and Morris's *Painted and Printed Fabrics,* Shoeser and Rufey's *English and American Textiles* and the catalogs of the Victoria and Albert Museum and the museums at Nantes, Mulhouse and Jouy, which are cited in the bibliography. Detailed photographs of original fabrics can be ordered from many textile study collections. There is no substitute for seeing the original example, however. Details and texture can seldom be conveyed accurately by photographs, and lens distortions may be misleading. Even studying the small scraps of fabric in well-preserved antique quilts can give you a feeling for the visual and textural character of the original documents, information that will be invaluable when judging the quality of a reproduction.

SELECTING REPRODUCTION FABRICS

The choice of a reproduction fabric should be guided by the results of historical research. However, one should understand that, no matter how expensive or how carefully the design and production have been supervised, fabric produced by modern methods will not exactly duplicate the original appearance of its historic counterpart. In addition, each restoration project will have specific economic and technical requirements that must be considered. Before attempting to choose from the fairly large selection of documentary reproduction fabrics currently on the market, it is crucial to define the variations of the original that are acceptable for the given project.

One might assume that the fiber must always be the same — that silk originals should be reproduced in silk, wool in wool, cotton in cotton. The possibility of using synthetic yarns, however, is likely to arise when the costs of silk or wool are considered and the durability of synthetics is compared with that of natural fibers. Persons responsible for restoration will have to decide whether they can afford the most technically accurate reproduction possible or whether a reasonably exact duplication of visual effect is the goal.

The current appeal of the "country" look has resulted in a large number of fabrics based on original period textiles but changed in such ways that they cannot be considered true reproductions. Handwoven coverlet designs have been printed on cotton. Embroidered and stenciled motifs from original pieces have been transposed onto printed fabric with little regard for the integrity of the original piece of which they were a part. Pieced and appliqued quilts, wall paintings, theorem paintings and hearth rugs have similarly been used as design sources with individual motifs carefully copied and repeated in yardage ad infinitum. Since the media have been changed and none of these original designs was intended to be used in endless repeats, these fabrics cannot be considered appropriate for restoration projects in which the goal is the accurate reproduction of the original visual effect. These designs are not listed in this book, but they may be found on the market with the names of prominent museums attached to them, a factor that may be misleading. The museums are well aware that these designs are adaptations; it is important that they be recognized for what they are and not used in serious restoration work until re-creating the period during which they have proven so popular — the 1980s.

In choosing a reproduction fabric, one should be aware of differences caused by the changing technology of textile production during the past 200 years. In no case can modern commercial spinning and weaving processes duplicate the appearance or texture of hand-production methods, nor can chemical dyes exactly duplicate the colors achieved by vegetable dyes. The silk-screen and steel-roller printing and the photoengraving methods usually used for reproductions cannot exactly duplicate the visual effects of the original block or copperplate printing or of hand engraving. Some reproductions using these methods do remarkably well, but inevitably some detail is lost.

The standard loom sizes also have changed; modern warps are longer and widths are greater than those of earlier periods. In some cases the original printed or woven designs can be doubled in width to fit the wider cloth, but more often they must be adjusted slightly in size in order to produce a unified design. Sometimes large copperplate designs cannot be reworked into modern widths; in those cases, the original design may be reproduced with large unprinted areas at the sides, or it may be significantly reduced in size. Woven silk designs are sometimes stretched horizontally to fit the specifications of commercial loom widths while the vertical dimension of the design is not enlarged. Damask designs may be reduced vertically by half, retaining only one of the original motifs.

Selecting the correct texture of goods for printing or yarns for woven designs is crucial to the success of a reproduction. Be aware that the original document has probably lost body through wear and cleaning. On the other hand, if too coarse a texture is selected for printed designs, design detail will be lost. Slubs, or lumps on threads, which in the past were regarded as undesirable imperfections in spinning, should not be arbitrarily added to modern goods in an attempt to make them look old. Reproduction of faded color or background discoloration through the use of "aged grounds" does a disservice to a design that was printed originally on white cotton or linen. Similarly, it is not necessary to dip a new fabric in tea to make it look old.

The use of undocumented colors is inappropriate in authentic restorations. In most commercial reproduction fabrics, the color of the original is reproduced and designated the document color, such as "document blue" or "documentary colorway." Most commercial reproductions are available in nondocumentary colors as well, in which case the original color is often listed as 1 in the catalog code number series for that fabric. One or two of the other available colors may have been possible historically, but in most cases the modern colors were unknown in the past and could not have been created with the dye technology then in use. An accurate restoration project must be designed within the framework of the technology of the restoration period, no matter how repetitious or strange it may seem.

Sometimes an acceptable reproduction is entirely inappropriate for use as a furnishing fabric because the document would not have originally been used as such. Some accurately reproduced clothing fabrics are currently available, but they are not usually suitable for interior restoration work. In rare cases, such a fabric might be used for a slipcover or a bed covering. Reproduction clothing fabrics are excellent, of course, for reproducing a pieced quilt. The key is to be sure that the reproduction fabric is used appropriately in the restoration context intended.

THE TRADE

Most of the fabrics listed in chapters 1–6 of this book are available only through design showrooms, which are accessible only to interior designers, architects and others in the trade. Some manufacturers will deal directly with curators, house committees and other authorized representatives of museums and historic houses. It is wise to determine a manufacturer's policy before appearing at a showroom and being turned away.

When writing to a manufacturer to request samples or a catalog, be sure to specify that the fabric sought is for restoration purposes. Some manufacturers will provide loan samples for restoration projects on request, and samples are also sometimes available through local interior designers. Before contacting a manufacturer, it is advisable to (1) assemble all data and photographs pertinent to the restoration, as well as any available original fabrics, and (2) com-

plete preliminary restoration plans, including specific requirements, such as the period to be re-created, the full
measurements of all surfaces to be covered, the planned use
of the room and the projected work schedule. When plac-
ing an order, be sure to check the accuracy of the number,
colorway, width and repeat. If the fabric is to be used for
drapery or bed hangings, give the length and number of
cuts in case the manufacturer finds it necessary to supply
goods in more than one piece. If you require delivery in one
piece, be sure to specify that on your original order. When
ordering a fabric not currently in stock, be sure to ask how
long the delivery time will be. It might be wise to add at
least two or three weeks to your own planning schedule be-
yond the time quoted by the manufacturer; sometimes delays will be even greater, particularly in the case of custom
weaving.

When ordering goods, be sure to request a current run
cutting — that is, a sample of the color currently available — in order to ensure that it is the exact same color as
the sample originally approved. At this time specify the
amount of yardage needed. It may be possible to reserve
that amount of fabric for 10 days while approving a run cutting, thus speeding up the order time and avoiding the possibility that available goods will be sold out while the cutting is approved. Check the cutting also for the quality of
printing; worn-out screens produce heavy blots of color
that are not desirable. When ordering handblocked goods,
expect some color variation even within one piece. When
an order is received, examine the entire yardage for any
flaws that would make it unacceptable. No manufacturer
accepts returns of goods that have been cut, and a premium
is charged for returns of custom-ordered goods.

CUSTOM REPRODUCTION WORK

When seeking the most exact reproduction possible of a
specific prototype fabric, a client usually has to arrange for
the custom manufacture of a limited amount of yardage and
the accompanying trimmings. It is also possible and somewhat less expensive to obtain special color runs of currently
available designs. A frequent illusion of historic house
restoration committees with cherished samples of original
fabric is that by offering a sample to a company for inclu-

sion in its commercial line, the company will in turn provide all the fabric needed for the restoration project as well as pay the owner a handsome royalty. This is very unlikely. Occasionally, a manufacturer can be persuaded to include a special design as part of the regular commercial line, paying a royalty at stated intervals. In such cases, the costs to the client are considerably less, but this situation rarely occurs. One should approach custom work with the clear-eyed expectation that it will be very expensive, it will take a long time, and there will be many difficult moments along the way. Be prepared to check artwork, threads, dyes, strikeoffs and samples at every possible juncture. You may find you have to reject several samples before an acceptable reproduction is made; some projects have taken four or five years. Do not be intimidated by the process, but remember that the company is doing one a favor to work to exacting specifications.

In custom work the client usually must bear the expenses of setting up the looms or cutting the printing screens and of reproducing the original color and design as well as the expenses of materials and labor. There are surcharges for every modification from standard commercial production. The price may vary also depending on the yardage required, small amounts of yardage being the most expensive. Often there is a minimum yardage requirement. In most cases, a 50 percent deposit is required. Negotiation for custom reproduction work is inevitably a highly personal experience. Among the few companies willing to undertake custom work on a limited basis are Brunschwig & Fils, Clarence House, Classic Revivals, Lee Jofa, Old World Weavers, Scalamandré and Schumacher. All are experienced in working with museums and can be commended for their cooperative attitude and excellent workmanship.

Signing a contract and paying a deposit are only the first steps in a long process. For a company to finish a custom-woven or custom-printed product can sometimes take 16 to 18 months or more, depending on the complexity of the design and your standard of accuracy. It is wise to check on the work at every step of production, carefully checking actual samples and color strikeoffs against the document. Be sure to approve or disapprove strikeoffs promptly in order to avoid being charged penalties designed to cover the cost of halted production or resetting looms or printing tables. If a long period of time goes by during which you do not hear from the company, inquire about progress and make certain that one or more of the essential approval steps has not been skipped over. Modern production methods and dyestuffs are not the same as those used to produce the original, so do not assume that the reproduction will be flawless just because it is called a reproduction or because the firm you are working with has done excellent work in the past. The client has the right to insist on as perfect a reproduction as possible, with full understanding and approval of any changes made by the company. Be sure to get a detailed estimate, so that you know the cost of special warps, wefts, ground cloths, special colors, artwork, setups and each strikeoff. Because of delays in the expected delivery time and other reasons, there still may be increased charges, so determine in advance whether the price estimate represents a maximum charge or whether allowance should be made for inflationary cost increases. Be sure to have firm price estimates in hand when fund raising and to allot a percentage of the budget for possible cost overruns.

Considering the high cost of quality custom reproduction as well as the large minimum orders and the extraordinary amount of time that may be required, it is often a good idea to work within the framework of available designs, considering only color changes. If price is a consideration, consider what effect you are seeking and what compromises are acceptable in reaching your goals.

In seeking to reproduce the appearance of the Yellow Chamber at the Moffatt-Ladd House in Portsmouth, N.H. (p. 34), for example, the committee decided that the cost of custom reproduction of the damask was prohibitive. It was decided that the most important visual qualities were the intense yellow color, the visual contrast of matte and shiny surfaces provided in the original document by silk and worsted threads, and the large scale of the design (66-inch repeat) with both major and minor motifs. To approximate these effects, a yellow damask fabric in silk and cotton with a 60-inch repeat and two vertical design motifs was selected from stock at Scalamandré. This choice offered all three of the sought-after visual qualities, with significant savings over the cost of custom reproduction.

Construction and Installation

Once the reproduction fabrics have been chosen, a number of questions remain. When actually making up the goods, decide on the degree of accuracy to which the reproduction furnishing must adhere. If an original curtain or bedspread was handstitched, unlined and perhaps fastened with iron tacks, should the modern reproduction be machine sewn, lined and fastened with Velcro? In making such decisions, keep in mind the purpose of the restoration. If the major goal is a decorative effect, by all means choose the best modern construction and installation methods. The fabrics will last longer and be much easier to clean. If, on the other hand, the goal is the interpretation of a way of life at a given moment, the completed work should be as faithful to the original as possible. To achieve this, all stitching should be a close approximation of the size and type of handwork or machine work done on original examples. Lining should be used only if there is a prototype. Original hanging methods should be duplicated if at all possible. If design motifs are not matched where widths are joined or if designs have been used upside down or sideways, these details should be carefully reproduced. The scale of the original fabric should be kept in mind, particularly if two repeats have been placed across a double width in a reproduction or if other alterations in scale have been made. It may even be necessary to cut a 54-inch-wide reproduction lengthwise, shift the panels slightly to distort the horizontal match and then sew them back together in order to replicate the number of seams and visual distortions of the original. Indeed, matching horizontal repeats in work for periods before 1840 and 1850 is seldom necessary, because it seems not to have been a standard practice at that time. When such practical details cannot be determined from an original example, careful study of existing documents and published designs and illustrations from the period may be necessary to provide guidelines for construction and installation.

How to Use the Catalog

The following catalog of fabrics suitable for use in historic buildings is divided into two parts. The first section presents documentary reproduction fabrics and is arranged by historical period. The second part, "Modern Textiles: Continuing a Tradition," lists nondocumentary and plain-woven fabrics and is arranged by type of fabric.

Individual catalog entries give the following information when it is available:

Manufacturer's catalog name for the fabric pattern

Country, date and method of manufacture of the original (unless the method is included in the pattern name, as in "Georgian Damask" or "French Brocade")

Fiber content of the reproduction fabric

Width of the reproduction fabric and repeat (length of one complete pattern motif)

Source of a published photograph of the document fabric if available (see bibliography for complete titles)

Technical or design changes made by the manufacturer in the reproduction

Organization or museum for which the fabric was reproduced

Information about the document and its location

Manufacturer's catalog number for the reproduction fabric

Manufacturer's name for the document color

Addresses of fabric manufacturers begin on p. 263.

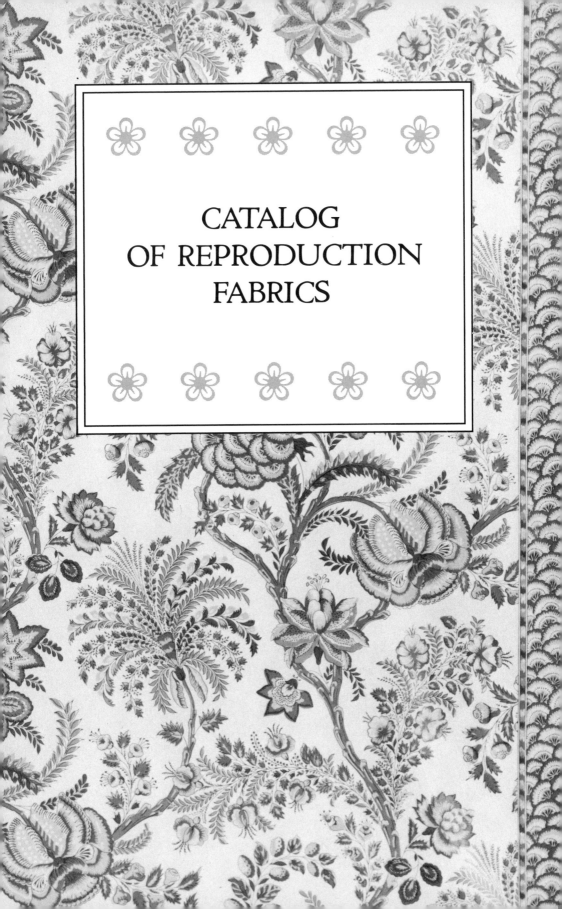

CATALOG
OF REPRODUCTION
FABRICS

1700 TO 1790:
A DEPENDENCE ON
IMPORTED FABRICS

Throughout the 18th century, most Americans depended on imported fabrics for furnishing their buildings. British fabrics predominated because they were protected by the high tariffs imposed by England on goods imported into the colonies from other countries. Indian goods also were imported under the protective arm of the British East India Company. The quality of British fabrics made for export varied, but for the most part these goods were far superior to anything made in colonial America. Although some colonial households produced woolen and linen goods for their own use and some professional weavers and a few linen stampers were able to make a living, throughout the colonial period domestic textiles usually were made for shirts and underclothing, children's garments, blankets and bed and table linen. Even in families where these goods were made at home, British imports were favored for formal clothing and decorative household furnishing alike.

The 18th century saw the beginnings of industrialization in textile manufacturing in England, but the new technology was a closely guarded secret that did not reach this continent until the end of the century. Not until after 1825 did American textile manufacturers begin to provide any serious competition for imported goods.

The removal of trade restrictions that accompanied the establishment of American independence broadened commercial networks and permitted importation of fabrics from around the world. Even then, British and, to some extent, French fabrics were favored for their superior quality, design and color.

Brilliantly colored and highly finished wools were among

Yellow Chamber,
Moffatt-Ladd House,
Portsmouth, N.H.
Restored to c. 1764–68
and installed 1981.

25

Bed hung with Brunschwig & Fils's moreen at the Raynham Hall Museum, Oyster Bay, Long Island, N.Y.

the most sought-after imports for both clothing and household furnishings. These were tightly spun, highly finished fabrics with a hard, crisp surface, totally unlike most modern wools. Silks were used primarily for clothing, although a few wealthy merchants, plantation owners and royal governors made use of silk draperies in their best chambers or parlors.

Colorful printed textiles were the primary vehicles by which all sorts of pictorial designs reached average Americans. People who might never see an illustrated book or an oil painting had an opportunity to see examples of fine rococo shellwork, exotic birds and flowers, pictures of balloon ascensions, portraits of national heroes or visions of distant Turkey or China. Throughout the period, designs were handprinted from cumbersome woodblocks; the colors were developed through a complex series of steps using mordants and natural dyestuffs. In the middle of the century, the introduction of printing from engraved copperplates directly on cotton or linen greatly expanded production and made possible the fine linear designs with large repeats that were especially well suited for use in household furnishing.

In both woodblock and copperplate printing, the colors were primarily deep indigo blues and the rich browns, blacks, purples, reds and pinks produced by using madder with one mordant or another. Many of the madder colors have faded to sepia or brown tones as a result of extensive exposure to the sun. In studying an antique fabric document to determine the original color, be sure to examine it carefully for areas that have been protected from the sun. A tiny space inside a seam or under a thread or border tape may preserve a surprisingly bright coloration. Details that appear to have been printed in brown may, in fact, have originally been purple.

In some 18th-century plate-printed textile designs, especially in France, additional colors were "penciled" or added with woodblocks to the monochromatic copperplate designs. As dye technology evolved, new colors were possible. It was not until 1814, however, that a good green could be printed directly on cloth. Before that time, green required a two-step process in which blue was printed over an area previously printed yellow. If the blocks for such a print were out of register, blue and yellow showed at the edges of all green areas. Frequently the yellow dyes were not as permanent as the blue, and as they faded, the green areas became blue. Many floral printed textiles that now appear to have been printed with blue stems and leaves were originally printed in green, but because of the fugitive nature of the yellow dye they now appear blue. Reproductions of such fabrics should duplicate the original green, but unfortunately they often do not.

Most reproductions of both plate-printed and block-printed textiles are manufactured today by the process of screen printing; only one or two firms continue to use the original methods. Although textile printing screens can be engraved photographically, most designs are redrawn in watercolor at the time the colors are separated for printing. Since few designers can resist the temptation to improve on the original artwork, one should try to compare any reproduction with a sample of the original fabric in order to judge the fidelity of the work. Some changes are made to simplify printing, thus coarsening the designs; other changes are made to enhance the visual qualities of the original, as when a second color screen is added to a plate-printed design in order to make the modern fabric appear richer.

Typical 18th-century block-printed designs for furnishing fabrics include large-scale flowers and birds on open white grounds, a style derived from imported Indian chintzes. After the middle of the century, delicate rococo scrolls and shells and some chinoiseries were added to the design vocabulary of textile printers. Large-scale arborescent designs, with their endless stems and handsome birds and flowers, predominated in the 1780s. During this period, fine dotted work was added to accentuate individual motifs or to fill in the entire background.

During the third quarter of the 18th century, some textiles with bold block-printed designs in deep indigo blue were printed by means of a resist process. Because the technology involved is relatively simple and the bold monochro-

Bed hung with Schumacher's "Carolina Toile" and valances edged with background motifs cut from Brunschwig & Fils's "Deborah Logan." The valance design was based on New England originals, c. 1770–75, in a private collection. Shown in the Stephen Chase House, Strawbery Banke Museum, Portsmouth, N.H.

matic designs are especially appealing to the modern eye, some authors have suggested that these fabrics might have been made in America. Indeed, many documented examples of blue resist-printed bed hangings and quilts have been found in areas of Dutch settlement in New York and along the south coast of New England. However, the discovery of an example at the Albany Institute of History and Art bearing the British excise mark for 1766 and the inclusion of proof designs in a British pattern book in the Baker Archive (illustrated in *From East to West*, fig. 22) confirm that these are also British goods, however popular they may have been in prerevolutionary America.

Both block and plate printing were done on bleached fabrics. Through time, many antique fabrics have become discolored, and the backgrounds now appear to be off-white or light tan in color. Reproductions of these often copy the discolored background, rather than the crispness of the original design. Fortunately, it is sometimes possible to have a reproduction fabric specially printed on a bleached white cloth rather than using what is known in the trade as an aged ground.

Fabric printing from engraved copperplates was invented by Francis Nixon at Drumcondra, Ireland, in 1752. By 1756 he had moved his operation to Surrey, England, where the technique was soon adopted by other textile printers. Their monochromatic designs included pastoral and classical landscapes, chinoiseries, rococo scrolls, birds, literary and theatrical subjects and commemorative designs. Some of these designs derived from contemporary prints; others were specially commissioned for textile printing.

The large scale of the plate-printed designs made them especially suitable for household furnishings, particularly for bed hangings and counterpanes. As early as 1761, the *Boston Gazette* carried an advertisement for "Cotton Copper Plate Furniture for Beds." Many examples of American bed hangings made of these fabrics have survived and should be studied in detail by those who wish to reproduce them. Such details as the width of the fabric, matching or mismatching of motifs, thread, size and type of stitches, trimmings and evidence of original hanging methods should all be noted in addition to the shape of the valances and style of curtains. A good example of a reproduction bed of this period is that at the John Brown House, Providence, R.I. (See p. 6.)

By the late 1770s copperplate printing began to be developed in France, especially by C. P. Oberkampf at Jouy. His work reached such a level of quality that the term *toiles de Jouy,* meaning cottons printed in Jouy, has become almost a generic term for copperplate-printed textiles. For many years the fact that this style of printing had originated in England was not known, and both French and English designs were referred to as toiles. Research by Peter Floud and Barbara Morris at the Victoria and Albert Museum in the 1950s clarified this issue; since that time the actual point of origin of many plate-printed designs has been identified.

After the American Revolution, some French plate-printed fabrics were imported into the United States and used as furnishing fabrics. These designs received a renewed interest at the end of the 19th century. For that reason many of the plate-printed textiles listed here are also suitable for restoration work at later periods, but in the catalog sections of this book they are listed only once, at the time of their introduction.

People re-creating colonial interiors have available a tempting yet misleading choice of fabrics. Many excellent reproductions of 18th-century dress silks, linens and printed cottons are available today, but there is little evidence to support their use in 18th-century American buildings for bed hangings, window curtains or furniture upholstery. For example, "Rivière Enchantée" by Brunschwig & Fils is an excellent reproduction of a beautiful early 18th-century Indian textile reflecting Javanese trade influence, but it is doubtful that it was ever imported into colonial America. "Tippoo Sahib's Tent" by Classic Revivals is another excellent reproduction, for which there is no imaginable use in 18th-century American restoration work.

Many reproductions of French 18th-century textiles are also available today, but it is important to recall the scarcity of these in colonial America. A less obvious problem is that created by the many silk damask designs that have been used so lavishly in "Georgian" interiors since the 1920s. Some of them are good reproductions, but few were used in 18th-century America.

Many 18th century–style silk designs available today have

been altered in scale to fit the size of modern looms. Original patterns measuring 18 or 21 inches wide have been stretched in width to fit two motifs across 48-inch goods. This change can present problems when an inexperienced upholsterer centers the modern fabric on a chair, for example, and thus moves the predominant woven motifs to the sides of the piece and leaves a design void in the center. In many of these same damask designs, a minor motif has been dropped to reduce the repeat from 60 inches or more to half or two thirds of that size. The resultant fabric may look as though it dates to the 18th century, but it should rightly be termed an adaptation, since it is only a portion of the original.

Exact reproductions of 18th-century silks are available, but they are usually handwoven to order and take a long time to complete. Such fabrics also present difficulties in matching patterns and generate expensive waste. Consider, for example, the original silk and worsted damask used in the Moffatt House in Portsmouth, N.H., in 1764 (pp. 24 and

Jaffrey Room, Museum of Fine Arts, Boston, with draperies in a Chinoiserie pattern by Schumacher, installed 1928. The armchair is covered with Mary Todd Lincoln Damask by Scalamandré. The lavish use of silk and the style of upholstery and drapery are typical of period room installations between 1924 and 1970.

Detail of the original yellow silk and worsted damask used in 1764 in the Yellow Chamber of the Moffatt-Ladd House. (National Society of the Colonial Dames of America in the State of New Hampshire)

32). The 18th-century fabric measures 18 inches wide and the repeat is 66 inches; the design has major and minor motifs. Exact reproduction of this fabric would be extraordinarily expensive, considering the size of the repeat and the difficulty in obtaining appropriate worsted yarns. In the installation of the goods, careful placement of the major motifs and attention to matching across seams would result in great waste. When one considers that even in the 18th century such fabrics were very expensive as well as difficult to use effectively, it is easier to understand why they were used only in the homes of the wealthy.

Many 18th-century woven silk or wool textile designs have been reproduced in other fibers. It is not uncommon to find 100 percent cotton, 100 percent rayon or cotton-rayon, cotton-linen combinations that look very much like their silk or woolen prototypes. If cost is a consideration, you would do well to consider using one of these less expensive fabric adaptations to achieve a period effect.

For those rare cases where site-specific research indicates the use of handwoven domestic wool or linen fabric, a custom reproduction can be made fairly easily by a skilled weaver. Some specialists are included in the list of suppliers

Bedroom, Mount Vernon. Brunschwig & Fils's "Creil," c.1775, has been used for bed hangings, drapery, curtains and chair upholstery. (The Mount Vernon Ladies' Association)

(pp. 263–67), but many others can successfully accomplish this work. Local weavers' guilds or regional craft associations can suggest qualified people. Take care to approve the threads selected and be sure to obtain a woven trial to ensure that the color and texture are close to that of the fabric to be reproduced. Some useful reference books are Constance Dann Gallagher's *Linen Heirlooms* and *More Linen Heirlooms*, John Hargrove's *The Weaver's Draft Book* and J. R. Bronson's *The Domestic Manufacturer's Assistant,* and for natural dyes of the period, Rita J. Adrosko's *Natural Dyes and Home Dyeing.*

How Furnishing Fabrics Were Used

Documentary evidence shows clearly that in the colonial period few houses were embellished with elaborate bed and window hangings or softly upholstered furniture in every room. Some people slept in pallet beds placed directly on the floor in rooms shared with children, cooking equipment, tools and storage containers. Statistical analyses of probate inventories, such as those published by Susan Schoelwer and Abbott Lowell Cummings, or upholsterers' account books, such as that published by Brock Jobe, make clear that even in seemingly spartan interiors imported textiles and the work of professional upholsterers played an important role in providing a modicum of comfort. Obviously, these same textiles provided color and design in spaces where there was little of either.

In many probate inventories, the value of beds with hangings far exceeds that of any other piece of furniture in the house. Bed hangings of woolen stuffs, such as harrateen, cheyney or moreen, were popular from the beginning of the 18th century. Green was the most common color, with crimson and scarlet the next most popular colors. In the early 1700s white linen was sometimes used for hangings, and soon colorful calicos and dramatic blue-and-white checks became more common. Copperplate-printed cottons were used during the last 40 years of the century, but wool continued to predominate, at least in the mid-Atlantic states and New England. Because of the work involved in their construction and the expense of the materials required, crewel embroidered, or "worked," curtains were rare.

Some bed hangings were imported ready made from London, but patterns for the latest designs also were imported by urban upholsterers and quickly copied. The typical shapes of bed valances changed several times throughout the 18th century, but the basic formula continued to be tester cloth, head cloth, valances and bases, all of which were nailed to the bed frame, and movable head and foot curtains, the latter usually twice the width of the former. The curtains might also be tacked to the tester frame, in which case they were drawn up with lines and pulleys or they might move freely with tape loops or iron rings passing along wooden rods. Bed curtains were seldom lined, and if there were selvages at the sides, they were not even hemmed. Often the scrolls of the valances were outlined with decorative border tapes or strips of fabric, but the remaining pieces might be plain.

Some bed chambers had window curtains of the same fabric and style as those of the bed curtains. The most luxurious had upholstered furniture to match. The "Yellow Chamber" of the Moffatt-Ladd House (1764) at Portsmouth, N.H., was furnished before 1768 with bed and window hangings of yellow silk and wool damask (pp. 24 and 32) in the "half drapery" style. Eight side chairs, an easy chair and three window-seat cushions also were covered in this fabric. The woodwork of the room was painted a dull mustard yellow, and the wallpaper had a yellow background as well. Color coordination was clearly important in the 18th-century interior.

Eighteenth-century window curtains were probably even more rare than fully hung beds. A committee or curator charged with the accurate restoration of a room interior of this period should be prepared to find that the room might not have had window curtains, even if 20th-century taste seems to require them. Fortunately, when restoring a period house or creating a period interior for private living, it is not necessary to re-create the original room; selection of appropriate reproduction fabrics and the use of period upholstery techniques will produce quite satisfactory results.

In the 18th century a curtain was defined as a piece of cloth that could be expanded or contracted at pleasure to admit or exclude light or air. Its purpose was considered functional rather than purely decorative. For that reason, few curtains of this period were fixed at the perimeters of the window frame. Until the invention in the 1790s of French rod curtains, which permitted curtain panels to be pulled apart horizontally, several systems of opening and closing curtains were employed. The curtains could be drawn up vertically in a style known as festoon, or, less frequently, Venetian curtains (the mechanism is exactly that of Venetian blinds), or they could be pulled up diagonally by cords threaded through rings and pulleys, resulting in the graceful swags of the drapery style, known today in England as reefed curtains. Such curtains could be made with single panels at each window (half drapery) or with two panels that could be drawn up in a single or double drapery, depending on whether one or two cords were used in each panel of fabric.

Bed or window curtains could be threaded on wire, string or iron rods; they could also be nailed to the bed or window frame or to a wooden lath that projected above the window at any height deemed suitable. The curtain panels could fall to the sill, spread onto the floor or stop almost anywhere in between. If threaded on a wire or rod, curtains were usually made with a tiny casing at the upper edge. Sometimes, window curtains were made with tiny tape loops (one-half inch or less) at the upper edge; bed curtains usually were made with longer loops (three or four inches), probably to make them easier to open or close by a person lying in bed.

In the last five years, festoon curtains have become extraordinarily popular; they are often very full and weighted down with thick ruffles or other trimming. In using this style for restoration work, it is important to replicate the spare proportion, hanging methods and trimmings of antique examples.

Recent careful analysis of surviving 18th-century furniture with its original upholstery has revealed much about upholstering techniques and the finished appearance of the work. Written sources have shown that the most common cover for chair seats that did not match bed or window hangings was black leather, rather than the colorful silk damasks often used on this style of furniture in the mid-20th century. One common practice of 18th-century artisans was to define the outlines of their work with rows of bright brass tacks or decorative tapes. Because of the type of stuffing and this use of tacks and tape, the furniture of this period had a taut outline, in contrast to the soft contours of modern spring seats and foam rubber padding.

Fortunately, the upholsterer's craft is seeing a revival, with a number of skilled workers who combine excellent scholarship and superb hand skills. These people have also become concerned about the damage done to wood furniture frames when they are nailed again and again in the application of fabrics by upholsterers. Robert Mussey, Richard Nylander and Elizabeth Lahikainen at the Society for the Preservation of New England Antiquities, Robert Trent at The Winterthur Museum, Wallace Gusler at Colonial Williamsburg and others have pioneered various forms of "tackless" upholstery that eliminate this damage to pieces that will be exhibited in museums and not be used as seating furniture.

In the 18th century, expensive fabric covers for seating furniture were often protected by loose cases or slipcovers of printed or checked cotton, dimity or linen. These cases were probably used most of the time, being removed only for the most important social occasions. Correctly made reproductions may appear sloppy to the modern eye, for the name "loose cases" aptly described their fit. Not only were they loose and wrinkled in appearance; they also were often attached with visible tapes or strings, tied together in floppy bowknots. The lower edges of the cases were often finished with a ruffle, sometimes extending to within a few inches of the floor.

Few original examples of 18th-century valances, curtains or loose cases have survived, and it would certainly be a mistake for every restoration to make slavish copies of these few. Rather, the originals should be carefully studied for their construction techniques and sewing details, which should be used to guide the cut and construction of appropriate fabric furnishings. The important point is not to use 20th-century techniques for this work. Pinch pleats, flannelette interlinings, wide loops or ties of double thicknesses of matching fabric, bias piping and skintight slipcovers were unknown in the 18th century. For accurate restoration work, it is as important to use appropriate construction techniques as to select the appropriate fabric.

BRUNSCHWIG & FILS

WOOLS

❀ BACCHUS WOOL DAMASK. English, c.1750–1800. 100% wool. 54" wide, 9½" vertical repeat, 7½" horizontal repeat. Adapted from the same documents at the Brooklyn Museum, Winterthur Museum and Maryland Historical Society on which "New Hambledon Damask" (below) is based. The size of the repeat has been reduced from 19¾". No. 63522.01 (French blue).

❀ HOGARTH WOOL STRIPE. English, c. 1750–1800. 100% wool. 54" wide, 1¾" horizontal repeat. Although not directly based on a document, this closely resembles 18th-century striped camlets. No.63531.01 (scarlet); No.63532.01 (indigo).

❀ NEW HAMBLEDON DAMASK. English, c.1750–1830. 73% cotton, 27% viscose. 50" wide, 19¾" repeat. Documents at Brooklyn Museum, Winterthur Museum and Maryland Historical Society. Original is a worsted woolen furnishing fabric with an embossed design intended to imitate damask; the modern fabric is an adaptation in which the design motifs have actually been woven as damask. Available colors: No.39674.01 (wintergreen); No.39672.01 (indigo).

❀ NORWICH WOOL STRIPE. English, c. 1760–1800. 100% wool. 54" wide, 2" horizontal repeat. Based on documentary samples of 18th-century callimancoes (see Montgomery, *Textiles in America*, pl. D-79). No.63511.01 (red).

❀ VERPLANCK WOOL DAMASK. English or Flemish, probably late 18th century. 100% wool. 19½" wide, 59" repeat. Document from the Verplanck family of New York; now owned by the Metropolitan Museum of Art, for whom it was reproduced. Document gold has been discontinued, but two other typical 18th-century colors are available: No.60294.01 (green); No.60291.01 (red). Cut by repeat only.

CLASSIC REVIVALS

Order fabrics by name and specify desired colors. Allow ample time for custom weaving.
❀ CAMLET. English, 18th century. 100% wool. 29½" wide, no repeat. Document privately owned in England. Custom colors.

SALEM STAMPED MOREEN, c.1750–85. Classic Revivals. Red.

❧ CHATHAM DAMASK. English, c.1765–70. 100% wool. 21" wide, 25½" repeat. Document privately owned in Yorkshire, England. Other extant examples of this design in both public and private collections are found in both wool and silk. This design can also be woven in silk and as an adaptation in 48" width. Custom colors.

❧ SALEM STAMPED MOREEN. English, c.1750–85. A woven worsted that has been watered and stamped (embossed). 100% wool. 27" wide, 24" repeat. Cummings, *Bed Hangings*, fig. 15. Document, owned by the Essex Institute, Salem, Mass., red bed furnishings believed to have been made at the time of the marriage of Daniel Saunders and Sarah Peele in 1770; another similar example, the original green upholstery of side chairs in the Jonathan Sayward House, York, Maine, owned by the Society for the Preservation of New England Antiquities. Red. Custom colors.

❧ TAMMY. English, 18th century. 100% wool, glazed. 29½" wide, no repeat. Document privately owned in England. No.105-1 (green); custom colors.

❧ WALPOLE DAMASK. French or Italian, c.1720–30. Can be woven in either 100% silk or 100% wool. 21" wide, 76" repeat. Silk document in Prelle Archives, Lyon, France; wool document owned by Guy Evans in England. Wool example at the Victoria and Albert Museum dated 1730–40. Perhaps the most popular damask design ever created; examples found in many English historic house collections. Custom colors.

SCALAMANDRÉ

❧ COLONIAL REPP. English, c.1750–1850. 100% worsted wool. 54" wide. Document owned by Scalamandré. No. 98309-1 (cardinal).

❧ CREOLE MOIRE'D MOREEN. Probably English, 18th or early 19th century. 40% linen, 60% wool. 50" wide. No.1946-3 (yellow).

❧ EARLY AMERICANA MOREEN. French, c.1760–1835. 25% linen, 50% wool, 17% cotton, 8% silk. 51" wide. Document at Schuyler Mansion, Albany, N.Y. No.1945-1 (old red strié, embossed); No.1945-2 (old red strié, not embossed).

❧ XVIII CENTURY ANTIQUE DAMASK. English, c.1750–1800. 94% wool, 6% nylon. 50" wide, 34" repeat. From a silk document owned by the National Society of the Colonial

Dames of America at its property Gunston Hall, Lorton, Va. No.90022B-12 (gold).

❀ INDEPENDENCE HALL BAIZE CLOTH. English, 18th or early 19th century. 100% wool. 50" wide. Document at Independence National Historical Park, Philadelphia. No.99243-1 (bottle green).

❀ MASSACHUSETTS TAFFETA MOREEN. English, c.1750–1825. 100% wool. 48" wide. Document privately owned. No. 99459-1 (bottle green).

❀ MOREEN BOUQUET. English, c.1750–80. 50" wide, 30" repeat. Cummings, *Bed Hangings,* fig.15. Printed adaptation of embossed documents such as the Saunders bed hangings owned by the Essex Institute and the Sayward House chairs owned by the Society for the Preservation of New England Antiquities. No.6906-3 (forest-on-forest).

❀ NEW ENGLAND DAMASK. English, c.1760–80. 100% wool. 49¾" wide, 44" repeat. Document an easy chair owned by New England Historic and Genealogical Society, Boston. No.97385-1 (gold). Special order only.

❀ RESTORATION MOIRE TAFFETA. English. c. 1750–1850, moreen. 46% wool, 48% cotton, 6% nylon. 58" wide. Document owned by Scalamandré. No.99374A-2 (Fredericksburg red); No.99374A-14 (river green); No.99374A-18 (cardinal).

❀ VERMICELLI. English, c.1750–1850. 48% cotton, 46% wool, 6% nylon. 48" wide, 28" repeat. Printed adaptation of an embossed moreen (or harateen) found on a privately owned Massachusetts easy chair in the Chippendale style, c. 1760–70. No.6831-1 (dark green); No.6831-4 (cardinal red).

SCHUMACHER
COLONIAL WILLIAMSBURG REPRODUCTIONS

All documents are owned by Colonial Williamsburg, Williamsburg, Va., and all are illustrated in *Williamsburg Reproductions.*

❀ PEYTON RANDOLPH WOOL DAMASK. English, c.1750–75. 100% wool. 52" wide, 26" vertical and horizontal repeat. No.53520 (document gold); consider also No.53524 (blue); No.53525 (teal); No.53523 (russet).

❀ WILLIAMSBURG WOOL MOREEN. English, c. 1750–1800. 51% wool, 49% cotton. 50" wide. No.90346 (green); nine additional colors.

top left
PEYTON RANDOLPH
WOOL DAMASK,
c.1750–75. Schumacher.
Blue, teal, russet.

top right
CREOLE MORIE'D
MOREEN, 18th or early
19th century.
Scalamandré. Yellow.

left
VERMICELLI, c.1750–
1850. Scalamandré.
Green, red.

❀ WILLIAMSBURG WOOL. English, c.1700–20. 100% worsted wool. 54" wide. Adapted from background of an early 18th-century worsted damask. No.86057 (Williamsburg blue); No.86055 (spruce).

STROHEIM & ROMANN

❀ CUMBERLAND. English, c. 1750–1800, woven damask. 100% cotton. 50" wide, 25" repeat. Adapted from original red woolen damask in textile collection of Winterthur Museum. No.39810-39817 (red).

PRINTS

BAILEY & GRIFFIN

❀ BIRD AND BOUGH. English, c.1770–90, block print. 100% cotton. 48" wide, 38½" repeat. Document privately owned. No.03475 (red and green on cream).

BRUNSCHWIG & FILS

❀ LES ARCADES INDOPERSIAN PANEL. Painted in Mazulipatan atelier and brought to France by Compagnie des Indes, c.1700–50. Hand painted in madder colors with blue. 100% cotton. 50" wide with 32" horizontal repeat, 73" high with 17" border of arcades above 70" colonnade. Document privately owned in France. No.174030.00 (multi).

❀ BIRD AND THISTLE. English, c.1780–85, copperplate print. 100% cotton. 54" wide, 32" half-drop repeat. Montgomery, *Printed Textiles,* pp.51 and 250; see also *From East to West*, p.147. Documents at Winterthur Museum and Brunschwig Archives. No.65751.01 (red); No.65752.01 (indigo).

❀ BROMELIA RESIST. English, c.1765, block-printed and resist-dyed cotton with border design. Montgomery, *Printed Textiles,* fig.192. 100% cotton. 44" wide with 2½" border on each side, 29" repeat. Document a quilt at Winterthur Museum. No.76862.04 (indigo).

❀ CHANTERAC COTTON AND LINEN PRINT. French, c. 1760, block print. 100% cotton. 56" wide, 30¼" repeat, 31¾" horizontal repeat. Document a block-printed Indienne with a red ground, privately owned in France; an early 19th-century paper proof with the same motifs but slightly larger is in the Brunschwig & Fils Archives. No.65031.01 (red).

❀ CREIL COTTON PRINT. French (Oberkampf Manufactory, Jouy), c.1775, block printed and painted on cotton. 100% cotton. 50" wide, 48" repeat. Moss, p.7. Document privately owned in France. Documents in Brunschwig & Fils Archives, Mount Vernon and Cooper-Hewitt Museum. No. 173610.00 (madder colors with blue on white ground).

�֍ DEBORAH LOGAN. Indian, mid- to late 18th century, block print. 100% cotton. 48" wide, 10¼" repeat. Document a quilt found at Stenton, home of James and Deborah Logan, Philadelphia. No. 73422.04 (indigo on off-white).

✖ DUBLIN TOILE. Irish, c.1760, copperplate print. 100% cotton. 38" wide, 33½" repeat, 36" horizontal repeat. Document a plate print on linen owned by the National Museum of Ireland; one of three known to have been printed by Robinson of Balls Bridge (the others are a chinoiserie at the Victoria and Albert Museum and another with hunting and genre scenes at the Baltimore Museum of Art). Document a faded brown that may have been aubergine (purple); this has not been reproduced, but other 18th-century colorways are available. Appropriate colors are No. 36632.01 (blue) and No. 36631.01 (red).

✖ DURAS PAINTED TAFFETAS. Chinese export, probably 18th century. 100% silk. 48" wide, 25½" repeat. Document in Textile Study Room, Metropolitan Museum of Art. No. 39130.00 (multi on cream).

✖ FLEURS INDIENNES COTTON AND LINEN PRINT. French, c. 1740, block print. 55% cotton, 45% linen. 39" wide, 53" repeat, 39" horizontal repeat; border fabric is composed of three stripes 11¼" wide with a 52½" repeat. Document privately owned in France. Yardage No. 172900.00, Border No. 17320.00 (both multi on cream).

✖ FOUR SEASONS LINEN PRINT. English, attributed to Francis Nixon, c.1770–80, copperplate print. 100% linen. 47" wide, 35½" repeat; width includes 1½" stripe on one side that was a separate applied border on the original. Blackburn, *Cherry Hill*, fig. 160. Document, printed on cotton, a bed valance and curtains for a field bed, all owned by Historic Cherry Hill, Albany, N.Y., for whom the reproduction was first done. Other examples (slightly different) owned by Winterthur Museum and Cooper-Hewitt Museum. No. 62011.01 (red).

✖ GRAND GENOIS PANNEAU. Indian, mid-18th century, printed and painted palampore made for European market. 100% cotton. 63" wide, 91% repeat (cut by panel only). Document privately owned. No. 173490.00 (multi on white).

FOUR SEASONS LINEN
PRINT, c. 1770–80.
Brunschwig & Fils.
Red.

LA VILLAGEOISE COTTON
PRINT, c. 1785.
Brunschwig & Fils.
Red; blue.

❀ Granville Ikat Stripe Cotton Print. English, c. 1745–55, block print. 100% cotton. 54" wide, 18" repeat, 5¼" horizontal repeat. Document, privately owned in England, a trompe l'oeil printed ikat stripe in tones of blue on white, used as back of a sidechair cover made by Mrs. Mary Delany. No. 78662.04 (blue).

❀ Hampton Resist. English, c. 1740–80, resist-dyed block print. 56% cotton, 44% linen. 46" wide plus 2" border on one side, 34" repeat. Document at Winterthur Museum. No. 77312.04 (blue).

❀ Kandahar Print, Kandahar Border. French, mid-18th century, madder and indigo block print. 100% cotton. Print 31" wide, 54¾" repeat; border 15½" wide, 31½" repeat. Document owned by manufacturer, Oberkampf, Alsace, France. Print No. 172300.00, Border No. 172310.00 (both multi on cream).

❀ La Fete Venitienne Cotton Print. French, 1785–89, block print. 100% cotton. 54" wide, 24" vertical repeat, 27" horizontal repeat. Document a paper proof of a fabric design by Jean-Baptiste Reveillon in an album now in the Musée des Arts Décoratifs in Paris. No. 62800.00 (multi on cream).

❀ La Tonnelle Enchantee Cotton Print. French, 1785–89, block print. 100% cotton. 53" wide, 9½" repeat, 7" horizontal repeat. Document a paper proof of a fabric design by Jean-Baptiste Reveillon now in the Musée des Arts Décoratifs in Paris. No. 62740.01 (multi).

❀ La Valette. Indian, early 18th century, printed and painted cotton made for the European market. 100% cotton. 40" wide, 13½" repeat. Document privately owned. No. 172750.00 (multi on cream).

❀ La Villageoise Cotton Print. French (Oberkampf Manufactory, Jouy), c. 1785, copperplate print. 100% cotton. 38" wide, 38" vertical repeat, 36" horizontal repeat. *Chefs d'Oeuvre...Mulhouse,* II, fig. 3; Clouzot, *Painted and Printed Fabrics,* pl. 18; Pitoiset, *Toiles Imprimées XVIIIe–XIXe siècles,* no. 299. Document privately owned in France; examples in many public collections. No. 62871.01 (document red) and 62872.01 (document blue); other colors can be custom printed.

❀ Le Jardin des Muses Cotton Print. French, 1785–89, block print. 100% cotton. 52" wide, 12½" repeat, 31" horizontal repeat. Document, a paper proof of a fabric design by Jean-Baptiste Reveillon in an album now in the Musée des Arts Décoratifs in Paris, shows both cream and yellow grounds. No. 62793.0l (multi on yellow); No. 62790.01 (multi on cream).

❀ LES FASTES PERSANS COTTON PRINT. French, 1785–89, block print. 100% cotton. 54" wide, 14½" repeat, 18" horizontal repeat. Document a paper proof of a fabric design by Jean-Baptiste Reveillon in an album now in the Musée des Arts Décoratifs in Paris. No.62760.01 (cream).

❀ LES INDES GALANTES COTTON PRINT. French, 1785–89, block print. 100% cotton. 55" wide, 17½" repeat, 17" horizontal repeat. Document a paper proof of a fabric design by Jean-Baptiste Reveillon in an album now in the Musée des Arts Décoratifs in Paris. No. 62785.0l (rose and lilac on cream).

❀ LES JARDINIERS COTTON PRINT. French (Oberkampf Manufactory, Jouy), c. 1770–1800, block print. 100% cotton. 58" wide, 33¾" repeat. Document in the Musée de Jouy. Scale slightly enlarged in screen-printed reproduction. No. 62380.01 (multi on cream).

❀ LES JEUX D'EAU COTTON PRINT. French, 1785–89, block print. 100% cotton. 54" wide, 16½" repeat, 13" horizontal repeat. Document a paper proof of a fabric design by Jean-Baptiste Reveillon in an album now in the Musée des Arts Décoratifs in Paris. No.62750.01 (cream).

❀ LES MENUS PLAISIRS COTTON PRINT. French, 1785–89, block print. 100% cotton. 53" wide, 14" repeat, 10½" horizontal repeat. Document a paper proof of a fabric design by Jean-Baptiste Reveillon in an album now in the Musée des Arts Décoratifs in Paris; a sample printed on cotton, possibly by Oberkampf at Jouy, also survives. No. 62773.01 (maize).

❀ L'EVENTAIL. French (Oberkampf Manufactory, Jouy), c. 1785, block print. 100% cotton. 50" wide, 5" repeat. Document privately owned. No.173224.00 (green).

❀ MANSARD COTTON PRINT AND BORDER. Indian, mid-18th century, block-printed and painted cotton. 100% cotton. 50" wide, 21" repeat. Border print 50" wide, 32" repeat; width of single border 12½". Document a panel with borders on all four sides, privately owned in France. Reproduced with field and border, each as a separate design.

LE JARDIN DES MUSES
COTTON PRINT, c. 1785–
89. Brunschwig & Fils.
Multi on yellow; multi
on cream.

LES MENUS PLAISIRS
COTTON PRINT, c. 1785–
89. Brunschwig & Fils.
Maize.

Originally printed in madder colors with blue and yellow to create green; yellow has now faded. Reproduction shows faded appearance with predominant blue. Yardage No. 174400.00, Border No. 174410.00 (both multi on cream).

❀ MIRANDE. French, c.1785–90, block print, 100% cotton. 48" wide, 16" half-drop repeat. Document privately owned. No. 37510.01 (cream ground).

❀ NEMOURS COTTON AND LINEN PRINT. Indian, c.1725–75, hand painted. 52% cotton, 48% linen. 51" wide, 36" repeat, 51" horizontal repeat. Document a painted linen used as chair seat covers in the Readbourne Stair Hall at Winterthur Museum. Reproduction fabric heavier than document but color, motifs and scale accurate. No. 78500.04 (crimson on ivory).

❀ PRANCING DEER. English, c.1750–80, resist-dyed block print. 56% cotton, 44% linen. 47" wide, 32½" repeat, 15" horizontal repeat with 2" border on both sides. Document a quilt at Winterthur Museum. No. 77332.04 (blue).

❀ QUEEN ANNE RESIST COTTON AND LINEN PRINT. English, c.1760–70, resist-dyed block print. 63% cotton, 37% linen. 54" wide, 17¾" half-drop repeat, 27" horizontal repeat. Document an 18th-century block-printed and resist-dyed cotton at Winterthur Museum used for upholstery on armchairs in the Queen Anne Dining Room. Original fabric printed with indigo; reproduction copies the now-faded appearance of the original. No. 78702.04 (French blue).

❀ RIVIERE ENCHANTEE. Indian, early 18th century, block print showing Javanese trade influence. 100% cotton. 49½" wide, 29" repeat. D'Allemagne, pls. 213 and 213B. Document privately owned in France. No. 174151.00 (red).

❀ SIKAR. Indian, mid-18th century, hand painted. 100% cotton. 50" wide, 20" repeat. Document privately owned. No. 172910.00 (multi on cream).

❀ SOMMERS TOILE. English (Jones, Old Ford), c.1775. 100% cotton. 54" wide, 17¾" repeat. Document a paper proof of an engraved copperplate originally used for textile printing by R. Jones at Old Ford, now owned by the Musée de l'Impressions sur Etoffe, Mulhouse. An 18th-century sample of cotton fabric, printed in red in this design, owned by the Victoria and Albert Museum. Reproduced in blue for the Museum of Early Southern Decorative Arts. Custom order only.

❀ SRINAGAR. Indian, mid-18th century, hand painted. 100% cotton. Yardage adapted from a panel with borders; 31" wide, 27½" half-drop repeat. Border 11" wide, printed with three stripes on 33"-wide fabric, 30" repeat. Document privately owned. Yardage No.172700.00, Border No.172710.00 (both multi on cream).

❀ TOILE DUPLEIX. Indian, late 18th century, madder and indigo block print, probably for the European market. 100% cotton. 51" wide, 46" repeat. Document at Victoria and Albert Museum. No.173640.00 (multi on white).

❀ UZES COTTON PRINT. French, 1781, block print. 100% cotton. 60" wide, 14¼" repeat. Document a block-printed paper proof of a design for a textile, in the Musée des Arts Décoratifs, Paris. No.62545.01 (rose stripe).

❀ VILLANDRY. French (Jouy), c.1785, block print. 50% linen, 50% cotton. 50" wide, 38" repeat. Document in Brunschwig & Fils Archives. No.172272.00 (blue).

❀ VILLEROY PRINT ON LINEN. French (Jouy), c.1785, block print. 56% cotton, 44% linen. 48" wide, 12½" repeat. Doc-

SOMMERS TOILE, c.1775. Brunschwig & Fils. Blue.

ument the lining of an 18th-century quilt made of Indian palampore, found in France; owned by the Cooper-Hewitt Museum. No.73930.04 (red and blue on cream ground).

CLARENCE HOUSE

❀ BUCKS COUNTY. Swiss-German, 18th century, resist-dyed block print. 60% linen, 40% cotton. 52" wide, field repeat ¼" with border repeat 12". Traditional design. No.32041-3 (blau).

❀ CORNE D'ABONDANCE. Indian, 18th century, block-printed and painted palampore. 100% cotton. 63" wide, 20" repeat. Handblocked. Document privately owned. No. 31762-1 (multi on bise).

❀ DEERFIELD. Swiss-German, 18th century, resist-dyed block print. 60% linen, 40% cotton. 51" wide, 12½" repeat. Traditional design. No.32042-3 (blau).

❀ L'ARBRE FLEURI. French, c.1750–1800, block print. 100% cotton. 60" wide, 43" repeat. Document privately owned. No.31854-1 (blanc).

❀ LES PAMPRES. French, late 18th century, block print. 100% cotton. 50" wide, 17½" repeat. Document privately owned. No.31783-1 (white).

CLASSIC REVIVALS

❀ ARDEN. French (Alsace), c.1780–90, block print. 100% cotton. 50" wide. Document owned by the British National Trust. No.TM 309-9 (mustard and wine).

❀ FELICIA. French or English, c.1780–95, block print. 100% cotton. 54" wide, 12½" repeat. Document privately owned. No.71000-002 (blue).

❀ LES TRAVAUX DE LA MANUFACTURE. French (Oberkampf Manufactory, Jouy), 1783–84, copperplate print. 100% cotton. 50" wide, 39⅜" repeat. Bredif, pp.44–45; Carlano and Salmon, fig.123; Edwards and Ramsey, *Etoffes Imprimées Françaises,* 18:1–9, Robinson, pl.23. Designed by Jean Baptiste Huet. Documents in many museum and private collections. The first design done by Huet for Oberkampf at Jouy; shows the various stages in the manufacture of printed cottons. Blue only; order by name.

❀ TIPPOO SAHIB'S TENT. Indian, c.1730–50, block printed and hand painted. 100% cotton. Made in panels 50" wide, 81¾" repeat. Document owned by the British National

Trust at Powis Castle, Wales. Panels originally composed the campaign tent of Tippoo Sahib, the last Moslem Sultan of Mysore, captured by Lord Clive at the seige of Seringapatam, May 4, 1799, and taken to Powis Castle as booty. Madder colors with blue on white; order by name.

COWTAN & TOUT

❀ POMEROY. English, c. 1780–90, copperplate print. 100% cotton. 54" wide, 25" repeat. Document privately owned in England. No. 5686 (red on cream).

DECORATORS WALK

❀ AMERICAN INDEPENDENCE. English, c. 1783–1800, copperplate print. 100% linen. 48" wide, 28¼" repeat. Schoeser and Rufey, chap. 2, fig. 1; Montgomery, *Printed Textiles*, fig. 300 ("Apotheosis of Benjamin Franklin and George Washington"); d'Allemagne, pl. 131. Document in many textile collections; 18th-century examples usually printed on cotton or a cotton-linen combination. No. L65058 (rust); No. L65055 (navy); No. L65059 (brown).

GREEFF FABRICS

❀ SHALIMAR. English, late 18th century, block print. 100% cotton. 56" wide, 3½" repeat. Document privately owned in England. No. 60400 (rose and gray-blue on sand).

LEE JOFA

❀ PEONY PRINT. English. c. 1780, block print. 100% cotton, glazed. 47" wide, 34½" half-drop repeat. No. 799600 (multi).
❀ TURF INN TOILE PRINT. English, c. 1780–95, copperplate print. 100% cotton. 54" wide, 30" half-drop repeat. Montgomery, *Printed Textiles*, fig. 270; Victoria and Albert Museum, *English Printed Textiles*, fig. 158. No. 729073 (blue); No. 729070 (red).

PIERRE DEUX

❀ CAMPAIGNE. French (Oberkampf Manufactory, Jouy), c. 1785–90, copperplate print. 100% cotton. 39" wide, 39" repeat. No. 9325-1 (red); No. 9325-3 (blue).
❀ FETE NAVALE. French (Petitpierre frères, Nantes), c. 1787, copperplate print. 100% cotton. 39" wide, 39" repeat. Carlano and Salmon, fig. 131; *Toiles de Nantes des XVIIIe et XIXe*

FETE NAVALE, c.1787.
Pierre Deux. Red.

FRAGONARD, c.1785–90.
Pierre Deux. Blue.

LAFAYETTE, c. 1783–84. Pierre Deux. Blue; red; aubergine.

LE BALLON DE GONESSE, c. 1784. Pierre Deux. Red; blue; brown.

siècles, fig. 6; d'Allemagne, pl. 141; Clouzot, pl. 71. Depicts the visit of Louis XVI to Cherbourg in June 1787. No. 1414-1 (red).

❀ FRAGONARD. French (Oberkampf Manufactory, Jouy), c. 1785–90, copperplate print. 100% cotton. 39" wide, 39" repeat. Designed by Jean-Baptiste Huet. No. 1471 (blue).

❀ LAFAYETTE. French (Oberkampf Manufactory, Jouy), c. 1783–84, copperplate print. 100% cotton, 39" wide, 39" repeat. Bredif, p. 141; Carlano and Salmon, fig. 125; Clouzot, p. 25; d'Allemagne, pl. 44. Designed by Jean-Baptiste Huet; also known as "L'homage de l'Amerique à la France." No. 1597-2 (blue); No. 1597-3 (red); No. 1597-4 (aubergine).

❀ LE BALLON DE GONESSE. French (Oberkampf Manufactory, Jouy), c. 1784, copperplate print. 100% cotton. 39" wide, 39" repeat. Bredif, p. 147. Designs based on two etchings illustrating "Panic among the inhabitants of Gonesse" after the crash of a hydrogen balloon and "An aerostatic globe dedicated to M. Charles," both illustrated in Bredif, p. 146. No. 1348-1 (red); No. 1348-2 (blue); No. 1348 (brown).

❀ MANUFACTURE. French (Oberkampf Manufactory, Jouy), 1785, copperplate print. 100% cotton. 39" wide, 39" repeat. Bredif, pp. 44–45; Carlano and Salmon, fig. 123; Edwards and Ramsey, *Etoffes Imprimées Françaises,* 18:1–9; Robinson, pl. 23. Designed by Jean-Baptiste Huet. More commonly known as "Les travaux de la manufacture, Oberkampf." Shows scenes in textile production: preparing the cotton, printing with engraved plates and wood blocks, laying out cloth to bleach on the grass near the town of Jouy, barrels for dyeing and fixing colors, smoothing with rollers and with presses, drawing designs, painting in additional colors, rinsing the finished cloth, the drying house and the Oberkampf factory itself. No. 13180 (blue or red).

SCALAMANDRÉ

❀ DON QUIXOTE TOILE. French (Nantes), c. 1785, copperplate print. 100% cotton. 34" wide, 38½" repeat. *Toiles de Nantes des XVIIIe et XIXe siècles,* fig. 36; d'Allemagne, pl. 160. Document owned by Scalamandré. No. 6445-1 (wine on beige). Special order only.

❀ FLOWER BASKET. English, c. 1770–80, resist-dyed block print. 100% linen. 50" side, 17½" repeat. Montgomery, *Printed Textiles,* fig. 189. Adapted from document at Metropolitan

Museum of Art. No. 6412-1 (blues on ecru). Special order only.

❀ FRENCH RESIST. French, mid-18th century, resist-dyed block print. 44% linen, 56% cotton. 48" wide, 22" repeat. Screen-printed adaptation from document in textile collection of Metropolitan Museum of Art. No. 6410-1 (indigo on natural). Special order only.

❀ ITALIAN COUNTRYSIDE. Irish (Drumcondra), c. 1752–57, copperplate print. 100% cotton. 51" wide, 35¼" repeat. Design attributed to Francis Nixon; first successful copperplate printing of textiles. No. 7588-3 (red on off-white).

❀ RESIST PRINT. English, c. 1776–85, resist-dyed block print. 100% linen. 46½" wide, 26" repeat. Montgomery, *Printed Textiles*, fig. 191 ("Pheasants"). Document at Metropolitan Museum of Art. No. 6218-1 (blue on white). Special order only.

❀ RODNEY. English, c. 1770–80, block print. 100% cotton. 36" wide, 34½" repeat. Document owned by Scalamandré.

RESIST PRINT, c. 1776–85. Scalamandré. Blue on white.

WASHINGTON-FRANKLIN
TOILE, c. 1783–1800.
Scalamandré.

No.6236-1 (red, blues and brown on tan). Special order only.
❀ WASHINGTON-FRANKLIN TOILE. English, c.1783–1800, copperplate print. 100% cotton. 33" wide, 33½" repeat. Schoeser and Rufey, chap. 2, fig. 1; Montgomery, *Printed Textiles,* fig. 300 ("Apotheosis of Benjamin Franklin and George Washington"); d'Allemagne, pl. 131, *Scalamandré,* no. 29. Document in many textile collections; known in blue, red and purple, printed on 100% cotton and cotton-linen combinations. Reproduction first introduced by Scalamandré in the 1940s. No.6012-11 (light red on cream.)

SCHUMACHER
COLONIAL WILLIAMSBURG REPRODUCTIONS

Unless otherwise cited, all documents are in the textile collection of Colonial Williamsburg, Williamsburg, Va., and all are illustrated in *Williamsburg Reproductions.*
❀ BANYAN PRINT. Indian, c.1775–90, mordant painted and dyed. 100% cotton. 54" wide, 18" repeat. Document a man's dressing gown. No.73790 (document red and blue).
❀ BOTANICAL CHINTZ. French, c.1765–1800, block print. 100% cotton. 54" wide, 26¾" repeat. No.72990 (document red and green.)
❀ CAROLINA TOILE. English, c.1775–90, copperplate print. 100% cotton. 54" wide, 36" repeat. Document a plate-printed cotton and linen fabric used as a counterpane. No. 78830 (red).
❀ CHINESE FLOWERS. French, c.1785, block print. 100% cotton. 54" wide, 25" repeat. No.75220 (multi).
❀ FLORAL STRIPE. French, c.1785–1810, block print. 100% cotton. 54" wide, 12½" vertical repeat. Linen and cotton document was originally used in France for quilted curtains and bed hangings. No.163600 (document red).
❀ FLORIBUNDA. French. c.1785–1800, block print. 100% cotton. 54" wide. 27" repeat. No.78750 (tobacco).
❀ INDIAN CHINTZ. Manufactured under Dutch patronage in India (Coromandel Coast) or Java (Batavia), c.1780–1820, printed and painted. 100% cotton, glazed. 54" wide, 8½" vertical repeat. Document in the Abby Aldrich Rockefeller Folk Art Collection, Colonial Williamsburg. No. 162940 (document red and blue).
❀ INDIAN FLOWERS. Indian, c.1750–60, block print. 100% cotton. 54" wide, 12¼" repeat. No.67754 (tile).

BOTANICAL CHINTZ,
c.1765–1800.
Schumacher. Red and
green.

FLORAL STRIPE, c.1785–
1810. Schumacher. Red.

CAROLINA TOILE,
c. 1775–90.
Schumacher. Red.

ONION RESIST,
c.1750–75.
Schumacher. Indigo.

❀ JONES TOILE. English, c.1761, copperplate print. 100% cotton. 40" wide, 77" repeat. Victoria and Albert Museum, *English Printed Textiles,* pl.4; Montgomery, *Printed Textiles,* fig.214. Vignette of shepherd seated on a fountain based on an etching by Nicholas Berghem, Flanders, 1652; see *Nancy Graves Cabot: In Memoriam,* pp.32–33. The earliest dated copperplate-printed textile; inscribed "R. JONES, OLD FORD, 1761." Design also produced in France in the 18th century and revived many times. Document a 19th-century reproduction of this design, once used for bed hangings at Colonial Williamsburg. No.50092 (brick red).

❀ ONION RESIST. French, c.1750–75, resist-dyed block print. 100% cotton. 54" wide, 27" repeat. Document originally used as a quilt. No.78730 (indigo).

❀ PLEASURES OF THE FARM. French (Oberkampf Manufactory, Jouy), c.1783, copperplate print. 100% cotton. 40" wide,

40" vertical and horizontal repeats. Bredif, p.29; Clouzot, pl. 18; Edwards and Ramsey, *Etoffes Imprimées Françaises*, no.98. Design by Jean-Baptiste Huet based on engravings by Claudine Bouzonnet Stella after Jacques Stella, Paris, 1667; see *Nancy Graves Cabot: In Memoriam*, pp.34–37. Williamsburg document originally used for bed hangings or slip covers; document also at Museum of Fine Arts, Boston. No.50428 (royal purple); No.50422 (regimental red).

❀ PONDI CHERRY. Indian (made for export), c.1770–95, block print, with mordant painting and dyeing. 100% cotton. 54" wide, 17½" repeat. Document originally used for women's clothing and bed hangings. No.65102 (lavender and pink).

❀ RALEIGH TAVERN RESIST. French, c.1760–1800, resist-dyed block print. 70% linen, 30% cotton. 54" wide, 42" repeat. No.178164 (blue).

PLEASURES OF THE FARM, c.1783. Schumacher. Royal purple; regimental red.

❀ SPRING FLOWERS. English, c.1775–1800, block print. 100% cotton. 54" wide, 21¾" repeat. No. 73810 (document blue).
❀ STENCIL FLOWERS. French, c. 1750–1800, resist-dyed block print. 66% linen, 34% cotton. 54" wide, 12½" vertical repeat, 8½" horizontal repeat. No. 66625 (indigo).
❀ TRACERY FLORAL. French, c.1770–1800, block print. 100% cotton. 54" wide, 12⅝" repeat. No. 73780 (document red).
❀ WILLIAMSBURG FLORAL TRAILS. English, c. 1770, copperplate print. 100% cotton. 54" wide, 32" repeat. Design attributed to the Ware Factory, Crayford, Kent. No. 60534 (blue).
❀ WILLIAMSBURG FLOWERING TREE. English, c.1775–1800, block print. 100% cotton. 54" wide, 34" repeat. Document originally used as a quilt. No. 60362 (ruby).
❀ WILLIAMSBURG IRIS. English, c. 1780–85, copperplate print. 100% cotton. 54" wide, 36½" repeat. Montgomery, *Printed Textiles,* fig. 238, pl. 23. Document, printed at Bromley Hall, Middlesex, originally used as a quilt. No. 67760 (document red).
❀ WILLIAMSBURG POMEGRANATE RESIST. Probably French, c.

TRACERY FLORAL, c.1770–1800. Schumacher. Document red.

1740–90, resist-dyed block print. 70% linen, 30% cotton. 50" wide, 20½" repeat. No. 162694 (blue).

❀ WYTHE HOUSE BORDER RESIST. English, c. 1740–60, resist-dyed block print. 100% cotton. 50" wide, 28" repeat. Document originally used as bed hangings. No. 162380 (blue).

BRUNSCHWIG & FILS

WOVEN DESIGNS

❀ AMPHORA DAMASK. French, c. 1700–15, damask weave. 62% cotton, 38% silk. 50" wide, 21" repeat. Document a silk woven in the "bizarre" style, privately owned in France. No. 190734.00 (green).

❀ BOSCOBEL STRIPED LAMPAS. French, late 18th century. Reproduced for Boscobel Restoration, Garrison-on-Hudson, N.Y. Document in Brunschwig & Fils Archives. Special order only.

❀ CASTETS SILK DAMASK. French, c. 1700–40. 70% silk, 30% cotton. 50" wide, 28" repeat. Document privately owned in France. No. 100581.00 (red); No. 100584.00 (green); No. 100583.00 (yellow).

❀ CHEVERNY LAMPAS. French, c. 1710–30. 68% rayon, 32% silk. 50" wide, 18½" repeat. Document privately owned in France. No. 190674.00 (multi on green).

❀ EDITH SILK DAMASK. French, c. 1750. 100% silk. 54" wide, 23" repeat, 13¾" horizontal repeat. Document in Brunschwig & Fils Archives is light blue, original repeat 13¼". No. 20060.02 (cream).

❀ FRAGIOLE BROCADE. French, c. 1750–75. 52% silk, 48% viscose. 51" wide, 2¾" repeat. Document a silk lampas privately owned in Italy. No. 190495.00 (rose and green).

❀ GRIGNAN BROCADED LAMPAS. French, c. 1760–70. 100% silk. 51" wide, 15¾" repeat, 10" horizontal repeat. Document a brocaded silk lampas with a moiré ground originally intended as a dress fabric, privately owned in France. No. 32592.00 (blue).

❀ LAUNAY DAMASK. French, c. 1750–90. 100% cotton. 51" wide, 26½" repeat. Document a silk damask privately owned in France. Design used in the 18th century at Chateau de Ceverny and rewoven in the 19th century for refurbishing the same chateau. No. 190724.00 (green, red and yellow).

❀ MONTRACHET PRINT ON MOIRE. French, c. 1750–70. 53% cotton, 47% rayon. 53" wide, 16" repeat, 10½" horizontal repeat. Adapted as a print from a brocaded silk privately owned in France. No. 174656.00 (apricot).

❀ MOULINS DAMASK. French, mid-18th century. 72" cotton, 28" silk. 48" wide, 18" repeat. Document privately owned in France. No. 31630.00, Color No. 7208 (vieux rouge).

❀ NEW TOILE DE VENCE. Southern France, c. 1750–1830, woven ikat. 67% linen, 33% cotton. 48" wide, 16" repeat, 16½" horizontal repeat. Document an indigo-and-white ikat cotton in Brunschwig & Fils Archives. Modern version printed but closely resembles the original; a style of fabric used only rarely in 18th-century America. No. 69592.01 (blue on natural).

❀ PENELOPE BROCADE. French, c. 1760–90, brocaded wool flowers on fustian. 38% wool, 27% cotton, 35% linen. 51" wide, 20½" repeat. Document privately owned in France. No. 32630.00 (cream).

❀ RONSARD PRINT ON MOIRE. French, c. 1760–70, brocaded silk. 53% cotton, 47% rayon. 53" wide, 32" repeat, 21" horizontal repeat. Adapted from a brocaded silk lampas privately owned in France. No. 174660.00 (cream).

❀ TOILE PROVENCALE. French, c. 1780–1800, brocaded wool flowers on fustian. 15% wool, 42% cotton, 43% linen. 51" wide, 15¾" repeat. Handwoven. Document privately owned in France. No. 32405.00 (pink stripes); No. 32402.00 (blue stripes).

❀ TUSCANY WOVEN STRIPE. Italian, c. 1775–1820. 56% linen, 44% cotton. 50" wide. Document a silk-and-linen, satin-faced stripe, privately owned in Italy. No. 63952.01 (midnight blue and rose).

CLASSIC REVIVALS

Order fabrics by name and specify desired colors. Allow ample time for custom weaving.

❀ BELTON DAMASK. French, c. 1690–1730. 100% silk. 21" wide, 53½" repeat. Document in Prelle Archives, Lyon, France. No. 6123.

❀ HOUGHTON DAMASK. French, English or possibly Italian, c. 1730. 100% silk. 21" wide, 85" repeat. *A Choice of Design,* fig. 216. Document in Prelle Archives, Lyon, France. First woven in 1730 for Houghton Hall, Sir Robert Walpole's house in Norfolk; rewoven by Prelle for Houghton in 1920. No. 7268.

❀ PATTERSON. French (Lyon), c. 1720, damask weave. 100% silk. 48" wide, 19¾" repeat. Document privately owned in France. No. TL 409-55. Custom colors.

far left
BELTON DAMASK,
c.1690–1730.
Classic Revivals.
Custom colors.

left
HOUGHTON DAMASK,
c.1730. Classic Revivals.
Custom colors.

❀ RANGERS DAMASK. English, c.1715. 100% silk. 21" wide, 24" repeat. "Bizarre" design. Document in the Victoria and Albert Museum. Handwoven. Custom colors.

❀ STRAFFON. French (Lyon), c.1765, damask weave. 100% silk. 48" wide, 71¾" repeat. Document privately owned in France. No. TL 407-53. Custom colors.

DECORATORS WALK

❀ CARLTON DAMASK. English or French, 1750–1800. 100% rayon. 56" wide, 21" repeat. From a privately owned silk document. No. P34880 (old rose); additional colors available.

❀ CASA SILK DAMASK. English or French, 1740–1800. 60% silk, 40% rayon. 50" wide, 23" repeat. From a silk document owned by J. H. Thorp and Company. No. T33700 (red).

❀ GAINSBOROUGH DAMASK. English, c.1740–90. 100% cot-

ton. 53" wide, 27⅜" repeat. From a privately owned silk document. No.P34812 (cranberry); eight additional colors.
❀ GEORGIAN DAMASK. English, c.1750–1800. 60% silk, 40% rayon. 50" wide, 25" repeat. From a silk document owned by J. H. Thorpe and Company. No.T34334 (peacock blue); additional colors available.
❀ TULLERIE BROCADE. French, c.1760–90. 54% rayon, 46% cotton. 49" wide, 25¼" repeat. From a privately owned silk document. No.T31695 (multi on ivory).
❀ WILLIAMSBURG DAMASK. English, c. 1740–1800. 100% silk. 50" wide, 27" repeat. Document privately owned. No. L56486 (red).

LEE JOFA

Handwoven damasks are available by special order in five qualities: 100% heavy silk; 100% silk; 56.5% cotton, 43.5% silk; and 100% cotton. Minimum order 22 yards. Any color can be matched. Usual delivery time is 12 to 16 weeks; fabric is woven in England. The following designs are especially good for 18th-century work:
❀ BINGHAM. English, mid-18th century. 50" wide, 55" repeat. Document privately owned in England. No.L53-4.
❀ HAMPTON COURT PALACE. English, c.1700–75. 50" wide, 44½" repeat. Document privately owned in England. No. L12-15A.
❀ LIVERPOOL DAMASK. English, c.1730–60. 50" wide, 44¾" repeat. Document privately owned in England. No. L6-1.
❀ PAVAI DAMASK. English, c.1740–70. 50" wide, 44¾" repeat. Document privately owned in England. No.L3-1.

OLD WORLD WEAVERS

❀ DECATUR DAMASK. Italian, 18th century. 80% silk, 20% rayon. 50" wide, 27½" repeat. Document owned by Old World Weavers. No.A-162-1808-1483 (color to order).
❀ DUQUESNE. French, 18th century. 40% silk, 60% rayon. 50" wide, 28" repeat. Document owned by Old World Weavers. No.S-5203 (gold).

SCALAMANDRÉ

❀ CHINOISERIE DAMASK. English, c.1730–50. 100% silk. 51" wide, 10" repeat. Document owned by Scalamandré. No. 90014-11 (old gold).

❀ CHINOISERIE DAMASK. English, c.1740–60. 33% silk, 67% cotton. 51" wide, 22½" repeat. Document owned by Scalamandré. No.99010-1 (beige and yellow).

❀ CHINOISERIE DAMASK. French, c.1730. 100% silk. 50" wide, 18" repeat. Document at the Louvre, Paris. No.2733-9 (ivory and pale blue); No.2733-000 (ivory).

❀ CHINOISERIE LAMPAS. French or Italian, c.1760. 100% silk. 50" wide, 53" repeat. Document owned by Scalamandré. No.1495-3 (gray and red); document green (special order only).

❀ DAMAS DE PARIS. French, 18th century. 100% silk. 51" wide, 21" repeat. Document owned by Scalamandré. No. 97416-4 (wine).

❀ 18TH CENTURY CHARLESTON DAMASK. English, mid-18th century. 100% silk. 51" wide, 46½" repeat. Document owned by Edmondston-Allston House, Charleston. No. 2099-2 (kelly green).

❀ XVIII CENTURY DAMASK. English, c.1750–1830. 100% silk. 50" wide, 14½" repeat. Document privately owned. No.2735-1 (crimson).

❀ XVIII CENTURY DAMASK. English, c.1750–1820. 100% silk. 52" wide, 31½" repeat. Document owned by Scalamandré. No.97430-2 (sea blue); No.97430-1 (bone).

❀ XVIII CENTURY GEORGIAN DAMASK. Italian, c.1730–60. 100% silk. 50" wide, 31" repeat. Document owned by Scalamandré. No.1228-6 (old ivory); No.1228-7 (deep rose on rose).

❀ FERRONERIE VELVET. Italian, c.1760. 40% silk, 60% cotton. 23" wide, 23" repeat. Document at Academy of Fine Arts, Philadelphia. Handwoven in Italy. No.3154-4 (blue, Gothic). Special order only.

❀ FLEUR RENAISSANCE. French or Italian, c.1750–70. 100% silk. 51" wide, 4⅛" repeat. Document owned by Scalamandré. No.370-16 (ivory and eggshell). Special order only.

❀ FRENCH DAMASK. French, c.1730–70. 100% silk. 50" wide, 36" repeat. Document at Musée des Tissus, Paris. No. 360-2 (red). Special order only.

❀ GEORGIAN ANTIQUE DAMASK. Italian, c.1650–1775. 40% silk, 60" linen. 50" wide, 24¼" repeat. Document privately owned. No.5138-20 (beige and white).

❀ GEORGIAN BROCATELLE. Italian, c.1750–90. 80% silk, 20% linen. 50" wide, 32" approximate repeat. Document owned

top left
GEORGIAN DAMASK,
c.1750–90. Scalaman-
dré. Emerald.

top right
LOUIS XVI DAMASK,
c.1770–1800. Scala-
mandré. Kelly green.

right
MARY TODD LINCOLN
DAMASK, c.1750–1800.
Scalamandré. Wine;
ivory and gold.

by Scalamandré. Same design more commonly found in damask weaves. No.895-21 (champagne).

❀ GEORGIAN DAMASK. English or Italian, c.1750–90. 100% silk. 50" wide, 24½" repeat. Scalamandré, no.15. Document owned by Scalamandré, which first reproduced the design in 1930; made in many colors and adapted to various sizes. No.1225-37 (emerald); other 18th-century colors available.

❀ LOUIS XV DAMASK. French, c.1750–80. 34% silk, 66% cotton. 50" wide, 25" approximate repeat. Document owned by Scalamandré. No.1182-9 (crimson).

❀ LOUIS XVI DAMASK. French, c.1770–1800. 89% silk, 11% cotton. 51½" wide, 32" repeat. Document owned by Scalamandré. No.97362-5 (kelly green).

❀ LOUIS XVI LAMPAS. French, c.1770–1800. 100% silk. 50" wide, 27" repeat. Document owned by Scalamandré, which first wove the design in the 1950s. Handwoven in Italy. No. 535-5 (tones of gold on light beige). Special order only.

❀ LOVE BIRD DAMASK. Italian, c.1650–1750. 100% silk. 50" wide, 18½" repeat. Document owned by Scalamandré, which first reproduced the design in 1930. No.1098-6 (Georgian red).

❀ MARY TODD LINCOLN DAMASK. French, c.1750–1800. 100% silk. 50" wide, 30¼" repeat. Document owned by Scalamandré. No.4986-3 (wine). Special order only. Also woven with a 23½" repeat; No.4986A-4 (ivory and gold).

❀ METROPOLITAN MUSEUM OF ART DAMASK. French or English, c.1750–1850. 30% silk, 70% cotton. 50" wide, 24" repeat. Document owned by Scalamandré. No.1348-14 (burgundy). Special order only.

❀ MET ORIENTAL DAMASK. French, c.1730–50. 32% silk, 68% cotton. 50¾" wide, 28¾" repeat. Document at Metropolitan Museum of Art. No.97383-1 (old gold). Special order only.

❀ NATCHEZ XVIII CENTURY LAMPAS. French or Italian, c. 1740–90. 100% silk. 50" wide, 29" repeat. Scalamandré, no.13. Document owned by Scalamandré, which first reproduced the design in 1962. No.1493A-1 (gold, yellow and ivory).

❀ POTTSGROVE DAMASK. French, 18th century. 100% silk. 50" wide, 17" repeat. Document owned by Scalamandré. No.166-7 (gold on platinum).

❀ PROVINCE STRIPE SATIN AND TAFFETA. French, c.1750. 100%

NATCHEZ XVIII CENTURY LAMPAS, c. 1740–90. Scalamandré. Gold, yellow and ivory.

silk. 50" wide. Document owned by Scalamandré. No. 154-1 (pale blue and peach).

❀ RESTORATION DAMASK. French or English, mid-18th century. 26% silk, 74% cotton. 50" wide, 53" repeat. Document owned by Scalamandré. No. 638-30 (gold). Special order only.

❀ RUTHMERE DAMASK. English, 18th century. 100% silk. 51" wide, 45" repeat. Document privately owned. No. 97292-2 (shrimp).

❀ SAN GALLEN DAMASK. French, c. 1700–50. 100% silk. 51½" wide, 20" repeat. Document owned by Scalamandré. No. 97415-7 (celadon).

❀ STRATFORD DAMASK. French or English, c. 1740–70. 100% silk. 50" wide, 21½" repeat. Document privately owned. No. 526-4 (pink).

❀ STRAWBERRY DESIGN STRIPED TAFFETA LISERE. French, c. 1750–90. 100% silk. 50" wide, 2¾" repeat. Document owned by Scalamandré. No.205-3 (multi on gold and ivory).

❀ VENETIAN DAMASK. Italian, c.1650–present. 77% silk, 23% rayon. 51" wide, 15" repeat. Document at Victoria and Albert Museum. No.97386-1 (beige on peach).

SCHUMACHER
COLONIAL WILLIAMSBURG REPRODUCTIONS

All documents are in the textile collection of Colonial Williamsburg, Williamsburg, Va., and all are illustrated in *Williamsburg Reproductions.*

❀ BRUSH EVERARD MOIRE STRIPE. European, c.1730–90. 65% cotton, 35% bemberg rayon. 50" wide, 5¼" horizontal repeat. Document made of bourette silk and cotton. No. 90010 (old red).

❀ BRUTON ADAPTATION DAMASK. c.1740–75, woven damask. 67% mercerized cotton, 33% silk. 52" wide, 21¼" repeat. Document 100% silk; scale of modern version slightly different. No.33101 (gold).

❀ CHINESE PEONY DAMASK. China, c.1740–50. 100% silk. 54" wide, 16¾" vertical repeat. No.36800 (persimmon).

❀ DOBBY WEAVE. American, c.1780–1820. 100% cotton. 54" wide. Document a 100% linen fabric of a type commonly used for tablecloths, napkins and towels. No.81729 (off-white).

❀ EDINBURGH CHECK. British, c.1750–1800. 100% linen. 48" wide, 2" vertical repeat, 1¼" horizontal repeat. No. 83174 (blue).

❀ GLOUCESTER DAMASK. European, c.1680–1700. 55% cotton, 45% linen. 56" wide, 28¼" vertical repeat, 13⅝" horizontal repeat. Document fabric 100% silk and used for curtains and chair upholstery. No.52841 (gold).

❀ HERRINGBONE STRIPE. English, c.1750–1800. 46% silk, 38% cotton, 16% rayon. 50" wide, 8½" horizontal repeat. Adapted from a bourette silk and hemp fabric. No.38594 (rust and blue).

❀ HERRINGBONE STRIPE. European, c.1750–1800. 46% silk, 38% cotton, 16% rayon. 50" wide. Document 100% silk. This type of fabric used for both furniture upholstery and curtains. No.84944 (rust).

❀ LUDWELL DAMASK. European, c.1725–50. 100% cotton.

53" wide, 18½" vertical repeat, 26¾" horizontal repeat. Document 100% silk. No. 52821 (blue).

❀ SHIR O'SHAKKAR. British or perhaps Indian, c.1750–1800. 100% cotton. 54" wide, 2" horizontal repeat. No. 81574 (periwinkle).

❀ TAVERN CHECK. American, c.1750–1800. 61% linen, 39% cotton. 54" wide, 3" vertical and horizontal repeats. Document 100% linen, originally used as a slipcover. No. 81508 (blue).

❀ WILLIAMSBURG GARDEN DAMASK. French, c.1750, woven damask. 100% cotton. 54" wide, 21" vertical repeat, 13½" horizontal repeat. Document 100% silk, originally used for a woman's garment. No. 51M620 (ivory).

❀ WILLIAMSBURG MULTI STRIPE. English, c.1780–1810. 100% cotton. 52" wide, 6½" horizontal repeat. Document woven of wool and cotton in a twill pattern with a prominent chevron design. No. 132962 (red).

❀ WILLIAMSBURG POMEGRANATE DAMASK. French or English, c.1740–90, woven damask. 63% cotton, 37% silk. 54" wide, 34" vertical repeat, 27" horizontal repeat. Continuously woven by Schumacher since 1902 (see p. 211); original 18th-century silk-and-linen document was given to the Colonial Williamsburg Foundation when this design was adopted for Schumacher's line of authorized Colonial Williamsburg reproductions in 1952. No. 53730 (red).

❀ WILLIAMSBURG SILK VELVET. European, c.1700–50. 100% silk. 50" wide. No. 42385 (deep rose).

❀ WILLIAMSBURG STRIPE. French, c.1750–1800. 65% cotton, 35% silk. 50" wide. Document a red-and-green bourette silk fabric used for upholstery or curtains. No. 31162 (red and green).

❀ WYTHE HOUSE STRIPE. Indian, c.1750–1800. 100% cotton. 50" wide, 6¾" horizontal repeat. No. 111342 (old red).

STROHEIM & ROMANN

❀ TOWNSEND. French or English, c.1725–75, damask weave. 100% cotton. 52" wide, 13½" repeat. Document a 100% silk damask in Winterthur Museum. No. 49114 (gold).

top left
BRUTON ADAPTATION
DAMASK, c.1740–75.
Schumacher. Gold.

top rght
HERRINGBONE STRIPE,
c.1750–1800. Schu-
macher. Rust and blue.

left
WILLIAMSBURG
POMEGRANATE DAMASK,
c.1740–90. Schumacher.
Red.

1790 TO 1815:
CHANGING TASTES
AND TECHNOLOGY

Toward the end of the 18th century and in the early years of the 19th century, mechanized textile production, one of the highlights of the Industrial Revolution, lowered fabric costs and brought furnishing fabrics, especially printed cottons and dimities, within the economic reach of many persons for the first time. Inevitably, fashion followed, and furnishing fabrics began to be used more widely and in greater abundance than before. Most fabrics were still imported from England, which had the most advanced textile technology, but American merchants also imported French, Indian and Chinese goods. The infant American textile industry was not yet a factor in providing fabrics for fashionable home furnishings. A few rural households continued to produce their own bed coverings and household linens, and some professional weavers with complex looms made wool and cotton coverlets and highly finished woolens, but neither group provided any serious competition for imported goods.

Although woolen bed hangings continued to be used in some households, colorful printed cotton chintz was now regarded as more stylish and had the added advantage of being easily washable. White cotton dimity was also popular. Both chintz and dimity were often trimmed with colorful silk or wool fringes or handmade knotted borders, both of which had to be removed for the fabric to be successfully laundered.

Bed valances were wider than they had been earlier in the 18th century, ranging up to 20 inches before the addition of the netting or fringe. The most elaborate designs for bed hangings included many additional pieces — extra valances, short curtains, swags and rosettes. The basic pieces also

Office, Homewood Museum, opened to the public in 1987 by The Johns Hopkins University, Baltimore. Brunschwig & Fils's "Bird and Thistle" has been used for the window curtain hung in double drapery and as slip covers. (Susan G. Tripp)

Parlor chamber, Lloyd Manor, Lloyd's Neck, N.Y. Scalamandré's "Documentary Print," custom printed on white ground, was used for the bed hangings.

were treated in a more elaborate fashion than before. Tester cloths could be shirred evenly or gathered into a radiating star, although many still were stretched flat. Head cloths could be hung straight in the traditional way, but they could also now be gathered to double fullness, reflecting the new sense of freedom in using greater quantities of fabric to achieve decorative effects. Bed valances were no longer straight pieces of fabric cut in stylized scrolls but could be cut in a series of repeating scallops, simply gathered on a string, or cut in swags and trapezoids and joined in the complex rhythm of French drapery. Bed skirts or bases no longer slavishly repeated the shape of the valances but were often gathered fully and either tied or nailed to the bed rails.

Field beds, also known as tent beds, became popular during this period, and they, too, were embellished with lavish fabric drapery. Most beds of this type were furnished with fully enclosing curtains, which could be drawn up in the daytime and secured by a loop and button or tied to the bedpost. Most bed hangings were unlined, perhaps to ensure that they would hang in graceful folds when drawn open during the daytime. In bedchambers, window curtains and upholstery still matched the color of the fabric and trimming of the bed hangings, although the counterpane could be made of a different fabric.

During this period certain fabrics were considered especially appropriate for specific kinds of furnishing purposes. Chintz was favored in parlors and drawing rooms, while wool was considered more suitable for dining rooms and libraries. As before, silk was used only in the parlors and best chambers of a few luxurious houses, but the number of these increased slightly. Wool, horsehair fabrics and leather continued to be used for furniture upholstery. Covering loose chair cushions in silk or chintz to match window curtains also was fashionable. Dimity, checks and chintzes were used for slipcovers.

Dimity was used extensively for the skirts of toilet tables; covers for these table tops were often embellished with Marseilles quilting.

Woolen fabrics continued to be highly finished worsteds in primary colors as well as green, while the usual furnishing silks were lightweight goods in plain weaves. Whichever was chosen the primary decorative effects were achieved by

French drapery from *Ackermann's Repository,* London, 1810.

77

well cut drapery and dramatically contrasting colors in linings, borders and trimmings. Bright green was often coupled with lilac and blue with buff or gold.

In block-printed cottons, the predominant color palette continued to be that derived from indigo or madder dyeing. From about 1799 to 1806, a "drab" style with quercitron-based brown, green and yellow colors was popular. (For color illustration, see Schoeser and Rufey, chap. 2, fig. 11.) Indigo blue backgrounds were popular at this same period; when enlivened by motifs in brilliant red, they were referred to as being in the "lapis" style. Red itself was a popular background color after about 1815, and "turkey red" designs were popular for decades.

In the mid-20th century, it was commonly believed that pale colors and chaste neoclassical motifs were characteristic of furnishing fabrics of the period 1790 to 1815. More recent research has shown, instead, a marked preference for dramatic printed designs and strong, almost glaring, colors — rich yellow, crimson, orange, scarlet and blue — often arranged in bold combinations. Unfortunately, few reproductions of this style are on the current market. (For illustrations of color of this period, see Richard C. Nylander, "The

Parlor, Lloyd Manor, Lloyd's Neck, N.Y. Restored to c.1795 and installed 1981–82. Brunschwig & Fils's "New Zinnia Toile" has been used for slip covers. (Society for the Preservation of Long Island Antiquities)

First Harrison Gray Otis House," *Antiques,* June 1976; Edward S. Cooke, *Upholstery in America and Europe,* pl. 11; and Schoeser and Rufey, *English and American Textiles,* chap. 2, figs. 19 and 55.)

BRUNSCHWIG & FILS

PRINTS

❀ ADELAIDE COTTON PRINT. Late 18th or early 19th century. 100% cotton. 50" wide, 18" repeat, 16" horizontal repeat. Document, in Brunschwig & Fils Archives, block printed in madder and indigo with overprinted green on a dense tabby woven cotton. No. 66441.01 (red and blue).

❀ FALCONET COTTON PRINT. French (Nantes), c. 1810–20, copperplate and block print. 100% cotton. 33" wide, 23¾" repeat. *Toiles de Nantes des XVIIIe et XIXe siècles,* pl. 108; d'Allemagne, *La Toile Imprimée,* pl. 86. Document, privately owned in France, an early-19th century version of a multicolored toile originally produced at Nantes by Favre, Petitpierre, et Cie in 1790 called "L'abreuvoir au pied des ruines." Document printed on cotton with a slightly smaller repeat; in modern version two motifs have been eliminated and some minor changes made in the drawing. No. 36260.01 (multi on cream).

ADELAIDE COTTON PRINT, late 18th or early 19th century. Brunschwig & Fils. Red and blue.

❀ FETE D'ETE COTTON PRINT. French, c.1800–30. 100% cotton. 58" wide, 13½" repeat. D'Allemagne, *La Toile Imprimée*, pl.174. Document a roller-printed cotton based on Pillement figure, in the Museum at Jouy. No.62721.01 (rose on gold); No.62723.01 (blue on gold); No.62722.01 (blues).

❀ FOLIE GEP GLAZED CHINTZ. French, c.1800. 100% cotton. 54" wide, 13¼" repeat, 26" horizontal repeat. D'Allemagne, *La Toile Imprimée*, pl.49. Document a roller-printed cotton privately owned in England. No.62902.01 (blue).

❀ GORE PLACE GLAZED CHINTZ. English, c.1805, block and roller print. 51" wide, 15⅜" repeat. *British Textile Design in the Victoria and Albert Museum*, no.364. Document with blue ground owned by Gore Place, Waltham, Mass.; a privately owned example has a saffron yellow ground, and the Victoria and Albert Museum has a sample with a tan ground that may be original or a faded version of the yellow. No. 36622.01 (blue); No.36623.01 (yellow).

❀ LES SPHINX MEDAILLONS. French, c.1810–20, plate and block print. 100% cotton. 37" wide, 10½" repeat. Document quilted and made into a set of bed hangings now owned by the Taft Museum, Cincinnati. Made originally as a custom order for the Taft Museum. No.36698.01 (aubergine and pale yellow).

❀ MATLEY GLAZED CHINTZ. English, c.1810–20, roller print with block-printed blotch. 100% cotton, glazed. 54½" wide, 12¾" repeat. *Chefs d'Oeuvre du Musée de l'Impression sur Etoffes, Mulhouse*, vol.2, pl.68. Documents owned privately in England, by Brunschwig & Fils and by the Musée de l'Impression sur Etoffes de Mulhouse. Documents printed in sepia with an acid yellow blotch, but motifs are copied exactly. Monochromatic fabrics, particularly in blue, are known in this style. Modern version is clearly an adaptation but could still be considered appropriate for restoration work. No.62392.01 (blue).

❀ NEW ZINNIA TOILE. French or English, late 18th century, copperplate print. 100% cotton. 55" wide, 39½" repeat. Document privately owned. No.67282.01 (blue on white).

❀ QUELUZ COTTON AND LINEN PRINT. French, c.1790, screen-printed copy of a block-printed indigo resist. 51% linen, 49% cotton. 52" wide, 4½" repeat. Document in Brunschwig & Fils Archives. No.785922.04 (indigo).

❀ SUN, MOON AND STARS GLAZED CHINTZ. English, c.1790–

FETE D'ETE COTTON
PRINT, c. 1800–30.
Brunschwig & Fils.
Rose on gold; blue on
gold; blues.

GORE PLACE GLAZED
CHINTZ, c. 1805.
Brunschwig & Fils.
Blue; yellow.

LES MISERABLES,
c.1780–1800. Clarence
House. Bleu; rouge.

1820, block print. 100% cotton. 49" wide, 9" repeat. Scale slightly altered. Document, in Winterthur Museum, has madder colors on aged ground. No.78402.04 (ochre on indigo); No.78409.04 (multi on blue) (both color adaptations). ❀ VILLEROY. French, late 18th century, block print. 56% cotton, 44% linen. 48" wide, 12½" repeat. Document in Brunschwig & Fils Archives. No.73930.04 (red and blue on cream).

❀ VIVIENNE. French, late 18th century, block print. 100% cotton. 50" wide, 8¼" repeat. Document privately owned in France. No.173620.00 (multi on cream).

CLARENCE HOUSE

❀ COMPAGNIE DES INDES. French, late 18th century, block print. 100% cotton. 46" wide plus 4½" border on each side, 26" repeat. Document privately owned. No.32043-1 (rouge). Minimum order two yards.

❀ LES MISERABLES. French, c.1780–1800, copperplate print. 100% cotton. 32½" wide, 34½" repeat. Document privately owned in France. No.32920-3 (bleu); No.32920-1 (rouge).

❀ LORD BYRON'S CHINTZ. French, 1808, block print. 100% cotton, glazed. 54" wide, 17¼" repeat. Schoeser and Rufey, chap 8, fig. 2; discussed as a reproduction on pp. 231–32. Document, privately owned in England, used as a bed hanging in the 1808 refurbishing of Newstead Abbey by Lord Byron. No. 32753-1 (document drab and green on green) with excellent success in reproducing blue on yellow overprint.

❀ PERSAN. French, late 18th century, block print. 100% cotton, glazed. 51" wide, 14¾" repeat. Document privately owned. No.31688-5 (ecru). Minimum order two yards.

❀ STRAIGHT LACE. English, c.1795–1810, block print in the drab style. 100% cotton, glazed. 54" wide, 6" repeat. Document privately owned. No.32602-2 (brown).

CLASSIC REVIVALS

❀ TRICHINOPOLY. French, c.1790–1800, block print (Indienne). 100% cotton. 50" wide, 14" repeat. Document owned by the British National Trust. No.TM 391-10 (madder colors with blue on ivory).

LEE JOFA

❀ BUCKINGHAM TOILE PRINT. English c.1790–95, copperplate print. 100% cotton. 34" wide, 34½" half-drop repeat. Document owned by Lee Jofa. No.8761-1 (blue); No.8763-1 (red).

SCALAMANDRÉ

❀ ANDREW JACKSON CHINTZ. French, c.1795–1810, block print. 100% cotton. 50" wide, 36" repeat. *Scalamandré*, no.

83

7. Document owned by The Hermitage, Nashville, Tenn.; another sample owned by Scalamandré, which first offered the design in 1952 and reissued it in 1985. No. 6046-1 (multi on dark brown).

❀ APHRODITE TOILE. English, c. 1790, copperplate print. 100% linen. 48" wide, 32½" repeat. Document privately owned; said to have been used by Thomas Jefferson at Monticello, Charlottesville, Va. No. 6281-14 (blue on white). Special order.

❀ BLIND MAN'S BLUFF. English, late 18th century, copperplate print. 100% linen. 50" wide, 32" repeat. Montgomery, *Printed Textiles*, fig. 288 (one motif). Document privately owned. No. 6065-1 (brown on tan). Special order only.

❀ CLIVEDEN, CHEW HOUSE PANEL. English, c. 1790–1800, block print. 100% cotton. 36" wide, 99" pattern repeat printed with 14" plain fabric at top and bottom; cut in 3½-yard panels only. Document a bed covering (perhaps originally window curtains) at Cliveden, Germantown, Pa., a property of the National Trust for Historic Preservation. No. 6811-1 (multi reds, blues, greens and browns on ecru). Special order only.

❀ CURWEN BED HANGING. English, c. 1805–10, block print. 100% cotton, glazed. 48" wide, 30" repeat. Document owned by Essex Institute, Salem, Mass. No. 6287-1 (reds and golds on white). Special order only.

❀ DOCUMENTARY PRINT. English, c. 1790–1800, block print. 100% linen. 42" wide, 34" repeat. Document privately owned. No. 6295-10 (pink, red and brown on beige); white ground available by special order only.

❀ ELIZA LUCAS FLORAL. English, c. 1750–60, block print. 100% cotton. 54" wide, 25¼" repeat. Document a bed hanging painted in the late 18th century by Eliza Lucas, owned by Historic Charleston Foundation, Charleston, S.C. No. 7780-1 (burgundies, browns, light blue and green on pongee).

❀ FERN AND THISTLE. English, late 18th century, copperplate print. 100% cotton. 48" wide, 37" repeat. Document privately owned. No. 6490-2 (blues on natural). Special order only.

❀ FLORAL DESIGN. English, c. 1790–1800, block print. 100% cotton. 48" wide, 27" repeat. Adapted from textile document in Metropolitan Museum of Art. No. 6533-7 (red, green, gold and brown on ecru). Special order only.

APHRODITE TOILE,
c.1790. Scalamandré.
Blue on white.

ANDREW JACKSON
FLORAL, c.1795–1810.
Scalamandré. Multi on
dark brown.

CLIVEDEN, CHEW
HOUSE, c.1790–1800.
Scalamandré. Multi on
ecru.

DOCUMENTARY PRINT, c.1790–1800. Scalamandré. Pink, red and brown on beige.

CURWEN BED HANGING, c.1805–10. Scalamandré. Reds and golds on white.

REVOLUTIONARY TOILE,
c. 1785–1800.
Scalamandré. Reds on
off-white.

QUAIL UNGLAZED
CHINTZ, c. 1815–35.
Scalamandré. Multi
on tan.

KENMORE TOILE,
c. 1790– 1800. Scala-
mandré. Blue on white.

❀ KENMORE TOILE. French, c. 1790–1800, copperplate print. 100% cotton. 48" wide, 30¼" repeat. *Scalamandré, no. 27.* Documents bed hangings owned by Kenmore, Fredericksburg, Va.; another example owned by Cooper Hewitt Museum. No. 6708 (blue on white). Special order only.

❀ QUAIL UNGLAZED CHINTZ. English, c. 1815–35, block print. 100% cotton. 47" wide, 15½" repeat. Document owned by Scalamandré. No. 6256-1 (multi on tan).

❀ REVOLUTIONARY TOILE. English, c. 1785–1800, copperplate print. 100% cotton. 50" wide, 30" repeat. *Scalamandré, no. 29;* Montgomery, *Printed Textiles,* fig. 301 ("America Presenting at the Altar of Liberty Medallions of Her Illustrious Sons"). Document owned by Scalamandré. No. 6247-4 (reds on off-white).

❀ WOODBURY PRINT. English, early 19th century, resist print. 100% cotton. 40" wide, 26" repeat. Document in American Wing, Metropolitan Museum of Art. No. 6673-1 (light blue and dark blue on cream). Special order only.

SCHUMACHER

❀ ANDROCLES. c.1800–20, copperplate print. Document in Schumacher Archives. No.163770 (red).

SCHUMACHER
COLONIAL WILLIAMSBURG REPRODUCTIONS

All documents are in the textile collection of Colonial Williamsburg, Williamsburg, Va., and all are illustrated in *Williamsburg Reproductions*.

❀ CHERUBINS. English or French, c.1790–1820, block print. 100% cotton, glazed. 54" wide, 13½" vertical repeat. No. 16111410 (brown).

❀ PARSLEY. Probably Dutch, c.1800. 100% cotton. 54" wide, 6" repeat. Document from a Dutch merchant's swatchbook. No.74250 (document blue).

❀ PILLEMENT. French, c.1790–1815, block print. 100% cotton. 48" wide, 16" repeat. No.70820 (document rose).

❀ TISSU FLEURI. French, c.1790, block print. 58% linen, 42% cotton. 54" wide, 18" vertical repeat, 25¼" horizontal repeat. No.161400 (red).

ANDROCLES, c.1800–20. Schumacher. Red.

CHERUBINS, c. 1790–1820. Schumacher. Brown.

TISSU FLEURI, c. 1790. Schumacher. Red.

WOVEN DESIGNS

BRUNSCHWIG & FILS

❀ AGEN BROCADE. French, c. 1800–15. 100% rayon. 50" wide, 5¼" repeat. Silk document privately owned in France. No.121230.00 (gold on cream ground); No.121231.00 (gold on red ground).

❀ BALTIMORE STRIPE. European, 1790–1830. 100% rayon. 50" wide. Silk document owned by Winterthur Museum. No.66765.01 (pink and green).

❀ GAURIAC STRIPED LAMPAS. French, c.1790–1810. 100% silk. 21" wide, 3" repeat. Document privately owned in France. No.33768.00 (brown).

❀ JULIANA FIGURED STRIPE. French, probably late 18th century. 52% cotton, 40% viscose rayon, 8% polypropylene. 50" wide, 12" repeat. Document, in Brunschwig & Fils Archives, linen with handembroidered clusters of flowers; reproduction has woven flowers. No.60612.01 (blue stripe).

❀ LAUREAL DAMASK. French, c.1790–1810. 60% spun rayon, 40% nylon. 52" wide, 27" repeat. Silk document at Museum of Early Southern Decorative Arts. No.10009.02 (white on beige).

❀ LESPARRE STRIPE. French, early 19th century, woven stripe. 100% rayon. 48" wide. Reproduced for Liberty Hall, Kenansville, N.C. Document a satin-faced stripe with silk warp and a linen weft, privately owned in France. No.30942.00 (blue and cream).

❀ LILA GLAZED TEXTURE. English, c.1790–1820. 66% viscose, 34% cotton. 54" wide, 2⅛" repeat, 4½" horizontal repeat. Montgomery, *Textiles in America,* pp. 356–58, pls. D-74-76, D-85. Document, in Brunschwig & Fils Archives, made of tabourat, a supplementary warp-glazed worsted in which the pattern is derived from warp shading. No. 60941.01 (coral).

❀ MONTMORENCI MOIRED STRIPE. European, 1790–1810. 66% cotton, 34% bemberg. 50" wide (no centerfold). Silk document owned by Winterthur Museum. No.63414.01 (pink and green).

❀ ST. CYR. French, c.1790–1810, brocaded satin. 70% spun rayon, 30% bemberg. 50" wide, 10¼" repeat. Silk document at Musée des Arts Décoratifs, Paris. No.142231.00 (red ground with black and white tails).

❀ SOMERSET WOVEN STRIPE. French or English, c. 1800–35, striped twill. 100% viscose. 53" wide, 11½" repeat. Adapted from a silk document at Winterthur Museum. No. 63591.00 (red and olive green).

❁ SPRIG AND STRIPE WOVEN TEXTURE. French, 1790–1800. 83% cotton, 17% spun rayon. 50" wide, 4½" repeat, 2¼" horizontal repeat. Document at Winterthur Museum, a handwoven linen with a woven indigo stripe, embroidered with a small sprig in ombred white and blue wool. Modern version has woven sprigs. No. 64962.01 (blues).

CLASSIC REVIVALS

Custom woven in your choice of colors. Order by name.
❁ FONTAINEBLEAU GOURGOURAND. French, 1806, woven damask. 100% silk. 21" wide. Can also be woven 48" wide, although this width is not authentic. Document in Prelle Archives, Lyon, France. First woven for the Palace of Fontainebleau in 1806.

FONTAINEBLEAU GOURGOURAND, 1806. Classic Revivals.

PALMES DE ST. CLOUD, c. 1802. Classic Revivals. Green.

❀ MELBOURNE DAMASK. English, c. 1820, woven damask. 100% wool. 21" wide, 6" repeat. Can also be woven 48" wide, although this width is not authentic. Document at Temple Newsam House, Leeds, Yorkshire.

❀ PALMES DE ST. CLOUD. French, 1802, woven *gros de tours* damask. 100% silk. 21" wide, 32½" repeat. Can also be woven 48" wide, although this width is not authentic. Document in Prelle Archives, Lyon, France. First woven in 1802 for the Library of the First Counsel Bonaparte at the Palace of St. Cloud. Known to have been used at Hopetoun House, Edinburgh, c. 1835. Rewoven recently for the British Embassy in Paris. Green.

DECORATORS WALK

❀ NAPOLEON BEE DAMASK. French, c. 1800–15. 100% silk. 50" wide, 3½" repeat. Document privately owned. No. L57835 (yellow and white).

MELBOURNE DAMASK, c. 1820. Classic Revivals.

CONCORDE EMPIRE LAMPAS, 1805. Scalamandré. Sofa panel. Royal gold on regal red.

SCALAMANDRÉ

❀ ADAM DAMASK. English, late 18th century. 100% silk. 50" wide, 18" repeat. Document privately owned. No. 1384-4 (grass green).

❀ "THE BEE" NAPOLEON LAMPAS. French or Italian, c.1790–1815. 25% rayon. 50" wide, 3½" repeat. Silk document privately owned in Italy. No. 96103-2 (beige and gold on oriental blue); No. 96103-1 (citron and gold on antique gray).

❀ CONCORDE EMPIRE LAMPAS. French, 1805. 100% silk. 50" wide, 16" repeat. *Scalamandré*, no. 38. Document privately owned in France. Reproduced for the White House Red Room during the Kennedy administration. Yardage No. 97052-1. Chair seat, 31" wide, 25" long, No. 97053-1. Chair backs, 26" wide, 25" long, No. 97054-1. Sofa panel, 2½ yards wide, 25" long, No. 97055-1. All royal gold on regal red. Special order only.

❀ DUMBARTON DAMASK. French or English, c. 1790–1820. 30% silk, 70% spun rayon. 51" wide, 5" repeat. Document owned by Scalamandré. No. 97382-6 (ginger).

❀ EAGLE LAMPAS. French, c. 1800–20. 100% silk. 50½" wide, 90" repeat. Document owned by Scalamandré; adapted slightly to make eagle less ferocious. Coordinates with "Medallion Chair Seat Lampas" and "Rosette Lampas." No. 97273-1 (gold on federal blue).

❀ FEDERAL LAMPAS. French, early 19th century. 75% silk, 25% cotton. 50" wide, 7¼" repeat. Document privately owned. No. 1951-1 (federal gold on sage). Special order only.

❀ GARDNER MUSEUM. French, early 19th century, lampas. 75% silk, 25% cotton. Reproduced for Isabella Stewart Gardner Museum, Boston, Mass. Chair back, 50" wide, 2½ yards long with two motifs across width and 9" plain satin between, 12" plain satin below and 62" plain satin above, No.97232-1. Chair seat, 50" wide, 2½ yards long, with two motifs across width and 9" plain satin between, 12" plain satin below and 62" plain satin above. Both cut by repeat only. Coordinating fabric "Emperor Lampas," 50½" wide, 4¼" repeat; No.97218-5. All white on grass green. All special order only.

❀ GERMANTOWN STRIPE. French or English, c.1790–1850, taffeta. 100% silk. 52" wide. Document at Cliveden, Germantown, Pa. No.99460-1 (cranberry and apple green).

❀ LE MANS EMPIRE LAMPAS. French, c.1805–30. 100% silk. 51" wide, 36" repeat. No.451-1 (yellow and Persian rose). Special order only.

❀ LOUIS XVI LAMPAS. French, late 18th century. 100% silk.

LOUIS XVI LAMPAS, late 18th century. Scalamandré. Blue and silver.

50" wide, 69" repeat. *Scalamandré,* no. 20. Document owned by Scalamandré. No. 1496 (blue and silver). Special order only.

❀ MEDALLION CHAIR SEAT LAMPAS. French, c. 1800–20. 100% silk. 50½" wide; woven in panels 2½ yards long with two motifs across each width. Document owned by Scalamandré. No. 97274-1 (gold on federal blue). Sold only by the panel.

❀ METROPOLITAN ROSETTE EMPIRE LAMPAS. French, late 18th century. 100% silk. 50" wide, 16" repeat. Document owned by Scalamandré. No. 97228-1 (golds on royal red).

❀ MUSEUM DAMASK. French, late 18th century. 26% silk, 74% cotton. 51" wide, 12½" repeat. Document owned by Scalamandré. No. 1622-3 (blue and ivory). Special order only.

❀ NAPOLITANO STRIPE. English, c. 1800–20. 35% silk, 65% rayon. 50" wide, 1" horizontal repeat. Document owned by Scalamandré. No. 2403-3 (French blue, peach and tan).

❀ OAK HILL DAMASK. Probably French, 1810–20. 100% silk. 51" wide, 12" repeat. Document owned by Essex Institute, Salem, Mass. No. 96398-1 (salmon).

❀ POMPEIAN MEMORIES DAMASK. English, c. 1790–1800. 70% cotton, 30% silk. 56" wide, 17" repeat. Document owned by Scalamandré. No. 97412-4 (grays on baby blue strié).

❀ ROSETTE LAMPAS. French, c. 1800–20. 100% silk. 50½" wide, 4½" repeat. Document owned by Scalamandré. No. 97275-1 (gold on federal blue). Coordinates with "Medallion Chair Seat Lampas."

❀ SHIRRED STRIPE TAFFETA AND REPP STRIPE. French, c. 1790–1800. 50" wide. Document owned by Scalamandré. No. 121-1 (peach and beige); No. 121-2 (pale blue); No. 121-8 (antique green and bronze).

❀ SIMBOLO STRIPED TAFFETA. English or French, c. 1790–1800. 100% silk. 50" wide. Document privately owned. No. 90010-2 (multi orange, gold, green and yellow); No. 90010-1 (multi peach, coral, green and gold).

SCHUMACHER
COLONIAL WILLIAMSBURG REPRODUCTIONS

All documents are in the collection of Colonial Williamsburg, Williamsburg, Va., and are illustrated in *Williamsburg Reproductions.*

❀ BRUTON DAMASK. English or French, c. 1790–1810. 33%

silk, 67% mercerized cotton. 52" wide, 21¼" repeat. Document in 100% silk. No. 33101 (gold).

❀ LIVERPOOL BIRDS. French, c. 1795–1812. 100% cotton. 52" wide, 7" vertical repeat, 8¾" horizontal repeat. No. 131123 (bois).

❀ WILLIAMSBURG MULTI STRIPE. French or English, c. 1790–1800. 100% cotton. 52" wide, 6½" horizontal repeat. Document at Colonial Williamsburg, Williamsburg, Va. No. 132962 (red).

STROHEIM & ROMANN

❀ AVENTINE. European, c. 1800–50, woven stripe. 60% spun rayon, 40% cotton. 52" wide. Adapted from a striped linen document at Winterthur Museum. No. 48260 (document).

❀ RHINEBECK STRIPE. European, c. 1790–1810, compound weave. 52% spun rayon, 48% polyester. 50" wide. Silk document owned by Winterthur Museum. No. 49250 (cream).

❀ SAVOYARD MOIRE STRIPE. European, c. 1790–1800, moiré with satin stripe. 64% linen, 21% cotton, 15% silk. 52" wide. Silk document owned by Winterthur Museum. No. 46874.

❀ SHERBROOKE MOIRE STRIPE. England, c. 1790–1815, taffeta with satin stripe. 60% filament rayon, 40% rayon. 54" wide. Silk document owned by Winterthur Museum. No. 49282.

1815 TO 1840:
TECHNOLOGICAL ADVANCES
AND COMPLEX DESIGNS

During the years 1815–40, the development of power looms, the perfection of cylinder printing and continuing improvements in dye technology greatly changed the textile industry in Europe and the United States. After 1820 the broad-scale adoption of the Jacquard selective shedding device for pattern weaving allowed increasing complexity in woven silk and woolen designs. The use of engraved metal cylinders for printing meant that design repeats were shorter and motifs often finely drawn. Popular designs included floral stripes, trompe l'oeil effects, shells and coral branches, birds and elaborately foliated pillar prints. The practice of outlining or emphasizing design motifs with clusters of small dots was even more common than in the previous period. For a time there was also a revival of monochromatic landscapes and commemorative designs in a style highly reminiscent of the earlier copperplate designs but now made much denser and with the shorter repeat defined by the circumference of the printing cylinder. Block printing continued to be used for large-scale floral chintzes. (For more details see Florence Montgomery, *Printed Textiles,* pp. 287–343, and Schoeser and Rufey, *English and American Textiles,* pp. 74–86.)

London and Paris continued to be the primary sources of new ideas about interior decoration. Travelers paid particular attention to the opulent interiors they visited, and they consulted with merchants, designers and fabric suppliers about appropriate styles and newly available goods. Sometimes Americans commissioned their friends or relatives who were traveling or living abroad to send them new fabrics or even new curtains and furniture coverings in the latest style, not knowing what they might receive.

Bedroom, Capt. Kyran Walsh House, Strawbery Banke Museum, Portsmouth, N.H., c.1830, with bed hangings made of "Oriole" by Brunschwig & Fils. Installed 1989.

The number of published design books also increased during this period. Volumes such as Pierre de la Messangere's *Meubles et Objets de Gout* and George Smith's *A Collection of Designs for Household Furniture* provided written descriptions as well as detailed illustrations, often in vivid colors, of the new styles of French drapery and Grecian, Egyptian or Gothic taste. The Grecian designs seem to have been most popular and featured strongly vertical arrangements of deep, even, tubular pleats, or conical pleats, interspersed with deep swags, which were known as "Roman drapery." Selections from the most notable design sources of this period are illustrated in Samuel J. Dornsife's "Design Sources for Nineteenth-Century Window Hangings," in Schoeser and Rufey, and several books and articles by Florence Montgomery.

In addition to books devoted exclusively to furniture and furnishing designs, fashionable periodicals featured illustrations of interior furnishings. Notable among them was Rudolph Ackermann's monthly *Repository of Arts, Literature, Commerce, Manufactures, Fashion and Politics* (London, 1809–28), which contained colored illustrations of fashionable clothing and furnishings, the latter often being window drapery. For a brief period, Ackermann even included actual textile swatches as emblems of British manufactures. Surviving today, unfaded between the pages of the magazine, they offer an excellent idea of the brilliant color and glossy finish deemed ideal in furnishing fabrics at this time.

During the 1820s there appeared the first of the domestic advice books, forerunners of the avalanche of helpful texts that now provide detailed information on American material culture and social behavior of the late 19th and 20th centuries. Among the earliest of these handbooks was *Domestic Duties, or Instructions to Young Married Ladies,* by Mrs. William Parkes. An American edition of this book was published in 1829, with few changes from the London original. Mrs. Parkes offered guidelines on the appropriateness of specific fabrics for specific rooms: light-colored chintz or silk drapery with muslin undercurtains was approved for parlors; in contrast, the more severe wool moreen curtains in crimson or scarlet were deemed appropriate for dining rooms. Moreen was also considered suitable for bedchambers, although light-colored chintz prints with contrasting linings were also regarded as handsome. Dimity was desirable for bedchambers, sometimes in combination with Marseilles spreads.

Paintings and drawings of American interiors began to be more common than they had been in the 18th century. These often depicted the use of textiles in decorating the parlors, sitting rooms and, occasionally, the bedchambers of middle-class and wealthy Americans. Woodcut illustrations in magazines and juvenile books also appeared with increasing frequency, often documenting the appearance of rooms of average Americans and sometimes those of lower socioeconomic levels. An excellent overview is given in *A Documentary History of American Interiors,* by Edgar Mayhew and Minor Myers.

The period 1815–40 saw the beginnings of the historical revival styles that were to characterize interior decorating throughout the remainder of the 19th century. Grecian and Egyptian designs had been used since the start of the century, but by the mid-1820s published designs for Gothic, Louis XIV, Louis XV and Elizabethan window drapery were also available. Such designs often made use of sheer white cotton curtains against the window panes; above these, special decorative effects were created by layers of heavier fabric and shaped valances, both in solid colors. Where French drapery continued to be used, the swags and cascades became increasingly complex, enhanced by the use of contrasting linings and elaborate trimmings.

In 1833 J. C. Loudon's *Encyclopaedia of Cottage, Farm and Villa Architecture and Furniture* offered specific illustrations of the currently popular styles adapted for people of varying economic levels. The simplest designs illustrated by Loudon are for straight hanging panels of heavy material, hung from large brass or wooden rings on visible rods with boldly turned finials. Straight or shaped valances could be hung over these to give Grecian or Gothic effects. These basic designs must have been especially popular in houses of middle-class Americans during the second quarter of the 19th century, for in both 1849 and 1860 they were still being illustrated as fashionable in *Godey's Lady's Book* and *Peterson's Ladies National Magazine.*

Apparently chintz and dimity were relegated to the bedchamber during most of this period, although, even there, embossed moreen, silk or other solid-colored fabrics might be used for bed and window hangings. As late as 1851, in an edition of the *Treatise on Domestic Economy,* Catherine Beecher was still urging that all fabric furnishings in a bed-chamber should correspond.

The use of bed hangings was a matter of individual choice that reflected patterns of fashion as well as philosophies of hygiene. Throughout the 1830s and 1840s controversy raged over the healthfulness of fully enclosing bed curtains. In 1839 Sarah Josepha Hale, editor of *Godey's,* wrote, "Bed hangings are unhealthy; they confine the air about us while we sleep." At the same time decorators and designers were publishing new designs for bed hangings, which were being used in both fashionable and common chambers. In some cases these were strictly a decorative display on the posts and tester frame, but some people continued the old-fash-ioned practice of closing bed curtains around them at night, especially during cold weather. Lightweight bobbinet or gauze was used in a similar way in southern climates as a protection against mosquitoes; often heavier curtains and valances were hung over the mosquito curtain in fashion-able drapery styles.

Research in probate inventories that record domestic fur-nishings in rural areas shows that throughout this period the houses of most middle-class people — both farmers and village artisans — still had no window curtains. If curtains were used at all, they were usually used in the parlor. In restoring and furnishing a simple rural house of this period, two approaches are correct: using no window curtains or using only single white cotton panels swagged to one side in a way reminiscent of the 18th-century style called half drapery.

Roller blinds were introduced at least as early as 1825. They were tacked to wooden dowels supported by simple brackets or fitted within fixed pulleys. The spring blind was not invented until the end of this period. The blinds could be made of plain white cotton or brown holland (un-bleached linen), or they could be embellished with colorful painted transparent landscapes. (Excellent reproductions of the latter style can be ordered through the Museum Gift Shop, Old Sturbridge Village, 1 Old Sturbridge Village Road, Sturbridge, Mass. 01566.)

The increasing use of upholstered furniture during this period resulted in some specific fabrics being made as furniture covers, but in many houses the same wools and silks were used for drapery in parlors or sitting rooms. Plain or patterned horsehair fabric was also used extensively for this purpose. Special panels were woven for the seats and backs of chairs and Grecian sofas; these are found in silk, wool and horsehair. No reproductions of the special wool or horsehair panels are currently available, but there is an excellent choice of woven silk panels. Also available are embossing designs that can be applied to wool or plush for use on seating furniture.

Slipcovers continued to be used in warm weather as a protection for expensive upholstery fabrics and to present a crisp, cool appearance. Undoubtedly, they were also used because they provided a much more comfortable sitting surface than wool or horsehair. Figured chintzes and dimity continued to be popular for this purpose, and by the mid-1830s crisp stripes of white and red, blue or green were also used.

The growing fashion for center tables in parlors fostered the production of specific kinds of woven or printed woolen table covers, none of which is reproduced today. Fortunately, some people made their own center table covers of plain woolen fabric trimmed with plain or patterned woven tapes, an effect easily re-created from commercially available goods.

The options for reproducing an accurate interior for the period 1815–40 are greater than for reproducing one of the earlier periods. Thus, it is even more important to decide in advance the purpose of the restoration and the point of view to be indicated in the fabric furnishings. A wide variety of handsome and appropriate effects can be created from period designs and available materials. Because so many effects are appropriate for this time period, selecting a focus is critical.

BRUNSCHWIG & FILS   PRINTS

❦ BELVOIR GLAZED CHINTZ. English, 1836, block print. 100% cotton, glazed. 54" wide, 39" repeat, 9" horizontal repeat. Document privately owned in England. No.66494.01 (yellow).

❦ CHINESE LEOPARD TOILE. French, 1825, roller print. 100% cotton. 36" wide, 15¼" repeat. Document privately owned. No. 70121.04 (shades of red and blue).

❦ CORAL BRANCH GLAZED CHINTZ. English, c. 1825–50, roller and block print. 100% cotton. 44" wide plus one 6¾" side border, 12¾" repeat. Document in Brunschwig & Fils Archives. No. 78221.04 (red and blue); No. 78225.04 (adaptation, pink and green).

❦ CORAUX GLAZED CHINTZ. French (Alsace), c. 1835, block print. 100% cotton, glazed. 51" wide, 5¾" repeat. Document at Musée des Arts Décoratifs, Paris. No. 61582.01 (blue).

❦ EDWINA GLAZED CHINTZ. English, c. 1820–50, roller printed. 100% cotton. 54" wide, negligible repeat. Document in Brunschwig & Fils Archives. No. 62281.01 (coral); No. 62282.01 (blue, based on other period examples).

❦ FILIGREE STRIPE GLAZED CHINTZ. English, c. 1835–45, roller print. 100% cotton, glazed. 53" wide, 31½" repeat. Design slightly enlarged and one motif added. Document owned by Winterthur Museum has a pink ground; an example with a beige filigree is at Cooper Hewitt Museum (see cover, Moss, *Printed Textiles*); and another privately owned document has a green ground. None of these has been reproduced, but blue indicated is convincing for the period. No. 65742.01 (blue).

❦ FLOREAL GLAZED CHINTZ. French (Alsace), c. 1838, block print. 100% cotton. 48¾" wide, 38¼" repeat. Document at Musée des Arts Décoratifs, Paris. No. 61640.01 (multi).

❦ ISMAELIA COTTON PRINT. English, c. 1830–40. 100% cotton. 52" wide, 14" drop repeat, 26" horizontal repeat. *Chefs d'Oeuvre du Musée de l'Impression sur Etoffes, Mulhouse,* vol. 2, no. 85. Document, privately owned in France, a roller-printed cotton in red and black with green added by wood block, probably made for the Portuguese market. Scene commemorates the arrival of the first giraffe in France, the gift to Charles X of France in 1826 from Mohamed Ali Pasha of Egypt. No. 174524.00 (green and persimmon).

❦ ORIOLE. English, c. 1830, roller print. 100% cotton, glazed. 48" wide, 15¼" repeat. Montgomery, *Printed Textiles,* fig. 380. Document owned by Winterthur Museum. No. 65810.01 (red and green on beige).

❦ ORMSEBY GLAZED CHINTZ. English, c. 1830–55, block and

roller print. 100% cotton. 55" wide, 4¾" repeat. Document a curtain fragment in Brunschwig & Fils Archives. No. 62314.01 (green and red).

❀ PARTERRE. French (Alsace), c. 1835, block print. 100% cotton. 49½" wide, 30¾" repeat. Document at Musée des Arts Décoratifs, Paris. No. 61700.01 (multi).

❀ PONTCHARTRAIN COTTON PRINT, PONTCHARTRAIN BORDER PRINT. French, c. 1835–60, block print. 100% cotton. Yardage 50" wide, 39" repeat; border 14½" wide per border, three of

FILIGREE STRIPE GLAZED CHINTZ, c. 1835–45. Brunschwig & Fils. Blue.

ORMSEBY GLAZED
CHINTZ, c. 1830–55.
Brunschwig & Fils.
Green and red.

which are printed side by side on fabric 53" wide, 22" repeat. Document a block print on cotton, privately owned in France. No. 174261.00 (red), Border No. 174271.00 (red).

CLARENCE HOUSE

✾ COLETTE. French, c. 1830–40, roller print. 100% cotton, glazed. 54" wide, 17" repeat. Document privately owned in France. No. 32097-1 (rose). Minimum order two yards.
✾ LA BELVEDERE. English, c. 1830–40, cylinder print. 100%

La Belvedere,
c. 1830–40. Clarence
House. Red.

cotton, glazed. 52" wide, 12" vertical repeat, 27" horizontal repeat. Document privately owned. No. 32937-1 (red).

CLASSIC REVIVALS

❦ ROSE CUTTINGS. English, c.1845–60, block and roller print. 100% cotton. 50" wide, 1½" repeat. Document privately owned in England. No.107-1 (rose and green on cream).

COWTAN & TOUT

❦ SEA CORAL. English, c.1835–50, block print with pin dot ground. 100% cotton, glazed. 51" wide, 4" repeat. Document privately owned in England. No.6035 (blues on off-white ground); No.6034 (reds on off-white ground).

DECORATORS WALK

❦ MENDHAM PRINTED CHINTZ. English, c.1820–40, block print. 100% cotton, glazed. 36" wide, 21¼" repeat. Document privately owned. No. T25123 (gold).

❦ PERCIER. English, c.1830–40, cylinder print. 100% cotton. 54" wide, 12½" repeat. Dots in fancy ground somewhat overemphasized in screen-printed version. Document privately owned; examples in many museum collections. No. L67010 (navy).

❦ COMPOSE. English, c.1830–40, block and roller print. 100% cotton, glazed. 50" wide, 24½" repeat. Document not located but appears to be an excellent presentation of color and design elements of dark-ground print featuring passion flowers, a design unavailable elsewhere. Printed in Brazil. No. 70485-A (green and cordovan).

SCALAMANDRÉ

❦ ESSEX GARDEN. English, c.1835–45, roller print. 100% cotton. 54" wide, 25¼" repeat. Document at Essex Institute, Salem, Mass. No. 7773-1 (multi on espresso).

❦ LADY OF THE LAKE. French, c.1830, roller print. 100% cotton. 30½" wide, 35" repeat. Reproduced for San Francisco Plantation, Garyville, La. Document privately owned. No. 6426-1 (charcoal on beige); No.6426-4 (bordeaux on beige). Special order only.

❦ MONIQUE. French, c.1820–30, block print. 100% cotton, glazed. 53" wide, 27" repeat. Document owned by Bibliothèque Forney, Paris. Design motifs slightly adapted. No. 6917-1 (multi roses and lilacs on ivory).

❀ NIPPONE. French, c. 1825–40, cylinder print. 100% cotton. 31" wide, 16" vertical repeat, 31" horizontal repeat. Printed with an original 19th-century engraved cylinder. No. 11014-2 (brick on cream); No. 11014-3 (black on cream).

❀ PILLAR. English, c. 1815–30, roller print. 100% cotton, glazed. 50" wide, 13" repeat. *Scalamandré*, no. 48. Document at Essex Institute, Salem, Mass. No. 7711-1 (multi on brown). Special order only.

PILLAR, c. 1815–30. Scalamandré. Multi on brown.

STAR CLOUDS SCREEN-
PRINTED GLAZED
CHINTZ, 1824. Stroheim
& Romann. Red, white
and blue.

PALMETTE DAMASK,
c.1815–30. Brunschwig
& Fils. Green.

❀ WILTON HOUSE FLORAL. English, c.1820–40, block print. 100% cotton. 49" wide, 15½" repeat. Document owned by National Society of the Colonial Dames of America in the State of Virginia. Reproduced for its property Wilton House, Richmond. No. 6364-1 (reds and greens on dark brown). Special order only.

SCHUMACHER

❀ THE QUEEN'S AVIARY. English, c.1830, block print. 100% cotton, glazed. 54" wide, 25" repeat. Document owned by Schumacher. Reproduced with endorsement of The Victorian Society in America. No. 73300 (document multi).

STROHEIM & ROMANN

❀ STAR CLOUDS SCREEN-PRINTED GLAZED CHINTZ. English, 1824, cylinder print. 100% cotton. 54" wide. Document at Winterthur Museum. No. 49126 (document red, white and blue).

BRUNSCHWIG & FILS

WOVEN DESIGNS

❀ DAVOUT SNOWFLAKE LAMPAS. French, early 19th century. 51% silk, 49% cotton. 48" wide, 8¼" repeat, 8¼" horizontal repeat. Reproduced for the Chillman Empire Parlor, Bayou Bend Collection, Houston. Document a silk lampas privately owned in France. No. 32261.00 (red); No. 32262.00 (blue); No. 32263.00 (gold); No. 32264.00 (green). Also available as coordinating panel design for chair seat and back and as plain yardage with wide or narrow borders and with coordinating plain satin.

❀ IVY VELVET. Italian, c.1815–30. 59% silk, 41% cotton. 24" wide, 25" repeat, 12" horizontal repeat. Document a silk cisele velvet privately owned in Italy. No. 121964.00 (green on cream).

❀ NEW HAMBLEDON DAMASK. (See p.37) This fabric is found on furniture of the period 1815–40 as well as earlier periods. No. 39674.01 (wintergreen); No. 39672.01 (indigo).

❀ PALMETTE DAMASK. French, c.1815–30. 100% cotton. 53" wide, 13" repeat. Document a silk damask in Brunschwig & Fils Archives. No. 82554.02 (green); some others colors, including some two-color damasks, useful for reproduction work.

❀ SOMERSET WOVEN STRIPE. European, c.1815–40. 100%

JULIETTE GORDON LOW DAMASK, c. 1815–30. Scalamandré. Antique gold.

viscose, 52" wide, 11½" repeat. Document a woven ikat stripe with a silk weft and a linen warp, in Brunschwig & Fils Archives. No. 63591.0l (red and olive green).

CLASSIC REVIVALS

❀ ARROWS DAMASK. French, c. 1820–30. 100% silk. 21" wide, 12" repeat. Document in Prelle Archives, Lyon, France. No. 7630. Custom colors.

❀ EMPIRE. French, 1823, damask. 100% silk. 20" wide, 11" repeat. Document privately owned. No. 8825-4099.

SCALAMANDRÉ

❀ CLASSICAL MEDALLION DAMASK, CHAIR BACK. French, c. 1820–35. 48% silk, 52% cotton. 52" wide, 33" repeat. Document owned by Scalamandré. No. 97443-1 (beige on Arabian red). Special order only. Cut by repeat only.

❀ CLASSICAL ROSETTE DAMASK. French, c. 1820–35. 48% silk, 52% cotton. 52" wide, 3½" repeat. Document owned by Scalamandré. No.97441-1 (beige on Arabian red). Special order only.

❀ CLASSICAL WREATH, CHAIR SEAT. French, c.1820–35. 48% silk, 52% cotton. 52" wide, 32½" repeat. Document owned by Scalamandré. No.97442-1 (beige on Arabian red). Special order only. Cut by repeat only.

❀ JOSEPHINE. French, c.1815–25. 100% silk. 54" wide, 10" repeat. Document found in Vizelle, France, now privately owned in London. No.11007-1 (jade and rust on lemon).

❀ JULIETTE GORDON LOW DAMASK. French, c.1815–30. 37% silk, 63% cotton. 51" wide, 25" repeat. Document owned by Juliette Gordon Low Birthplace, Savannah, Ga. No.97428-1 (antique gold).

❀ MONARCH LAMPAS. French, mid-19th century. 100% silk. 49" wide, 30½" repeat. Document at Lyndhurst, Tarrytown, N.Y. No.97124-1 (golden orange). Special order only.

❀ XIX CENTURY DAMASK. French, mid-19th-century revival of a mid-18th-century rococo design. 15% silk, 74% cotton. 51" wide, 23" repeat. Document a drapery panel from Sorrel-Weed House, Savannah, Ga. No.97371-4 (slate blue).

❀ XIX CENTURY STRIPE. French or English, c.1830-45. 32% silk, 68% cotton. 53" wide. Document owned by Sorrel-Weed House, Savannah, Ga. No.99440-1 (beige, rose and charcoal).

❀ PERIGORD LAMPAS. French, c.1825–40. 100% silk. 51" wide, 48" repeat. Document owned by Scalamandré. No. 410-1 (blue and ivory on green). Special order only.

STROHEIM & ROMANN

❀ TIVERTON MOIRE STRIPE. European, c.1830–60, striped silk taffeta. 55% filament rayon, 45% spun rayon. 54" wide, 6" repeat. Silk document at Winterthur Museum. No.49270 (document).

1840 TO 1870:
INCREASING DIVERSITY
IN FURNISHING FABRICS

I n the mid-19th century, the use of textiles to decorate American houses was lavish, reflecting both the availability of a wide variety of fabrics in many price ranges and the interest women took in the appearance of their homes. Fashionable fabrics included silk, velvet, damask, plush, rep, plain satin and figured chintz. Twentieth-century interest in the handsome chintzes of this period has resulted in an abundance of excellent reproductions, but it should be remembered that at its height of fashion in the mid-19th century, chintz was used primarily in bedchambers or as a summer covering.

These years saw the rise of furnishing warehouses in large cities. Such firms employed design consultants and provided furnishings for all aspects of a domestic interior, drapery as well as furniture. A good example is the firm of Leon Marcotte, in New York City, which served clients in every part of the country. Similar firms were established in Boston, New York, Philadelphia, Baltimore, Washington, Cincinnati, Chicago, St. Louis and New Orleans.

Popular magazines and domestic advice books made it possible for those who did not or could not employ professional decorators or upholsterers to make their own fashionable curtains and bed hangings as well as a host of decorative accessories such as antimacassars, doileys, lamp rugs, table carpets, netted curtains and fireplace lambrequins. Advice was even given on ways to create comfortable and fashionable upholstered furniture from packing crates and barrels. Miss Eliza Leslie, in *The House Book* (1840), Sarah Josepha Hale, in *Godey's Lady's Book* (published monthly from 1830 to 1892), and Catherine Beecher and Harriet Beecher Stowe, in *The American Woman's Home*

Parlor, Wickham-Valentine House, Richmond, Va., with "Victorian Damask" by Brunschwig & Fils used for drapery and upholstery. Installed c.1970. Dismantled before 1988 to permit restoration to an earlier period. (© Richard Cheek for Historic Richmond Foundation).

(1869), all stressed the importance of women's personal involvement in home decorating. Rooms embellished with the products of women's hands were considered symbols of successful attention to domestic duty.

Both Mrs. Hale and the Beecher sisters provided written descriptions and practical illustrations for creating inexpensive but fashionable interiors that fulfilled the ultimate goal — a "homelike" setting. All three authors urged women not to lament their situation but to use their innate talent to create an attractive and welcoming domestic atmosphere at little expense to their husbands. They insisted, for example, that less than a dollar's worth of fabric could be fashioned into handsome curtains, an important component of the domestic interior, which enclosed the family circle and set it aside from the rigors of the workaday world. The influence of these ideas and suggestions can be seen in the middle-class interiors illustrated in Edgar Mayhew and Minor Myers's *A Documentary History of American Interiors*, William Seale's *The Tasteful Interlude* and, especially, Katherine C. Grier's *Culture and Comfort*.

As in previous decades, high-style interior design was characterized by historical revival styles; often, different periods were reflected in different rooms within the same house. The basic formula for window curtains remained unchanged — layered curtains, with sheer undercurtains, heavy side draperies and a shaped valance that might be distinctively Greek, Gothic, Moorish or Jacobean. Beginning in 1838, flat, shaped valances stiffened by buckram or paper were introduced, although the complex folds and swags derived from the earlier French drapery style continued in use. The exposed pole with large brass or wooden rings also was still used as were decorative cornices above concealed curtain rods. The heavy curtain panels were often lined with chintz, sometimes in a color corresponding to or harmonizing with the fabric of the curtain panel but often in beige or tan. The tops of these panels were usually arranged in a series of flat pleats, usually stitched down for two or three inches and bound across the top with tape of some kind. Simple brass hooks were sewn in the back of the pleats; these hooks were then passed through small rings on a pulley device on a concealed rod or at the bottom of the large exposed rings, which slid freely on decorative curtain poles.

Parlor, White House of the Confederacy, showing "Crenshaw" by Scalamandré used for drapery and upholstery. Installed 1989.

Woolen damask, velvet, rep and moreen as well as silks were used for parlor and sitting room curtains, which could be arranged in two or three layers of different color and texture with additional embellishment in the braid, fringe, cord and tassels. Tiebacks usually were made of one of these decorative trimmings, almost never of matching fabric. Splendid examples of mid-19th-century drapery and trimmings survive at the Morse-Libbey House in Portland, Maine; one of these is illustrated in Mary Schoeser and Celia Rufey, *English and American Textiles,* chap. 3, fig. 61.

Undercurtains could be sheer cotton muslin, either plain or embellished with embroidery. After the invention of the lace curtain machine in 1846, more and more people selected lace curtain panels for this purpose.

The fashion for heavier fabrics continued to prevail in the

treatment of dining rooms and libraries; wool rep and velvet were especially popular for these rooms. Crimson continued to be used extensively, and deep olive green was also popular; these dark colors were often enhanced by gold braid and cords.

Many 17th- and 18th-century woven silk designs in the baroque and rococo styles, enlarged and somewhat coarsened, were used as the basis for jacquard woven patterns. In selecting reproduction fabrics it is important to use these for mid-19th-century work, not for earlier periods when they would not have been woven on jacquard looms.

Samuel J. Dornsife illustrates some specific designs for this period in "Design Sources for Nineteenth-Century Window Hangings"; others are illustrated in William Seale's *The Tasteful Interlude,* Edgar Mayhew and Minor Myers's *A Documentary History of American Interiors* and Mary Schoeser and Celia Rufey's *English and American Textiles.* Many of these effects can be achieved today by using a solid-colored silk, rep, moreen or velvet with an appropriate variety of braids, fringes and trimming. Although few documentary reproductions of these plain materials are available, an excellent selection of appropriate fabrics can be found. Some suggestions are given in the chapter on modern textiles, but do not hesitate to use others if they look right. Reproductions of appropriate curtain rods, rings and cornices are much more difficult to find; indeed, they may require custom work. If such accessories are unavailable and no specific design prototype for the situation at hand exists, it might be wise to select a curtain treatment that makes use of a concealed rod.

During the mid-19th century, kitchen curtains began to be used extensively for the first time. They usually were made of simple cotton muslin, lightweight checked dimity or dotted swiss. The styles tended to be straight panels with a narrow casing at the top, hung on a rod, wire or string, often covering only the lower half of the window opening.

Dotted swiss and specially made lace panels were used to curtain windows in exterior doors. Roller blinds continued to be popular, the bold transparent landscapes of the earlier decades giving way to more chaste designs of flowers or landscapes in small central medallions or simple gilded moldings that were sometimes enhanced with applied mica crystals.

Bedchambers were decorated in a variety of ways. Colorful printed chintzes were recommended by professional upholsterers and designers, yet some of the best chambers were fitted up with heavy silk or wool window drapery in the styles used in parlors, with bed hangings to correspond. In some homes, dimity continued to be used for bed and window curtains, bedroom slipcovers and toilet table covers.

These years saw the first flowering of American pieced and appliqué quiltmaking, in which the beauty of individual printed cottons was superseded by artful arrangement and precise stitching. Colorful quilts provided a focal point of design in the humblest interior.

During this period jacquard woven coverlets of bleached cotton and colorful wool were manufactured by professional weavers, especially in Pennsylvania, New York, Ohio, Indiana and Illinois. Some reproductions of these are currently available and custom reproduction of specific designs is now possible.

In this period upholstered furniture became much more dominant in the domestic interior, providing comfort and a sense of luxury unknown in previous generations. Deep spring seats and lavish use of cushions were characteristic. In some cases the upholstery completely overran the furniture frame, reducing it to nothing more than a set of wooden legs supporting fabric-covered cushions.

Plain or patterned horsehair was used extensively for upholstery of sofas, chairs and stools, but moreen and silk or wool damask were also used. A new fabric was a lightweight twilled wool challis printed in colorful floral designs that could be used for drapery as well as upholstery. "Longfellow House" is a good reproduction of this type of material, the original of which was chosen by Henry Wadsworth Longfellow and his bride, Fanny Appleton Longfellow, for their parlor in the old Craigie House at Cambridge, Mass., in 1842.

This period saw a growing fashion for needlework upholstery or upholstery incorporating embroidered strips or medallions. Examples are illustrated in Katherine C. Grier, *Culture and Comfort,* pls. 36 and 37. Such work was a perfect vehicle for a woman's personal involvement in the complexity of the fashionable interior, reflecting the ideals of domesticity in a visible and concrete way. Some of the designs for needlework upholstery and upholstery elements were published in sewing manuals or needlework magazines; thus, they may be easily copied today if appropriate materials are selected. Some of the designs were sold as embroidery kits; these may be more difficult to reproduce, especially if they should incorporate cut steel beads.

Loose cushions began to be used extensively on sofas, and the number of tables, footstools and ottomans with upholstered tops multiplied as well. In most cases, the fabrics used corresponded with those used on the other upholstered furniture in the rooms, but needlework designs were sometimes chosen for these pieces.

Because the variety of designs considered appropriate continued to increase, careful research is the most important element in re-creating an accurate site-specific interior. Many designs can be easily copied or successfully interpreted in modern materials. The hardest part is selecting designs and fabrics that accurately reflect the tastes and economic situation of the original owner. Persons seeking to achieve an appropriate period effect have a much simpler task, made easier by the fact that the work of interior designers has been studied and published and some of the domestic advice books of this period have been reprinted.

PRINTS

Baker Decorative Fabrics

❀ Chelsea. English, c.1850–65, block print. 100% cotton. 54" wide, 25" repeat. Document in Baker Archive, London. No.84-111 (blue-9); No.84-112 (green-6).

❀ Honeycomb. German, c.1840–55, block and cylinder print. 100% cotton, glazed. 54" wide, 27" repeat. Document privately owned. No.52-150 (brown-2).

Brunschwig & Fils

❀ Albertina Glazed Chintz. English, c.1850–70, block print. 100% cotton, glazed. 55" wide, 15¾" repeat. Document in Brunschwig & Fils Archives. No.36222.01 (blue stripe).

❀ Antibes Glazed Chintz. French (Alsace), c.1850, block print. 100% cotton, glazed. 65" wide, 51" drop repeat. Design by Jean Ulrich Tournier. Document privately owned in France. No.171470.00 (multi on white).

❀ Ardentes Cotton Print. French, c.1850–70, block print.

100% cotton. 55" wide, 25¼" repeat. Document a block-printed wool privately owned in France. No. 174559.00 (black).

❈ AUGUSTA GLAZED CHINTZ. English, c. 1870–80, block print. 100% cotton, glazed. 53" wide, 35" vertical repeat, 13" horizontal repeat. Believed to be a redrawing of a block-printed design introduced in England about 1840 (see Frank Lewis, *English Chintz,* pl. 81). Document privately owned in England. No. 66340.01 (cream).

❈ BEGONIA TREE GLAZED CHINTZ. English, c. 1840–50, block print. 100% cotton, glazed. 53" wide, 27⅞" repeat. Document privately owned in England. No. 61815.01 (rose bouquet on pink).

❈ BORROMEA COTTON PRINT. English, c. 1840–60. 100% cotton. 54" wide, 16¼" vertical repeat, 54" horizontal repeat. Document a block-printed cotton privately owned in Italy. This type of design was made for the Portuguese market, but samples have been found in mid-19th-century New England quilts, so it must have been available in the United States as well. No. 62342.01 (blue).

ARDENTES COTTON PRINT, c. 1850–70. Brunschwig & Fils. Black.

CAHIR GLAZED CHINTZ, 1864. Brunschwig & Fils. Green.

❧ CAHIR GLAZED CHINTZ. English, 1864. 100% cotton. 45" wide field plus one 8" border on left side, 9½" repeat. Document a gouache on paper drawing for a textile, dated December 12, 1864, privately owned in England. No. 36584.01 (green).

❧ CALIPH COTTON PRINT. English, c. 1860–75, block print. 100% cotton. 54" wide, 13" vertical repeat, 18" horizontal repeat. Document a block-printed cotton privately owned in England. Motifs slightly enlarged in reproduction. No. 36184.01 (green and teal).

❧ CAMBALUC COTTON PRINT. French, c. 1850–60, block print. 100% cotton. 60" wide, 17¼" repeat with a 2" off-straight join. Document privately owned in France. No. 174580.00 (cream).

❧ CASHEMIRE COTTON. French (Thierry-Mieg, Mulhouse), 1865, roller print. 100% cotton. 51½" wide, 12½" repeat. *Chefs d'Oeuvre du Musée de l'Impression sur Etoffes,* Mulhouse, vol. 1, fig. 99. Document at Musée de l'Impression sur Etoffes, Mulhouse, France. No. 61251.01 (red).

❧ CAVENDISH GLAZED CHINTZ. English, c. 1850. 100% cotton. 54" wide, 19¾" repeat. Document a block-printed cot-

ton with roller-printed fancy ground now in Brunschwig &
Fils Archives. No.62320.01 (beige stripe).

❀ CECILY GLAZED CHINTZ. French (Thierry-Mieg, Mulhouse), c.1845–50. 100% cotton. 53" wide, 27¾" repeat.
Document a block-printed cotton chintz in Brunschwig &
Fils Archives; it still retains manufacturer's label. No.
65862.01 (rose and blue ribbons).

❀ CHANTAL GLAZED CHINTZ. French, c.1850–65. 100% cotton, 48" wide, 26" repeat. Document, privately owned in
France, a block-printed cotton that was probably inspired
by a late 18th-century brocaded silk. No.170392.00 (blue
ribbon).

❀ CHATHAM COTTON PRINT. American, c.1850–80. 100%
cotton. 34" wide, 14½" vertical repeat, 23" horizontal repeat. Document, in Brunschwig & Fils Archives, a block-
printed discharge print on cotton, inspired by Kashmir and
Paisley shawl patterns. No.75811.04 (turkey red).

❀ CLAN ROSE GLAZED CHINTZ. English, c.1855–65, block
print. 100% cotton, glazed. 55" wide, 17¾" repeat. Inspired
by Queen Victoria's fascination with Balmoral and the en-
suing fashion for things Scottish. Document privately

CLAN ROSE GLAZED
CHINTZ, c.1855–65.
Brunschwig & Fils.
Brown.

owned in England. Design motifs slightly enlarged in reproduction; original was not glazed. No. 36529.01 (brown).

❀ COALBROOK GLAZED CHINTZ. English, c. 1840–60, block print. 56" wide, 8¾" vertical repeat, 34½" horizontal repeat, plus 8" border on both sides. Document, possibly designed by S. Ackerman, privately owned in England. Probably designed for use as a roller blind. No. 62374.01 (dark green).

❀ CORALIE GLAZED CHINTZ. French, c. 1850–70, block print. 100% cotton, glazed. 49" wide, 31" repeat. Document at Musée des Arts Décoratifs, Paris. No. 62527.01 (burgundy).

❀ CORDELIA COTTON PRINT. English, c. 1845–55, block and roller print. 100% cotton. 54" wide, 21" vertical repeat, 26½" horizontal repeat. Document a cotton curtain panel in Brunschwig & Fils Archives. No. 62833.01 (gold).

❀ DYSART GLAZED CHINTZ. English, c. 1850–75. 100% cotton. 56" wide, 17¾" repeat. Document a block-printed cotton privately owned in England. No. 62362.01 (blue stripe).

❀ EBURY. English, c. 1850–70, block print. 100% cotton, glazed. 53" wide, 16" repeat. Document privately owned in England. No. 61601.01 (red).

❀ ERIN GLAZED CHINTZ. English, 1859, block print. 100% cotton, glazed. 54" wide, 8¼" repeat. Introduced January 24, 1859; originally printed at Bannister Hall, Preston, England. Document a gouache on paper drawing for a textile privately owned in England. No. 36474.01 (rose and green).

❀ ESCARPOLETTE COTTON PRINT. English, c. 1830–40, block and roller print. 100% cotton. 54" wide, 13¾" repeat. Document at Musée de l'Impression sur Etoffes, Mulhouse, France. *Chefs d'Oeuvre du Musée de l'Impression sur Etoffes, Mulhouse,* vol. 2, no. 83. No. 62156.01 (sage on rust).

❀ FERN AND ANEMONE GLAZED CHINTZ. English, c. 1860–75, block print. 100% cotton, glazed. 54" wide, 31½" repeat. Document privately owned in England. Scale of repeat reduced from 29½" when transferred to screen printing. No. 62681.01 (red stripe).

❀ FOLLY GLAZED CHINTZ. English, c. 1840–60. 100% cotton. 53" wide, 17¾" vertical repeat, 25½" horizontal repeat. Document a block-printed cotton chintz privately owned in England; minor color adaptations in two details. No. 36280.01 (white ground).

❀ HADDON HALL GLAZED CHINTZ. English, 1848, block and

COALBROOK GLAZED
CHINTZ, c. 1840–60.
Brunschwig & Fils.
Dark green.

ERIN GLAZED CHINTZ,
1859. Brunschwig &
Fils. Rose and green.

JAMMU COTTON AND
LINEN PRINT, c.1840–
60. Brunschwig & Fils.
Red and blue.

IVY ORNE GLAZED
CHINTZ, 1866.
Brunschwig & Fils.
Rose and green.

roller print. 100% cotton, glazed. 51" wide, 43" repeat. Document a block and roller print in Brunschwig & Fils Archives; original drawing for the design privately owned in England. The original tea-colored ground has been slightly lightened. No.61873.01 (pale yellow).

❀ HAMPSTEAD GLAZED CHINTZ. English, c.1860–80, block print, 100% cotton. 53" wide, 51" repeat. Document a block-printed cotton privately owned in England. No.61994.01 (aqua stripe).

❀ HIDCOTE GLAZED CHINTZ. English, c.1850–60, block print. 100% cotton, glazed. 51" wide, 35" drop repeat. Document privately owned in England. No.61124.01 (green).

❀ HONORIA GLAZED CHINTZ. English, c.1850, block print. 100% cotton, glazed. 52" wide, 40⅜" repeat. Document in Brunschwig & Fils Archives. No.62038.01 (rose on taupe).

❀ IVY ORNE GLAZED CHINTZ. English, 1866. 46" field plus 4" border on left, 5¼" repeat. Document, privately owned in England, a gouache-on-paper drawing for a textile, dated June 12, 1866. No.36491.01 (rose and green).

❀ JAMMU COTTON AND LINEN PRINT. French (probably Provencal), c.1840–60, block print. 56% linen, 44% cotton. 58" wide, 9¼" repeat. Document in Brunschwig & Fils Archives. Scale slightly reduced to fit modern fabric widths; original repeat is 10½". No.62710.01 (red and blue).

❀ LA FLORE. French, mid-19th century, roller print. 100% cotton. 50" wide, 19⅝" repeat. Document at Musée de l'Impression sur Etoffes, Mulhouse, France. No.67841.01 (red).

❀ LA PORTUGAISE. English (for the Portuguese market), mid-19th century, block print. 100% cotton, glazed. 50" wide, 34" repeat. Document privately owned in England. No.172630.00 (multi on aubergine).

❀ LEIGHTON HOUSE GLAZED CHINTZ. English, 1839. 100% cotton. 54" wide, 31½" repeat. Document, privately owned in England, a hand-drawn, gouache-on-paper textile design. No.62434.01 (green).

❀ LILY OF GALTEE GLAZED CHINTZ. England, 1859. 44" field plus a 6" border on right side, 6¼" repeat. Document, privately owned in England, a gouache-on-paper drawing for a textile, dated July 2, 1859. No.36465.01 (pink ribbon).

❀ LONGLEAT COTTON PRINT. English, c.1850–65. 100% cotton. 57" wide, 13¾" vertical repeat, 38" horizontal repeat. Document a block-printed cotton in Brunschwig & Fils

Archives. Scale slightly reduced in screen-printed reproduction; color and motifs are exact. No. 36290.01 (multi).

❀ MILLICENT GLAZED CHINTZ. French (Alsace), c.1855, block print. 100% cotton, glazed. 54" wide, 40" vertical repeat, 27" horizontal repeat. Document at Musée de l'Impression sur Etoffes, Mulhouse, France. Motifs slightly altered so that the smaller bouquet and ribbon stripe repeat halfway between the large bouquets on the other stripes. No. 64255.01 (pink stripe).

❀ MOIS DE MAI GLAZED CHINTZ. French (Alsace), c.1840, block print. 100% cotton, glazed. 50% wide, 31" repeat. Original design by Jean Ulrich Tournier. Document in Brunschwig & Fils Archives and at Musée de l'Impression sur Etoffes, Mulhouse, France. No. 61090.01 (white).

❀ MON JARDIN GLAZED CHINTZ. French (Alsace), c.1850, roller print. 100% cotton, glazed. 63" wide, 38½" repeat. *Chefs d'Oeuvre du Musée de l'Impression sur Etoffes, Mulhouse*, vol.1, fig.93. Original design by Jean Ulrich Tournier. Document in Brunschwig & Fils Archives and at Musée de l'Impression sur Etoffes, Mulhouse, France. No. 610700.00 (multi on ivory).

❀ NEW ROSES ET RUBANS GLAZED CHINTZ. American, c.1860, block printed on challis. 100% cotton, glazed. 54" wide, 32" vertical repeat, 18" horizontal repeat. Document in Brunschwig & Fils Archives. Modern version has been slightly enlarged from original 30¼" repeat, and black outlines around flowers have been eliminated. No. 79068.04 (deep brown).

❀ NOSEGAY STRIPE GLAZED CHINTZ. French, c. 1860–80, block print. 100% cotton, glazed. 51" wide, 14¼" vertical repeat, 8¾" horizontal repeat. Document a block-printed chintz used at the Codman House, Lincoln, Mass., now owned by the Society for the Preservation of New England Antiquities. No. 62142.01 (blue).

❀ POND LILY GLAZED CHINTZ. English, mid-19th century, block print. 100% cotton, glazed. 53½" wide, 35" repeat. Document retained at print works in England. No. 66250.01 (red and green on cream).

❀ PONDICHERRY COTTON PRINT. French, c.1850–80, block print. 100% cotton. 54" wide, 25" vertical repeat, 26½" horizontal repeat. Document a gouache-on-paper design for a block-printed fabric from Thierry-Mieg at Mulhouse, now owned by Musée de l'Impression sur Etoffes at Mulhouse, France. Design reduced from 27⅜" vertical repeat. No. 36314.01 (green).

❀ REDOUTE GLAZED CHINTZ. French, c.1850–70, block print on roller-printed or plain ground. 100% cotton. 65" wide, 35½" repeat. Documents in Brunschwig & Fils Archives. No. 36350.01 (beige with fancy ground); No. 36353.01 (yellow with plain ground).

❀ ROCKINGHAM GLAZED CHINTZ. English, c. 1855–65, block print. 100% cotton, glazed. 53" wide, 36½" repeat. Document privately owned in England. No. 62640.01 (cream).

❀ ROSES AND LEAVES GLAZED CHINTZ. English, mid-19th century, block print. 100% cotton, glazed. 48½" wide, 35" repeat. Handblocked. Document privately owned in England. No. 61554.01 (red and emerald).

❀ ROSES AND PANSIES GLAZED CHINTZ. English, c.1845, block print. 100% cotton, glazed. 54" wide, 27½" repeat. Document privately owned in England. No. 66070.01 (multi).

❀ ROSES ET LILAS GLAZED CHINTZ. French (Alsace), c. 1850–60, block and roller print. 100% cotton, glazed. 51" wide, 32¼" repeat. Document, in Brunschwig & Fils Archives, a block-printed cotton chintz with a roller-printed fancy ground (dotted stripes alternating with moiréd stripes also formed of tiny dots) by Jean-Ulrich Tournier, Alsace. Modern version lacks the fancy ground and has been enlarged slightly horizontally. No. 36670.01 (cream).

❀ ST. CROIX COTTON PRINT, ST. CROIX BORDER PRINT. French (Alsace), c. 1850–65, block print. 100% cotton. Cotton yardage 32" wide, 38" repeat. Border print 13" wide, fabric 28", 20" repeat. Available either as single border or two side by side. Document a block print on cotton privately owned in France. No. 174350.00 (cream); Border No. 174360.00 (cream).

❀ SARAH JANE GLAZED CHINTZ. English, 1842, block print. 50" wide, 25¼" repeat. Originally printed at Bannister Hall, Preston, England, and introduced July 23, 1842. Documents a gouache-on-paper drawing for a textile and a block-printed cotton chintz, both privately owned in England. Original fabric has a fancy ground of overlapping tiny dots not indicated on the drawing; this detail has not been reproduced. No. 36053.01 (yellow).

❀ SUMMERHOUSE GLAZED CHINTZ. French (Alsace), 1855–

56, block print. 100% cotton. 49" wide, 25½" half-drop re-peat. Designed by Jean Ulrich Tournier for Schwartz & Hu-guenin at Mulhouse-Dornach. *Chefs d'Oeuvre du Musée de l'Impression sur Etoffes, Mulhouse,* vol.1, no.97. Document a block-printed cotton in Brunschwig & Fils Archives. No. 78333.04 (coral and blue on yellow).

❀ TANTE ROSE GLAZED CHINTZ. French (Alsace), c.1850, block print. 100% cotton. 49" wide, 28¾" drop repeat. Doc-ument owned by Musée des Arts Décoratifs, Paris. No. 62537.01 (red on aubergine).

❀ VICTORIAN GARDEN GLAZED CHINTZ. English, c.1850, block print. 100% cotton, glazed. 50" wide, 30½" half-drop repeat. Document owned by Winterthur Museum. No. 65807.01 (rose and blue on aubergine).

❀ VIVIENNE COTTON PRINT. French, c.1840, block print. 100% cotton. 50" wide, 19½" repeat. Document, privately owned in France, a block-printed cotton based on a hand-painted Louis XVI period original. No.173620.00 (multi on cream).

CLARENCE HOUSE

Minimum order two yards.

❀ BABYLONE. English, c.1855–65, block print. 100% cot-ton, glazed. 54" wide, 25¼" vertical repeat, 27" horizontal repeat. Document privately owned in England. No.32881-3 (green),

❀ BAILEY ROSE. English, c.1850–70, block print. 100% cot-ton, glazed. 53" wide, 39" repeat. Jones, Colefax & Fowler, p.96. Document owned by Colefax & Fowler, London. No. 31925-1 (pink).

❀ EUGENIE. English, c.1860–70, block and roller print. 100% cotton, glazed. 52" wide, 31" repeat. Document privately owned in England. No.32033-1 (red and green).

❀ FRAGONARD. English, c.1850–65, block print. 100% cot-ton, glazed. 56" wide, 26½" repeat. Document owned by Clarence House. Late 19th-century window curtains made of this design are now in the collections of the Society for the Preservation of New England Antiquities. No.32089-3 (framboise).

❀ GALLICA. English, c.1845–60, block and roller print. 100% cotton, glazed. 52" wide, 26" repeat. Document pri-vately owned in England. No.32066-1 (red and turquoise).

FRAGONARD, c. 1850–65. Clarence House. Framboise.

❀ LA VIE EN ROSE. English, c.1850–60, block print. 100% cotton, glazed. 55" wide, 22" vertical repeat, 18" horizontal repeat. Document privately owned. The Society for the Preservation of New England Antiquities owns period window curtains made of this fabric and a curtain rod covered with the same fabric (see Grier, *Color and Comfort,* pl.29; Cooke, *Upholstery in America and Europe,* fig.207). No. 32777-3 (aubergine).

❀ LETTRES DE MON JARDIN. French, c.1860–70, block print. 100% cotton, glazed. 54" wide, 31½" repeat. No.32725-1 (original).

❀ L'OPERA CHINOIS. English, c.1850–70, block print. 100% cotton. 51" wide, 15" repeat. Document owned by Clarence House. No.31929-61 (ecru, unglazed); No.31929-1 (ecru, glazed).

❀ MUSSET. French, c.1845–70, block print. 100% cotton, glazed. 51" wide, 30¼" repeat. Document privately owned in France. No.31015-5 (parme).

❀ NOAILLES. English, c.1850–70, block print. 100% cotton, glazed. 58" wide, 25½" repeat. Document privately owned. No.32074-2 (celadon).

❀ PASSION FLOWER. English, c.1845–60, block print. 100% cotton, glazed. 48" wide, 14" vertical repeat, 22¾" horizontal repeat. Jones, *Colefax & Fowler,* p. 96. Document owned by Colefax & Fowler, London. No.32507-03 (blue).

❀ POLESDEN LACY. English, c.1855–65, block print. 100% cotton, glazed. 52" wide, 25½" repeat. Document privately owned in England. No.32638-3 (celadon).

❀ RAYURE PICHET. French, c.1845–55, roller print with fancy ground. 100% cotton, glazed. 51" wide, 14¼" vertical repeat, 25½" horizontal repeat. Document privately owned in Germany. No.32862-1 (document).

❀ ROPE LATTICE. English, c.1860, block print. 100% cotton, glazed. 48" wide, 24" repeat. Document owned by Clarence House. No.2505178 (creme); No.2552855 (green).

❀ ROSA MUNDIE. English, c.1850–65, block print. 100% cotton, glazed. 54 1/2" wide, 21½" repeat. Document privately owned in England. No.32032-2 (blue); No.32032-15 (black).

❀ ROSE SPRIG. English, c.1840–50, block and roller print. 100% cotton, glazed. 52" wide, 13" repeat. Document privately owned. No.32067-2 (turquoise).

LETTRES DE MON JARDIN, 1860–70. Clarence House. Original.

L'OPERA CHINOIS, 1850–70. Clarence House. Ecru.

NOAILLES, c. 1850–70.
Clarence House.
Celadon.

RAYURE PICHET, c. 1845–
55. Clarence House.
Document.

136

❀ TONBRIDGE. English, c.1845–60, block print. 100% cotton, glazed. 54" wide, 11¾" repeat. Document privately owned in England. No. 32760-1 (green).

❀ TREE POPPY. English, c.1850–65, block and roller print. 100% cotton, glazed. 52" wide, 29" repeat. Document privately owned in England. No. 32130-1 (red and green).

❀ ULVERSTON. English, c.1850–65, block and roller print. 100% cotton, glazed. 54" wide, 11" vertical repeat, 9" horizontal repeat. Document privately owned. No. 32700-1 (green).

CLASSIC REVIVALS

❀ CHELSEA FLOWERS. English, c.1845–55, block print with fancy ground. 100% cotton. 54" wide, 12½" repeat. Document privately owned. No. 50500-010 (green).

COWTAN & TOUT

Minimum order two yards.

❀ ALEXANDRA CHINTZ. English, c.1840–50, block and roller print. 100% cotton, glazed. 54" wide, 18" repeat. Document owned by Cowtan & Tout. No. 6422 (reds and greens on beige ground).

❀ ARBOR ROSE. English, c.1855–65, block print. 100% cotton, glazed. 50" wide, 18" repeat. Document privately owned in England. No. 8152 (multi on green).

❀ AVALON. English, c. 1855–70, block and roller print. 100% cotton. 51" wide, 25" repeat. Document privately owned in England. No. 9201 (multi on beige).

❀ BERMUDA CORAL. English, c.1845–60. 100% cotton. 48" wide, 2" repeat. Document owned by Cowtan & Tout. No. 1108 (navy).

❀ BAILEY ROSE. English, c.1860–90, block print. 100% cotton, glazed. 50" wide, 38" repeat. Jones, Colefax & Fowler, p.96. Document owned by Colefax & Fowler, London. No. 7180 (reds, pinks and greens on white ground).

❀ BRAMFIELD. English, c.1850–65, block and roller print. 100% cotton. 54" wide, 12" repeat. Document owned by Cowtan & Tout. No. 2490 (multi on red), No. 2491 (multi on black).

❀ CORAL BRANCHES. English, c.1845–60. 100% cotton. 54" wide, 2" repeat. Document owned by Cowtan & Tout. No. 5454 (red and green); No. 5455 (red and brown).

❀ CROCUSES. English, c. 1845–65, block with pin dot ground. 100% cotton, glazed. 54" wide, 3½" repeat. Document owned by Cowtan & Tout. No. 4100 (pinks and blue on white ground).

❀ DIANTHUS. English, c. 1850–65, block print with fancy ground. 100% cotton, glazed. 54" wide, 11" repeat. Document privately owned in England. No. 1350 (reds and blues on cream ground).

❀ FLORAL BOUQUET AND RIBBON. English, c. 1860–1900, block print. 100% cotton, glazed. 53" wide, 39" repeat. Document privately owned in England. No. 2033 (reds, pinks and greens on ivory ground).

❀ MAYFAIR. English, c. 1855–65, block and roller print. 100% cotton, glazed. 52" wide, 28" repeat. Document privately owned in England. No. 7550 (multi with tan underprint).

❀ PEARL STRIPE AND RIBBON. English, c. 1860–70, block print. 100% cotton, glazed. 52" wide, 25" repeat. Document owned by Cowtan & Tout. No. 5054 (pink and white with green stripes).

❀ RANBUTEAU. French, c. 1850–70, block print. 100% cotton. 33" wide, 46" repeat. Document privately owned in France. No. 2476 (blue and white); No. 2477 (beige and cream).

❀ REBECCA. English, c. 1850–60, roller print. 100% cotton. 53" wide, 2" repeat. Document a curtain lining owned by Cowtan & Tout. No. 1147-03.

❀ ROSE AND LABURNUM. English, c. 1855–70, block print with roller printed squiggle ground. 100% cotton, glazed. 50" wide, 29" repeat. Document owned by Cowtan & Tout. No. 7040 (reds and lilac on fancy squiggle ground).

❀ STAFFORDSHIRE. English, c. 1850–70, block and roller print. 100% cotton, glazed. 54" wide, 24" repeat. Document privately owned in England. No. 2496 (multi on cafe with dots).

❀ VICTORIA. English, c. 1860–80, block print. 100% cotton, glazed. 50" wide, 18" repeat. Document owned by Cowtan & Tout. No. 9701 (rose and green with blue stripes on white ground).

❀ WINDSOR ROSE. English, c. 1860–90, block print. 100% cotton, glazed. 55" wide, 35½" repeat. Document privately owned in France. No. 82000-1F (multi on off-white); No. 82000-2F (multi on aqua).

❀ WINFIELD. English, c.1855–70, block print. 100% cotton. 53" wide, 30½" repeat. Document owned by Cowtan & Tout. No.1644 (blue ribbon on blue upright).

FONTHILL

❀ LILAS. English, c.1855–70, block print. 100% cotton, glazed. 62" wide, 45" repeat. Document owned by Fonthill. No.1533-6 (green ground).

❀ OLD GUERNSEY. English, c.1850–65, block and roller print. 100% cotton. 52" wide, 32½" repeat. Document in Baker Archive, London. No.1731-1 (pink).

❀ WENTWORTH. English, c.1855–65, block and roller print. 100% cotton. 50" wide, 32" repeat. Document privately owned. No.1613-1 (celadon and lavender).

GREEFF FABRICS

❀ HATHAWAY HOUSE. English, c.1860, block print. 100% cotton. 36" wide, 16" repeat. Document privately owned in England. No.55835 (red).

❀ KENDRICK. English, c.1860, block print. 100% cotton, glazed. 56" wide, 36" repeat. Document privately owned in England. No.60873 (old rose and lilac on ivory).

HALLIE GREER

❀ CHURCHILL. English, c.1865–75, block print. 100% cotton. 54" wide, 21" repeat. Document in Hallie Greer Archives. No.F-16 (documentary peach, rose and green).

❀ LETIZIA. French, c.1850–65, block print. 100% cotton. 54" wide, 16" repeat. Document a watercolor rendering of a design for a textile now in Hallie Greer Archives. No.F-25 (documentary, lavender ground).

LEE JOFA

❀ GRANVILLE PRINT. English, c.1860, block print. 100% cotton, glazed. 54" wide, 29½" repeat. Document owned by Lee Jofa. No.789030 (multi on cream).

❀ HOLLYHOCK AND RIBBON PRINT. English, c.1850–75, block print. 100% cotton, glazed. 49–50" wide, 36" half-drop repeat (cut by repeat only). Document privately owned. No. 799820 (ivory).

❀ HOLLYHOCK MINOR. English, c.1850–60, block and roller print. 100% cotton, glazed. 52" wide, 23½" repeat. Docu-

top left
CHURCHILL, c. 1865–75.
Hallie Greer. Document
peach, rose and green.

top right
HOLLYHOCK, c. 1850–60.
Lee Jofa. Whites, reds,
turquoise.

right
LETIZIA, c. 1850–65.
Hallie Greer. Lavender
ground.

ment owned by Lee Jofa. No.9395-0 (green, rose and spruce).

❀ HOLLYHOCK PRINT. English, c. 1850–60, block print. 100% cotton, glazed. 47" wide, 40¼" repeat (cut by repeat only). Schoeser and Rufey, *English and American Textiles,* chap. 7, fig. 22; cited as "possibly the most beautiful chintz on the market" (1955) and "one of Sir Henry Cole's examples of false principles of design" (1852). Handblocked. Document privately owned in England. No. 7131 (white, reds and turquoise).

❀ LEAVES PRINT. English, c.1850, block print. 100% cotton, glazed. 52" wide, 36½" repeat. Document privately owned. No.809201 (rose on buff).

❀ LUDLOW PRINT. English, c.1850–60, block print. 100% cotton, glazed. 48-49" wide, 24½" half-drop repeat. Document privately owned in England. No. 789010 (multi on cream); No.789011 (multi on white).

❀ PORCELAIN FLOWERS PRINT. English, c. 1850–60, block print. 100% cotton, glazed. 50" wide, 27¾" repeat. Handblocked. Document privately owned in England. No.99348 (white, red and turquoise).

❀ ROSEBANK PRINT. English, c.1850–60, block print. 100% cotton, glazed. 49–50" wide, 36" repeat. Document privately owned in England. No.789000 (white and red).

❀ ROSEDALE PRINT. English, c.1860, block print. 100% cotton, glazed. 50" wide, 24" repeat. Document privately owned in England. No.659080 (red and white).

❀ TRENTHAM HALL PRINT. English c.1850–60, block print. 100% cotton, glazed. 53" wide, 36" half-drop repeat. Document privately owned in England. Recently converted from handblocked print to rotary screen. No.647205 (beige and multi).

❀ WHIPPETS PRINT. English (probably Lancashire), c. 1850–60, block print. 100% cotton, glazed. 53–54" wide, 25¼" repeat. *From East to West,* fig.67. Adapted slightly to make animal elements less ferocious and eliminate a dead hare between the paws of the dog in the foreground. Document owned by Lee Jofa. No.769040 (multi on cream).

ROSE CUMMING CHINTZES

❀ GENGES. English, c.1850–65, cylinder print. 100% cotton, glazed. 53" wide, 15" repeat. Document privately owned. No.5031-1 (beige).

❀ GRAND CHINOIS. French, c. 1830–45, roller print. 100% cotton, glazed. 44" wide, 18" repeat. Schoeser and Rufey, *English and American Textiles,* chap. 2, figs. 41–43; Montgomery, *Printed Textiles,* fig. 51. Pattern often known as "Open Window." Documents in Baker Archive, London, Winterthur Museum, Old Sturbridge Village and other collections. Known in red, blue and multicolored versions, probably from different printers. No. 5060-1 (blue and white).

❀ LILAC. French, continuous from c. 1860, block print on striped pin-dot ground. 100% cotton. 46" wide, 37" repeat. Example owned by Society for the Preservation of New England Antiquities. RC 1602-1 (creme).

❀ ROSALYNDA. English, c. 1860–75, block print with fancy ground. 100% cotton, glazed. 54" wide, 9" repeat. Document privately owned. No. 5084-1 (taupe).

RUE DE FRANCE

❀ BONIS. French, c. 1845–70, block print. 100% cotton. 59" wide, 1" repeat. Document privately owned in France. No. 78-4 (rouge).

❀ INDIANAIRE. French, c. 1845–70, block print. 100% cotton. 59" wide including 2½" border on each side. Document privately owned in France. No. 64-4 (rouge).

❀ ISLAMABAD. French, c. 1860–80, block print. 100% cotton. 59" wide. Document privately owned in France. No. 103-81 (cerise).

SCALAMANDRÉ

❀ LONGFELLOW HOUSE. English, c. 1840, printed wool. 100% wool twill. 55" wide, 10¼" repeat. Document a printed wool fabric purchased in 1842 by Henry Wadsworth Longfellow and Fanny Appleton Longfellow from James Paul and Company, Boston; used for window drapery and furniture upholstery in their parlor in Cambridge, Mass. Document owned by Longfellow National Historic Site. Adaptation on 100% cotton, glazed. No. 7795-3 (pinks, yellows and greens on off-white).

❀ MULHOUSE FLORAL. French (Thierry-Mieg, Mulhouse, Alsace), c. 1850–60, block print. 100% cotton. 48" wide, 31½" repeat. Document at Musée de l'Impression sur Etoffes, Mulhouse, France. No. 6838-1 (multi on ivory).

❀ SWAN LAKE. English, c.1845–55, roller print. 100% cotton. 50" wide, 14" repeat. Document at Essex Institute, Salem, Mass. No. 6277-5 (wine, purple, blues and gold). Special order only.

SCHUMACHER

❀ FERNDALE. Probably English, c.1850, printed wool. 50% rayon, 37% cotton, 13" wool. 48" wide, 28¼" repeat. Document owned by Cooper-Hewitt Museum. Endorsed by the Victorian Society in America. No. 73370 (document multi).

❀ ST. GREGORY'S STRIPE. English or American, c.1840–60. 100% cotton. 54" wide, 18" repeat. Document a glazed cotton window valance in the Schumacher Archives. No. 162820 (document tan and green).

❀ VERMICELLI. English or American, c.1840–70, cylinder

SWAN LAKE, c.1845–55. Scalamandré. Wine, purple, blues and gold.

VICTORIA AND ALBERT
CHINTZ, c. 1854.
Stroheim & Romann.
Red on white.

print. 100% cotton. 54" wide, negligible repeat. Document a glazed chintz in the Schumacher Archives. No. 162738 (stone).

STROHEIM & ROMANN

❀ VICTORIA AND ALBERT CHINTZ. English, c.1854, block print. 100% cotton. 50" wide, 31" repeat. Designed for the first royal yacht of Queen Victoria; design contains profiles of Victoria and Albert. Document privately owned in England. No. 34370 (red on white).

BRUNSCHWIG & FILS

❀ ALICIA WOVEN TAPESTRY. French. c.1850–70. 100% cotton. 51" wide, 13" vertical repeat, 6¼" horizontal repeat, reversible. Document a jacquard woven cotton privately owned in France. No. 63661.01 (terracotta and beige).

❀ DIANORA WOVEN TEXTURE. French (Lyon), c.1850–60. 76% wool, 24% cotton. 55" wide, 5½" repeat. Document a shawl in Brunschwig & Fils Archives. Successful adaptation to yard goods, although slightly less colorful than the original and no longer a tapestry twill weave. No. 63239.01 (red and black).

❀ MARCOTTE DAMASK. French, 19th century. 100% silk. 53" wide, 18½" repeat. Reproduced for American Wing, Metropolitan Museum of Art, which owns the document. Also called "Centennial Damask." Special order only.

❀ NACY TAPESTRY. American, c.1850–70, needlepoint. 98% cotton, 2% nylon. 51" wide, 3½" repeat. Adapted from an embroidered wool-on-canvas document in Brunschwig & Fils Archives. Scale of reproduction slightly enlarged and colors somewhat muted. No. 63434.01 (spruce).

❀ PRINCE NOIR TAPESTRY. Italian, c.1850–75, needlepoint. 74% cotton, 26% wool. 51" wide, 15" repeat. Adapted from an embroidered wool-on-canvas document privately owned in Italy. No. 190819.00 (black and green).

❀ ROANNE SILK DAMASK. European, mid-19th century. 100% silk. 48" wide, 19½" repeat (cut by repeat only). Reproduced for Belter Parlor (1845–70), Bayou Bend Collection, Houston. Document in Brunschwig & Fils Archives. No. 31620.00 (vieux rose, color no. 7009).

❀ SERGE WOVEN STRIPE. American, c.1850. 60% linen, 40% cotton. 55" wide, 6" horizontal repeat. Documents from a

WOVEN DESIGNS

ARUNDEL BROCATELLE,
1841. Classic Revivals.
Custom colors.

merchant's sample collection or pattern book now in Brunschwig & Fils Archives. No.63871.01 (raspberry and cream); No.63872.01 (marine blue and cream); No.63874.01 (green and cream); No.62877.01 (marine blue and raspberry).
❁ VICTORIAN DAMASK. English, c.1840. 58% cotton, 30% wool, 12% rayon. 51" wide, 20" repeat. Document a set of wool draperies from a Virginia plantation; now at Valentine Museum, Richmond. No.10705.02 (pink).

CLASSIC REVIVALS

Not all fabrics have order numbers; specify name of desired design. All are custom woven after order is placed.
❁ ARUNDEL BROCATELLE. French, 1841. Silk-linen blend. 21" wide, 24" repeat. Document, dated July 30, 1841, in Prelle Archives, Lyon, France. Brocatelle in this design was supplied by Morant in 1846 for Queen Victoria's bed at Arundel Castle. No.4084. Custom colors.

146

BROCATELLE NO. 18,
c. 1860. Classic Revivals.
Custom colors.

✿ BROCATELLE NO. 18. English, c.1860, handwoven jacquard. 100% silk. 21" wide, 43" repeat. *A Choice of Design*, no.18. First woven by Daniel Keith & Co., London. Document in Warner Archive, London. Custom colors.

✿ BROCATELLE NO. 4563. French, c.1850–80. 60% silk, 40% linen. 21" wide, 37½" repeat. Document in Prelle Archives, Lyon, France, a mid-19th-century reproduction of a 17th-century Italian brocatelle. No.4563 (custom colors).

✿ CAVENDISH BROCATELLE. English, c.1840–50. 60% linen, 40% silk. 21" wide. Woven for the Speaker's Bed, Palace of Westminster. Document owned by the Palace of Westminster. Handwoven by the Humphries Weaving Company. Custom colors.

✿ CURRANT. English, c.1860, damasquette. 100% silk. 42" wide, 28" repeat. *A Choice of Design*, no. 6. First woven by Daniel Walters & Sons, Braintree, Essex, England. Document in Warner Archive, London. Custom colors.

❀ EGYPTIAN. English, c.1860–80, silk tissue. 100% silk. 21" wide, 27" repeat, six strips of borders woven across a single fabric width. *A Choice of Design,* no.54. Document in Warner Archive, London. Custom colors.

❀ FERRIERES DAMASK. France, c.1850–65. 100% silk. 21" wide, 28" repeat. Document in Prelle Archives, Lyon, France. Originally woven for the Chateau de Ferrieres. Rewoven recently for a Belter-style sofa at Victoria and Albert Museum. Custom colors.

❀ GOSFIELD BROCATELLE. English, c.1850–60. 60% linen, 40% silk. 21" wide. Document owned by the British National Trust. Used for window curtains at Gawthorpe Hall, Lancashire, England. Custom colors. Handwoven by the Humphries Weaving Company.

❀ GOTHIC DAMASK. French, 1853. 100% silk with silver thread. 21" wide, 7" repeat. Document, dated January 20, 1853, in Prelle Archives, Lyon, France. First woven for Burton, London, possibly for ecclesiastical use. No.4390. Custom colors.

❀ HIBISCAN. English, c.1860, silk tissue. 100% silk. 21" wide, 31" repeat. *A Choice of Design,* fig.25. First woven by Daniel Walters & Sons, Braintree, Essex, England. Document in Warner Archive, London. Custom colors.

❀ HINDLEY. English, c.1860, damasquette. 100% silk. 21" wide, 46" repeat. *A Choice of Design,* fig.17. First woven by Keith & Co. for Messrs. Hindley & Co. Exhibited at the International Exhibition, London, 1862 (see *Art Journal Illustrated Catalogue,* p.142). Document in Warner Archive, London, stamped "K & Co." Custom colors.

❀ OWEN JONES BROCATELLE. English, c.1855. silk and cotton blend, exact proportions unknown. 21" wide, 21½" repeat. Document in Prelle Archives, Lyon, France. No.9119 (blue, gold and cream).

❀ PALERMO. English, c.1860, damasquette with satin and rep figuring. 100% silk. 27" wide, 27" repeat. *A Choice of Design,* fig.4. First woven by Daniel Walters & Sons, Braintree, Essex, England. Document in Warner Archive, London, stamped "DW & S." Custom colors.

❀ P. 62. English, c.1860, damask. 100% silk. 20" wide, 29" repeat. Schoeser and Rufey, *English and American Textiles,* chap.3, fig.5; *A Choice of Design,* fig.3. Design used for hangings at Queen Victoria's coronation in 1838; varies slightly

CURRANT, c. 1860.
Classic Revivals.
Custom colors.

GOTHIC DAMASK, 1853.
Classic Revivals.
Custom colors.

top left
HIBISCAN, c. 1860.
Classic Revivals.
Custom colors.

top right
HINDLEY, c. 1860.
Classic Revivals.
Custom colors.

right
PALERMO, c. 1860.
Classic Revivals.
Custom colors.

150

from a French silk damask of c.1806. Modern version based
on a sample woven by Daniel Walters & Sons, Braintree,
Essex, England. c.1860, now in Warner Archive, London.
Custom colors.

❀ SILK BROCATELLE. English, c.1845. 100% silk. 21" wide,
54" repeat. *A Choice of Design,* fig.20. Designed by A. W. N.
Pugin. Woven by Keith & Co. Document in Warner Archive, London. Custom colors.

❀ VATICAN. English, c.1865–70, damask. 100% silk. 63"
wide. 52" repeat. *A Choice of Design,* fig.14. First woven by
Daniel Walters & Sons, Braintree, Essex, England. Document in Warner Archive, London. Custom colors.

❀ VENETIAN. English, c.1860, brocatelle. 100% silk. 42"
wide, 52" repeat. *A Choice of Design,* fig.21. First woven by
Daniel Walters & Sons, Braintree, Essex, England. Exhibited at the International Exhibition, London, 1862. Document in Warner Archive, London. Custom colors.

❀ WALTHAM. English, 1859, damasquette. 100% silk. 21"
wide, 49" repeat. *A Choice of Design,* fig.24. Design registered
October 23, 1859. Woven by Keith & Co., London and Sudbury. Document in Warner Archive, London. Custom colors.

P. 62, c.1860.
Classic Revivals.
Custom colors.

SILK BROCATELLE,
c.1845. Classic Revivals.
Custom colors.

LEE JOFA

❁ SCOTTISH TARTANS. Traditional. 100% wool. 54" wide, re-
peats vary. Clans available:
ANCIENT CAMPBELL. No.4723-1.
ANCIENT HUNTING MACRAE. No.4730-1.
ANDERSON. No.4710-0.
BLACK WATCH. No.4636-0 (blue and green).
BLACK WATCH MUTED. No.4641-0 (gray and mink).
BLUE DOUGLAS MUTED. No.834055X.
BROWN SCOT. No.4720-1
CLAN CAMERON. No.4712-1.
DARK JOHNSTON. No.4725-1
DRESS MACDUFF. No.4727-1.
DRESS MACKENZIE. No.834052X.
DRESS MACKENZIE MUTED. No.4738-1.
DRESS MENZIES. No.4716-1.
ELLIOTT. No.4724-1.

GREEN BARCLAY. No.4639-0 (navy and green).

GREEN DOUGLAS. No.4719-1.

GREY DOUGLAS. No.4732-1.

HOME. No.834051X.

HUNTING CHISHOLM. No.4648-0 (brown and green).

HUNTING FRASER. No.4713-1.

HUNTING MACINNES. No.4728-1.

HUNTING MACINTOSH. No.4634-0.

HUNTING MACINTOSH MUTED. No.4737-1.

HUNTING MACLEOD. No.4715-1.

HUNTING MENZIES. No.4638-0 (red and green).

KENNEDY. No.4714-1.

LINDSAY. No.4643-0 (maroon and green).

MACBETH. No.834050X.

MACKELLAR MUTED. No.4736-1.

MACLENNAN. No.4729-1.

MUTED HUNTING STEWART. No.4647-0 (brown).

MUTED RED HUNTING CHISHOLM. No.4640-0 (brown, light blue, red).

PRINCESS MARY. No.4718-1.

PRINCESS MARY MUTED. No.4740-1.

RED MACINTOSH. No.4644-0 (red and navy).

STEWART OF FINGASK. No.834054X.

WALLACE. No.4731-1.

❀ WYMONDHAM DAMASK. English, c.1845–70. 56.5% cotton, 43.5% silk. Document privately owned in England. No.K211. Special order only; colors to order.

OLD WORLD WEAVERS

❀ METROPOLITAN MUSEUM. Probably Italian, mid-19th century. 59% rayon, 45% cotton. 50" wide, 3½" repeat. Reproduced for American Wing, Metropolitan Museum of Art. Previously known as "Brocatello Museo." No.A2474B (royal blue and gold).

SCALAMANDRÉ

❀ BALLROOM SATIN. c.1855–70. 42% silk, 58% cotton. 50½" wide. Suitable texture for formal drapery and upholstery. Document owned by Scalamandré. No.99450-1 (champagne).

❀ BROCKENBROUGH DAMASK. French, c.1860–65. 43% wool, 57% silk. 48½" width, 20½" vertical repeat, 12¼" horizontal repeat. Document a lambrequin used in a hallway, now owned by the White House of the Confederacy. Richmond, Va. No. 97461-1 (golden rod on brick red). Special order only; minimum order 50 yards.

❀ BUTTERFLY DAMASK. French, c. 1850–60. 100% silk. 51" wide, 22" repeat. Document owned by Scalamandré. No. 1051-16 (oyster gray). Special order only.

❀ CRENSHAW DAMASK. French, c. 1850–60. 60% wool, 40% silk. 49" wide, 18½" vertical repeat, 12¼" horizontal repeat. Document a portiere, now owned by the White House of the Confederacy, Richmond, Va. Scale significantly reduced in adaptation of design; vertical repeat reduced from 27", horizontal repeat from 18¼". No. 97460-1 (gold on wine). Special order only.

❀ DAVIS BROCATELLE. French, c. 1850–65. 75% silk, 25% linen. 48" wide, 60¼" vertical repeat, 23¾" horizontal repeat. Document owned by the White House of the Confederacy, Richmond, Va. No. 97459-1 (green and gold).

❀ LINCOLN HOUSE BROCATELLE. French, c. 1850–65. 51% wool, 49% silk. 51" wide, 23" vertical repeat, 17" horizontal repeat. Document owned by National Park Service, Abraham Lincoln House, Springfield, Ill. Scale enlarged in adaptation. No. 20028-1 (rust and gold). Special order only.

❀ LOUIS XVI LAMPAS. c. 1855–75. 65% silk, 35% cotton. 50" wide, 26¾" repeat. Document owned by Scalamandré. No. 586-12 (gold and silver on royal blue). Special order only.

❀ MUSEUM OF THE CITY OF NEW YORK DAMASK. c. 1870. 100% silk. 51" wide, 9" repeat. Reproduced for Rockefeller Room, Museum of the City of New York. Document owned by Scalamandré. No. 97201-1 (cardinal red). Special order only.

❀ PATRICK BARRY BROCATELLE. c. 1850–65. 65% silk, 35% linen. 50" wide, 26½" repeat. Document owned by Scalamandré. No. 97120A-1 (bronze, French gray and white). Special order only.

❀ STAN HYWET BROCATELLE. c. 1850–70. 36% silk, 64" linen. 50" wide, 27¾" repeat. Document owned by Scalamandré. No. 97321A-1 (slate blue strié). Special order.

left
BROCKENBROUGH DAMASK, c. 1860–65, Scalamandré. Golden rod on red brick.

bottom left
CRENSHAW DAMASK, c. 1850–60. Scalamandré. Gold on wine.

bottom right
LINCOLN HOUSE BROCATELLE, c. 1850–65. Scalamandré. Rust and gold.

1870 TO 1900:
NEW INFLUENCES
AND VARIETY

M any American houses during the years 1870–1900 were characterized by heavy window drapery and luxurious upholstery, lavish ornaments and abundant use of table covers, lambrequins and purely decorative textile accents. The fabrics used included richly textured brocatelle, brocade, lampas and damask; delicate shades of soft silk and satin; elaborately patterned cretonne, cashmere and tapestry; and highly polished chintz. During the summer months, many of these heavy decorative elements were carefully stored away and replaced by lighter window curtains, rush mats and rugs and brightly colored chintz slipcovers.

Throughout the period solid-colored window curtains were still popular for primary rooms. Complex decorative effects were achieved through the use of many layers of fabric and contrasting colors and trims. These elaborate window curtain designs were set off nicely by the crisp white muslin or lace curtains used next to the window panes and the window shades beneath them.

The heavy winter window hangings were often made of solid-colored wool or velvet panels trimmed with decorative woven tapes or bands of embroidery. Damask and moreen were also used. There might also be a layer of lighter silk curtains between the heavy outer pair and the lace curtains nearest the glass. The curtains were usually surmounted by decorative lambrequins and cornices and further set off by elaborate fringes, tassels and tiebacks. The curtain panels themselves were often stiffened with flannel interlinings that had not been used previously. Because of the elaborate folds in window valances and curtains, stiff rep was used less frequently than in the previous decades.

"Style of Decoration and Hangings for Windows," from *How to Build, Furnish & Decorate: The Cooperative Building Plan Association*, 1883.

157

For simpler houses, one or more of these layers might be omitted and less expensive fabrics and trimmings substituted. Some of the cheaper fabrics could be made to simulate those of richer texture by the use of extra lining and interlining. As a substitute for costly trimmings, attractive decorative accents could be made at home. One authority suggested using gray linen damask curtain panels bordered with embroidered flowers or figures cut from scarlet, blue or green cloth and appliqued to the linen. Figures cut from chintz or cretonne could also be used to embellish simple curtains. One author even suggested gluing bands of colorful autumn leaves to strips of muslin and using these as curtain borders, adding a thin tree branch as a cornice. This combination was thought to create a truly medieval appearance and could be expected to last at least one season.

In addition to window drapery, additional interior embellishment was introduced in the form of portieres, which were interior curtains hung in doorways. These could be hung from thick wooden rods on exposed rings or above the door frame on an apparatus concealed by an elaborate lambrequin. Closely woven fabrics, such as wool rep, were favored for portieres as the most effective means of stopping drafts between rooms. In many cases portieres were trimmed with horizontal bands of appliquéd velvet or embroidery, the placement of which could reflect the architectural divisions of the adjacent walls. Less commonly, the portieres matched the window drapery within a room.

Decorating conventions dictated appropriate colors for the various rooms in a house. Parlors should be opulent, adorned with the most expensive fabrics in jewellike colors, while family sitting rooms were to be furnished with colorful chintz and cretonne in luxurious shades of blue, drab, gray or pale rose. Libraries and dining rooms were still decorated in more somber colors such as brown, stone, dark green, crimson or dull red; wool damask and velvet were the fabrics considered especially well suited to these rooms.

Bedchambers could be decorated in silks and damasks as rich as those used in parlors, but many people favored lighter effects achieved with cretonne, sateen, cashmere or chintz in brighter colors and more lively prints. Beds were once again hung with elaborate drapery, although seldom with fully enclosing curtains. Light and airy netted canopies were introduced during this period as a decorative covering for old high-post bedsteads. Even simple brass beds were adorned with curtains hung from a rod or boxed frame fixed to the wall above the headboard.

In summer heavy window drapery, portieres and table covers were packed away to protect them from moths and make way for light-colored, gaily patterned, washable fabric furnishings. Light- or white-ground chintzes and cretonnes in bright floral prints were highly favored, although those with buff or blue grounds were also used. In some houses, ruffled swiss muslin or dotted swiss cotton was used for window curtains, slipcovers, dressing tables and bed drapery. If color was desired, the white cotton could be lined with a chintz of a bright, contrasting color or embellished by colored ribbons drawn through broad hems or used as informal tiebacks. Summer textiles might be made of simpler fabrics, but they were not necessarily used in simple ways. In *Beautiful Homes* (1878), Henry T. Williams and Mrs. C. S. Jones proclaimed that "exquisite puffs and neatly fluted ruffles" in abundance were still the order of the day.

Lace curtains could be used year round, alone in summer time and covered by heavy, colorful curtains in winter. In selecting Nottingham lace curtains, people were advised to choose those of a soft, yellowish cream color rather than those of glaring bleached white. Small-figured designs and delicate motifs were recommended, among them fine fern sprays, conventional flowers, ivy sprays and imitations of old laces. Various qualities were available, the cheapest weighing less than eight ounces and costing as little as fifty-nine cents per pair in 1895 when the best lace curtains weighed nearly three pounds and could cost as much as fifteen dollars per pair. The center of lace curtain manufacture was Nottingham, England, but by 1885 machine-woven laces for curtains, pillow shams and edgings were made in the United States as well. Mail-order houses such as Sears, Roebuck and Montgomery Ward regularly offered lace curtains, and their illustrated catalogs are today among the best sources for dating changing tastes in curtain patterns among the middle classes. In the 19th century curtains were regularly made in pieces three and half yards long; lace curtains today are offered in various lengths and usually are finished with a rod pocket at the upper edge.

Chair at The Grange, Lincoln, Mass., home of the Codman family. Brunschwig & Fils's "New Berry Chintz," a silk-screened reproduction of the original block-printed chintz first used in this room by the Codman family in the 1920s, covers the chair. This design was first printed in the 1850s and has never gone out of production. (Society for the Preservation of New England Antiquities)

In 1895 Montgomery Ward offered both Irish point and Brussels net lace curtains that were slightly more expensive than the Nottingham designs. The company stated that this was the first time such curtains had been available in the United States for "people of moderate means." Clearly, this type of curtain should not be used in 19th-century restoration work except in the most expensive contexts; at the same time, Nottingham lace curtains seem to be appropriate for almost all economic levels.

Roller blinds or window shades of buff holland were chosen for the warm color they gave to the light passing through them. However, some people thought that white cotton or linen shades harmonized better with other drapery and upholstery, and they had the further advantage of being easier to launder. Painted window shades continued to be used, most often simple panels of ivory, gray or lavender embellished with gilded panels with corner scrolls or a single central motif of a vase of fruit or flowers. On some of the more expensive shades, these ornamental elements might be highlighted with mica.

Several books and many articles in popular periodicals gave precise instructions for cutting, sewing and installing fashionable drapery and upholstery. Anyone attempting to re-create an interior of this period should survey the contemporary literature. The books written by Henry T. Williams and Mrs. C. S. Jones, such as *Beautiful Homes*, are especially well illustrated, highly descriptive and practical.

Throughout these years, ornamental needlework was extensively used in curtain and upholstery borders and accents and on decorative accessories such as cushions, lamp rugs, footstools, lambrequins, mantel drapery, table covers, doilies, antimacassars and wall pockets. Patterns for such items were published in all the popular ladies' magazines and individual books of instruction as well. Needlework kits with designs prestamped on appropriate fabrics and the colors of the embroidery silks or wools charted could be purchased. For modern reproduction of these accessories and trimmings, see Sophia Caulfeild and Blanche Saward's *The Dictionary of Needlework* (1882) or *The Lady's Handbook of Fancy Needlework* (1880), both of which have been reprinted. For a different point of view, see Constance Cary Harrison's *Women's Handiwork in Modern Homes* (1881) or the various works of Candace Wheeler.

As in earlier times, printed fabrics intended for use in home furnishing were distinctive in color and scale. Often the ground cloth was slightly heavier than that used for dress goods and the weave was often a twill or sateen. Usually the designs were larger and more elaborate and employed more colors than those of dress fabrics. The complexity of the designs and the associated production costs contributed to the less frequent introduction of new designs and longer periods of popularity for furniture prints. Rich, three-dimensional floral designs predominated in this market, although oriental motifs, exotic scenery, romantic ruins and sentimentalized groups of people were also available.

In the late 19th century, the design and use of printed furnishing fabrics reflected several new influences. The design reform movement produced advocates, practitioners and publications as well as the distinctive flat-patterned fabrics in the style of William Morris.

The Morris-style fabrics seem to have a special appeal to the late 20th-century eye and have been reproduced by several companies. Unfortunately, many of the "Morris fabrics" currently on the market are copies of wallpaper designs. They are excellent interpretations of design and color, but since they were not printed as textiles by Morris and Company in the 19th century, they are not appropriate for restoration work where authenticity is the goal. Bear in mind also that Morris fabrics were not widely distributed in their own time. They were expensive, handprinted textiles sold in the United States through only a few interior design firms, such as A. H. Davenport of Boston. They usually were used in highly structured interiors, not highlighted in flat panels as examples of fine design or casually strewn about as pillow covers.

Toward the end of the 19th century, there was a revival of interest in American colonial and Federal period motifs. A related development was a few early reproductions of 18th-century French "toiles." Some of the reproductions of 18th-century copperplate-printed fabrics, particularly the French ones listed earlier in this book, may be useful for persons trying to create the appearance of the early Colonial Revival. Simple ruffled muslin curtains were used in bedchambers of this style; in some New England houses, they were even used in parlors. These curtains were known as "Priscillas," an allusion to Longfellow's heroine thought to make them seem more antique. Like the netted bed canopies and hooked rugs that were part of the same style, these curtains were new elements crafted to give the appearance of simplicity and great age.

During the 1880s exotic interests resulted in a distinct but fairly short-lived passion for Japanese designs. Only a few reproductions that reflect this taste are available, but suitable effects can be achieved with plain fabrics and appropriate design and trimming.

The late 19th century also saw a move toward classicism in high-style interior decoration, explained most fully in Edith Wharton and Ogden Codman's book *The Decoration of Houses* (1897), with its emphasis on classical perfection as expressed in the Italian Renaissance and Louis XIV periods. Wharton and Codman did not require slavish reproduction, but they felt certain that perfect design would naturally result from the use of classical principles and archeologically correct detail. In their work decoration was most closely related to architecture, and fabrics were not the primary feature of any interior.

Not surprisingly, Wharton and Codman suggested treating windows in a distinguished architectural way rather than concealing them with elaborate drapery. They advocated the use of muslin curtains only as a transparent screen intended to provide privacy in an interior. They denounced the currently popular lace curtains as an obstruction of the exterior view and an attempt to show off the luxury of the interior to passersby.

Despite the best efforts of the reformers, American pop-

Paneled room at The Grange, Lincoln, Mass. The French toile used here, "L'Escarpolette," was custom reproduced in 1989. The fabric was first used by Ogden Codman in this room in 1897. (Society for the Preservation of New England Antiquities)

ular taste continued to favor lavish textile furnishings in domestic interiors. Many textile merchants imported expensive reproductions of antique textiles, particularly French toiles, brocades, watered silks and fabrics woven with gold and silver threads. F. Schumacher & Company, established in 1889, opened its own mill in Patterson, N.J., in 1895 for custom weaving of all sorts of lavish fabrics. The early Schumacher sample books reveal damask, lampas, brocatelle, satin and taffeta weaves in historical designs ranging from the Renaissance to Adamesque, all woven in the popular 1890s colors of red and old rose.

The taste for elaborate fabric furnishings is well documented in the illustrations published in *Harper's Weekly,* as sheet music covers or as accompaniment to contemporary fiction. Current fascination with the period has produced many useful compendia of period photographs, among them Nicholas Cooper's *The Opulent Eye,* William Seale's *The Tasteful Interlude* and a number of regional studies.

Interiors of the period 1870–1900 have received increasing attention from preservationists and designers. As a result, some documentary reproduction fabrics for this period have been made available. Bear in mind, however, that most of these have been commissioned for specific restorations. Although for the most part they are well done, they do not necessarily represent the most typical fabrics available at that time; they are a reflection more of modern circumstances than period taste. Careful research may dictate that none of these fabrics is appropriate for a particular restoration project. Fortunately, many late 19th–century design details can be re-created from solid-colored fabrics of suitable texture combined with appropriate trimmings. In some cases, however, custom reproduction may still be necessary.

PRINTED DESIGNS

BRUNSCHWIG & FILS

❀ AUTUMN ROSE GLAZED CHINTZ. English, c. 1890–1900, block print. 100% cotton, glazed. 52" wide, 32" vertical repeat, 52" horizontal repeat. Document privately owned in England. No.65700.01 (red and blue on cream).

❀ CHENIER WARP PRINT ON TAFFETAS. French, c.1880–1900. 100% silk. 51" wide, 20½" repeat. Document privately owned in France. No. 39420.00 (cream ground).

❀ DAFFODIL AND VINE GLAZED CHINTZ. English, 1870, block

DAFFODIL AND VINE
GLAZED CHINTZ, 1870.
Brunschwig & Fils.
Black green.

print. 100% cotton, glazed. 54" wide, 37" vertical repeat, 18"
horizontal repeat. Document a privately owned textile design in gouache on paper inscribed "Thomas Clarkson, Bannister Hall, nr. Preston, Lancastershire March 17, 1870."
Width doubled in reproduction. No.61979.01 (black green).
❀ FAR PAVILION COTTON PRINT. Probably English, 1880–90,
block print. 100% cotton. 55" wide, 14¼" vertical repeat,
25½" horizontal repeat. Document in the Brunschwig &
Fils Archives. No.36441.01 (burgundy).
❀ GRENELLE PRINTED TAFFETA. French, c.1880–1900, block
print. 100% silk. 48" wide, 24½" repeat. Document privately owned in France. No.35650.00 (cream ground).
❀ LA BONNE FORTUNE COTTON PRINT. Indo-Portuguese
(probably printed in France), c.1870, block and roller print.
100% cotton. 54" wide, 13⅜" repeat. Document privately
owned in Italy. Width doubled in reproduction. No.66540.01
(ecru).
❀ LA PORTUGAISE GLAZED CHINTZ. English, c.1892, block
print. 100% cotton, glazed. 50" wide, 16¼" drop repeat,
33" horizontal repeat. Document a block-printed cotton

from Cummersdale, England, now privately owned in England. No.172630.00 (multi on cream, brown stripe).

❀ LES FAISANS GLAZED CHINTZ. French, c.1875–90, block print. 100% cotton, glazed. 63" wide, 46" vertical repeat, 31" horizontal repeat. Document privately owned in France, probably based on an earlier Chinese design. No.173860.00 (multicolored on cream).

❀ LES PAPILLONS EXOTIQUES. French, c.1885–1900, roller print. 100% cotton. 51" wide, 17" repeat. Document privately owned. No.173418.00 (multi on brown).

❀ MARIGOT GLAZED CHINTZ. English, c.1880–1910, block print. 100% cotton, glazed. 54" wide, 25" vertical repeat, 17¾" horizontal repeat. Document, in Brunschwig & Fils Archives, a block-printed chintz used in a pair of window curtains. No.62302.01 (red and blue).

❀ MARINET GLAZED CHINTZ. English, c.1880–1910, roller print. 100% cotton. 54" wide, 1³⁄₁₆" vertical repeat, 2½" horizontal repeat. Document, in Brunschwig & Fils Archives, a roller-printed chintz used as the lining of a pair of window curtains. Curtain fabric reproduced as "Marigot Glazed Chintz." No.62292.01 (blue).

MARINET GLAZED CHINTZ. Brunschwig & Fils. Blue.

❀ MUSTIQUE GLAZED CHINTZ. French, c. 1870–80, block print. 100% cotton, glazed. 54" wide, 41" repeat. Document privately owned in France. No. 36409.01 (charcoal).

❀ NAPOLEON TROIS. French, c. 1870–90, roller print. 100% cotton. 50" wide, 24" half-drop repeat. Document privately owned in France. No. 66334.01 (multi on green trellis).

❀ NARCISSUS. American, c. 1885–90, block print. 100% cotton. 54" wide, 15½" repeat. Original design by Candace Wheeler. Adaptation of 100% linen original. Available by special order only.

❀ NEW BERRY COTTON PRINT. French, c. 1880–present, block print. 100% cotton glazed. 62" wide, 36⅝" repeat. Metcalf, *Ogden Codman,* pl. 1. Document a block-printed cotton owned in France by company that has produced it since about 1880. Design was block printed by hand until 1985; since then it has been screen printed in a double width. Ogden Codman extensively used this fabric, which he called "Les Roses." No. 174546.00 (peach stripe).

❀ OLEANDER GLAZED CHINTZ. English, c. 1875–95, block and roller print. 100% cotton, glazed. 53" wide, 25" vertical repeat, 26½" horizontal repeat. Document in Brunschwig & Fils Archives. No. 62620.01 (red on cream).

❀ PAULETTE GLAZED CHINTZ. French, c. 1870–1900, block print. 100% cotton, glazed. 57" wide, 9¾" repeat. Document in Brunschwig & Fils Archives. No. 62403.01 (gold stripe).

❀ SAVANNAH GLAZED CHINTZ. Chinese, c. 1885–1900. 100% cotton, glazed. 53" wide, 28¾" repeat. Document, in Brunschwig & Fils Archives, a gouache drawing for a textile design. No. 618600.00 (cream).

❀ SEYCHELLES COTTON PRINT. French, c. 1870, roller print. 100% cotton. 55" wide, 25½" repeat. Document a roller print in Brunschwig & Fils Archives, a gift from the original printer of the design. Scale slightly enlarged in transfer to screen print. No. 62206.01 (coral).

CLARENCE HOUSE

❀ RUBENS. French, c. 1880–1900, block print. 100% cotton, glazed. 51" wide, 47" repeat. Document privately owned in France. No. 31777-2 (cream); No. 31777-12 (cream; 60% linen, 40% cotton).

SHELLS AND RIBBONS,
c. 1890. J. R. Burrows.
Yellow and sepia.

COWTAN & TOUT

❀ BOUQUET AND LATTICE. English, c. 1880–1900, block print. 100% cotton, softly glazed. 50" wide, 19½" repeat. Document privately owned. No. 4403 (rose and greens on white ground).

❀ GLYNDEBOURNE. English, c. 1880–1900, block print. 100% cotton, glazed. 54" wide, 27" repeat. Document privately owned. No. 5666-7 (lilac and rose on white ground).

❀ HANDBLOCKED LILY AND AURICULA. English, c. 1880–1900, block print. 100% cotton, glazed. 48" wide, 32" repeat. Handblocked. Document privately owned in England. No. 5045 (red, beige and white on aqua ground).

J. R. BURROWS

❀ SHELLS AND RIBBONS. American, c. 1890, block print. Designed by Candace Wheeler of Associated Artists, New York. 100% cotton. 56" wide, 11" repeat. Document at Mark Twain Memorial, Hartford, Conn. Scale reduced about 10% in screen-printed version. Order by name. Yellow and sepia.

LEE JOFA

❀ BALMORAL PRINT. English, c. 1890–1900, block print. 100% cotton, glazed. 49–50" wide, 19½" repeat. Document owned by Lee Jofa. No. 789203 (mauve, pink and aquarelle).

SANDERSON

❀ CRAY. English, 1884, block print. 100% cotton. 54" wide, 36" repeat. Clark, *William Morris Wallpapers and Chintzes,* no. 28; Parry, *William Morris Textiles,* cat. no. 57 (p. 157). Document owned by Sanderson. Original design by William Morris, printed at Merton Abbey. Inspired by a 17th-century velvet, the rich effect of this design is achieved by the use of a large number of wood blocks. Width expanded from 17½" to 54". No. PR 7325-3 (100% cotton; dark blue on green ground with corals); No. PR 7325-4 (53% linen, 35% cotton, 12% nylon; dark blue on green ground with corals). Minimum order 2 yards.

❀ ROSE. English, 1883, block print. 53% linen, 35% cotton, 12% nylon. 54" wide, 17¼" repeat. Clark, *William Morris Wallpapers and Chintzes,* no. 27; Parry, *William Morris Textiles,* cat. no. 53 (p. 156). Document owned by Sanderson. Original design by William Morris; registered December 8, 1883. Printed by indigo discharge at Merton Abbey. Inspired by the same 16th-century Venetian silk and gold brocade used by Morris as the design source in 1880 for a woven silk called "Rose and Lily." Scale altered from original 20" width, 17" repeat. No. PR7255-2 (pink, blue). Minimum order 2 yards.

SCALAMANDRÉ

❀ BROTHER RABBIT. English, 1882, indigo discharge and block print. 100% cotton. 49½" wide, 12½" repeat. Clark, *William Morris Wallpapers and Chintzes,* no. 14; Parry, *William Morris Textiles,* cat. no. 38. Original design by William Morris; registered May 20, 1882. Document owned by North American Branch of William Morris Society. No. 6785-1 (wine red on off-white).

❀ DAFFODIL. English, c. 1891, block print. 100% cotton. 48" wide, 12¾" repeat. Clark, *William Morris Wallpapers and Chintzes,* no. 37; Parry, *William Morris Textiles,* cat. no. 76. Original design by William Morris (his last chintz design). Document owned by North American Branch of William Morris Society. No. 6794-1 (greens, pink, yellow and rust on off-white). Special order only.

❀ LODDON. English, 1884, indigo discharge and block print. 100% cotton. 48" wide, 19³⁄₁₆" repeat. Clark, *William Morris Wallpapers and Chintzes,* no. 29; Parry, *William Morris Tex-*

BROTHER RABBIT, 1882.
Scalamandré. Wine red
on off-white.

DAFFODIL, c.1891. Scalamandré. Greens, pinks, yellow and rust on off-white.

LODDON, 1884. Scala-mandré. Light blue, pinks, yellow and olive green on beige.

tiles, cat. no. 54. Original design by William Morris. Document owned by North American Branch of William Morris Society. No. 6802-1 (light blue, pinks, yellow and olive green on beige).

✽ STRAWBERRY THIEF. English, 1883, block print. 100% cotton. 49" wide, 19⁷⁄₁₆" repeat. *Scalamandré,* no. 85; Clark, *William Morris Wallpapers and Chintzes,* no. 22; Parry, *William Morris Textiles,* cat. no. 46. Original design by William Morris; the first successful indigo discharge printing by Morris at Merton Abbey. Document owned by North American Branch of William Morris Society. No. 6792-1 (light blue, pink, yellow and moss green on deep blue).

✽ VANDERBILT MANSION BLUE ROOM. French, c. 1896, roller print. 56% cotton, 44% linen. 50" wide, 26" repeat. Document a printed version of an 18th-century silk brocade used in 1896 in Blue Room of the Vanderbilt Mansion, now Vanderbilt Mansion National Historic Site, Hyde Park, N.Y. No. 6818-1 (roses, oranges, greens and tans on beige).

✽ WILLOWY FIELDS. English or American, c. 1890, block print. 100% cotton, glazed. 48" wide, 27" repeat. Document privately owned. No. 6809-4 (multi on eggshell).

SCHUMACHER

✽ GERTRUDE'S BOUQUET. English, c. 1895, block print. 100% cotton, glazed. 54" wide, 18" repeat. From an original cretonne selected by Ogden Codman for Gertrude Vanderbilt Whitney's bedroom at The Breakers, Newport, R.I. Document owned by Preservation Society of Newport County. No. 75M970 (document rose).

✽ MUSICAL GARLANDS. English or American, c. 1895, block print. 100% cotton. 48½" wide, 28" repeat. From an original cretonne selected by Ogden Codman for Gertrude Vanderbilt Whitney's dressing room walls and curtains at The Breakers, Newport, R.I. Document owned by Preservation Society of Newport County. No. 75M940 (document rose and green).

✽ RIBBON FLORAL. English or French, c. 1895, block print. 100% cotton, glazed. 54" wide, 14" repeat. From an original chintz selected by Ogden Codman for The Breakers, Newport, R.I. Document owned by Preservation Society of Newport County. No. 75M980 (document rose).

✽ VANDERBILT FLORAL. French or English, c. 1895, block

WILLOWY FIELDS,
c. 1890. Scalamandré.
Multi on eggshell.

VANDERBILT MANSION
BLUE ROOM, c. 1896.
Scalamandré. Roses,
oranges, greens and
tans on beige.

CANTON, c. 1870.
Classic Revivals.
Custom colors.

print. 100% cotton, glazed. 46" wide, 36" repeat. From an original chintz selected by Ogden Codman for Gertrude Vanderbilt Whitney's bedroom walls at The Breakers, Newport, R.I. Document owned by Preservation Society of Newport County. No.75M950 (document rose and green).

❦ WHITNEY FLORAL. French or English, c.1895, block print. 100% cotton. 54" wide, 28" repeat. From an original cretonne selected by Ogden Codman for Gertrude Vanderbilt Whitney's bedroom at The Breakers, Newport, R.I. Document owned by Preservation Society of Newport County. No.75M960 (document rose).

STROHEIM & ROMANN

❦ EASTBOURNE SCREEN PRINT. English, c.1870–1900, roller print. 100% cotton. 54" wide, 25" repeat. Document, in madder colors with indigo on cream, at Winterthur Museum. No.49658 (document).

❦ WORTHING SCREEN PRINT. English, c.1870–1900, roller print. 100% cotton. 54" wide, 18" repeat. Document, in madder colors on cream, at Winterthur Museum. No. 49651 (document).

BRUNSCHWIG & FILS

❦ DRUMMOND COTTON PRINT. French, c.1885–1900, printed version of a woven silk and linen damask. 100% cotton. 54" wide, 17" vertical repeat, 13¼" horizontal repeat. Document in Brunschwig & Fils Archives. Reverse of the damask was used because it had a greater contrast; therefore the motifs are reversed. No.78831.04 (rose and green).

CLASSIC REVIVALS

Order by name. Allow ample time for custom weaving after your order is confirmed.

❦ ACORN. English, c.1875, damasquette. 100% silk. 62" wide, 30" repeat. *A Choice of Design,* no.27. First woven by Daniel Walters & Sons, Braintree, Essex, England. Document in Warner Archive, London. Custom colors.

❦ ADAMITE. English, 1874, silk tissue. 100% silk. 21" wide, 44" repeat. *A Choice of Design,* fig.36. Document in Warner Archive, London. Custom colors.

❦ CANTON. English, c.1870, silk tissue. 100% silk. 21" wide, 50" repeat. *A Choice of Design,* fig.40. First woven by War-

WOVEN DESIGNS

ACORN, c. 1875.
Classic Revivals.
Custom colors.

ner, Sillett & Ramm, London. Document in Warner Archive, London. Custom colors.

❀ CULROSS/CASHMERE. English, August 15, 1870, damask. 100% silk. 21" wide. Designed by Owen Jones. Document in Warner Archive, London. Custom colors.

❀ CYNOSE. English, c. 1870, damask. 100% silk. 63" wide, 36" repeat. Designed from a Greek-style ornament, possibly by Owen Jones. First woven by Daniel Walters & Sons, Braintree, Essex, England. Document in Warner Archive, London. Custom colors.

❀ DAMASK 6105. French, c. 1885–1900, woven damask. 100% silk. 21" wide, 12¾" repeat. Document in Prelle Archives, Lyon, France, a late 19th-century reproduction of a 15th-century Italian damask design. No. 6105. Custom colors.

❀ FLOWER GARDEN. English, 1879. 100% silk. 54" wide, 15¾" repeat. A Choice of Design, no. 133; Parry, William Morris Textiles, cat. no. 31. Designed by William Morris and first woven at Queen Square in silk and wool. First produced by Warner & Company in silk tissue with silver and

CULROSS/CASHMERE (design), 1870. Classic Revivals. Custom colors.

CYNOSE, c. 1870. Classic Revivals. Custom colors.

top left
DAMASK 6105, c. 1885–
1900. Classic Revivals.
Custom colors.

top right
FLOWER GARDEN, 1879.
Classic Revivals.
Custom colors.

right
JAVA, c. 1880. Classic
Revivals. Custom
colors.

gold thread, 1911. Document in Warner Archive, London. Custom colors.

❀ JAVA. English, c.1880, damask. 100% silk. 21" wide, 22" repeat. *A Choice of Design,* no.33. First woven by Daniel Walters & Sons, Braintree, Essex, England. Document in Warner Archive, London. Custom colors.

❀ LAMPAS 6499. French, November 11, 1899, woven lampas. 100% silk. 50" wide, 18½" repeat. Document in Prelle Archives, Lyon, France. Designed by Colonna for Bing. No. 6499. Custom colors.

❀ LAMPAS 6502. French, 1900, woven lampas. 100% silk. 21" wide, 13½" repeat. Document in Prelle Archives, Lyon, France. Designed by de Feure for Bing. No.6502. Custom colors.

❀ MARES. English, c.1880, damasquette. 100% silk. 63" wide, 31" repeat. *A Choice of Design,* fig.31. First woven by Daniel Walters & Sons, Braintree, Essex, England. Document in Warner Archive, London. Custom colors.

❀ NIZAM. English, August 15, 1870. 100% silk. 21" wide. Designed by Owen Jones and used as wall hangings in

LAMPAS 6499, 1899. Classic Revivals. Custom colors.

LAMPAS 6502, 1900.
Classic Revivals.
Custom colors.

Clarence House, the house of the Duke of Edinburgh, as part of the refurnishing by Waller & Sons, begun 1873–74. Document in Warner Archive, London. Custom colors.

❦ OXEYE DAISY. English, 1879, damasquette. 100% silk. 22" wide, 38" repeat. *A Choice of Design*, no.47. Designed by G. C. Hate for T. W. Cutler. Document in Warner Archive, London. Custom colors.

❦ SATSUMA. English, 1879, silk tissue. 10% silk. 21" wide, 36" repeat. *A Choice of Design,* no.35. Possibly designed by E. W. Godwin for Warner & Ramm. Document in Warner Archive, London. Custom colors.

❦ SICILY. English, c.1870–1873, silk tissue. 100% silk. 21" wide. Designed by Owen Jones. First woven August 24, 1877. Document in Warner Archive, London. Custom colors.

❦ SILK DAMASQUETTE. English, c.1880. 100% silk. 21" wide, 53" repeat. Designed by Morris and Company from an Italian velvet, c.1550. Document in Warner Archive, London; acquired from Cowtan & Sons, 1927. Custom colors.

❦ STANMORE. English, 1895, silk tissue. 100% silk. 63" wide, 36" repeat. *A Choice of Design*, no.73. Document in Warner Archive, London. Custom colors.

top left
NIZAM (design) 1870.
Classic Revivals.
Custom colors.

top right
STANMORE, 1895. Classic
Revivals. Custom
colors.

left
MARES, c. 1880.
Classic Revivals.
Custom colors.

❀ TURENNE. English, c.1870, damask. 100% silk. 61" wide, 37" repeat. *A Choice of Design,* fig.16. First woven by Daniel Walters & Sons, Braintree, Essex, England. Document in Warner Archive, London.

DECORATORS WALK

In addition to the fabrics listed here, Decorators Walk has many other late 19th- to early 20th-century revivals of 18th-century silk lampas and brocade designs that are suitable for this period.

❀ BUCKINGHAM PALACE LINEN DAMASK. Low Countries, c. 1870–1900. 100% linen. 56" wide, 27" repeat. Revival of an early 18th-century design. Document privately owned. No. L58690 (natural). Special order only.

❀ FLORAL LINEN DAMASK. Low Countries, c.1870–90. 100% linen. 60" wide, 14¼" repeat. Revival of a mid-18th-century design. Document privately owned. No.P35685 (natural).

❀ JACOBEAN LINEN DAMASK. Low Countries, c.1870–1900. 100% linen. 56" wide, 27" repeat. Revival of a 17th-century design. Document privately owned. No.L58260 (natural). Special order only.

❀ MEDICI LINEN DAMASK. Low Countries, c. 1870–1900. 100% linen. 56" wide, 27" repeat. Revival of a 17th-century design. Document privately owned. No.L58100 (natural).

❀ PALAIS LISERE. French, 1880–1900. 78% cotton, 22% spun rayon. 49" wide, 29⅛" repeat. Revival of an 18th-century

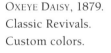

OXEYE DAISY, 1879. Classic Revivals. Custom colors.

SATSUMA, 1879.
Classic Revivals.
Custom colors.

SICILY, c. 1870–73.
Classic Revivals.
Custom colors.

TURENNE, 1870. Classic Revivals. Custom colors.

EDISON VELVET, c. 1890– 1900. Scalamandré. Brown on gold.

design. Document privately owned. No. T31568 (multi on white).

❀ SURREY. Low Countries, c. 1885–1920. 100% linen. 60" wide, 26¾" repeat. Document privately owned. No. T46415 (oatmeal).

SCALAMANDRÉ

❀ EDISON VELVET. Italian, c. 1890–1900. 40% cotton, 60% silk. 25½" wide, 16" vertical repeat. Document upholstery on a library chair owned by Thomas A. Edison House, Glenmont, West Orange, N.J. No. 96962-2 (brown on gold).

❀ 1890 HOUSE DAMASK. French or Italian, c. 1890–1900. 23% silk, 77% cotton. 51" wide, 20" repeat. Document owned by Scalamandré. No. 97405-1 (beige).

❀ IOLANI BROCATELLE. Country of origin unknown, 1884. 46% silk, 54% linen. 48½" wide, 18" repeat. Document provided by A. H. Davenport of Boston for the Throne Room chairs at Iolani Palace, Honolulu, Hawaii. Document owned by Iolani Palace. No. 97395-1 (red). Special order only.

❀ LITTLE ROCK DIAMOND MOIRED LISERE. French or Italian, c. 1890–1910. 50" wide, 5" repeat. Document privately owned. No. 96383-1 (beige on moss).

❀ MARBLE COLLEGIATE DAMASK. French, 1891. 100% wool. 48½" wide, 9½" repeat. Document owned by Marble Collegiate Reformed Church, New York, N.Y. No. 96482-1 (rust).

❀ MARBLE HOUSE DAMASK. Italian or French, c. 1890–1900. 100% silk. 50" wide, 50" repeat. Document upholstery and drapery originally used at Marble House, Newport, R.I., owned by Preservation Society of Newport County, R.I. No. 20011-1 (gold).

❀ MONTEGO BAY DAMASK. Probably French or Italian, c. 1870–95. 100% silk. 50½" wide, 62" repeat (cut by repeat only). Document owned by Scalamandré. No. 97178-2 (cream on ming gold). Special order only.

❀ THOMAS EDISON HOUSE STRIPED DAMASK. American, c. 1890–1900. 30% silk, 70% cotton. 51" wide, 25½" repeat. Document sofa upholstery owned by Thomas A. Edison House, Glenmont, West Orange, N.J. No. 91297-6 (rose, beige and yellow).

❀ VANDERBILT. Country of origin unknown, c. 1890–1900. 35% silk, 65% cotton. 50½" wide. Document owned by Vanderbilt Mansion National Historic Site, Hyde Park, N.Y. No. 97429-1 (aqua and pale yellow).

THE TWENTIETH CENTURY: INNOVATION AND TRADITION

R apidly changing technology and tides of taste have characterized the production of furnishing fabrics and their use in 20th-century interiors. There is an abundance of documentary material in published form, particularly in magazines such as *Ladies' Home Journal, Good Housekeeping, Modern Priscilla, House and Garden, House Beautiful* and *The Magazine Antiques,* as well as in books on interior design and mail-order catalogs. With the development of home economics, interior design and museum studies as professional fields have come textbooks, professional libraries, photographic archives and specialized journals. Because of the rapidity with which new styles have been introduced by designers and manufacturers, it is particularly important to undertake detailed research on a specific situation and develop an informed point of view before reviewing available goods. Although general patterns of taste may be discerned and certain goods dominated the market in each decade, economic circumstances, individual innovation and the possibility of stark conservatism should be considered as well.

At the beginning of the century, many traditional designs and some documentary reproductions were produced by English, French and American firms to satisfy market demand. Interest in neoclassical taste manifested itself in revivals of Adam, Colonial, Empire and Louis XVI styles, some of which were quite academic in interpretation while others were more generic. These interiors featured pastel colors, especially green, blue and pink, often with white walls. Straight hanging window curtains, usually with simple valances and some form of sheer undercurtain, predominated. Both woven silks and mid-19th-century chintz designs were popular, although the latter were mistakenly

LES GAZELLES AU BOIS, 1927–34. Schumacher. Cream and black; cream and slate.

thought by many to be 18th century in origin. Empire furniture was often labeled "colonial" during these years, and reproductions of classic designs were available at several levels of price and quality.

Popularizing the ideas formulated by Edith Wharton and Ogden Codman in *The Decoration of Houses,* Elsie de Wolfe established in 1904 what was to become one of America's most influential decorating firms. Her ideas were summarized in her 1913 book, *The House in Good Taste,* which emphasized simplicity, harmonious colors and good proportion. This style manifested itself in rooms with light-colored walls, Louis XVI–style furniture and abundant use of chintz. Window curtains were often straight hanging panels that reached to either the sill or the floor and were hung with simple scalloped valances or none at all. Tapestry and embroideries were used for upholstery in the best rooms, while chintz was always an option.

In simple middle-class interiors and summer houses, plain white curtains of checked dimity, dotted swiss or organdy were used. The Priscilla style continued to be popular, while others used the "Bonne Femme" style, which was essentially the same as an 18th-century festoon or Venetian curtain and somewhat more restrained than the late 20th-century versions of the pull-up curtains popularly known as Austrian shades.

Lace curtains continued to be used against the window glass, with floral motifs predominating. In some rooms, lace curtains were used alone, whereas previously they had been used in combination with heavier overcurtains, either in straight hanging or drapery style. In 1908 Sears, Roebuck offered trompe l'oeil lace designs that simulated the appearance of layered window curtains, Bonne Femme curtains and rope valances, all of which had been widely used in the preceding 20 years in materials other than lace but now had largely disappeared in stylish interiors.

A simpler style known as Arts and Crafts was explained and illustrated in Candace Wheeler's *Principles of Home Decoration* (1903) and *The Craftsman* magazine. For these interiors rough denim, coarse linen and theater gauze were recommended for simple curtains and portieres, which were sometimes accented by embroidery. Leather and leather cloth were used for upholstery and denim for couch covers. Clear, natural colors were preferred, especially shades of red, gold, green and indigo blue. Wheeler recommended the use of sheer silk curtains in gold or apricot to warm a cold north room.

Related to both the Arts and Crafts movement and the Colonial Revival was an interest in 17th-century interiors, which were loosely termed Jacobean or Tudor. Although most rooms in this taste were English in inspiration, some were Spanish in feeling. In all such rooms the textiles were apt to be machine-woven tapestries, printed cretonne and heavy linen, all in muted colors chosen to suggest great age. This taste was featured in a 1908 article in *Needlecraft and Monthly Magazine,* which urged the use of reproductions of Jacobean and late Tudor embroideries for curtains, spreads and drawing room ornaments. This article spurred a revival of Elizabethan and Jacobean styles of crewel embroidery and promoted the use of cretonne on which the printed motifs could be highlighted by crewel embroidery.

At the same time that traditional interiors continued to be popular, printed and woven textiles were somewhat influential in carrying the modern designs introduced by the Glasgow School of Art and the Weiner Werkstatte in Vienna. Although these were not widely distributed in their own time, they have gained considerable popularity in recent revivals.

Protected and encouraged by the McKinley Tariff of 1890, American textile firms began to hold a firm place in the world markets for furnishing fabrics. The Cheney Silk Mills of Manchester, Conn; and Arnold Print Works at Adams, Mass., were notable, as were a number of Philadelphia mills that specialized in woven upholstery goods.

After importing expensive French furnishing silks to New York for six years, Frederick Schumacher established his first silk mill in Patterson, N.J., in 1895 and launched a successful business. One of his earliest patterns, "Regal Damask," now known as "Williamsburg Pomegranate Damask," was introduced in 1902 and has been made continuously since that time. Seven years earlier, Schumacher's "Pattern No. 162," based on a mid-18th-century document and introduced in 1895, was used by Ogden Codman at Chateau sur Mer and in 1898 in the main dining room of the Waldorf Astoria; later this same design was selected for the Wil-

Wrought-iron fireplace screen from the Exposition Internationale des Arts Decoratifs, Paris, 1925, which inspired "Les Gazelles au Bois," a fabric designed by Pierre Pozier for Schumacher in 1927.

liamsburg line and renamed "Bruton Damask." This kind of traditional textile was in great demand during the first quarter of the 20th century and, with continued imports of European silks and French toiles, formed a solid basis for the Schumacher business.

The American taste for traditional fabrics, especially silks, was further fostered by the success of Franco Scalamandré, who began his business in Long Island City in 1929. His interest in historic interiors led to collaboration with many historical restoration projects. Skilled craftworkers and designers at the Scalamandré mill still produce some of America's finest reproduction fabrics.

Some furnishing textiles in the 1920s began to reflect contemporary design trends. In 1925 Schumacher introduced its first major collection of Moderne textile designs, inspired by work included in the Paris Exposition International des Arts Décoratifs of that year. These designs remained influential for a decade, reflecting the style known as Art Deco and moving the reputation of the firm away from exclusively traditional designs. Several reproductions of these new designs were included in the Schumacher centennial collection in 1989, partially in response to the current interest in Art Deco design.

Until the Depression, furnishing fabrics were usually sold through department stores and furniture warehouses, with ample yardage readily available in stock. Today's system of selling through showroom samples, was developed in response to the economic hardships of the Depression. This system permits a manufacturer to stock all patterns and colors in a central warehouse and reduces inventories at the point of sale. Not incidentally, this system also makes it economically feasible to offer a much wider range of patterns and colors with relatively short order times.

During the 1930s conservative taste favored solid colors for draperies and upholstery. Textiles considered modern or streamlined were produced in limited color ranges with design elements that tended to be geometric and severe. After World War II the use of natural forms increased, and the use of solid colors continued. Modern designers recommended incorporating a variety of colors and textures in interiors. Traditional interiors continued to be popular at all levels because of mass-produced fabrics, a growing body of design literature and the beginnings of department store decorating advice. To enhance the aged quality of traditional interiors, some fabrics were specially treated to make them appear old. Slubs and bumps were introduced to suggest hand spinning. Faded colors were popular, and some fabrics were made with pseudo-worn spots, which were actually woven in repeat. The backgrounds of printed cottons were tinted beige or the finished goods were dipped in tea, and strié effects were used in woven silks to suggest age. Adaptations were developed to make traditional textile designs more adaptable to the size of modern houses: damasks that originally had two motifs in a vertical repeat, for example, were scaled down to just one motif, thereby reducing the size of the repeat and permitting placement and matching of motifs with much less waste.

During the 1950s and 1960s, a number of museum cura-

191

Lisere loom, Scalamandré mill. The shuttle is automatically thrown across the open shed created by lifting of warp yarns by the jacquard head motion. Lisere is a fabric woven with two warp beams — one, the "pallette," which is usually multi-colored, creates the pattern on the face of the fabric, and another, using a filler yarn, weaves in the background. Here, the fabric is No. 213 "Bee."

tors and interior designers began to study furnishing textiles and investigate the way in which they were actually used. Two seminal conferences were held, one on bed hangings at the Society for the Preservation of New England Antiquities in 1960 and another on upholstery and drapery at the Museum of Fine Arts in Boston and Old Sturbridge Village in 1979. Each conference featured an exhibition and resulted in a publication (see bibliography). Since that time other conferences and exhibitions have been held, notably "Culture and Comfort" at the Strong Museum in Rochester, N.Y., in 1988 and a conference on upholstery conservation at Colonial Williamsburg in 1990, and the field's body of literature is growing.

Since the 1930s many independent firms have imported and manufactured furnishing textiles. Britain and France have tended to be the primary sources of imported goods, although Italy, Germany, India and China have also supplied goods used in historic interiors. Some fabric suppliers have employed their own designers or have contracted with independent designers such as Vera or Dorothy Draper.

Block printing continued throughout the period but was largely replaced by screen printing for large volume. Only a few fabrics are still block printed commercially today. The reason is simple: block printing of some of the most complex designs is cumbersome and slow; some designs use as many as 30 colors and require more than 150 individual blocks.

Copper roller printing continues to be used for some designs with small repeats and more limited colors. This printing technique is much faster than block printing and has been used since the 1820s for increased speed in production and lower market cost. Up to 12 colors can be printed consecutively by one cylinder printing machine. Because of the high cost of engraving rollers and setting up machines, this printing technique has been used only for mass-produced goods, now usually those manufactured in runs of 10,000 yards and more.

Both block and cylinder printing have been largely replaced by screen printing. This inexpensive new technique, widely adopted in the 1930s, enabled manufacturers to pro-

Screen printing the fabric "Cliveden, Chew House" in the Scalamandré mill.

duce designs in smaller quantities and change designs frequently. Because the screens are larger than the surface area of printing rollers, the typical scale of furnishing fabrics has expanded. In screen printing the color is forced through a taut silk screen, very much like a stencil, the mesh of the silk being so fine that it does not show on the printed cloth. Screen printing requires separate screens for each color; usually not more than 21 can be accommodated. Exact registration of the screens is necessary for perfect development of the design; if even one screen is out of register, the finished design will appear fuzzy, with certain elements out of place. Printing screens last a long time, but eventually they will lose some detail and produce blotchy results. This is something to watch for in selecting a commercially available reproduction: some of the most popular designs have been in production for a long time, and if the screens are badly worn the appearance of the finished goods will not be close to the original.

In the late 1950s screen printing was mechanized, and metal mesh largely replaced silk; since 1963 automated rotary screen machines have been widely adopted. Designs can be transferred to the screens through a photographic process and so are almost limitless in variety and detail. While flat screen machines can produce roughly 350 yards of printed goods per hour, a rotary screen machine can produce roughly 2,400 yards per hour in up to 20 colors. Flat screens continue to be used for small yardages and custom printing.

With the opening of the American Wing at the Metropolitan Museum of Art in 1924 and a growing awareness of the American decorative arts, traditionalism in American interiors received even greater encouragement. In Nancy McClelland's *Furnishing the Colonial and Federal House* (1936), the elements of Jacobean interiors were summarized and recommended as appropriate for 17th-century or oak-paneled rooms. For formal Georgian interiors, silk damask upholstery and straight hanging curtains were recommended, together with oriental rugs. For less formal 18th-century rooms with maple or mahogany furniture, bright glazed chintz, calico or cotton taffetas were recommended as brighter and gayer than silks. The use of informal cotton textiles, patchwork quilts, fishnet curtains and canopies, rag or hooked rugs, maple furniture, painted paneling and ruffled curtains defined a style that soon became known as early American and was to continue in popularity well into the 1960s, only to give birth to a more cluttered version of the same, known today as American country.

To feed the demand for early American designs, many fabrics have been produced that have been inspired by historic documents or popular conceptions of historic design. In these, authentic replication of color and detail was not the primary goal. The thousands of "early American" calico or chintz designs produced in this way would be perfectly appropriate for use in restoring some mid- to late 20th-century interiors, but they should not mislead one who is seeking to re-create the look of an earlier period.

Concern for authentic reproduction at first grew slowly among museum curators, antique dealers and interior designers, but in recent years it has become almost obsessive. An early expression of this concern was combined with smart marketing when Colonial Williamsburg began its "authorized" reproductions in the 1930s. The first Williamsburg reproduction fabrics were printed goods produced by Cy Clark and woven designs by Scalamandré. After 1939, Schumacher began to produce the Williamsburg printed textiles and after 1951 the woven designs as well.

Scalamandré and Schumacher's successful collaboration with Colonial Williamsburg prompted other historic collections and reproduction work. Scalamandré tended to work with individual museums to reproduce textiles and trimmings needed for specific restoration projects offering these designs as part of its general line. Schumacher preferred to market seasonal collections based on textile documents or inspired by other decorative arts in museum collections. In spring 1951 it produced a collection in conjunction with the Farmer's Museum at Cooperstown, N.Y., and that fall another with the Henry Ford Museum and Greenfield Village; these were followed by many others. In recent years Brunschwig & Fils has produced excellent reproductions for a number of museums, especially the Winterthur Museum and the Society for the Preservation of New England Antiquities.

For further information on the history of textile design and the use of fabrics in 20th-century interiors, see Mary Schoeser and Celia Rufey's *English and American Textiles from 1790 to the Present,* pp. 137–243.

In selecting fabrics for the catalog listing in this book, only documented examples that have been recently revived have been included. Many manufacturers produce fabrics that have been available for decades; any of these could be considered for restoring mid- to late 20th-century interiors.

PRINTS

BRUNSCHWIG & FILS

❀ ARBRE JAPONAIS GLAZED CHINTZ. French, c. 1920–40, pochoir print. 100% cotton, glazed. 48" wide, 63" vertical repeat, 43" horizontal repeat. Document a pochoir print based on 19th-century painted Chinese silk privately owned in France; another example is also in Brunschwig & Fils Archives. Slight adaptation, with metallic accents of the pochoir print omitted. No.171910.00 (multi on cream).

❀ BUTTERFLY COTTON AND LINEN PRINT. French, c.1920–35, stencil print. 69% linen, 31% cotton. 53" wide, 27" repeat. Document a stencil-printed linen privately owned in France. No.62449.01 (forest and navy on natural).

❀ CAMABLUC COTTON PRINT. French, c. 1920–30, stencil print. 100% cotton. 60" wide, 17¼" repeat, 2" off straight join. Document a stenciled reproduction of a mid-19th-century block-printed cotton, both privately owned in France. No.174580.00 (cream).

❀ CHINESE BLOSSOMS GLAZED CHINTZ. French. c.1920–40, pochoir print. 100% cotton, glazed. 49" wide, 45½" repeat. Document, at the Cooper-Hewitt Museum, an 18th-century handpainted silk satin adapted as a pochoir print in the 1920s and 1930s. No.77365.04 (mauve on natural).

❀ EDENWOOD GLAZED CHINTZ. English, 1920–40, block print. 100% cotton, glazed. 49" wide, 29½" vertical repeat, 23" horizontal repeat. Document, privately owned in England, continuously printed since first introduced; many colorways have been produced through the years. No.66110.01 (rose on white); No.66112.01 (rose on blue); No.66113.01 (coral on yellow).

❀ ILLYRIA GLAZED CHINTZ. English, 1900–25, block print. 100% cotton, glazed. 38" wide, 58" repeat. Document in Brunschwig & Fils Archives. No.36257.01 (red on aubergine).

❀ LA PORTUGAISE. (See p.129.) Widely used by Elsie de Wolfe, Billy Baldwin and Mark Hampton in elaborate domestic schemes. Probably used more in American rooms in the 20th century than when first produced. No.172630.00 (multi on aubergine).

❈ MANDALAY GLAZED CHINTZ. French, c.1920–30, stencil print. 100% cotton. 48" wide, 28½" repeat. Document, privately owned in France, based on 18th-century Chinese hand-painted silk designs. No.72100.04 (multicolor on beige).

❈ MARISA GLAZED CHINTZ. French, 1925–40, block print. 100% cotton, glazed. 54" wide, 8" vertical repeat, 7¾" horizontal repeat. Document in Brunschwig & Fils Archives. No.64241.01 (rose and pink).

❈ WESTBURY BOUQUET COTTON AND LINEN PRINT. English, c.1900–25, block print. 65% linen, 35% cotton. 53" wide, 35½" vertical repeat, 53" horizontal repeat. Document a block-printed linen used for sofa slipcovers in the conservatory at Old Westbury Gardens, N.Y. No.61057.01 (blue and sand on aubergine).

CLARENCE HOUSE

❈ OLD ROSE. English, c.1920–30, block print. 100% cotton, glazed. 50" wide, 17½" repeat. Document privately owned in England. No.31745-1 (rose and cream).

BUTTERFLY COTTON AND LINEN PRINT, c. 1920–35. Brunschwig & Fils. Forest and navy on natural.

WESTBURY BOUQUET COTTON AND LINEN PRINT, c.1900–25. Brunschwig & Fils. Blue and sand on aubergine.

❀ ROSE CUMMING CHINTZ. English, c.1920–30, block print. 100% cotton, glazed. 51" wide, 35½" repeat. Document privately owned. No.31410-01 (multi on ice blue).

HALLIE GREER

❀ ELIZABETH GREER. English, c.1900–15. 100% cotton. 54" wide, 52" repeat. Document, used at Blenheim Palace, now at Hallie Greer Archives. No.F-18. Documentary red and pink with green.

IAN WALL

❀ DIABOLO. Austrian, 1911. 52% cotton, 48% viscose. 50$\frac{7}{10}$" wide, ½" repeat. Design by Otto Prutscher. Document privately owned. No.69N903 (gray/black).

❀ HARLEIKEN. Austrian, 1908. 100% viscose. 50$\frac{7}{10}$" wide, 3$\frac{7}{10}$" repeat. Design by Josef Hoffmann. Document privately owned. No.625503 (black/white).

❀ HENRY VAN DE VELDE. Belgian, 1904. 8% viscose, 32% cotton. 50$\frac{7}{10}$" wide, 2¾" repeat. Design by Henry Van De Velde. Document privately owned. No.200-2 (light green); No.200-1 (silver).

❀ HOFFMANN. Austrian, 1907. 58% viscose. 50$\frac{7}{10}$" wide, 3¾" repeat. Design by Josef Hoffmann. Document privately owned. No.6528031 (black/white).

❀ NORA. Austrian, 1906. 100% viscose. 50$\frac{7}{10}$" wide, 3½" repeat. Design by Franz Safonith. Document privately owned. No.633606 (green/yellow).

❀ SONNENAUFGANG. French, 1901. 74% viscose, 26% polyester. 50$\frac{7}{10}$" wide, 19½" repeat. Design by Atelier Ruepp. Document privately owned. No. 61B706 (green/cream); No.61B707 (green/rose).

❀ STREBER. Austrian, 1904. 100% viscose. 50$\frac{7}{10}$" wide, 5$\frac{3}{10}$" repeat. Design by Josef Hoffmann. Document privately owned. No.631017 (rose/cream); No.631003 (gray/cream).

❀ TRAUBE. Austrian, 1908. 63% viscose, 37% cotton. 50$\frac{7}{10}$" wide, 3$\frac{7}{10}$" repeat. Design by Josef Hoffmann. No.631303 (blue/blue).

❀ VINETA. Austrian, 1903. 78% viscose, 22% polyester. 50$\frac{7}{10}$" wide, 8$\frac{1}{5}$" repeat. Design by Gustav Jungichel. Document privately owned. No. 651805 (brown/blue); No. 651806 (gold/black).

❀ Zickzack. Austrian, 1907. 100% viscose. 50$^7/_{10}$" wide, 3$^7/_{10}$" repeat. Design by Josef Hoffmann. Document privately owned. No.626113 (gray/cream).

Lee Jofa

❀ Trentham Hall. (See p.141.) Current production of this design is favored by 20th-century designers for its soft, faded appearance.

Rose Cumming Chintzes

❀ Kensington. English, c.1930–40, screen print. 100% cotton. 55" wide, 40" repeat. Document privately owned. No.RC 5019-3 (pink with screen).

❀ Marlborough. English, c.1920–45, block print with fancy ground. 100% cotton, glazed. 50" wide, 22" repeat. Document privately owned in England. No.RC 408-1 (rose and green on white).

❀ Swainson. English, c.1930–50, screen print. 100% cotton. 54" wide, 36" repeat. Document privately owned. No. RC 427-3 (pink); No.RC 427-2 (green).

❀ Wilton. English, c.1930–50, cylinder print. 100% cotton. 49" wide, 15" repeat. Document privately owned. No. RC 406-7 (aqua and peach).

❀ Windsor Rose. English, c.1935–50, screen print. 100% cotton, glazed. 54" wide, 24" repeat. Document privately owned. No.RC 420-2 (white).

Scalamandré

❀ Birr Castle Peony. English, c.1900–30, block print. 70% cotton, 25% linen. 54" wide, 35$^1/_4$" repeat. Document an early 20th-century chintz drapery used in a library, owned by Birr Castle, Ireland. No.7807-1 (multi on pale taupe).

❀ Leixlip Castle. English, c.1920–40, block print. 100% cotton, glazed. 54" wide, 36$^1/_4$" vertical repeat, 27" horizontal repeat. Document owned by Leixlip Castle, Ireland. No. 7824-1 (multi on oatmeal).

Schumacher

❀ Asia. American, 1930–40, screen print. 100% cotton, glazed. 54" wide, 25" vertical repeat. Design by F. Schumacher & Company. Document in Schumacher Archives. No.77070 (document onyx).

CENTENNIAL BOUQUET, c. 1926. Schumacher. Document red and blue.

❀ CENTENNIAL BOUQUET. American, c. 1926, block print. 100% linen. 53" wide, 62" repeat. Design by F. Schumacher & Company. Document in Schumacher Archives. Modern version, now a screen print that uses 28 screens, lacks the monochromatic leaf borders of the 1926 original. No. 162750 (document red and blue).

❀ CHRYSANTHEMUM AND FERN. English, 1940–70, block print, 100% cotton, glazed. 53" wide, 36" repeat. Document, in multi-reds and greens on white, in Schumacher Archives; modern version now a screen print using 20 screens. Used in the family quarters of the White House during the Truman and Eisenhower administrations. No. 162770 (document).

❀ DESIGN 102. American, 1950–60, screen print. 58% linen, 42% cotton. 54" wide, 27" vertical repeat. Design by F. Schumacher & Company. Document in Schumacher Archives.

CHRYSANTHEMUM AND
FERN, 1940–70. Schu-
macher. Document.

Adapted from a design by Frank Lloyd Wright and distributed by Schumacher in the 1950s as part of its Taliesen
line; 1989 version is slightly altered in scale. No. 160020
(document blue).

❀ FLORAL GROVE. English, c. 1940–50, block print. 100%
cotton, glazed. 54" wide, 25¼" repeat. Document, in Schumacher Archives, a glazed chintz known in the 1940s as
"Beaconsfield" and popular in the 1940s for 18th century–
style rooms; printed linen version was also available. No.
162740 (document).

❀ MAGNOLIA BLOSSOMS. American, 1938, screen print. 100%
cotton, glazed. 54" wide, 25¼" vertical repeat. Design by F.
Schumacher & Company. Document in Schumacher Archives. No. 161770 (magnolia white).

❀ METROPOLIS. American, 1920–40, screen print. 58% linen,
42% cotton. 54" wide, 25¼" repeat. Adapted from docu-

DESIGN 102, 1950–60. Schumacher. Document blue.

TREE OF LIFE, c. 1925–40. Schumacher. Document; pink and green.

ment in Schumacher Archives. No. 16M1940 (sunset).

❦ STAFFORD. American, c.1950, screen print. 100% cotton. 54" wide, 25¼" repeat. Design by F. Schumacher & Company. Document in Schumacher Archives; design originally known by this name. No. 656050 (colonial).

❦ TREE OF LIFE. American or English, c.1925–40, block print. 52% linen, 48% cotton. 54" wide, 48" half-drop repeat. Document, in madder reds, pinks and browns with green on cream, in Schumacher Archives; based on 18th-century tree of life embroideries. No. 162780 (document); No. 162782 (pink and green). Both are documentary colors.

❦ WILLIAMSBURG GRAPES. American, 1942–present. 100% cotton, 54" wide, 17" repeat. Design by F. Schumacher & Company. Document in Schumacher Archives. No. 64920 (amber and green).

WAVERLY FABRICS

❦ FLIRTATION. American, 1947. 100% cotton. 54" wide, 27" vertical and horizontal repeat. Design by Waverly Fabrics. Document in Schumacher Archives. No. 65M6120 (document).

BAKER DECORATIVE FABRICS

❦ BERLIN. European, c.1925–40. 100% wool. 54" wide, ½" repeat. Document privately owned. No. 74-112 (burgundy).

❦ DORTMOND. European, c.1925–40. 100% wool. 54" wide, ¾" vertical repeat, 3⅛" horizontal repeat. Document privately owned. No. 74-132 (burgundy).

BRUNSCHWIG & FILS

❦ BELMONT WOOL TEXTURE. European, 1930–40, uncut velvet. 58% wool, 20% cotton, 9% dralon, 7% viscose, 6% modal. 51" wide, 7" repeat. Document a wool uncut velvet used for upholstery on banquettes on the S.S. *Coronna*. No. 63001.01 (red with cream).

❦ LEOPARD VELVET. French, 1920–30. 55% silk, 31% linen, 14% cotton. 25" wide, 30½" repeat. Document owned by the mill that made this fabric in the 1920s and has revived production. No. 36500.00 (natural).

❦ LOUDEAC TAPESTRY. French, c.1890–present, machine-woven version of a late 16th- or early 17th-century tapestry. 100% cotton. 48" wide, 24½" repeat. Document privately

WOVEN DESIGNS

BELMONT WOOL
TEXTURE, 1930–40.
Brunschwig & Fils.
Red on cream.

NICE STRIPE, 1910–30.
Brunschwig & Fils. Red
stripe on beige.

owned in France. No. 180350.00 (multi, unfaded colors as shown on reverse of document); No. 180353.00 (multi on yellow, colors of the faded front of the document).

❀ NICE STRIPE. French, 1910–30. 56% cotton, 44% linen. 52" wide, 4¾" horizontal repeat. Document, now in Brunschwig & Fils Archives, a striped linen twill used as seat upholstery and canopy of a beach chair. No. 66881.01 (red stripe on beige).

❀ RAYURE MODERNE. American, 1928–29. 75% rayon, 25% silk. 50" wide, 20" vertical repeat, 12" horizontal repeat. Document, upholstery on a tubular steel chair, designed by Donald Deskey and now owned by the Metropolitan Museum of Art. Reproduced for the Metropolitan Museum of Art. No. 63429.01 (black and gray).

❀ SEDAN CLOTH. European, c. 1925. 100% wool. 52" wide, ⅝" vertical repeat, ⅜" horizontal repeat. Document, now in Brunschwig & Fils Archives, upholstery in a 1925 Mercedes automobile. No. 60698.01 (nutria and cranberry).

❀ TIGER VELVET. French, 1920–30. 55% silk, 31% linen, 14% cotton. 25" wide, 30" repeat. Document owned by the mill that made this fabric in the 1920s and has revived production. No. 36530.00 (natural).

CLASSIC REVIVALS

❀ ADAMITE. English, 1913, silk tissue. 100% silk. 21" wide, 44" repeat. Schoeser and Rufey, *English and American Textiles,* chap. 5, fig. 40. Revival of 1873 design. Document in Warner Archive, London. Custom colors.

❀ BROCATELLE 7038. French, 1911, woven brocatelle. 50% silk, 50% linen. 21" wide, 41" repeat. Document in Prelle Archives, Lyon, France, based on a late 16th- or early 17th-century Italian document and woven July 1911 for Gill and Reigate.

❀ DAMASK 7308. French, 1921. 50% silk, 50% linen. 21" wide, 19" repeat; can also be woven 48" wide. Design from 16th-century original. Document in Prelle Archives, Lyon, France, based on a Renaissance design of either French or Italian origin and woven July 1921. No. 7308. Custom colors.

❀ LULLINGSTONE. English, 1937 and c. 1950, damask. 50% silk, 50% cotton. 50" wide, 47" repeat. *A Choice of Design,* no. 98. Design by Herbert Woodman based on a 15th-century Italian damask intended for ecclesiastical use. Document in Warner Archive, London. Custom colors.

❀ WARHAM. English, 1921, damasquette. 100% silk. 51" wide, 54" repeat. Design by F. E. Howard based on 15th-century Italian designs. Made for Warham Guild, founded in 1912 to supply vestments and church ornaments. Document in Warner Archive, London. Custom colors.

❀ WOBURN ARMURE. English, 1901, brocade on armure ground. 15" wide, 26" repeat. Reproduced from 1841 document in the state rooms at Woburn Abbey. Document in Warner Archive, London. Custom colors.

DECORATORS WALK

❀ IMBERLINE DAMASK. American, c. 1925–40. 63% bemberg rayon, 37% cotton. 50" wide, 17½" repeat. No. T 7653 (gold); No. T 7651 (blue); No. T 7650 (red).

SCALAMANDRÉ

❀ DIANA DAMASK. American, c. 1930–40. 38% silk, 62% spun rayon. 50" wide, 13½" repeat. Design by Scalamandré. Based on a late 16th-century French or Italian design. No. 276-5 (henna).

SCHUMACHER

❀ CENTENNIAL DAMASK. Italian, c. 1920–30, woven damask. 75% cotton, 25% silk. 51" wide, 26" vertical repeat, 25" horizontal repeat. Document, in Schumacher Archives, a Renaissance design revived in both the 18th and 19th centuries. Woven with an iridescent strié ground typical of the 1920s. No. 53600 (green).

❀ FLANDERS. Belgian, 1925, woven tapestry. 58% linen, 42% cotton. 54" wide, 25¼" repeat. Document in Schumacher Archives. No. 162710 (harvest).

❀ IMPERIAL TRIANGLE. American, 1956, damask. 58% cotton, 42% rayon. 53" wide, 8¼" vertical repeat, 6¾" horizontal repeat. Design by F. Schumacher & Company. Document, in Schumacher Archives, a two-color damask distributed in the 1950s under the name "Design 513" as part of the Taliesen line and adapted from a 1922 silk design used in the Imperial Hotel, Tokyo. No. 52990 (indigo).

❀ JACOBEAN DAMASK. American, 1915. 72% cotton, 28% silk. 51" wide, 43" vertical repeat, 25½" horizontal repeat. Design by F. Schumacher & Company. Silk document in

top left
ADAMITE, 1913.
Classic Revivals.
Custom colors.

top right
BROCATELLE 7038, 1911.
Classic Revivals.
Custom colors.

left
DAMASK 7308, 1921.
Classic Revivals.
Custom colors.

right
JACOBEAN DAMASK,
1915. Schumacher.
Midnight.

bottom left
LULLINGSTONE, 1937
and c.1950. Classic
Revivals. Custom
colors.

bottom right
WOBURN ARMURE, 1901.
Classic Revivals.
Custom colors.

WARHAM, 1921.
Classic Revivals.
Custom colors.

IMPERIAL TRIANGLE,
1956. Schumacher.
Indigo.

RIGATO OMBRE,
1920–30. Schumacher.
Terra rosa; indian blue.

Schumacher Archives was inspired by 18th century–style tree of life embroideries. No.53720 (midnight).

❀ La Chambre. American, 1910, woven check. 75% cotton, 25% silk. 54" wide, repeat negligible. Design by F. Schumacher & Company. Document in Schumacher Archives. No.91512 (clove).

❀ La Vigne. American, 1910, woven. 77% cotton, 23% silk. 54" wide, 1¼ vertical repeat, 2" horizontal repeat. Design by F. Schumacher & Company. Document in Schumacher Archives. No.91491 (dark red).

❀ Les Gazelles au Bois. American, 1927–34, woven design. 57% cotton, 43% silk. 54" wide, 10" vertical repeat, 13½" horizontal repeat. Originally designed in 1927 by Pierre Pozier, who was inspired by the Art Deco metalwork of French designer Edgar Brant, shown at the 1925 Exposition International des Arts Décoratifs in Paris; the scale of Pozier's original design (pattern 915) was much larger. Two colorways of this design in this scale (pattern 1118) were woven by Schumacher for the Waldorf Astoria Ballroom in 1934. Document in Schumacher Archives. No.22270 (cream and black); No.22271 (cream and slate).

❀ Park East Matelasse. German, 1920–30, woven design. 100% cotton. 54" wide, 9¾" vertical repeat, 6¾" horizontal repeat. Woven adaptation of a brocaded document in Schumacher Archives. No.53M327 (burgundy).

❀ Persian Botanical. Belgian, c.1890–1930, tapestry. 67% cotton, 28% wool. 54" wide, 19½" vertical repeat, 13½" horizontal repeat. Document an 18th-century botanical tapestry in Schumacher Archives. No.27410 (black).

❀ Rigato Ombre. American, c.1920–30, woven striped design with moiré surface. 50% linen, 50% rayon moiré. 51" wide, 18¼" horizontal repeat. Design by F. Schumacher & Company. Document, in Schumacher Archives, originally advertised as appropriate for upholstery in limousines, airplanes and yachts. No.53712 (document terra rosa); No. 53713 (document indian blue).

❀ Williamsburg Pomegranate Damask. (See p.73.) Reproduction of an 18th-century silk damask. Fabric continuously woven by Schumacher since 1902; used in the U.S. Supreme Court in 1920.

MODERN TEXTILES: CONTINUING A TRADITION

S ome modern textiles that have changed little or not at all are entirely appropriate for restoration work. Commercial sources for some of these fabrics — including plain-woven checks, cottons and linens, baize, diaper, dimity, plush, rep and horsehair — are provided in the following sections. In addition, a number of handweavers who excel at reproduction work have been listed. The fabrics and people listed here are intended only as an elementary guideline for identifying appropriate fabrics or as a shortcut to ordering suitable goods. Because many similar fabrics are available in retail shops throughout the country, you should feel free to search elsewhere for traditional fabrics that are still being manufactured or for those that visually resemble the products of an earlier time. For exact reproduction of a handwoven document, you are encouraged to work closely with a skilled local weaver who may not be listed here. While purists may wish to use natural fibers exclusively for restoration work, in some cases compromise on this point can result in visual similarity at greatly reduced cost.

BAIZE

True baize is fairly heavy and has a long nap. It is most often dyed a dark olive green. Several modern fabrics, listed here, serve the purpose well.

BLATT BILLIARDS

❀ BILLIARD CLOTH. 75% wool, 25% nylon. 62" wide. Avocado.

DECORATORS WALK

❀ BILLIARD CLOTH. 70% acrylic, 30% wool. 59–60" wide. T41950 (several shades of green).

Checked linen bed curtains and counterpane, c. 1790–1810, used by the Copp Family, Stonington, Conn. (Smithsonian Institution)

THE DORR MILL STORE

❀ RUG WOOL. 100% wool. 60" wide. No. 44 (green); No. 6307 (dark blue); 32 other colors available.

CONSTANCE LA LENA, SUNFLOWER STUDIO

❀ CARPET BAIZE. 100% wool. 36" wide. A heavy weight especially suitable for crumb cloths. Handwoven. No. X18.12 (cream white). Can be dyed to order; range includes 7 shades of green.
❀ FLANNEL BAIZE. 100% wool. 36" wide. A lighter weight more appropriate for table coverings and quilt tops. Handwoven. No. C14.11 (cream white). Can be dyed to order; range includes 7 shades of green.

SCALAMANDRÉ

❀ INDEPENDENCE HALL BAIZE CLOTH. (See p. 40.)
❀ SHELBOURNE CASEMENT. 50% wool, 50% cotton. 50" wide. No. 99412-1 (white). Also available in 5 colors. Dyed width 47". Consider especially No. 99412-5 (bottle green). Special order only.

BLANKETS

ALEXANDRA'S TEXTILE

Checked and plaid blanketing by the yard. 100% wool. 60" wide. Based on handwoven blankets, c. 1830–40. No. BW blue woven plaid; No. BW red woven plaid; No. BW blue check; No. BW red check. All illustrated in color in catalog.

BETSY BOURDON

Handwoven blankets in windowpane checks and a variety of plaids. Twill or tabby weaves. Woven in wool dyed with your choice of colors in vegetable or chemical dyes. Custom sizes.

JANENE CHARBENEAU

❀ ROSE BLANKETS. 100% wool. 80" wide, 100" long. A plain weave with a narrow black stripe at each end and embroidered medallions in each corner.
   Also, handwoven blankets custom woven to your specifications are available in a variety of colors, either plain or pattern woven, custom or commercial dyeing.

KATHLEEN B. SMITH

Handwoven blankets in plain or windowpane checks. Your choice of vegetable-dyed colors. Custom sizes.

MARY WORLEY

Custom weaving of handwoven blankets in checks and a variety of plaids. Twill or tabby weaves. Woven in wool dyed with natural dyes, primarily indigo, madder and black walnut, and available primarily in single-ply yarns.

BORDERINGS

During the period 1750–1880, some bed and window valances and curtains were made with applied borders of printed fabric. (See Montgomery, *Printed Textiles,* figs. 239, 244.) These were constructed of strips cut from yard goods, the raw edges of which were folded under and the resulting piece of fabric applied to the edge of the valance. The raw edges of the valance itself were folded up "to the right side" and completely covered with the appliquéd strip of cloth. This treatment gave a neatly finished look to the valance, providing no visible hems, a clean finish on the inside and a well-defined outline to the shaped valance on the outside. Early in this period, some fabrics were intentionally printed in a series of stripes with broad areas between them so that the stripes could be cut apart and used for borderings. (See Montgomery, *Printed Textiles,* fig. 428.) Not everyone used these specific fabrics for this purpose, however, and especially from the 19th century on there are numerous examples of valances bordered with strips of printed cotton of allover design. It is not difficult to achieve these effects with modern materials. "Williamsburg Liner Stripe" is an excellent reproduction of the type of bordering specially printed to be cut apart. The other fabrics listed here include documentary and nondocumentary prints considered especially appropriate for this use.

BRUNSCHWIG & FILS

❀ EDWINA GLAZED CHINTZ. English, c. 1820–50, roller print. 100% cotton, glazed. 54" wide, negligible repeat. Document in Brunschwig & Fils Archives. No. 62281.01 (coral); No. 62282.01 (blue).

❀ FOUR SEASONS LINEN PRINT. English, c. 1770, copperplate and block print. 100% linen. 47" wide, 35½" repeat. Document owned by Historic Cherry Hill, Albany, N.Y. Striped motif originally a separate piece of block-printed fabric applied and used as a border. Although printed as an integral part of "Four Seasons Print," this motif could be cut off and used for bordering. No. 62011.01 (red).

PEAWEED COTTON PRINT.
Brunschwig & Fils.
Raspberry; other
colors.

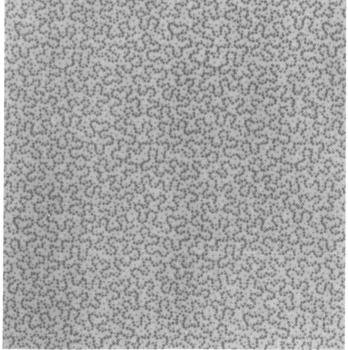

VERMICELLI, c. 1830–60.
Schumacher. Fawn.

216

❀ MANSARD STRIPE PRINT. Indian, c. 1750–80, block print. 100% cotton. 36½" wide. Document, privately owned in France, has these stripes as part of a larger design. No. 174420.00 (multi on beige).

❀ PEAWEED COTTON PRINT. 100% cotton. 48" wide, 3½" repeat. No. 66201.01 (raspberry); other colors available.

COWTAN & TOUT

❀ ONDINE. 100% cotton. 54" wide, 3" repeat. No. 8749 (blue and cream). Minimum order 2 yards.

❀ SQUIGGLE CHINTZ. 100% cotton, glazed. 54" wide, 4" repeat. No. 5605 (blue and cream); No. 5611 (red and white); other colors available. Minimum order 2 yards.

❀ WEXFORD. 100% cotton. 54" wide, 2" repeat. No. 5454 (red and green); No. 5455 (red and brown). Minimum order 2 yards.

SCHUMACHER

❀ VERMICELLI. English or American, c. 1830–60, roller print. 100% cotton. 54" wide, negligible repeat. No. 162737 (fawn).

CHECKS

Plain-woven checks and simple plaids have changed little in the last 200 years. The tabby-woven patterns of regular or irregular repeats of squares were relatively easy to establish on hand looms, and a surprising variety of decorative effects was achieved within this basic design formula by changing the arrangement of colors or introducing twill textures. From the earliest days of settlement in America, checks were used for clothing as well as for bed and window curtains and loose cases or slipcovers for furniture. In the last half of the 18th century, simple checks of large scale (i.e., with repeats of 2 or 2½ inches) were especially popular for bed and window hangings.

The earliest examples of checks were handwoven of 100 percent linen, and although they could be made on home looms, they were also imported in enormous quantities. Checks and stripes were among the first products of American cotton textile mills, and these fabrics, too, were used in household decoration as well as for more utilitarian items such as mattress and pillow ticking in addition to clothing. Many of the cotton checks prized as "homespun" today are actually products of the early 19th-century textile mills. Even though the patterns are simple and the colors somewhat limited, these factory products were widely used for bed tickings, pillow and bolster covers, counterpanes, aprons, curtains and quilt linings. With the introduction of machine printing in the early 19th century, some checks also were printed; these were often of an inferior quality, on cheap goods with the design seldom aligned with the straight grain of the fabric.

To judge from surviving examples dating before the mid-19th century, blue and white was the most common color combination, although red, green and various shades of gold and brown were also combined with white. Sometimes the gold or brown was combined with blue as well as white; this color combination seems to have been favored especially by German settlers in Pennsylvania, Ohio and North Carolina. Until the mid-19th century, the texture of cotton check was somewhat heavier than that of modern gingham, and the heavier checks seem to have always been preferred for household furnishings; indeed, they have often been referred to as "furniture checks." In the 18th century, French upholsterers and those trained in France traditionally used large-scale checks as coverings for the backs of even the most high-style furniture. Small-scale checks, with repeats as tiny as $\frac{1}{4}$ inch, were usually used for aprons rather than for household furnishings. In the 19th century small checked ginghams were favored for children's clothing, work gowns and handkerchiefs. For illustrations of early checks, see Montgomery, *Textiles in America,* pls. D-23, D-44 and D-45 and fig. D-28.

Many textile firms carry checks as part of their regular stock, although it is surprisingly difficult to find a plain blue-and-white checked linen with a repeat of 2 or $2\frac{1}{2}$ inches, despite the fact that this was probably the most common type used in 18th-century America for bed hangings. Although checks are represented in almost every museum and historical society collection, some authorized museum reproduction checks are available on the modern market. It is not difficult for a handweaver to reproduce a checked pattern, providing threads of suitable texture can be found.

ALEXANDRA'S TEXTILE

❀ HOMESPUN ORIGINALS. 33 patterns of handwoven 100% cotton check. Documents privately owned, mostly late

18th-century handwoven and early 19th-century factory woven cotton checks. Catalog and samples available.

BRUNSCHWIG & FILS

The following fabrics are based on French provincial checks of the 18th or 19th century.

✿ BRISTOL CHECK. 56% rayon, 44% linen. 51" wide, 1" repeat. No. 69883.01 (yellow).

✿ ISIGNY CHECK. 47% cotton, 37% rayon, 16% linen. 55" wide, 2" repeat. No. 140422.00 (royal blue and off-white); No. 140442.00 (navy).

✿ LONGCHAMPS CHECK. 43% cotton, 40% rayon, 17% linen. 56" wide, $1\frac{3}{8}$" repeat. No. 668399.01 (medium blue and white).

✿ POTOMAC LINEN CHECK. 62% linen, 38% cotton. 54" wide, 3" repeat. No. 69051.01 (red on cream); No. 69052.01 (blue on cream).

✿ VALERAS CHECK. 100% cotton. 55" wide, $4\frac{5}{8}$" vertical repeat, 5" horizontal repeat. No. 63180.01 (beige and cream); No. 63182.01 (blue and cream).

JEANNE CHARBENEAU

✿ FURNITURE CHECKS. 100% linen or 100% cotton. Custom-woven checks based on your document or published sources.

CLASSIC REVIVALS

✿ CASE CLOTH. 100% linen. 48" wide, 8" repeat. Taken from a group portrait of the governors of the Kings Hospital, Dublin, c. 1765.

RABBIT GOODY

Handwoven cotton checks based on privately owned documents or published sources. Can work directly from your document as well.

CONSTANCE LA LENA, SUNFLOWER STUDIO

✿ COLONIAL CHECK LINEN. 100% linen. 30" wide, 2" repeat. No. C7.1 (indigo blue and cream white only). Handwoven.

✿ COUNTRY CHECK LINEN. 100% linen. 30" wide, 1" check, 2" repeat. No. B6.1 (indigo blue and cream white only). Handwoven.

CASE CLOTH. Classic Revivals.

❀ LINSEY-WOOLSEY CHECK. 82% linen, 18% wool. 30" wide, 1" repeat. No.D8.1 (available in 35 colors, each with white). Handwoven.

❀ VILLAGE CHECK LINEN. 100% linen. 30" wide, ⅜" repeat. No.C5.1 (indigo blue and cream white only). Handwoven.

OSBORNE & LITTLE

❀ MIREPOIX. 100% cotton. 55" wide, 1" repeat. A regular plaid with herringbone woven texture in the large white squares. No.F183-02 (blue and white).

PIERRE DEUX

❀ LARGE PLAID. 49% cotton, 36% viscose, 15% linen. 54" wide, 2⅜" balanced repeat. No order numbers. Good color variety, excellent blue and white.

❀ SMALL PLAID. 100% cotton. 56" wide, ¾" balanced repeat. No order numbers. Good color variety, excellent blue and white.

SCALAMANDRÉ

❀ COUNTRY PLAID. 57% cotton, 43% linen. 51" wide, 1¾" repeat, 2" horizontal repeat. No.99473-1 (slate blue and off-white).

220

SCHUMACHER
COLONIAL WILLIAMSBURG REPRODUCTIONS

Documents are in the textile collection of Colonial Williamsburg, Williamsburg, Va.

❀ CHECKS. 18th or early 19th century. 55% linen, 45% cotton. 48" wide, ¾" vertical and horizontal repeat. No.118883 (maple sugar).

❀ EDINBURGH CHECK. 100% linen. 48" wide, 2" vertical and horizontal repeat. No.83174 (blue).

❀ TAVERN CHECK. American, c.1750–1800. 61% linen, 39% cotton. 48" wide, 3" vertical and horizontal repeat. Document originally used as a slipcover for a settee cushion. No. 81508 (blue).

KATHLEEN B. SMITH

❀ HANDWOVEN SMALL CHECKS. 100% cotton. 45" wide. No. 228. Assorted patterns and colors. Write for samples.

WAVERLY FABRICS

❀ CRANSTON CHECK. 100% cotton. 54" wide, ¾" repeat. Document an early 19th-century handwoven linen apron at Old Sturbridge Village. No.60M3240 (indigo).

❀ CRANSTON PLAID. 100% cotton. 54" wide, 1½" repeat. Document an early 19th-century cotton bolster cover at Old Sturbridge Village. No.645692 (indigo).

MARY WORLEY

Handwoven checks custom woven in a wide variety of 18th- and 19th-century patterns. Usually uses single-ply linen, although will also do cotton-and-linen combinations for toweling and curtains. Natural dyes, including indigo.

CHINTZ

BRUNSCHWIG & FILS

❀ ALBI PLAIN GLAZED CHINTZ. 100% cotton. 50" wide. No. 6569.01 (103 colors).

❀ MAJA FIGURED CHINTZ. 100% cotton, glazed. 50" wide, No.6571.01 (80 colors).

CLARENCE HOUSE

❀ PARIS CHINTZ. 100% cotton, glazed. 52" wide. No.32726 (65 colors).

CRANSTON PLAID.
Waverly Fabrics.
Indigo.

DECORATORS WALK

❀ FRENCH GLAZED COTTON. 100% cotton. 48" wide. No. T41800 (31 colors).

FONTHILL

❀ MOIRE STRIPE. 100% cotton, glazed. 54" wide, 2" repeat. No. 1540-5 (green); No. 1540-2 (scarlet).

LEE JOFA

❀ CHINTZ CAMILLE. 100% cotton, glazed. 51" wide. No. 824300 series (34 colors).

SCALAMANDRÉ

❀ PARIS SPRING. 100% cotton, glazed. 48½" wide. No. 98189 series (19 colors).

STROHEIM & ROMANN

❀ LAMPYRE GLAZED CHINTZ. 100% cotton. 54" wide. No. 46600 series (48 colors).
❀ SUNGLOW GLAZED CHINTZ. 50% cotton, 50% polyester. 48" wide. No. 49400 series (84 colors).

WAVERLY FABRICS

❀ STARLIGHT CHINTZ. 50% cotton, 50% polyester, glazed. 45" wide. No. 30M1120 series (28 colors).

COTTONS

Plain-woven cottons and synthetic-cotton blends of good texture are available from a number of manufacturers listed in this book as well as in drapery and clothing fabric shops throughout the country. Some examples suitable for restoration work are listed here:

AMAZON VINEGAR & PICKLING WORKS DRYGOODS

❀ DRILL. 100% cotton. 39" wide. Twill weave. White.
❀ DUCK. 100% cotton. 36" wide. 10 oz. weight. Natural.
❀ NAINSOOK. 100% cotton. 45" wide. White only.
❀ SHEETING. 100% cotton. 100" wide. White only.
❀ WHITE COTTON. 100% cotton. 45" wide.

BRUNSCHWIG & FILS

❀ COTTON VOILE. 100% cotton. 55" wide. No. 8568.01 (cream); No. 85680.01 (white).

❀ HEATHER DOTTED SWISS. 100% cotton. 54" wide. No. 66820.00 (white); No.668200.01 (cream).

❀ ORGANDY COTTON. 100% cotton (preshrunk). 43" wide. No.8556.02 (white).

❀ PERCALE. 100% cotton. 61" wide. No.8570.02 (white).

❀ PLAIN CLOTH. 56% linen, 44% cotton. 48" wide. No. 8554.02 (white).

❀ POLISHED COTTON. 100% cotton. 51" wide. No.8566.01 (natural).

❀ SAILCLOTH. 100% cotton. 55" wide. No.8560.02 (white).

❀ STRIPED VOILE. 100% cotton. 55" wide. No.85690.01 (white).

COWTAN & TOUT

❀ SHEER STRIPE. 100% cotton. 55" wide. No.5849 (ivory). Minimum order 2 yards.

DECORATORS WALK

❀ BATISTE. 100% polyester. 47–48" wide. No. HC81660 (white); No.81661 (oyster).

❀ BATISTE II. 100% polyester. 48" wide. No.HC76552 (oyster); No.76550 (white).

❀ BROADCLOTH. 65% polyester, 35% cotton. 45" wide. No. HC78497 (white).

❀ COTTON BATISTE. 100% cotton. 45" wide. No.HC78495 (white).

❀ COTTON VOILE. 100% cotton. 50" wide. No.HC79250 (white).

❀ DOTTED SWISS. 65% polyester, 35% cotton. 45" wide. No. HC70590 (white).

❀ EMBROIDERED BATISTE. 65% polyester, 35% cotton. 43" wide. No.HC80065 (white).

❀ MARQUISETTE. 100% polyester. 118" wide. No.HC70311 (white); No.HC70312 (eggshell). 114" wide. No.HC74420 (white).

❀ ORGANDY. 100% cotton. 44" wide. No.HC9255 (white).

❀ PERMANENT FINISH ORGANDY. 100% cotton. 42–43" wide. No.HC77049 (white).

❀ POPLIN CLOTH. 100% cotton. 56" wide. No.IS399-1 (oyster).

❀ SWISS LAWN. 100% cotton. 51" wide. No.Q2949 (white).

❀ Verti Crash. 80% polyester, 20% cotton. 48" wide. No. HC81579 (bone and 4 other colors available).

❀ Woven Dotted Swiss. 65% polyester, 35% cotton. 45" wide. No. HC78470 (white).

Gohn Brothers

Order by name of goods.

❀ Bed Sheeting. 100% cotton (heavyweight). 90" wide. Unbleached.

❀ Birdseye Diaper Cloth. 100% cotton. 36" wide. White only.

❀ Buckram. 100% cotton. 20" wide, white only. 30" wide, black or white.

❀ Burlap. 100% cotton. 36" wide. Natural only.

❀ Cloth of Gold Percale. 100% cotton. 45" wide. White and 38 colors available.

❀ Crinoline. 100% cotton. 39" wide. Black or white.

❀ Fiesta Amish Percale. 100% cotton. 45" wide. White and 21 colors available.

❀ Frontier Cloth (Drill). 100% cotton. 45" wide. Natural only.

❀ Georgaire Voile. 100% cotton. 48" wide. White only.

❀ Huck Toweling. 100% cotton. 15" wide. White only.

❀ Imported Organdy. 100% cotton. 39" wide. White only.

❀ Lawn. 100% cotton. 44" wide. White only.

❀ Muslin. 100% cotton. "Economy Muslin," 39" wide, natural. "Muslin," 45" wide, white and unbleached. "Candlewicking Muslin," 48" wide, unbleached.

❀ 100% Cotton Denim. 60" wide; 10 or 13 oz. weight. 45" wide, 6 oz. weight. Navy only.

❀ Quilt Sheeting (Muslin). 100% cotton. 90" or 108" wide. White or unbleached.

❀ Unbleached Drill. 100% cotton. 40" or 60" wide.

❀ Unbleached Duck Cloth. 100% cotton. 47" wide.

❀ White American Organdy. 100% cotton. 45" wide. White only.

❀ Zephyr Batiste. 100% cotton. 45" wide. White only.

Greeff Fabrics representing E.C. Carter

❀ Embroidered Batiste. This firm specializes in embroidered batiste designs. More than 60 designs are available, some of them in colors on white. These fabrics come in either 10- or 15-yard pieces that must be purchased entire. Many of these designs are suitable for late 19th-century restoration work. No. 33975. 65% Dacron, 35% cotton. 45" wide, 2" repeat. White. No. 33750, a design of 2 sizes of white dots embroidered on white. 65% Dacron, 35% cotton. 44–45" wide, 3" repeat. White. Consider also Nos. 34070, 33935, 34125, 33945 and 34135.

❀ EMBROIDERED DOTTED BATISTE. 65% Dacron, 35% cotton. 43" wide, 2" repeat. No. 30534 (white).

❀ EMBROIDERED STRIPED BATISTE. 65% Dacron, 35% cotton. 39" wide. No. 33620 (white).

❀ EYELET EMBROIDERED BATISTE. 65% Dacron, 35% cotton. 45" wide, 2" repeat. No. 34130 (white on white).

RUE DE FRANCE

❀ VOILE. 65% polyester, 35% cotton. 42" wide. No. VL (white).

SCALAMANDRÉ

❀ COLONIAL BATISTE. 100% cotton. 51" wide. No. 98230-1 (white).

❀ FRENCH VOILE. 100% cotton. 52" wide. No. 4213-0 (white).

❀ SUMMER NET VOILE. 100% cotton. 55" wide. No. 98235-1 (white).

TIOGA

❀ MUSLIN. 100% cotton. 45" wide. Natural. Order by name.

WILSON'S

Stocks an inexpensive unbleached white cotton called tobacco cloth. When washed in hot water and bleached, it shrinks at least 4 inches per yard. The bleached fabric is soft and resembles some 19th-century Indian muslins.

❀ TOBACCO CLOTH. 100% cotton. 45" wide. Natural. Order by name.

COTTONS, HANDWOVEN

JANENE CHARBENEAU

❀ BIRD'S EYE. 100% cotton. Various widths. Custom woven.

❀ HUCKABACK. 100% cotton. Various widths. Custom woven.

ANDREA CESARI

Custom weaving of late 17th- to early 19th-century cotton designs from published weavers' drafts or original samples. Can weave widths up to 40 inches and patterns using up to 8 harnesses. Established patterns include Hargrove's "English Huckaback," "Plain Cord," "Dimity" and "No. XXXVII" with corrected treadling.

KATHLEEN B. SMITH

❀ FINE SHEER. 100% cotton. 42" wide. No. 208 (white).
❀ HUCKABACK. 100% cotton. 22" wide. No. 223 (white).
❀ MUSLIN. 100% unbleached cotton. 47" wide, 18" long. Especially suitable for mounting antique textiles. Fabric has been woven, washed and dried on stretchers; has never had any finish or sizing applied to it. No. 433.

VIRGINIA GOODWIN   COUNTERPANES

❀ KNOTTED SPREADS. Popularly known as "Candlewick" spreads, these counterpanes are hand embroidered in 100% cotton heavy yarn on 100% cotton ground cloth. White or natural. "Diamond Star Pattern" dates from c. 1820 and has been made continuously since that time. Other traditional patterns include "Bowknot and Thistle," "Napoleon's Wreath" and "Basket of Fern and Daisies."

KATHLEEN B. SMITH

100% wool counterpanes woven in 16-harness patterns, vegetable dyed colors. Two patterns available: "Small Bird's Eye" and "Double Diamond."

ANDA BIJHOUWER   COVERLETS

Can weave overshot or summer-winter coverlets from your pattern or from published designs. The following designs are standard in her work. Each can be ordered with or without fringe.
❀ FLOURISHING WAVE. Overshot weave. Cotton and wool. Indigo blue and white (other colors to your specifications).
❀ JOHANN SPECK'S DESIGN. Pennsylvania German design in overshot weave. Cotton and wool. Document privately owned. Indigo blue and white (other colors to your specifications).

❀ PHIPPSBURG. Overshot weave. Cotton and wool. Document an old coverlet found in a former shipbuilder's home in Phippsburg Center, Maine. Reproduction in Smithsonian Institution collection. Indigo blue and white (other colors to your specifications).

❀ PINE TREE AND SINGLE SNOWBALL. Summer-winter weave. Cotton and wool. Indigo blue and white (other colors to your specifications).

❀ SUNRISE. Overshot weave. Cotton and wool. Indigo blue and white (other colors to your specifications).

❀ WHIG ROSE. Summer-winter weave also known as "Wedding Bands." Cotton and wool. Indigo blue and white (other colors to your specifications).

ANDREA CESARI

❀ SNAILS TRAIL AND CAT'S TRACK. Overshot design. 20/2 cotton and 2/12 worsted wool, 30 epi. Indigo and white.

FAMILY HEIRLOOM WEAVERS/DAVID A. KLINE

❀ BIRD AND BUSH COVERLET. Cotton and wool. Double (76" wide, 90" long, plus 3" side fringe), queen (76" wide, 105" long, plus 5" side fringe), king (112" wide, 105" long, plus 5" side fringe) or child's size (39" wide, 38" long, plus side fringe). Document a jacquard coverlet woven in 1838 by Andrew Kump of Hanover, Pa. Reproduction has personalized signature block, date and weaver's name.

❀ HOUSE BORDER COVERLET. Cotton and wool. Double (76" wide, 100" long, plus 3" side fringe), queen (76" wide, 100" long, plus 5" side fringe) or child's size (38" wide, 33" long, plus side fringe). Document a jacquard coverlet woven in 1848 by H. and A. Seifert of Mechanicsburg, Pa. Reproduction has personalized signature block, date and weaver's name.

VIRGINIA GOODWIN

❀ HONEYCOMB. Design taken from a dated pattern of 1849. 100% cotton. Single (82" wide, 112" long) or double (94" wide, 112" long), including fringe. Creamy white only.

❀ LOVER'S KNOT. 19th-century summer-winter weave. Cotton and wool. Delft blue and white; navy blue and white; red and white.

❀ MORNING STAR. Overshot design. 48% virgin wool, 52% cotton. Double (90" wide, 108" long). Indigo or delft blue with white. Also 100% cotton in creamy white on white.

❀ WHIG ROSE. Overshot design. c. 1820–present. Cotton and wool. Delft blue and white; navy blue and white.

RABBIT GOODY

Custom-woven coverlets based on your document or those in her own collection.

JSP DESIGNS

Custom-woven coverlets in overshot and summer-winter weave structures. Standard line includes "Rosepath" and "Wheel of Fortune" designs. Custom colors.

MAGGIE KENNEDY

❀ DOUBLE CHARIOT WHEELS. Overshot design. Cotton and wool. Twin (72" wide, 100" long), double (94" wide, 106" long), queen (100" wide, 108" long) or king (104" wide, 110" long) sizes. Navy and white.

❀ BLOOMING LEAF. Overshot design. Cotton and wool. Twin (72" wide, 100" long), double (94" wide, 106" long), queen (100" wide, 108" long) or king (104" wide, 110" long) sizes. Navy and white.

❀ LEE'S SURRENDER. Overshot design. Cotton and wool. Twin (72" wide, 100" long), double (94" wide, 106" long), queen (100" wide, 108" long) or king (104" wide, 110" long) sizes. Navy and white.

❀ PINE BLOOM. Overshot design. Cotton and wool. Twin (72" wide, 100" long) double (94" wide, 106" long), queen (100" wide, 108" long) or king (104" wide, 110" long) sizes. Navy and white.

❀ WHIG ROSE AND LOVER'S KNOT. Overshot design. Cotton and wool. Twin (72" wide, 100" long), double (94" wide, 106" long), queen (100" wide, 108" long) or king (104" wide, 110" long) sizes. Navy and white.

LAURA COPENHAVER INDUSTRIES

❀ HONEYCOMB. c. 1820–present. 100% cotton. Can be ordered with or without hand-tied netted fringe with 3" or 5" tassels.

❀ LOVER'S KNOT PINE TREE BORDER. 19th-century summer-winter weave. Cotton and wool. Delft blue and white.

❀ WHIG ROSE. Overshot design. c. 1820–present. Cotton and wool. Delft blue and white.

WILLIAM A. LEINBACH

Handwoven overshot coverlets in traditional designs, including "Rose in the Woods," "Blooming Leaf," "Sixteen Roses," "Pine Burr," "Double Compass," "True Love's Knot" and "Whig Rose." All coverlets have woven borders and fringed ends. Made of cotton and worsted wool in your choice of either commercial colors or natural dyes. Available in various sizes: child's (36" wide, 42" long), keepsake (42" wide, 42" long), double (90" wide, 90" long), queen (90" wide, 108" long), king (104" wide, 108" long) and super king (104" wide, 120" long). All coverlets are signed and dated by the weaver.

MARY WORLEY

Overshot coverlets custom woven to reproduce your document or another pattern. Uses natural dyes — indigo, madder and black walnut — for wool combined with natural or bleached cotton.

CURTAIN LININGS

Through the years a variety of simple fabrics has been used for lining window curtains to protect them from fading and rotting caused by exposure to the sun's ultraviolet rays. Coarsely woven wool tammies were sometimes used in the 18th century, although many curtains of this period were not lined at all. Lightweight glazed chintzes were commonly used for curtain linings throughout the 19th century. In the period 1810–30, sharply contrasting lining colors were employed in the fashionable French draperies. During the years 1800–60, beige, tan, tea-colored and even black chintzes were commonly used for curtain linings. From the middle of the 19th century onward, some people made use of finely printed, monochromatic chintz designs, usually harmonizing with the primary color of the curtains.

For tammy, see Classic Revivals, p.39. For printed curtain linings, consider "Edwina" (p. 216),"Mansard Stripe" (p. 217) by Brunschwig & Fils, or some of the "squiggle chintzes" by Cowtan & Tout (p.217).

BASSETT MCNAB

❀ CURTAIN LININGS. 100% cotton. 54" wide, 6¼" repeat. No.7170-7 (tan); No.7170-17 (blue).

BRUNSCHWIG & FILS

❀ MARINET GLAZED CHINTZ. (See p. 166.)

CLARENCE HOUSE

❀ FANCY LINING. 100% cotton, glazed. 48" wide, ⅜" repeat. No. 32863-2 (blue).

SCHUMACHER

❀ VERMICELLI. 100% cotton. 54" wide, repeat negligible. No. 162737 (fawn).

In the 18th and early 19th centuries in the United States, "diaper" referred to patterned woven cottons and linens that were often used for table linens, napkins and toweling. Rarely is evidence found of their having been used for curtains. These designs can easily be copied by handweaving using published drafts. An excellent selection is given in the two books by Constance Dann Gallagher. **DIAPER**

SCALAMANDRÉ

❀ CAMEO CLOTH. 100% cotton. 50" wide. No. 97711-1 (white).

SCHUMACHER

❀ WILLIAMSBURG DOBBY WEAVE. American, c. 1780–1820. 100% cotton. 54" wide. Document, owned by Colonial Williamsburg, originally used for table cloths and napkins or toweling. No. 81729 (off-white).

In the 18th and early 19th centuries, dimity was a heavy cotton cloth distinguished by various patterns of vertical ribs, either regular or irregular. Dimity was used for bed curtains, window curtains, counterpanes, dressing or toilet table covers and slipcovers or loose cases for seating furniture (often called "furniture dimities"). By the late 1820s, dimity was also made in a lighter version that was used mainly for clothing; this was usually referred to as "cap dimity" or "checked dimity," to distinguish it from the heavier furniture dimity. The new fabric also used woven ribs as its primary design characteristic, but the cloth was much lighter in weight and the ribs were spaced more regularly in small stripes or checks. Both dimities were **DIMITY**

Furniture Dimity,
c. 1800–20, used by the
Copp Family, Stoning-
ton, Conn. (Smithso-
nian Institution)

232

available from about 1825 until the end of the 19th century. In the last quarter of the 19th century, the lighter type of dimity began to be used for curtains in kitchens, bedchambers and summer cottages. Curtains made of lightweight dimity were used extensively in late 19th-century and early 20th-century Colonial Revival interiors, although the fabric was unknown in the 18th century. It eventually superseded the heavier furniture dimity and has never gone out of production. Lightweight 100 percent cotton dimity is difficult to find today, but cotton-polyester blends are available in many department and fabric stores. Available types of the heavier furniture dimity are listed below.

All dimities can be washed, but those made of 100% cotton will shrink. It is wise to wash a sample yard before cutting unwashed cloth. Furniture dimity will shrink in length an inch or more per yard. Because of the nature of the woven vertical ribbing in furniture dimity, the horizontal shrinkage will be much greater, as much as seven inches per yard. This amount can be reduced somewhat by vigorous ironing, which also reduces the characteristically puffy vertical ribs of the freshly laundered fabric.

BRUNSCHWIG & FILS

❀ NEW RICHMOND DIMITY. 100% cotton. 46½" wide. No. 69400.01 (white).

JANENE CHARBENEAU

❀ DIMITY. 100% cotton. 32" wide. Weave structure based on published designs. Can also do custom reproduction.

SCALAMANDRÉ

❀ BETSY ROSS DIMITY. 100% cotton. 52" wide. No. 98246-1 (white).
❀ DIMITY. 100% cotton. 50" wide. No. 1657-1 (colonial white).
❀ DIMITY. 100% cotton. 50" wide. No. 1658-1 (colonial white).

EMBOSSING

Brunschwig & Fils, Clarence House, Old World Weavers and Scalamandré can emboss designs using 19th-century rollers. Several hundred patterns are available, and selections can be made from illustrated catalogs in the show-rooms. Embossed designs are particularly effective on plush or velvet; they can also be used on some silks and wool moreens.

FUSTIAN

CONSTANCE LA LENA, SUNFLOWER STUDIO

❀ DOUBLE FUSTIAN. 56% linen (warp), 44% cotton (weft). 30" wide. Handwoven. No. D1.1 (cream white); No. E1.1 (35 colors available).
❀ JEAN FUSTIAN. 65% linen (warp), 35% cotton (weft). 30" wide. Handwoven. No. C1.2 (cream white or dyed; 35 colors available).

HORSEHAIR

Beginning in the mid-18th century, plain and patterned horsehair fabrics in black, green, red, blue and white were used for upholstery. Judging by surviving examples, black seems to have been used most commonly. Colonial Williamsburg, the Wadsworth Athenaeum and the Connecticut Historical Society have mid-18th-century examples with a satin woven stripe alternating with a ribbed stripe. Eighteenth-century horsehair fabric with alternating half-inch satin and tabby stripes can be seen on some New York chairs now at Monticello, Charlottesville, Va. Documents of plain satin weave and various diaper woven designs can be dated as early as the late 18th century. Examples are in the collections of Strawbery Banke, Portsmouth, N.H., the Society for the Preservation of New England Antiquities, Boston, Historic Deerfield, Deerfield, Mass., Monticello, the American Wing of the Metropolitan Museum of Art and the Henry Francis duPont Winterthur Museum.

All of these styles continued to be made for the next hundred or more years; special medallions for chair seats and sofa upholstery were also made during the 19th century. Examples are in the collections of the Old York Historical Society, York, Maine, at the Elizabeth Perkins House; the Strong Museum, Rochester, N.Y.; and Old Sturbridge Village. Old Sturbridge Village has a set of sofa panels and chair seats in a blue-and-white diaper design with red, green and yellow brocaded medallions; these are dated 1844. Throughout the mid-19th century, plain black satin weave was the most common type of horsehair upholstery; it was sometimes tufted.

Authentic horsehair fabrics and accurate reproductions are made with a cotton or linen warp, the weft being made of actual tail or mane hair. The width of the fabric is thus limited by the length of the horsehair, usually from 25 to 30 inches. Nylon imitations of horsehair are usually made wider. Because of the narrow width of authentic horsehair goods, visible seams are often a necessity.

A variety of horsehair patterns is currently available; almost all of them are imported. Bear in mind that cuttings or loan samples are seldom available and that orders of horsehair fabrics are apt to have a long delivery time, sometimes as much as 18 months. When ordering horsehair fabric in solid colors, expect some variation in colors because of the natural variation in the way the hair may absorb the dye.

BRUNSCHWIG & FILS

❀ CHAMFORT HORSEHAIR TEXTURE. A woven design of alternating octagons and diamonds. 60% horsehair, 40% cotton. 27" wide, 2" repeat. No. 190279.00 (black); No. 190274.00 (dark green).

❀ CHRISTIANE HORSEHAIR TEXTURE. A woven design of alternating octagons and diamonds. 30% horsehair, 40% hemp, 30% cotton. 27" wide, 1½" repeat. No. 190021.00 (red); No. 190028.00 (brown and gold).

❀ CORDAY HORSEHAIR TEXTURE. A woven design with diamonds in a contrasting color. 30% horsehair, 30% cotton, 40% hemp. 27" wide, ¾" repeat. No. 190282.00 (blue and gold); No. 190289.00 (black); 5 other colors available.

❀ PALOMINO HORSEHAIR TEXTURE. A woven design of circles alternating with diaper diamonds. 60% horsehair, 40% cotton. 27" wide, 2" repeat. No. 190399.00 (black).

❀ RAINCY HORSEHAIR TEXTURE. A satin weave. 60% horsehair, 40% cotton. 27" wide. No. 180274.00 (green); No. 180278.00 (brown).

❀ SALINS HORSEHAIR TEXTURE. A satin weave. 60% horsehair, 40% cotton. 27" wide. No. 180599.00 (black).

CLARENCE HOUSE

❀ HORSEHAIR. 50% horsehair, 50% hemp. 25" wide. No. 1500 series (33 patterns and color combinations currently available).

Decorators Walk

❀ Horsehair. 50% horsehair, 50% cotton. 16" to 27" wide. 7 patterns and various color combinations; also nylon imitations, which are wider.

❀ Horsehair Bronze and Black Diamond. 50% horsehair, 50% cotton. 21" wide, 1¼" repeat. Bronze warp imitates discoloring often found on old horsehair; may be useful for repairs or for filling in a set of chairs. No. P20209

Lee Jofa

❀ Horsehair Damask. 68% horsehair, 32% cotton. 24" wide; can be ordered 26–27" wide for a slight additional charge. No. 664226 (blue). A woven pattern of alternating octagons and diamonds. 2" repeat. Also No. 664227 (green).

❀ Horsehair Sateens. 68% horsehair, 32% cotton. 24" wide; can be ordered 26–27" wide for a slight additional charge. No. 664238 (black).

Old World Weavers

❀ Christiane. 30% horsehair, 40% hemp, 30% cotton. 27" wide. No. N-42 (noir).

❀ Gael. 30% horsehair, 40% hemp. 30% cotton. 27" wide. No. N-30 (green and noir).

❀ Nircel. 30% horsehair, 40% hemp. 30% cotton. 27" wide. No. N-344 (noir).

Scalamandré

❀ Holmes Horsehair Damask. 60% horsehair, 40% cotton. 25" wide, ¾" repeat. No. 96535-1 (black).

❀ Horsehair Damask. 60% horsehair, 40% cotton. 26" wide, ¾" repeat. No. 96409-1 (black).

❀ Horsehair Repp. 60% horsehair, 40% cotton. 26" wide. No. 98208-2 (green warp with black hair).

❀ Horsehair Sateen Document Texture. 60% horsehair, 40% cotton. 26" wide. No. 98207-1 (grays).

❀ La France Horsehair Document. 60% horsehair, 40% cotton. 27" wide. A woven diaper design of small diamonds. No. 98164-1 (black).

❀ Meeks Horsehair Damask. 60% horsehair, 40% cotton. 22½" wide, 1" repeat. Reproduction of 19th-century design. No. 96536-1 (black); No. 20040-1 (pearl gray).

❀ Nineteenth-Century Horsehair Document. A satin weave. 60% horsehair, 40% cotton. 26" wide. No. 98206-1 (black).

❀ Phyfe Horsehair Damask. 60% horsehair, 40% cotton. 25" wide, ⅞" repeat. No. 96533-1 (black).

❀ Sheraton Horsehair Damask. 60% horsehair, 40% cotton. 26" wide, 1½" repeat. No. 96531-1 (off-white).

Sheer white undercurtains are essential for a successful layered window treatment for any period after about 1815. Although plain cotton batiste (called mull or muslin in the period) was used throughout the 19th century, machine-made embroideries became popular after about 1835 and machine-made lace panels after about 1850. No documentary reproductions of these are available, but some firms carry "traditional" yardage or panels that are appropriate. In the last five years there has been a great revival of interest in lace curtains, and many old patterns are now available. Some of these designs were introduced fairly soon after machine-made laces were introduced and have never gone out of production.

LACE AND NET CURTAINS

Decorators Walk

❀ Bobbinet. 100% polyester. Used for a mosquito bar in the restoration of San Francisco Plantation, Garyville, La.; also appropriate for late 19th-century window curtains. No. HC74660, 70" wide, white. No. HC74662, 70" wide, ecru. No. HC69221, 136–140" wide, white. No. HC69223, 136–140" wide, ecru. No. HC74661, 216" wide, white.

❀ Diamond Lace. Nottingham lace, c. 1875–1940. 100% cotton. 47" wide, 4½" repeat. No. TT34465 (oyster).

❀ Fernery. 100% polyester. 47" wide, 26¼" repeat. No. 77116 (eggshell); No. 77117 (snow); No. 77118 (cream).

❀ Jacquard II. Nottingham lace, c. 1855–1900. 100% cotton. 75" wide, 24¼" repeat. No. HC86210 (white).

❀ Lace Curtains. 70% polyester, 30% cotton. 57" wide, 98" long. No. HC78690 (eggshell). Sold in pairs only.

❀ Lace Net. 100% polyester. 118" wide (can be used either horizontally or vertically). No. HC74721 (white).

❀ Leaf Elegance. Nottingham lace, c. 1880–1910. 100% cotton. 60" wide, 34¼" repeat. No. HC80000 (champagne).

❀ LIMERICK LACE. Nottingham lace, c. 1865–1920. 100% cotton. 48" wide, 2" repeat. No. T34641 (white).

❀ OLD FASHION. Nottingham lace, c. 1885–1910. 100% cotton. 72" wide, 22¼" repeat. No. HC84001 (ivory).

❀ POINTE DE SPRIT. 100% polyester. 112" wide (can be used either horizontally or vertically). No. HC81425 (white); No. HC81426 (eggshell).

❀ STARFLAKE LACE. 70% polyester, 30% cotton. 47" wide, 7¼" repeat. No. T34456 (ecru).

❀ VICTORIAN I LACE PANEL. 70% polyester, 30% cotton. 95" wide, 118" long. No. HC78790 (champagne). Sold in pairs only; can be ordered twice this width.

❀ VICTORIAN II LACE PANEL. Scotland, c. 1880–1920. 70% polyester, 30% cotton. 59" wide, 118" long. No. HC81595 (champagne); No. HC81596 (white). Sold in pairs only; can be ordered twice this width.

❀ VICTORIAN III LACE PANEL. Nottingham lace, c. 1850–80. 70% polyester, 30% cotton. 95" wide, 118" long. No. HC78785 (champagne). Sold in pairs only; can be ordered twice this width.

❀ WHITE TAMBOUR NET CURTAINS. 100% polyester bobbinet with batiste appliqué. 44" wide, 108" long. No. HC77092 (white). Sold in pairs only; can be ordered twice this width.

GREEFF FABRICS

❀ AVIARY LACE. 100% cotton. 70" wide, 126" long. No. 400900 (ivory).

❀ IVORY BIRDS PANEL. 100% cotton. 60" wide, 106" repeat. No. 401015 (ivory).

❀ KENSINGTON LACE. 100% cotton. 68" wide, 36" repeat. No. 39800 (ivory).

❀ NOTTINGHAM LACE NET. 100% cotton. 48" wide. Ivory or eggshell. No. 38720; No. 38724; No. 38712; No. 39552; No. 39553; No. 38981; No. 39303.

J. R. BURROWS

❀ COTTAGE PANEL PAIRS. Scotland, c. 1900–20. 95% cotton, 5% polyester. Nottingham lace panels have scalloped border motif on three sides. Available in panels 34" wide, 48" long; 34" wide, 54" long; 34" wide, 60" long; 34" wide, 72" long; 34" wide, 84" long; 34" wide, 90" long. Sold only in 68" wide pairs that are joined at the top of the rod pocket; they may be easily separated. No. LCE-308 (ecru); No. LCW-308 (white).

Pattern also available as "Cottage Yardage." 36" wide, 15½" repeat. No. LCE-008 (ecru); No. LCW-008 (white).

❊ EDWARDIAN LACE BEDSPEAD. Scotland, c. 1900–20. 89% cotton, 11% polyester. Single 74" wide, 104" long; full 94" wide, 104" long; queen/king 100" wide, 110" long. No. LCE-120 (ecru); No. LCW-120 (white).

❊ FLORAL YARDAGE. Scotland, c. 1880–1900. 73% polyester, 27% cotton. 60" wide, 12" repeat. No. LCE-005 (ecru); No. LCW-005 (white).

❊ NEO-GREC PANELS. Scotland, 1870–80. 95% cotton, 5% polyester. Nottingham lace panels have scalloped border motif on three sides. Available in panels with rod pocket at top 60" wide, 72" long; 60" wide, 84" long; 60" wide, 90" long; 60" wide, 102" long; 60" wide, 108" long; and 60" wide, 144" long. Design reproduces one that won acclaim

IVORY BIRDS PANEL, Greeff Fabrics. Ivory.

NEO-GREC PANEL,
1870–80. J. R. Burrows.
Ecru; white.

at the 1876 Centennial Exhibition in Philadelphia. No. LCE-103 (ecru); No. LCW-103 (white). Pattern also available as "Neo-Grec Yardage." 60" wide, 31" repeat. No. LCE-103 (ecru); No. LCW-103 (white). Also available as yardage with border on two sides only. No. LCE-003 (ecru); No. LCW-003 (white).

❦ VICTORIAN PANELS. Scotland, 1880–95. 95% cotton, 5% polyester. Nottingham lace panels have scalloped border motif on three sides. Available in panels 60" wide, 72" long; 60" wide, 84" long; 60" wide, 90" long; 60" wide, 102" long; 60" wide, 108" long; and 60" wide, 144" long. No. LCE-101 (ecru); No. LCW-101 (white). Pattern also available as "Victorian Yardage." 60" wide, 23" repeat. No. LCE-001 (ecru); No. LCW-001 (white). Also available as yardage with border on two sides only. No. LCE-001 (ecru); No. LCW-001 (white).

240

LEE JOFA

❀ EDWARD LACE. 100% cotton. 55" wide, 5" repeat. No. 823010 (bone).

❀ ROSEBUD LACE. 100% cotton. 59" wide, 13" repeat. No. 803010 (off-white).

❀ TOMASINA LACE. 100% cotton. 55" wide, 15" repeat. No. 82300 (bone).

LONDON LACE

❀ ASHFIELD. Scotland, originally produced in 1860. 95% cotton, 5% polyester. 24" wide, 84" long with a rod pocket at the top. White or ivory.

❀ BLENHEIM. Scotland, originally produced in 1890. 95% cotton, 5% polyester. 37" wide, 63" long and 37" wide, 78" long, each with a rod pocket at the top. White or ivory.

❀ KENSINGTON. Scotland, originally produced in 1905. 95% cotton, 5% polyester. 36"-deep horizontal yardage with rod holes in the upper edge. Intended for half curtains (cafe curtains). White or ivory.

❀ SANDBOURNE. Scotland, originally produced in 1875. 95% cotton, 5% polyester. 54" wide, 103" long with a scalloped top. White or ivory.

❀ TOWN AND COUNTRY. Scotland, originally produced in 1910. 95% cotton, 5% polyester. Horizontal yardage 24" long, intended for use as a valance, with rod holes in upper edge. White or ivory.

❀ VICTORIAN CHERUB. Scotland, originally produced in 1880. 95% cotton, 5% polyester. 52" wide, 103" long, with a scalloped top. White or ivory.

❀ WILDREST. Scotland, originally produced in 1910. 95% cotton, 5% polyester. 52" wide, 63" long and 52" wide, 84" long, each with rod pocket at the top. White or ivory.

❀ WINDERMERE. Scotland, originally produced in 1885. 95% cotton, 5% polyester. 60" wide, 103" long with a scalloped top. White or ivory.

❀ WINDSOR. Scotland, originally produced in 1895. 95% cotton, 5% polyester. 60" wide, 84" long with a rod pocket at the top. White or ivory.

RUE DE FRANCE

❀ GRAND MERE. French, c. 1890–1990, has appearance of hand crochet. 100% dralon. 24" or 36" wide, 5" repeat. No. EYD (natural or beige).

❀ OLD CALAIS. French, c. 1880–1940. 100% dralon. 33" wide. No. DYD (pure white or beige).

❀ POINT D'ESPRIT. French, c.1850–1990. 100% dralon. 94" wide. No. GYD (natural). Also available as curtain panels: No. GPSP (54", 63", 72", 84" or 90" long).

SCALAMANDRÉ

❀ EGYPT LACE PANEL. 100% cotton. 60" wide, 126" repeat. Document (c.1870–90) privately owned in England. No. 96432-1 (off-white).

❀ ROSALIE LACE PANELS. Possibly French, c.1850–80. 100% cotton. 53" wide, 137" repeat. *Scalamandré*, no.14. Document owned by the Mississippi Chapter of the Daughters of the American Revolution at its headquarters, Rosalie, Natchez, Miss. No.96530-1 (off-white).

❀ ROSE SWIRL. 95% cotton, 5% polyester. 50" wide, 8¼" repeat. Document privately owned in England. No.98210-1 (ecru).

❀ VICTORIAN LACE. 30% cotton, 70% polyester. 50" wide, 14" repeat, plus 2½" border on each side. Document (c. 1890–1910) privately owned in England.

❀ VICTORIAN WINDOW. 100% cotton. 24" wide, 51" long. Document a late 19th-century Nottingham lace panel window shade privately owned in England. No.96430-1 (off-white).

❀ WHITE HOUSE OF THE CONFEDERACY PANELS. Possibly French, c. 1850–80. 100% cotton. 53" wide, 137" vertical repeat, 53" horizontal repeat. Document owned by the White House of the Confederacy, Richmond, Va. No.20079-1 (off-white).

STROHEIM & ROMANN

❀ CHANTILLY. English, c. 1875–1910. 95% cotton, 5% polyester. 51" wide, 102" long, plus pattern borders on three sides. Sold as panels only. Document privately owned in England. No.7810-195.

❀ OPUS. English, c.1890–1910. 95% cotton, 5% polyester. 59" wide, 102" long. Sold as panels only. Document privately owned in England. No.7859-192.

❀ VIVALDI. English, c.1850–75. 95% cotton, 5% polyester. 59" wide, 102" long. Sold as panels only. Document privately owned in England. No.7998-172.

BAKER DECORATIVE FABRICS

❊ MILAN. 60 square feet per hide. No. 96-600 series (24 colors).

SCHUMACHER

❊ WILLIAMSBURG LEATHER. Full top grain. Hand finished and antiqued. Available in full and half hides; full hides average 50–55 square feet; half hides average 24–27 square feet. No. 195068 (black glazed); 13 other colors available.

STROHEIM & ROMANN

❊ WINTERTHUR LEATHER. Available in full and half hides. Reproduced for Winterthur Museum. No. 01390 (Essex Room green); No. 01391 (Marlboro Room red); No. 01392 (Tappahanock Room brown); No. 01392 (Wentworth Room brown); No. 01395 (Lancaster Room black); No. 01396 (Centreville Room brown).

LEATHER

BRUNSCHWIG & FILS

❊ GENT LINEN CASEMENT. 100% linen. 48" wide. No. 69410.01 (white).
❊ LINEN. 100% linen. 52" wide. No. 8565.01 (white).
❊ LINEN CANVAS. 100% linen. 52" wide. No. 8564.01 (natural).

CLASSIC REVIVALS

❊ TISSAGE GANDER. 100% linen. 60" wide. No. 13 (unbleached); No. 14 (bleached); No. 70 STR (red and white striped); No. 4 STR (blue and white striped); No. 4 (blue and white plaid); No. 2 (blue and white plaid).

DECORATORS WALK

❊ HANDKERCHIEF LINEN. 100% linen. 46" wide. No. HC4850 (white).
Other linen samples available on request.

SCALAMANDRÉ

❊ PRINT CLOTH. 100% linen. 51" wide. Warp 16 ends per inch, weft 12 ends per inch. No. L-10 (white). Can be dyed any color as a special order only. Minimum order 15 yards.

SCHUMACHER
COLONIAL WILLIAMSBURG REPRODUCTIONS

❊ GOVERNOR'S PALACE TABLE LINENS. British or Flemish, c. 1780–1800, damask weave. 100% linen. Document owned

LINENS

by Colonial Williamsburg. Tablecloths No. 73397, 72" wide, 72" long; No. 73398, 72" wide, 98" long; No. 73999, 72" wide, 110" long; No. 73400, 72" wide, 128" long; No. 73401, 72" wide, 146" long. Napkins No. 73396, 24" wide, 24" long.

STROHEIM & ROMANN

❀ PLAIN LINEN. 100% linen. 54" wide. No. 47007 (natural)

HAMILTON-ADAMS
ULSTER WEAVING COMPANY

Both Hamilton-Adams and Ulster stock dozens of types of white, brown and dyed linen in a variety of colors, textures, widths and weaves, including fine cambrics. The best procedure is to write describing what you want and to request samples and a piece list. At Hamilton-Adams the minimum order is 50 yards; at Ulster Weaving Company the minimum order is five yards, but a premium of $1 per yard is charged for orders of less than 25 yards. Still, the variety and quality are almost impossible to find elsewhere.

BETSY BOURDON

Handwoven linen made to your order in checked or plain designs, twill or tabby weave. 100% linen or cotton-linen mixtures.

CAROL BROWN

❀ HANDKERCHIEF LINEN. 100% linen. Various widths. Request sample of current stock before ordering.

ANDREA CESARI

Custom weaving of linens in widths up to 40 inches of patterns requiring up to 8 harnesses. Uses commercially dyed yarns, although custom dyeing with vegetable dyes can be arranged. Weave structures based on published period drafts or your document.

JANENE CHARBENEAU

Custom reproduction of handwoven linens in checked, textured or plain designs. Natural, bleached or custom dyed.

MARY ELVA ERF

Custom reproduction of handwoven linens in natural or bleached threads. Specializes in documented 18th-century and Shaker drafts.

RABBIT GOODY

Custom reproduction of handwoven linens in checked and textured designs. Can work from your sample or published weavers' drafts. Natural, bleached or custom dyed.

❀ M's AND O's. Among the most popular early 19th-century handwoven table linen patterns. Documents in many collections. See also Gallagher. Available in 100% linen or 100% cotton for table cloths, towels and napkins. White.

CONSTANCE LA LENA, SUNFLOWER STUDIO

❀ CANVAS LINEN. 100% linen. 30" wide. Handwoven. No. B3.4 (cream white).

❀ LINEN DRILL. 100% linen. 30" wide. Twill. Handwoven. No. C1.3 (cream white).

❀ PURE LINEN. 100% linen. 30" wide. Handwoven. No.B3.2 (cream white).

❀ TOWCLOTH. 100% linen. 30" wide. Woven of 50% flax linen and 50% tow. Handwoven. No. A4.2 (brown only).

THE SCARLET LETTER

Unbleached and lightly bleached linens, green linen and linsey-woolsey, some handwoven. Balanced weaves especially suitable for counted thread embroidery; 25, 30, 35 and 45 count.

KATHLEEN B. SMITH

❀ COMMON LINEN. 100% linen. 36" wide. No. 220 (creamy bleached).

❀ DYED LINENS. 100% linen. Medium and common weights. 54–60" wide. No. 227. Write for samples.

❀ FINE LINEN. 100% linen. 36" wide. No. 207 (white).

❀ FINE SHEER. 100% linen. 46" wide. No. 224 (natural).

❀ FINE SHEER. 100% linen. 36" wide. No. 225 (white stripe).

❀ HUCKABACK. 100% linen. 22" wide. No. 223 (white linen).

❀ MEDIUM WEIGHT LINEN. 100% linen. 36", 54" or 72" wide. No. 206 (white).

❀ NATURAL GRAY AND WHITE STRIPED LINEN. 100% linen. 58" wide. No. 222.

MARY WORLEY

Handwoven linens custom woven based on your document or other published historical patterns. Uses single-ply linen

Handwoven toweling, three cotton-linen plaids and M's and O's. Mary Worley.

and natural dyes. Checks and plaids as well as various patterns derived from weave structures such as twill, "M's and O's," "Birdseye" or "Huckaback." Suitable for bed and table linens, curtains and toweling.

LINSEY-WOOLSEY

Despite its extreme popularity as a romantic symbol of the frugal, homespun American, linsey-woolsey actually was not a common fabric in the early years of this country. For those whose documentation requires it, good sources are listed here.

BETSY BOURDON

Custom handwoven linsey-woolsey. Your choice of colors.

CONSTANCE LA LENA, SUNFLOWER STUDIO

❀ HEAVYWEIGHT LINSEY-WOOLSEY. 50% linen, 50% wool. 30" wide. Handwoven. No. A4.1 (cream white); 35 additional colors available.

❀ LIGHTWEIGHT LINSEY-WOOLSEY. 50% linen, 50% wool.

LIGHTWEIGHT LINSEY-WOOLSEY, Sunflower Studio. Cream white and other colors.

30" wide. Handwoven. No. B3.1 (cream white); 35 additional colors available.
❀ LINSEY-WOOLSEY TWILL. 50% linen, 50% wool. 30" wide. Handwoven. No. C1.4 (cream white); 35 additional colors available.

KATHLEEN B. SMITH
❀ LINSEY-WOOLSEY. 50% linen, 50% wool. Up to 54" wide. Custom woven in your choice of colors.

MADRAS MUSLINS

Madras muslins are pattern-woven curtain fabrics woven on jacquard looms in Scotland from c. 1870. The industry centered in Glasgow and in towns in the Irvine Valley. The cloth is characterized by a fine gauze ground with pattern motifs woven into it with extra threads. The area between the pattern motifs is at first covered with floating weft threads, but these are then cut away, leaving the characteristic short, soft, fringelike edges on the wrong side of each pattern motif.

Decorators Walk

❀ Formal Madras. 58% cotton, 42% polyester. 81" wide, 46¾" repeat. No. HC83385 (cream).

Greeff Fabrics, representing E. C. Carter

Most of the madras designs currently available through Greeff are suitable for window curtains for mid-20th-century interiors.

❀ Fairlie. Scotland, c.1870–1920. jacquard madras. 100% cotton. 48" wide, 19" repeat. No. 32495 (ivory).

❀ Hurlford. Scotland, c. 1870–1920, jacquard madras. 100% cotton. 48" wide, 29" repeat. No. 32490 (ivory).

❀ Kirkmichael. Scotland, c.1870–1920, jacquard madras. 100% cotton. 48" wide. No. 32500 (ivory).

MARSEILLES WEAVES

Marseilles weaves are adaptations of late 18th- and early 19th-century machine-woven bed coverings. In many ways these are not appropriate for restoration use because individual design elements have been taken from units originally composed as large rectangles and have been rearranged to create continuous yardage. They are listed here only as suggestions for use in certain high-traffic or low-budget projects where a handmade reproduction of a white bed covering cannot be obtained.

Brunschwig & Fils

❀ Bedford Quilt. 100% cotton. 50" wide, 10½" repeat. No. 8065.02 (natural).

❀ March Bank Cotton Matelasse. 100% cotton. 54" wide, 13" repeat. Adapted from a textile document at Winterthur Museum. No. 8202.02 (natural).

NETTED CANOPIES

Netted canopies were a popular means of covering bed tester frames in the late 19th and 20th centuries. Little or no evidence has been found for use of netted canopies prior to the mid-19th century. It appears that they were used to decorate bed frames after the fashion for fully enclosing fabric bed hangings began to disappear.

Carter Canopies

Hand-tied canopies in 100% cotton, either bleached white or natural. "Double Diamond," "Single Diamond," "Straight

DOUBLE DIAMOND
NETTED CANOPY,
c. 1880–present. Carter
Canopies. Bleached
white or natural.

SINGLE DIAMOND
NETTED CANOPY,
c. 1880–present. Carter
Canopies. Bleached
white or natural.

Edge," "Large Scallop" and "Lover's Knot." Designs in twin, double, queen and king sizes.

Virginia Goodwin

Hand-tied canopies provided in any size from doll bed to modern king-size bed. Send exact measurements when ordering and indicate if bed has flat or arched tester. 100% cotton, 2-ply cotton thread in cream or white. Made with 16" deep valance; additional depth may be ordered. Standard patterns include "Single Diamond," "Double Diamond," "Straight Edge Diamond" and "Round Scallop."

Margery Howe

Hand-tied canopies custom made in 2-ply 100% cotton thread, bleached or unbleached. Experienced netter can reproduce complex designs for canopies and fringes as well as standard single and double diamond patterns.

Laura Copenhaver Industries

Hand-tied canopies in 100% cotton thread available in either natural cream or bleached white. When ordering, give exact length and width of canopy frame. Two traditional designs are "Single Diamond Point Canopy" and "Double Diamond Point Canopy."

The Log Haus

Hand-tied canopies in 2-ply 100% cotton thread in both white and off-white. Sized to fit standard twin, double, queen- or king- size beds. "Single Diamond Pattern," "Double Diamond Pattern."

OSNABURG

Amazon Vinegar & Pickling Works Drygoods

❀ Osnaburg. 100% cotton. 44–45" wide (natural).

Gohn Brothers

Order by name of goods.
❀ Osnaburg. 100% cotton. 45" wide. Unbleached.

Constance La Lena, Sunflower Studio

❀ Brown Osnaburg. 100% linen. 30" wide. Handwoven. No. B3.3 (natural brown).

TIOGA

❀ OSNABURG. 100% cotton. 48" wide. Natural. Order by name.

Although no documentary museum reproductions of plush are currently available, one can safely use any densely woven wool or mohair velvet with a deep pile, preferably at least ³⁄₁₆ inch or ¼ inch. Plush can also be embossed (see Embossing).

BAKER DECORATIVE FABRICS

❀ COLOGNE. 100% mohair. 54" wide. No. 74-170 series (8 colors).

BRUNSCHWIG & FILS

❀ METROPOLITAN MOHAIR VELVET. 51% cotton, 49% mohair. 55" wide. No. 6313.01 series (20 colors).

CLARENCE HOUSE

❀ VELOURS MOHAIR. 64% mohair, 36% cotton. 50" wide. No. 10379 (33 colors).

CLASSIC REVIVALS

❀ MOHAIR VELVET. 100% mohair. 50" wide. No. 344-3200 series (20 colors).

DECORATORS WALK

❀ DENSEPILE PLUSH. 52% mohair, 25% cotton, 24% polynosic (100% mohair pile). 50" wide. No. IS1100 series (36 colors).
❀ MOHAIR PLUSH. 60% mohair, 40% cotton (100% mohair pile on 100% cotton back). 54" wide. No. T34100 series (36 colors).
❀ WOOL PLUSH. 50% cotton, 50% wool. 50" wide. No. T38555-38574 (20 colors).
❀ WOOL PLUSH. 50% wool, 50% rayon face, 100% cotton back. 54" wide. No. T40390-40428 (38 colors).
❀ WOOL PLUSH. 100% wool pile, 100% cotton back. 55" wide. No. T41266-41270 (5 colors).

LEE JOFA

❀ MOHAIR VELOUR. 61% cotton, 39% mohair (100% mohair

pile on a 100% cotton back). 50" wide. No. 805120 series (14 colors).

OLD WORLD WEAVERS

❀ PLUSH. 75% mohair, 25% cotton. 50" wide. No. J-11229-C (colors to order).

SCALAMANDRÉ

❀ BARONS PLUSH. 47% wool, 53% cotton. 51" wide. No. 98633-7; special colors to order.

STROHEIM & ROMANN

❀ DUSSELDORF. 100% mohair pile; backing 75% cotton, 25% rayon. 51" wide. No. 30800 series (33 colors).

PONGEE

CAROL BROWN

❀ PONGEE. 100% silk. Various widths. Request samples of current stock before ordering.

DECORATORS WALK

❀ PONGEE. 100% silk. 45" wide. No. HC63381 (off-white); No. HC63380 (natural).
❀ PONGEE. 100% silk. 50" wide. No. T35771 (natural); No. T35770 (white).

FAR EASTERN FABRICS

❀ PONGEE. 100% silk. 45" wide. Order by name. Write for current samples.

QUILTS

Reproductions of antique quilts are difficult to make, because the originals usually incorporated a number of different fabrics, most of which were clothing fabrics that have no counterparts on the modern market. Local and regional quilters guilds can be helpful with specific problems, and a few quilt reproductions are commercially available.

LAURA COPENHAVER INDUSTRIES

Offers quilts that are pieced, appliquéd and quilted by hand in standard color combinations or your choice of colors. Standard sizes are twin, double, queen or king; other sizes can be custom ordered. Other custom quilting services available, including quilting your own quilt top.

❀ FLOWER POT. Pieced in red and green, c.1850–1940.
❀ GOOSE TRACKS. Pieced in red and white, c.1850–1900.
❀ VIRGINIA BEAUTY. An appliqué design, c.1860–1940.
❀ WILD ROSE. An appliqué design, c.1860–1940.

When using rep cloths for reproduction work, bear in mind that 19th-century reps were woven with the ridges in a vertical dimension; in commercially woven modern reps the predominant ridges are horizontal. The visual effect of 19th-century reps can be replicated by correct placement of the ribs.

REP

JANENE CHARBENEAU

❀ REP. Handwoven adaptation of a wool-and-linen warp-faced fragment originally handwoven in Richmond, Va., and used for upholstery fabric. Document owned by the Valentine Museum, Richmond.

LEE JOFA

❀ HIGHLAND RIB CLOTH. 90% wool, 10% nylon. 59" wide. No.795350-795360 (20 colors).
❀ LUCIEN REP. 96% wool, 4% other fiber. 51" wide. No. 924300-924311 (6 colors).

SCALAMANDRÉ

❀ REGENT REP. 100% cotton. 52" wide. No.99754 series (22 colors).
❀ WOOL REP. 100% wool. 52" wide. No.99447 (7 colors).

CONSTANCE LA LENA, SUNFLOWER STUDIO

SERGE

❀ UPHOLSTERY SERGE. 100% wool. 36" wide. Handwoven. No. X14.12 (cream white); can be dyed to order, 36 colors available.

Plain and textured silks have never disappeared from production. Many excellent failles, moirés, satins and taffetas are available from companies specializing in drapery fabrics. Brunschwig & Fils, Scalamandré and Schumacher have designated certain of their patterns as museum reproductions, primarily because of criteria relating to texture. In addition, Clarence House, Classic Revivals, Decorators Walk, Old World Weavers and other companies have excellent

SILKS

silks. The variety is tremendous, making careful selection of a prototype essential. When working with a limited budget, one might also want to consider certain synthetics or fiber blends that closely resemble silks.

STRIPES

BRUNSCHWIG & FILS

❀ COURTISANNE SILK STRIPE. English, c.1840. 100% silk. 51" wide. Document, privately owned in Italy, originally used for a visiting dress. No.190659.00 (green).

❀ DE WOLF STRIPE. 100% cotton. 54" wide. No.7864.04 (8 colors), No.7865.04 (8 color combinations).

❀ MONTABERT TAFFETAS STRIPE. 59% viscose rayon, 41% acetate. No.30163.00 (gold and cream).

❀ NICE STRIPE. French, 1910–30, woven twill stripe. 56% cotton, 44% linen. 52" wide, 4¾" repeat. Document, in Brunschwig & Fils Archives, used as the seat upholstery and canopy for a beach chair.

❀ NORWICH WOOL STRIPE. 100% wool, woven stripe with twill face. 54" wide. No.63511.01 (red).

❀ SERGE WOVEN STRIPE. Probably American, c.1850, woven twill stripe. 60% linen, 40% cotton. 55" wide, 6" repeat. From a collection of merchant's or manufacturer's samples in No.63874.01 (green and cream); No.62877.01 (marine blue and raspberry).

COWTAN & TOUT

❀ CANDY STRIPE. Mid- to late 19th century. 100% cotton, glazed. 54" wide. No.88049-5 (blue on white ground); No. 88049-3 (red on white ground). Minimum order 2 yards.

❀ COLE STRIPE. 19th century. 100% cotton, glazed. 54" wide, ⅛" horizontal repeat. No. 8240 (blue); No. 8239 (beige).

❀ TURNBULL STRIPE. Mid- to late 19th century. 100% cotton, glazed. 54" wide. No.1210 (light blue). Minimum order 2 yards.

OLD WORLD WEAVERS

❀ ORGEVAL. 100% cotton. 51" wide, 4⅛" repeat. No. FV-56175 (moired navy with seafoam and gold).

Rose Cumming Chintzes

❀ STRIPES. Mid- to late 19th century. 100% cotton, glazed. 54" wide. No.316-7 (red); No.316-2 (blue).

SCALAMANDRÉ

❀ DIRECTOIRE. 34% silk, 66% cotton. 50" wide. A taffeta texture. No. 1908-007 (rose and off-white).

❀ STRIPED SATIN. 100% silk. 50" wide. No. 1236-1 (coral and bone).

SCHUMACHER
COLONIAL WILLIAMSBURG REPRODUCTIONS

Documents at Colonial Williamsburg, Williamsburg, Va.

❀ WILLIAMSBURG LINEN STRIPE. American, 18th century. 55% linen, 45% cotton. 54" wide, 1" repeat. Document has linen warp and wool weft. No. 86552 (fern).

❀ WILLIAMSBURG STRIPE. 18th century. 100% cotton. 50" wide. No. 132962 (red).

❀ WYTHE HOUSE STRIPE. Indian, c. 1750–1800. 100% cotton. 50" wide. No. 111342 (old red).

DECORATORS WALK

TAMBOUR CURTAINS

❀ EMBROIDERED CURTAINS. 100% cotton. 48" wide, 108" long. No. HC77095 (ivory); No. HC77094 (white). Sold in pairs only.

❀ TAMBOUR CURTAINS. 100% cotton net. 67" wide, 126" long (made with adjustable open tops). No. HC85091 (champagne).

❀ TAMBOUR CURTAINS. c. 1895–1930. 100% cotton net. 52" wide, 126" long (made with adjustable open tops). No. HC84395 (white).

❀ TAMBOUR CURTAINS. 100% cotton batiste. 52" wide, 108" long, plus 8" border on lower edge and one side. No. HC85145 (white). Sold in pairs only.

❀ WHITE TAMBOUR CURTAIN. 100% polyester. 44" wide, 108" long. Sheer woven fabric with allover repeated motif that resembles Indian Chikan work. No. HC77069.

❀ WHITE TAMBOUR CURTAINS. 100% cotton batiste. 44" wide, 108" long. No. HC77094. Sold in pairs only.

GREEFF FABRICS

This firm stocks a variety of tambour curtain designs that are suitable for late 19th-century work.

SCALAMANDRÉ

❀ ROSALIE. 100% cotton. 53" wide, 137" long. Designs chain stitched on net. Document at Rosalie, Headquarters of the

Mississippi Society of the Daughters of the American Revolution, Natchez, Miss. No. 96530-1 (off-white). Sold as panels in pairs only, one right, one left. No cuttings available.
❀ WHITE HOUSE OF THE CONFEDERACY. 100% cotton. 53" wide, 137" long. Designs chain stitched on net. Document owned by the White House of the Confederacy, Richmond, Va. No. 20079-1 (off-white). Sold as panels in pairs only, one right, one left. No cuttings available.

TAPES

During the years 1730–1860 and even later, the edges of curtains and the seams in seat upholstery and loose cases were often covered with applied tapes. Usually made of cotton or linen, the tapes often were striped in more than one color. Some mid-18th-century examples feature floral sprig in warp floats. A sample card illustrating typical stripes is illustrated in Carlano, *French Textiles*, fig. 13.

Such tapes are seldom reproduced commercially, and handweavers have difficulty finding threads of appropriate dimensions. The weave structures themselves are not particularly difficult.

SCALAMANDRÉ

❀ STRIPED TAPE. 100% cotton. The closest representation on the commercial market to the handwoven striped tape commonly used for binding chintz curtains, valances and bed coverings c. 1820–50. No. V-203-1 (multi).

KATHLEEN B. SMITH

❀ COTTON TAPE, TABBY WEAVE. 100% cotton. $\frac{3}{16}$", $\frac{3}{8}$", $\frac{5}{8}$" or 1" wide; 1" heavyweight. No. 301 (white).
❀ COTTON TAPE, TWILL WEAVE. 100% cotton. $\frac{1}{4}$", $\frac{3}{8}$", $\frac{1}{2}$", $\frac{5}{8}$", $\frac{3}{4}$" or 1" wide. No. 302 (white or black).
❀ LINEN TAPE, FINE DUTCH TABBY WEAVE. 100% linen. $\frac{1}{4}$", $\frac{3}{8}$", $\frac{1}{2}$", $\frac{5}{8}$" or $\frac{3}{4}$" wide. No. 311 (natural brown or bleached).
❀ LINEN TAPE, TABBY WEAVE. 100% linen. $\frac{1}{4}$", $\frac{3}{8}$", $\frac{1}{2}$", $\frac{3}{4}$" or 1" wide. No. 310 (natural brown or bleached).
❀ SILK RIBBON. 100% silk. 4mm, $\frac{3}{16}$" or 7mm wide (white).
❀ SUPER HOLLAND RIBBED TAPE. 100% linen. $\frac{1}{2}$" or $\frac{5}{8}$" wide. No. 314 (white).
❀ WORSTED TAPE. 100% wool. $\frac{3}{4}$", 1" or $1\frac{1}{4}$" wide. Handwoven. No. 335 (colors to your specifications, using natural or vegetable dyes).

ULSTER WEAVING COMPANY

❀ COTTON TAPE. 100% cotton. Tabby weave. 1" wide. White only. Sold in rolls of 50M (54.68 yards). Order by name. Linen tape is no longer available from this firm.

TICKING

Closely woven cotton and linen fabrics used for bed ticking have always come in a variety of patterns, usually stripes. Modern blue-and-white striped bed ticking is little changed in appearance since the late 18th century. Waverly's "Cranston Plaid" (p. 223) is a documentary reproduction of a factory-woven, early 19th-century bed ticking in the textile collection at Old Sturbridge Village, Sturbridge, Mass. For those who wish to use handwoven ticking, one pattern of stripes is given in Grace Rogers Cooper's *The Copp Family Textiles*. Documented examples from the Robbins Family of East Lexington, Mass., can be found in the collections of the Society for the Preservation of New England Antiquities. The Wintherthur Museum and Colonial Williamsburg have other examples.

ALEXANDRA'S TEXTILE

❀ TICKING. 100% cotton. Three different patterns available. Catalog has color illustrations of all.

Early 19th-century ticking, used by the Copp Family, Stonington, Conn. (Smithsonian Institution)

Netted cotton fringes, c.1790–1810, used by the Copp Family, Stonington, Conn. (Smithsonian Institution)

JANENE CHARBENEAU

❊ TICKING. 100% cotton. Various widths. Custom woven. Pattern of colors and stripes can reproduce your document or published sources.

GOHN BROTHERS

❊ PILLOW TICKING. 100% cotton. 32" wide, striped. 36" wide, ivory.

CONSTANCE LA LENA, SUNFLOWER STUDIO

❊ LINEN TICKING. 100% linen. 30" wide. No. E2.1 (blue and cream).

RABBIT GOODY

❊ TICKING. 100% linen. Custom woven to your specifications.

KATHLEEN B. SMITH

❊ BLACK STRIPE TICKING. 100% cotton. 56" wide. No. 219.
❊ BLUE STRIPE TICKING. 100% cotton. 32" wide. No. 215.
❊ WHITE HERRINGBONE TICKING. 100% cotton. 56" wide. No. 221.

TRIMMINGS

Many historic fabric treatments, especially in the 19th century, made use of complex trimmings. Custom reproduction of these is almost always possible, but it is very expensive. For simple fringes, braids, cords or tapes, it is wise to check available stock before contracting for custom reproduction. Fine trimmings are displayed in the showrooms of Brunschwig & Fils, Clarence House, Cowtan & Tout, Decorator's Walk, Osborne & Little, Schumacher, Scalamandré and others. Some independent showrooms offer imports from Manuel Canovas or Louvet et Mauny in Paris.

Custom work is often necessary to match an example of original trimming. Several firms will undertake this kind of work, notably Scalamandré, Brunschwig & Fils, Clarence House and Old World Weavers. Scalamandré has specialized equipment and trained personnel in their American mill to undertake this kind of work. They are in great demand, so there may be significant delays. The same guidelines one would observe for custom reproduction of any furnishing fabric should be carefully observed in order to assure a satisfactory result.

Eighteenth-century tapes and fringes were handwoven on simple looms, and a modern handweaver can reproduce them without difficulty, provided the correct yarns are available. Hand-tied or netted fringes can also be reproduced easily with cotton threads. One style can also be ordered directly:

CARTER CANOPIES

❀ HAND-TIED FRINGE. 100% cotton, 5" deep. No. ECIO (natural cream or white).

LAURA COPENHAVER INDUSTRIES

❀ HAND-TIED COTTON FRINGE. 100% cotton. Available in 3" or 5" "peacock tail" style or as insertion. Order by name (natural cream or white).

VELVET

Plain and figured velvets have scarcely changed. They are readily available in mohair, cotton, linen and silk from most drapery fabric manufacturers. Washable synthetic velvets are also available. They are sometimes an acceptable inexpensive substitute for silk velvet if the color and texture are similar. Velvets can be embossed in a wide variety of period designs (see Embossing). A few velvets have been designated museum reproductions:

SCALAMANDRÉ

❀ GRAND CANAL VELVET. Suitable for late 19th-century upholstery and drapery. 100% cotton. 54" wide. No. 98655 series (27 colors).

STROHEIM & ROMANN

❀ WINTERTHUR VELVET. 100% cotton. 54" wide. No. 40488-40498 (11 colors).

WOOLS

The texture and finishing of woolen fabrics have changed considerably over the last 200 years. For restoration work focusing on the period before 1850, unless color simulation is the sole criterion, it is necessary to use documentary reproductions (such as those listed on pp. 37–42) or handwoven wool fabrics using tightly spun yards.

BRUNSCHWIG & FILS

❀ WOOL CASEMENT. 100% wool. 53" wide. No. 69320.01 (natural).

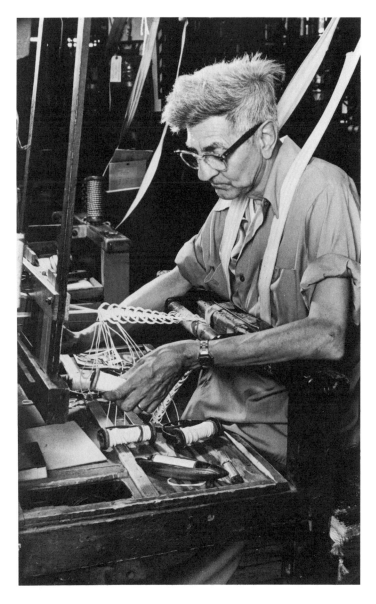

Handweaving trim-
mings at the Scalaman-
dré mill on a specially
re-created loom.

DECORATORS WALK

❀ IMPERIAL WOOL WORSTED. 100% wool. 54" wide. No.
IS1376-00 (21 colors).

SCALAMANDRÉ

❀ ITALIAN CHALLIS WOOL CASEMENT. English, c. 1840–60.
100% wool. 53" wide. Document owned by Historic Hudson Valley, Tarrytown, N.Y. No.98094-1 (cream).

WOOLS,
HANDWOVEN

BETSY BOURDON

❀ WOOL TWILL. 100% wool. Handwoven in yarns colored with your choice of colors in either vegetable or chemical dyes.

ANDREA CESARI

❀ FLANNEL. 100% wool in 2/38 worsted, 48 epi. Can be done in solid color or check, either natural wool or your choice of available colors.

RABBIT GOODY

Custom reproduction of documented wool textiles. Has successfully reproduced kersey, ticksett, fustian and similar weaves. Can work from your sample or from written documentation and her considerable experience in this field.

CONSTANCE LA LENA, SUNFLOWER STUDIO

Can supply several of the early types, including camlet, worsted, serge and shalloon. Custom woven in your choice of colors. Minimum order 20 yards.

KATHLEEN B. SMITH

❀ WOOLEN TWILL. 100% wool. 57" wide. No. 212 (natural or your choice of vegetable-dyed colors).
❀ WORSTED TWILL. 100% wool. 45" wide. No. 211 (natural or your choice of vegetable-dyed colors).
❀ WORSTED WARP, COTTON WEFT. 50% wool, 50% cotton. 45" wide. No. 213 (natural or your choice of vegetable-dyed colors).

MARY WORLEY

Custom handweaving of woolens in twill and tabby weave. All natural dyes.

APPENDIX

The suppliers marked with an asterisk (*) in the following list sell directly to the public through their shops or catalogs.

Most of the remaining firms listed are manufacturing firms that operate their own wholesale showrooms that are open "to the trade only." This means that their fabrics are sold only through architects, interior designers and the decorating departments of fine retail and furniture stores. In some cases, the manufacturers will sell goods directly to nonprofit institutions such as museums, historical societies, preservation agencies and state-owned historic properties. When ordering or requesting information about a specific fabric, begin by writing to the main office of a firm. It may choose to deal with clients directly or may refer them to a local agent. Arrangements for custom reproductions should always be made through the main office; personal consultation is usually more satisfactory than correspondence.

*AMAZON VINEGAR & PICKLING WORKS DRYGOODS. 2218 East 11th Street, Davenport, Iowa 52803 (319) 322-6800 or (309) 786-3504

BAILEY & GRIFFIN. 1406 Mermaid Lane, Philadelphia, Pa. 19118 (212) 836-4350

BAKER DECORATIVE FABRICS. Subsidiary of Baker, Knapp & Tubbs

BAKER, KNAPP & TUBBS, INC. 917 Merchandise Mart, Chicago, Ill. 60654 (312) 329-9410

BLATT BILLIARDS. 809 Broadway, New York, N.Y. 10013 (212) 674-8855

BASSETT MCNAB COMPANY. 1032 Arch Street, Philadelphia, Pa. 19107 (215) 922-8717

*CAROL BROWN. Putney, Vt. 05346 (802) 387-5875. Supplier of natural fiber fabrics, specializing in those for clothing. Often has Indian cottons, imported linens, pongee, tussah silk and a wide variety of cotton prints.

BRUNSCHWIG & FILS. 979 Third Avenue, New York, N.Y. 10022 (212) 838-7878

CLARENCE HOUSE. 211 East 58th Street, New York, N.Y. 10022 (212) 752-2890

*CLASSIC REVIVALS. One Design Center Place, Boston, Mass. 02210 (617) 574-9030

COWTAN & TOUT. 979 Third Avenue, New York, N.Y. 10022 (212) 753-4488

DECORATORS WALK. 171 East 56th Street, New York, N.Y. 10022 (212) 319-7100 Representing: Lee Behren Silks, The Henrose Company, Henry Cassen, Peter Schneiders' Sons and Company, J. H. Thorpe and Company.

*DORR MILL STORE. Guild, N.H. 03754 (603) 863-1197

*FAR EASTERN FABRICS. 171 Madison Avenue, New York, N.Y. 10016 (212) 683-2623

FONTHILL. Showroom: 979 Third Avenue, New York, N.Y. 10022. Main Office: 578 Nepperhan Avenue, Yonkers, N.Y. 10701 (914) 376-2000

*GOHN BROTHERS. Box 111, 105 South Main Street, Middlebury, Ind. 46540-0111 (219) 825-2400

GREEFF FABRICS. Showroom: 155 East 56th Street, New York, N.Y. 10022. Main Office: 200 Garden City Plaza, Garden City, N.Y. 11530 (800) 223-0357. Representing: Warners of London, E. C. Carter & Son, Inc.

HALLIE GREER. Cushing Corners Road, P.O. Box 150, Freedom, N.H. 03836 (603) 539-5012

*HAMILTON-ADAMS. 104 West 40th Street, 8th floor, New York, N.Y. 10018 (212) 221-0800

*THE HUMPHRIES WEAVING COMPANY. De Vere Mill, Queen Street, Hedingham, Halstead, Essex, England CO9 3HA (0787) 61193

IAN WALL, LTD. 979 Third Avenue, New York, N.Y. 10022 (212) 758-5337

*J. R. BURROWS & COMPANY. P.O. Box 1739, Jamaica Plain, Mass. 02130 (617) 524-1795

LEE JOFA INC. Showroom: 979 Third Avenue, New York, N.Y. 10022. Main Office: 800 Central Boulevard, Carlstadt, N.J. 07072 (201) 438-8444

*LONDON LACE. 167 Newbury Street, Boston, Mass. 02116
(617) 267-3506

OLD WORLD WEAVERS. 979 Third Avenue, New York, N.Y.
10022 (212) 355-7186

OSBORNE & LITTLE. Showroom: 979 Third Avenue, New
York, N.Y. 10022 (212) 751-3333. Main Office: 65 Commerce Road, Stamford, Conn. 06902 (203) 359-1500

*PIERRE DEUX. Showroom: 870 Madison Avenue, New York,
N.Y. 10021. Main office: 147 Palmer Avenue, Mamaro-
neck, N.Y. 10543. 17 stores across the United States; write
for nearest location.

ROSE CUMMING CHINTZES. 232 East 59th Street, New York,
N.Y. 10022 (212) 758-0844.

*RUE DE FRANCE. 78 Thames Street, Newport, R.I. 02840
(800) 777-0998

SANDERSON. 979 Avenue, New York, NY 10022 (212) 319-7220

SCALAMANDRÉ. Showroom: 950 Third Avenue, New York,
N.Y. 10022. Special order division: 37-24 24th Street, Long
Island City, N.Y. 11101 (718) 361-8500

*THE SCARLET LETTER. P.O. Box 397, Sullivan, Wis. 53178
(414) 593-8470

F. SCHUMACHER AND COMPANY. Showroom: 939 Third Avenue,
New York, N.Y. 10022 (212) 415-3900. Main Office: 79
Madison Avenue, New York, N.Y. 10016 (212) 213-7900.

STROHEIM & ROMANN. Showroom: 155 East 56th Street,
New York, N.Y. 10022 Main Office: 3111 Thomason Avenue, Long Island City, N.Y. 11101 (212) 691-0700

THEODORE MEREWITZ TEXTILES, INC. 415 West Huron Street,
Chicago, Ill. 60610 (telephone unlisted). Supplier of trimmings, will do custom work.

*TIOGA. 200 South Hartman Street, York, Pa. 17403 (717)
843-5139

*ULSTER WEAVING COMPANY. 148 Madison Avenue, New
York, N.Y. 10016 (212) 684-5534

WAVERLY FABRICS. 79 Madison Avenue, New York, N.Y.
10016 (212) 213-8100

SPECIALTY
SOURCES

HANDWOVEN FABRICS

Weavers guilds in many cities and regions can provide information about persons who will undertake custom reproduction of handwoven yard goods and coverlets. Several who have specialized in these are:

*ALEXANDRA'S TEXTILE. 5606 State Route 37, Delaware, Ohio 43015 (614) 369-1817. Also known as The 1817 Shoppe and The Seraph East-West (614) 369-1817

*ANDA BIJHOUWER. Box 16, Phippsburg Center, Maine 04562 (207) 389-2033

*BETSY BOURDON. Scribner Hill, Wolcott, Vt. 05680 (802) 472-6508

*ANDREA CESARI. P.O. Box 123, Nobleboro, Maine 04555 (207) 832-5088

* JANENE CHARBENEAU. 3426 Stuart Avenue, Richmond, Va. 23221 (804) 358-0417

*MARY ELVA ERF. 127 Carriage Drive, Glastonbury, Conn. 06033 (203) 633-4244

*FAMILY HEIR-LOOM WEAVERS, DAVID KLINE. RFD No. 3, Box 59E, Red Lion, Pa. 17356 (717) 246-2431

*RABBIT GOODY WOOLS & CASHMERE, BRAMBLE BRIDGE WEAVE SHOP. 21 Main Street, Cherry Valley, N.Y. 13320 (607) 264-8400

JSP DESIGNS. 235 North Street, Route 112, Saco, Maine 04072 (207) 283-4408

*CONSTANCE LA LENA, SUNFLOWER STUDIO. 2851 Road B1/2, Grand Junction, Colo. 81501. (719) 243-3409. All fabrics are custom woven and require a minimum order of 20 yards

*KATHLEEN B. SMITH. P.O. Box 48, West Chesterfield, Mass. 01084 (413) 296-4437

*THE C. S. SMUCKERS. R.R. 1, State Route 287, West Liberty, Ohio 43357 (513) 465-2507

*MARY WORLEY. Mountain Road, Cornwall, R.D. 2, Middlebury, Vt. 05753 (802) 462-2315

COVERLETS

*VIRGINIA GOODWIN. Route 2, Box 770, Big Hill Road, Boone, N.C. 28607 (704) 264-7704

*MAGGIE KENNEDY, OZARK WEAVING STUDIO. P.O. Box 286, Camp Hill, Ariz. 72717 (501) 824-3920

*LAURA COPENHAVER INDUSTRIES, INC. P.O. Box 149, Marion, Va. 24354 (800) 227-6797; in Va. (703) 783-4663

*WILLIAM LEINBACH. 356 Royers Road, Myerstown, Pa. 17067 (717) 866-5525

NETTED BED CANOPIES AND EDGINGS

*CARTER CANOPIES. Elsie M. Carter, P.O. Box 808, Route 2, Box 270-G, Troutman, N.C. 28166-0808 (704) 528-4071

*PATRICK DORMAN. 115 Bellevue Avenue East, No. 301, Seattle, Wash. 98122 (206) 322-5890. Edgings only.

*VIRGINIA GOODWIN. Route 2, Box 770, Big Hill Road, Boone, N.C. 28607 (704) 264-7704

*MRS. SHELDON HOWE. 4 Lorita Lane, Northfield, Mass. 01360 (413) 498-2007. Traditional Deerfield designs; custom orders only

*LAURA COPENHAVER INDUSTRIES. P.O. Box 149, Marion, Va. 24354 (800) 227-6797; in Va. (703) 783-4663

*THE LOG HAUS. Route 1, Box 272, Blowing Rock, N.C. 28605 (704) 264-5664

SHAKER CHAIR TAPE

*SHAKER WORKSHOPS. P.O. Box 1028, Concord, Mass. 01742. 100% cotton tape ⅝" and 1" wide. 11 solid colors and 2 stripes in 5- and 10-yard rolls. Free color samples available.

TOBACCO CLOTH

*WILSON'S. Personal Shopper, 285 Main Street, Greenfield, Mass. 01301 (413) 774-4326

GLOSSARY

Identification of textiles referred to in early documents is complicated by the ways in which the meaning of the names has changed over time. Fabrics denoted by certain names have changed in texture and appearance or even in characteristic fiber content, making it important to understand the definition of the names at specific historical periods. In addition, subtle differences that were once commonly understood by manufacturers, merchants and consumers are now extremely difficult to discern. In some cases, several different names were used for the same type of goods, with the name denoting a place of manufacture rather than a distinctly different type of fabric. The best way to begin to determine the meaning of a specific name at a particular period is to consult a contemporary dictionary, encyclopedia or merchant's guide. In addition to works of a broad general interest, the following specialized publications are particularly helpful:

Beck, S. William. *The Draper's Dictionary, A Manual of Textile Fabrics, Their History and Applications.* London, 1882.

Brown, C. M., and C. L. Gates. *Scissors and Yardstick; or, All About Dry Goods. Hartford.* Conn.: C. M. Brown and F. W. Jacqua, 1872.

Cole, George S. *A Complete Dictionary of Dry Goods.* Rev. ed. New York: Textile Publishing Company, 1892.

Dickinson, William, ed. *A General Commercial Dictionary Comprehending Trade, Manufactures and Navigation, Also Agriculture as Far as It Is Connected with Commerce.* 2d ed. London, 1819.

Montgomery, Florence. *Textiles in America, 1650–1870.* New York: W. W. Norton, 1984.

ANILINE DYES. Dyes made from coal tars that produce characteristic strong shades of purple, blue, green and fuchsia; the first English patent for the process was issued in 1856.

APPLIQUÉ. An ornamental technique in which a design motif of one layer of cloth is cut out and sewn or glued onto a larger layer, which serves as the background.

ARMURE. Curtain fabric with designs woven on a rep ground, usually cotton. Can be made of a solid color or a combination of colors. Used in the late 19th and early 20th centuries for portieres and couch covers.

BAIZE. Coarsely woven woolen cloth in a tabby weave, finished with a long nap to imitate felt. Used in the 18th and 19th centuries as a protective cover for carpets, tables and bookcases as well as for clothing, especially the lining of cloaks and coats. Not particularly successful as a writing surface unless glued down but sometimes used in this way despite its soft texture. Green appears to have been the most common color, although brown, blue and red were also used. Long napped baize is illustrated in Montgomery, *Textiles in America,* pl. D-98.

BATISTE. Fine lightweight cotton or bleached white linen, usually cotton.

BATTING. Large sheets of carded fibers that are used for interlining in quilts, comforters and some clothing. Historically either cotton or wool; now polyester and other fibers are also used.

BEMBERG. Trade name for rayon made by a special process owned by the American Bemberg Company. Occasionally loosely used to refer to any rayon.

BIRD'S EYE. A woven spot or figure thought to resemble a bird's eye. A popular motif in table linens and cotton toweling, also in coverlets and blankets. In 20th-century commercial bird's eye fabrics, the filling yarns are loosely spun to make the fabric more absorbent. Illustrated in Montgomery, *Textiles in America,* pl. D-101.

"BIZARRE" STYLE. A style of woven silk, c. 1705–20, with characteristic twisted columns and grand scrolls ending in delicate flowers.

BLOCK PRINTING. Handprinting technique by which dyestuffs and mordants are transferred to fabric by means of handcarved wood blocks. This technique has been almost completely replaced by cylinder or screen printing.

BLOTCH. In printing textiles, background color applied with the areas intended for the design reserved (i.e., left white) to heighten the color contrast.

BOBBINET. Machine-woven or "imitation" cotton lace, having a nearly hexagonal mesh. The foundation of machine-made lace. First successfully made in 1809 by John Heathcoat in England. Also refers to curtains with machine-woven insertion and edgings appliqued to a machine-made net ground cloth.

BOCKING. Coarse wool flannel or baize cloth, named for its

place of origin, a city in Essex, England, well known in the 18th and 19th centuries for the manufacture of this type of cloth.

BOLTON COUNTERPANE. A bed covering woven in white cotton with looped pile forming geometric designs. Named for the town in Lancashire that specialized in their production. Illustrated in Montgomery, *Textiles in America,* fig. D-19. Similar counterpanes were produced by Elizabeth Wildes Perkins Bourne in Kennebunk, Maine, c. 1810–20. See Sprague, *Agreeable Situations,* pp. 217–18, fig. 5-4.

BOURETTE. A slubby silk usually spun from flawed cocoons; can be twill or plain weave.

BROADCLOTH. Firm tabby woven wool, fulled tightly, napped and shorn to a smooth, velvety surface. Woven on wide looms that produced goods up to 63 inches wide. Illustrated in Montgomery, *Textiles in America,* pl. D-102.

BROCADE. A figured fabric in which the design is woven in additional contrasting color wefts restricted to the area of the design and not extended from selvage to selvage; these threads appear on the surface only in the areas required by the design. The background fabric can be tabby, twill or satin weave. The designs are frequently flowers or sprays of foliage. Most brocades are silk, although they can be woven in other fibers and the patterns can be woven in gold or silver threads. Illustrated in Montgomery, *Textiles in America,* fig. D-23.

BROCATELLE. A special form of lampas with a pattern in one weave on a ground of a contrasting texture, sometimes a satin weave. Often, heavy linen is used for extra ground wefts, which contrast with the silk pattern wefts but do not appear on the surface of the fabric. The cloth is woven tightly, thus sometimes causing the design elements to appear puffy; it can be made flat by adjusting the weaving tensions for the different fibers. In the last quarter of the 19th century, inexpensive brocatelles were made of silk and cotton or of cotton alone and used for curtains, upholstery and carriage linings. Illustrated in Schoeser and Rufey, *English and American Textiles,* pp. 95, 96, 98 and 127.

BROWN LINEN. Unbleached linen, ranging through various shades of tan to dark brown.

BRUSSELS CURTAINS. Finely embroidered designs on fine-gauge

cotton net. The enclosed surfaces of the design motifs are filled in with embroidery of still finer threads. The finest Brussels curtains were known as duchesse curtains at the end of the 19th century.

BUCKRAM. Coarse plain-woven scrim, often stiffened with glue. Used for stiffening in clothing and valances from the 17th century. Sometimes made of hemp; can also be cotton.

BURLAP. Coarse, tabby woven fabric of jute, hemp or cotton, usually natural (brown) color.

CALAMANCO. A glazed worsted fabric in a satin weave, either solid color or woven with figured designs or stripes in brilliant colors resembling silk brocades. See Cummin, "Calamanco," p.184. Figured calamancoes are illustrated in Montgomery, *Textiles in America,* pls. D-30, D-63–64, D-79–80; a solid color quilt is shown in fig. D-25.

CALENDER. A cloth-finishing machine using two or more heated cylinders through which the fabric is passed. Calendering gives an impermanent, smooth, even surface to the fabric. If one cylinder rotates faster than the other, one side of the fabric will have a shiny, or glazed, surface. If one cylinder has a pattern raised on it, the surface will be embossed with the pattern; this may be an overall watered, or moired, design or a specific motif such as flowers and ribbons or Gothic arches. This technique is especially suitable for embellishing moreens and velvets.

CALICO. Cotton cloth with patterns printed in one or more colors. In the 18th and early 19th centuries, calico referred to the printed cloth imported from India and sometimes to any plain-woven cotton — woven, printed, checked or striped. Now it usually refers to cotton prints with small, stylized patterns.

CAMBRIC. Originally, fine bleached linen; later, a fine cotton of plain weave with a highly glazed surface. Cheaper cotton cambric of a very loose weave is used for underupholstery on seat furniture.

CAMLET. Unglazed worsted fabric of a plain weave, often including goat hair. Descriptive of a group of 18th-century materials including harrateen and china (cheyney); the variations depend on different methods of hot-press finishing. See Cummin, "Camlet," pp. 309–12.

CANVAS. Stiff and heavy cotton or linen fabric with an even weave.

CASEMENT CLOTH. Name for many kinds of sheer, open fabrics used for window curtains.

CHALLIS. Soft wool or a wool-cotton combination, usually twill. Introduced about 1832 and used for upholstery as well as dressmaking. Often printed with floral or paisley motifs.

CHENILLE. Yarn of silk, wool, cotton or rayon from which pile protrudes on all sides. Chenille cloth was often used for curtains and portieres as well as table and couch covers in the late 19th century. Also a kind of rug or carpet. Chenille table covers are illustrated in Greir, *Culture and Comfort*, pls. 6, 7.

CHEYNEY. A plain worsted fabric whose name is apparently derived from a phonetic spelling of a colloquial pronunciation of "China." Sometimes watered, the usual colors in the 18th century were green, red, blue, yellow and purple.

CHIKAN WORK. Tambour embroidery in white cotton thread on fine white cotton cloth. A specialty of craftspeople in Lucknow, India.

CHINA (see CHENEY).

CHINTZ. Glazed cotton cloth of plain weave. In the 18th and 19th centuries, always block printed. First manufactured in India, then imitated elsewhere. Printed designs usually have at least five colors and are frequently large-scale floral patterns. In the 19th century often synonymous with "furniture print." Now also refers to solid-colored, glazed cottons with a fine thread count.

CISELE VELVET. Patterned velvet distinguished by a pattern of cut and uncut loops.

CLOTH. In 18th-century sources, usually denotes finely spun and woven woolen broadcloth.

COCHINEAL. Bright red dye derived from the dried bodies of female cochineal insects.

COLORWAY. One standard color combination of a style or pattern.

CORNELY EMBROIDERY. Tambour work on net or muslin. It has the appearance of chain stitch.

COUNTERPANE. Defined by Thomas Sheraton in *The Cabinet Dictionary,* 1803, as "The utmost of bed clothes; that under which all the rest are concealed." Actually can be a blanket, quilt or woven coverlet, hemmed or fringed piece of cloth, lined or unlined.

CRASH. Coarse cotton or linen with a rough texture caused by weaving with various sized yarns. Used for table linen and window drapery in the late 19th and 20th centuries.

CRETONNE. A stout cotton cloth, usually unglazed, printed on one or both sides, usually in dark, rich colors. Popular in the last half of the 19th century for window curtains, sofa covers and chair coverings. At the present time it is unavailable in the United States. Illustrated in Grier, *Culture and Comfort,* pls. 18, 40.

CREWEL. Loosely spun, two-ply worsted yarn favored for embroidery. Used for bed furnishings in the 18th century and revived, especially 1950–80, for restoration work.

CYLINDER PRINTING. Textile printing done with engraved metal cylinders, a technique first developed in 1783 and perfected in the early 19th century. Each color element of a design requires a separate cylinder and is printed directly on the cloth. In cylinder printing the height of each design repeat is limited to the circumference of the cylinder; the range is usually 14 to 22 inches. Also referred to as roller printing or machine printing.

DAMASK. A fabric with reversible, solid-colored, woven designs on contrasting glossy and dull fabric surfaces; can be woven of any fiber or combination of fibers, most commonly silk or linen. Illustrated in Montgomery, *Textiles in America,* pls. D-56-C, D-68, D-73, D-89; fig. D-36.

DAMASQUETTE. A compound weave with an additional warp matching the color of the weft, thus creating areas of solid but contrasting color that would not be possible in a multicolored damask.

DARNIX (also DORNICK). Heavy linen cloth; usually refers to checked or damask-woven table linen.

DIAPER. Fabric containing motifs of small woven geometric patterns in linen or cotton white goods, typically diamonds, bird's eyes, arrowheads or chevrons. Eighteenth-century uses included clouting (infant's napkins), table cloths, napkins and toweling; diaper patterns continue to be made for table linen and toweling. It was not until nearly the middle of the 19th century that infants' clouts were called diapers.

DIMITY. White cotton cloth with woven patterns that may be pictorial or ribs with a pattern of either stripes or checks. In the late 19th-century dimity was sometimes printed with small-figured designs, but it is usually white. For more detail, see Cummin, "What Was Dimity in 1790?" pp. 23–25. Documentary samples are illustrated in Montgomery, *Textiles in America,* figs. D-40 and D-41 and pl. D-25. See also pp. 231–233 and illustration on p. 232.

DISCHARGE PRINTING. A technique that produces a pattern on a ground of a solid color. The cloth is first piece dyed and then block printed with a chemical discharging agent, which removes the color from the areas of the design, leaving a solid background.

DOCUMENT. A historic fabric or fabric design, the source of color and design for a reproduction.

DOCUMENTARY COLORWAY. A modern manufacturers' term used to indicate that the colors of a reproduction fabric are those of the original document.

DOUBLE-NET CURTAINS. Curtains made with one layer of fine-gauge, machine-made net embroidered on another, the ground of the upper layer then being entirely cut away, leaving the net doubled only in the area of the designs. In many cases, hand embroidery was used for additional embellishment.

DOUBLE WOVEN. Two ply, or made with two layers interwoven at regular intervals.

DRAB STYLE. A style of printed furnishing fabrics, popular c. 1798–1810, characterized by the colors produced by quercitron when used in combination with various mordants — olive, tan, khaki and dark brown.

DRAW LOOM. Prior to the invention of the Jacquard loom, the draw loom used a selective shedding device, operated by a draw-boy, to produce complex, nonrepeating weaves, such as damasks and brocades.

DRILL. Strong cotton fabric with a twill weave.

DROP REPEAT. A large-scale design that can be matched lengthwise only by alternating motifs in a diagonal pattern across two widths; requires extra yardage. Also called a drop match.

DRUGGET. Durable wool or linen and wool used to protect expensive floor coverings after c. 1825.

DUCK. Strong fabric in plain or ribbed weaves, historically linen, but in the 20th century usually cotton. Similar to canvas.

DURANT. A glazed woolen fabric, better quality than tammy. Folded lengthwise during calendering, therefore having a characteristic sharp center crease. Illustrated in Montgomery, *Textiles in America,* pl. D-60.

ELL. A long measure, mainly for cloth, of different length in different countries. An English ell equals 45 inches, or 1¼ yards.

EPI. Ends per inch. An indication of fabric weight and texture.

FELT. Woolen cloth made without weaving; a matted layer of randomly arranged woolen fibers.

FILLING. Threads woven from selvage to selvage crosswise on the loom. Also called weft.

FLAX. Fibers of the flax plant, the substance of linen.

FRISE. Uncut velvet.

FUGITIVE COLORS. Those dyes that fade most rapidly as a result of exposure to sunlight or laundry solutions.

FULLING. A finishing technique for woolen fabrics in which they are scoured in water and pressed firmly before having the nap raised on the surface.

FURNITURE. A term commonly used in the 18th century to denote the full equipment of something. Hence, the term "bed and furniture" meant the mattress, bolster, pillows, sheets, pillow cases and sometimes the blankets and curtains; "tea table and furniture" referred to the table as well as its accompanying ceramic and metal objects for the service of tea. In the case of "window curtain and furniture," the term "furniture" referred to the rods, hooks, rings and pulleys, as well as the cloth. The term also is used to denote any of the whole class of furnishing fabrics.

FURNITURE CHECK. A kind of checked linen or cotton used from the 17th century to the present for loose cases or slipcovers, window curtains, bed hangings and underupholstery on seating furniture. Checks of various sizes were used for this purpose, but they were usually in units of at least one-half inch. Smaller checks were usually intended for use in clothing and were often referred to as "apron checks." Note that 18th-century references to "furniture" do not necessarily specify check.

FUSTIAN. In the 18th century, refers to any of a wide variety of linen-and-cotton or occasionally all-cotton textiles, which can be herringbone, ribbed diaper or plain-woven.

In the early 19th century, fustians were commonly ribbed on one side; in the 18th century, they were most commonly used for work clothing.

GALLOON. Originally a narrow worsted tape or binding. By the end of the 19th century, it might also be made of wool, silk, cotton, gold or silver threads.

GAUFRAGE. An embossing technique in which a heated metal cylinder with a raised design on it is pressed against the pile of a plain fabric, such as plush or velvet, thereby transferring the pattern.

GAUZE. Thin, plain-woven fabric having an openwork effect. Used for mosquito nets or bed canopies, especially in the southern colonies and West Indies. Also used for covering paintings, looking glasses and chandeliers to protect them from fly specks.

GENOA VELVET. Velvet with bold floral designs composed of many colors of both cut and uncut pile, a specialty of Genoa, Italy, but also a generic name for velvets in this style.

GIMP. A flat trimming made by twisting silk, worsted or cotton threads around a foundation thread or wire and then worked in an open design; frequently used for valance and curtain edging as well as for furniture trimming. Often used in colors that contrast brightly with those of the fabric to which the gimp is attached. Adhesive gimps, patented in 1887, are illustrated in Geier, *Culture and Comfort,* pl. 15.

GLAZED. Having a smooth and lustrous surface on the exposed, or right, side only. Cotton fabrics may be glazed with starch, glue, paraffin or shellac and polished with a hot roller; these finishes do not survive washing.

GROS DE TOUR DAMASK. A damask pattern having a ribbed ground caused by using a weft much heavier than the warp.

GROUND. Background.

HARRATEEN. In 18th-century England and colonial America, a worsted moiré, hot pressed, sometimes embossed. Most often green, red, blue or yellow; also tan and slate colored. Illustrated in Montgomgery, *Textiles in America,* pl. D-27 A-D.

HERRINGBONE. A twill weave in which a stripe of short diagonal lines is juxtaposed to another in which the short lines go in the opposite direction, thus forming an overall zigzag effect.

HOLLAND. An 18th- and early 19th-century term for closely woven linens, first manufactured in Holland but later made throughout Europe and the British Isles. In the mid- and late 19th century, the term also referred to starched cotton cloth that was heavily glazed; it was used most commonly for window shades. "Brown holland" refers to unbleached linen.

HOLLAND SHADE CLOTH. Plain linen or cotton that is sized and finished with oil in order to make it opaque.

HOMESPUN. Normally refers to fabric that is handspun and handwoven. Sometimes in modern manufacturing slubs or bumps are added to machine-spun yarns in an attempt to suggest handwork, but fine hand spinning is not usually characterized by lumpy texture.

HORSEHAIR FABRIC (also HAIR CLOTH). Fabric woven of horse mane and tail hairs with a cotton, linen or worsted warp. Used for sofa upholstery and chair seats; can be tabby, satin or pattern woven. Black horsehair fabric is made with dyed black and gray hairs, while the lighter colored hairs are dyed green, claret, crimson or, less frequently, blue or gold. Illustrated in Montgomery, *Textiles in America,* fig. D-55.

HUCK. A finely patterned weave with warp and weft floats on the opposite sides, especially popular for toweling. Illustrated in Montgomery, *Textiles in America,* fig. D-57.

INDIENNE. Styles imitating those of imported Indian textiles.

IKAT. Fabric woven of warp threads that were bundled together and dyed in sections, creating distinctive blocks of color as patterns in the finished goods. In the 18th century, calamancoes woven in this technique were referred to as "clouded"; these are illustrated in Montgomery, *Textiles in America,* fig. D-30.

INDIGO. Plant that produces strong blue dye; also the color produced by this dyestuff.

IRISH POINT LACE CURTAINS. Cotton net panels with appliqué designs; the areas between the designs are cut away and the opening bound with embroidery and crossed by cords or threads sometimes fastened together in designs called spiders.

JACQUARD. A selective shedding device added to looms. Developed in France by M. Jacquard, who received a medal for it in Paris in 1801 and continued to refine the system, perfecting it in 1803; first brought to America in 1823. Originally used extensively for silk weaving but soon also for carpets, coverlets, table linens and all other types of textiles. The jacquard device uses needles to read punched cards and automatically control the action of the harnesses on the loom, greatly simplifying the weaving of complex patterns. Still used today for pattern weaving.

JASPE. Furnishing fabric with a series of stripes of several shades of the same color woven together.

JEAN. Strong, twilled cotton, a little lighter than drill. Solid or with woven stripes.

JUTE. Rough, brown fiber from a plant grown in India. Used for burlap and rope.

LAMPAS. A figured fabric of satin weave using additional wefts and warps to form a design in one texture on the ground of another; the additional threads are woven into the back of the fabric. The ground may be tabby, twill, satin or damask. The design effect on the front is that of a two-color damask, but the fabric is not reversible. Illustrated in Schoeser and Rufey, *English and American Textiles,* pp. 23, 122, 142 and 189.

LAWN. Thin cotton fabric, usually white.

LINSEY-WOOLSEY. A coarse fabric with a linen warp and woolen weft. Usually homespun and handwoven. Since linen and wool are affected differently by the same dyestuffs, linsey-woolsey is characterized by a speckled, uneven color. Less common in colonial America than recent romantic history would suggest. Many antique fabrics that are called "linsey-woolsey" are found, on careful examination, to contain no linen at all.

LISERE. A fabric woven with the warp wound on two separate beams. On one of them, usually called the palette, the threads are multicolored; these threads are brought to the surface of the fabric and form the design. The second warp beam carries strong filler yarns that form the background of the goods. See illustration, p. 194.

LUTESTRING (also LUSTERING). Lightweight silk with a rich sheen achieved by pulling dampened silk threads during the weaving process. Used for women's clothing, firescreens and some curtain linings. Illustrated in Thornton, *Baroque and Rococo Silks,* pls. 84B, 84A and 91B; Rothstein, *A Lady of Fashion,* (original album) pp. 3, 5, 10, 11, 13, 14, 15, 16, and 19.

MADDER. Eurasian herb used in dyeing to produce a moderate to strong red or shades of purple, brown and pink, depending on the mordant used; also the color produced by this dyestuff.

MARSEILLES (also MARCELLA). A heavy, corded cotton fabric with a pattern woven in the goods; usually white, it resembled hand quilting. Used primarily for bed coverings from the late 18th to the early 20th century; also used for petticoats and vesting in the mid-19th century.

MATELASSE. A double-woven cloth that simulates quilting by interlocking in some areas to produce a puckered effect.

MERCERIZE. A treatment of cotton with caustic soda to increase strength, enhance receptiveness to dyes and impart a characteristic shine. Patented in 1850 by John Mercer, an English calico printer.

MESH. In embroidery canvas, bobbinet or netting, one hole; in lace, the entire background.

MOHAIR. Hair of the angora goat, having a silky appearance and easily dyed. Used for filling, or pile, in the finest furniture velvets, also called Utrecht velvets in the 19th century. Because of the extraordinary durability of mohair plush fabrics, they were favored for seat upholstery and used even in railroad and trolley cars.

MOIRÉ. Clouded or watered effects on ribbed wool or silk fabrics, achieved by the application of intense but uneven pressure to the dampened fabric.

MOMIE CLOTH. Rough cloth with cotton or silk warps with wool filling. Thought to resemble cloth found on Eqyptian mummies. Popular in the 20th century for upholstery and drapery.

MONK'S CLOTH. Unbleached cotton or linen cloth with some additional rough flax or jute; basket-woven and thought to resemble the cloth used for the habits of monks in medieval times.

MOREEN. In the 18th century, a stout worsted or mohair fabric; by the late 19th century, often wool with a cotton warp. Sometimes plain but more often embossed with a design of fancy flowers or other elaborate figures, sometimes with a watered background in imitation of moiré. These effects are achieved by passing the fabric over a hot brass roller on which is engraved the design. Used extensively for upholstery and heavy curtains for beds and windows. Illustrated in Montgomery, *Textiles in America,* pl. D-104; fig. D-74.

MOQUETTE. A soft, velvetlike carpet sometimes used for upholstery work in the 19th century.

MOSQUITO NETTING. Commercial types made in the late 19th century included a coarse cotton gauze with large open mesh; usually bobbinet and gauze were used for this purpose.

M's AND O's. A popular pattern for handwoven linens utilizing squares and rectangles to produce two characteristic design blocks. See Gallagher, *Linen Heirlooms,* pp. 32–35 and chap. 10.

MULL. A thin, almost transparent soft cotton muslin; often used for clothing.

MULTI. A modern manufacturers' term for a fabric design containing many colors.

MUSLIN. A fine thin cotton cloth with downy nap on its surface. Generally plain but sometimes decorated with openwork or embroidery. In recent years, somewhat more coarse in texture.

NAIL. In English cloth measure, 2¼ inches, or 1/16 yard. Appears as the abbreviation "N" or "n" in sewing instructions.

NAP. The surface fibers of felt and woven cloth; may be raised by brushing.

NAUGAHYDE. Trade name for vinyl, resin-coated fabrics made by the U.S. Rubber Company, usually upholstery fabric.

NET. An open textile fabric of any fiber, tied or woven with a mesh of any size. Nets are formed by threads being wound around each other and knotted. Made by hand until the invention of the bobbinet machine in 1809. The term "net" is also used for light, woven fabrics, such as gauze.

NOTTINGHAM LACE CURTAINS. Panels of machine-made lace with integral designs; so called because they are made on a lace curtain machine invented in Nottingham, England, which was also the principal place of their manufacture during the last half of the 19th century. Throughout its history, this fabric has always been available in various designs and qualities.

OIL CLOTH. Cotton coated on one side with a mix of oil, pigment and a clay filler. Used especially for table and shelf coverings, c. 1850–1980.

ORGANDY. Thin, transparent, crisp cotton cloth. Formerly had to be starched after each laundering; can now be chemically treated to retain stiffness.

OSNABURG. A kind of plain-woven coarse linen originally made in Osnabruck, Germany, but later imitated in England and elsewhere. Sometimes spelled "Ozenbriggs." By the second half of the 19th century, the name referred to coarse cottons, often unbleached.

OVERSHOT. A woven design defined by extra weft yarns that pass in geometric patterns over the tabby woven foundation cloth. In coverlets these extra yarns are often heavy colored wools, while the foundation is white or natural cotton or linen. Apparently uncommon in colonial times, the earliest documented American example (at Winterthur) is dated 1773.

PALAMPORE. A cotton bed covering from India, usually printed or painted with large-scale, highly naturalistic designs, often a tree of life. See especially Beer, *Trade Goods*.

PANNE VELVET. Velvet with an unusually high pile.

PASSEMENTERIE. Edgings or trimmings, especially those made out of gimp, braid or cords; may be silk, cotton, wool or metallic threads.

PATCH. Printed cottons, usually chintz furnishing fabrics. A term frequently encountered in New England manuscripts and printed documents, c. 1750–1850. Used for bed and window curtains, slip covers and counterpanes. After 1840 fabrics printed with trompe l'oeil patchworks were also called patch.

PERCALE. Medium-weight cotton with a firm finish; can be either a solid color or printed.

PIECE DYED. After weaving, cloth dyed "in the piece," in contrast to cloth woven of colored yarns or printed on one surface only. Has equal color on each side of finished goods, but may have undyed areas within if dyestuff has not saturated the goods fully.

PILE. Regular close nap made of threads standing at right angles to the web. Usually sheared to form a smooth and even surface. The textured furry surface of velvet or plush.

PIN MARKS. Small printed dots placed at regular intervals to guide the textile printer in the placement of each block or screen; also called "register marks."

PINTADO. Inexpensive block-printed cotton cloth imported from India in the 17th and 18th centuries.

PLUSH. A fabric with an even pile, longer and less dense than that of velvet. Used for upholstery in the mid- to late 19th century. May be silk, mohair or wool. Can be embellished with woven patterns or embossed designs; the "crushed plush" illustrated in Grier, *Culture and Comfort,* pls. 21 and 22 features rich reflections of light in irregular patterns.

PLY. The number of strands of which a yarn is made. Also, a thickness or layer of cloth.

POCHOIR PRINTING. A textile printing technique using metal stencils, or *pochoirs,* which produced rather soft, sketchy designs. More efficient than block printing by hand, but not as fast or effective as screen printing, which replaced it as a technique. Especially popular in France, late 19th and early 20th century.

PONGEE. Thin, soft, uncolored natural, or raw, silk.

PORTIERE. A heavy curtain hung at a doorway to prevent drafts, to provide privacy or to enhance the decorative effect of an interior scheme. Usually hung on large rings that slide on a pole placed above the doorway. A good example is illustrated in Grier, *Culture and Comfort,* pl. 34.

QUALITY BINDING. Wide worsted tape, used for carpet binding. Often referred to in 19th-century documents simply as "quality."

QUARTER. A measurement of a quarter yard (nine inches). A 12-4 (twelve-quarter) lace curtain is three yards long; a 12-4 blanket is three yards wide.

QUILTING. In the 18th century, can refer to tufting in upholstery of chairs or cushions. Normally, however, a bed cover made of two layers of fabric having wadding or batting between them and stitched together in geometric or fancy patterns.

RAYON. Name used since 1924 for a particular kind of artificial silk made of cellulose. Rayon is less expensive, stiffer and more lustrous than silk.

REP. Fabric with closely woven, crosswise ribs. Wool or worsted rep in solid colors was popular from about 1835 for upholstery and heavy curtains. In the late 19th century "furniture rep," a flowered cotton in a thin weave, was also manufactured. Silk reps were usually but not always used for clothing. In the 19th century the ribs of rep fabrics were vertical; in modern reps they are horizontal, extending from selvage to selvage. Illustrated in Montgomery, *Textiles in America,* fig. D-86; Grier, *Culture and Comfort,* pl. 8; chap. 7, fig. 18.

REPEAT. The linear measurement of one complete pattern motif. Manufacturers have customarily provided information about the vertical repeat of their fabric designs; recently some manufacturers have also given the measurements of the horizontal repeat as well.

RESIST PRINTING. An 18th-century method of indigo printing in which a resist paste inhibited the dye. See Montgomery, *Printed Textiles,* pp. 194–211.

ROLLER PRINTING. Continuous machine printing from engraved metal cylinders, not from a handheld roller. See cylinder printing.

ROSE BLANKET. Blanket with large embroidered geometric motifs, called "rosings," in each corner. See cat. no. 250, "Rose Blanket," in *The Great River,* pp. 381–82; Montgomery, *Textiles in America,* p. 170, figs. D-17, D-18.

RUSSELL. Worsted damask, usually calendered to create a shiny surface. Illustrated in Montgomery, *Textiles in America,* pl. D-8, D-103.

RUSSIA LEATHER. In the early 18th century, seal or goat skin dyed black, imported from Russia for upholstery; later widely imitated.

SATEEN. A smooth, satin-weave cloth usually made of mercerized cotton. Used for window hangings, bed coverings and occasionally as a ground for embroidery in the last half of the 19th and early 20th centuries.

SATIN. A fabric that is shiny on one side and dull on the other, created by a special weave leaving numerous warp floats on the surface. Usually silk; also wool and linen. Eighteenth-century brocaded satins are illustrated in Montgomery, *Textiles in America,* fig. D-90.

SATIN-DE-LAINE. Printed wool in satin weave, popular for furniture upholstery c. 1850–90. Illustrated in Grier, *Culture and Comfort,* chap. 7, fig. 12.

SCREEN PRINTING. A printing technique for textiles or paper that is essentially the same as stenciling. When first introduced commercially in the 1930s, screen printing was done with silk screens that had been stretched on wooden frames and through which the dyestuff was forced by

means of a scraper or squeegee. Since the screens themselves were relatively inexpensive, this method of printing
permitted economical production of small amounts of fabric in a given design, thereby greatly increasing variety
and giving manufacturers more flexibility. Most screen
printing is now done with rotary screens, cylindrical in
form, on which the design to be printed has been etched
photographically. In both flat and rotary screen printing,
a separate screen is required for each color. With flat
screens, great care is needed to assure proper registration
of the colors. Rotary screen printing is a continuous process, and any error that occurs is apt to be repeated.

SCRIM. Loosely woven cotton, sometimes with a heavy weave,
used in the late 19th century for window curtains and
drapery.

SELVAGE (also SELVEDGE). The lengthwise edges of a piece of
cloth, often of a different color and heavier threads, sometimes even a different weave. Intended to prevent ravel-
ing. Also called list.

SERGE. A strong, twill-woven wool fabric with a pronounced
diagonal rib, made in various qualities. After leather and
turkeywork, the third most popular chair covering in late
17th- and early 18th-century America.

SHADE CLOTH. Heavy cotton cloth treated with oil and starch
to make it opaque; used for roller blinds.

SHALLOON. A lightweight twilled wool or worsted fabric. Illustrated in Montgomery, *Textiles in America,* pl. D-33.

SHEERS. Thin, pliable, translucent cotton or linen textiles.
Since about 1810, these types of fabric have been used for
undercurtains; today, lightweight curtains themselves are
often called sheers.

SILESIA. Twilled, thin linen cloth or a cotton imitation thereof.

SLUBS. Lumps on thread, formed by careless spinning. De-
liberate use of slubs to give an antique effect to finished
cloth is inappropriate for restoration purposes.

STORMONT. A textile pattern introduced in the factory of Sir
Robert Peel in the 1780s. The design is characterized by
a background of dots of color. At first these were sprayed
from a broom; later, brushes were used. Eventually the
dots were produced by metal teeth in a wooden roller. Illustrated in Rothstein, *A Lady of Fashion,* (album) p. 29.

STRIE. Mottled effects achieved by dying each of two parts

of a skein of yarn a different color before weaving.

STUFF. Any woven woolen cloth without nap, usually a worsted.

SWISS LACE. Machine-made lace manufactured in Nottingham, England, of coarse cotton in imitation of 16th-century Swiss laces. Favored for household furnishing uses by Charles Eastlake in *Hints on Household Taste*, 1868.

TABBINET. A silk and wool fabric with a watered surface, used for upholstery. A superior type was called tabaret; it was characterized by alternating stripes of watered and satin surfaces in different colors.

TABBY. A plain-woven structure in which one warp passes over and then under a single weft thread. The warp and weft threads are the same size and are set with the same number per inch, thereby giving a balanced weave. Also, a fabric woven in this way.

TAFFETA. A closely woven, firm fabric of even weight and tension, known by its glossy surface. Usually silk but can be linen. There is no difference between the two sides. Illustrated in Montgomery, *Textiles in America*, fig. D-96.

TAMBOUR. Embroidery worked on fine cotton cloth using a small hook on the upper side and bringing threads up through the cloth to form a chain stitch on the upper surface. Continues to be done on yard goods in India to this day. Machine-embroidered curtain panels have been made in this stitch since the mid-19th century. The center of their manufacture continues to be Switzerland.

TAMMY. A loosely woven wool of medium quality.

TAPES. Woven narrow strips, plain or striped, used to bind raw edges of fabric, cover seams and accent the outline of upholstery goods of all sorts. "Garters, Quality Bindings & Tapes of all Sorts" dating from 1771 are illustrated in Montgomery, *Textiles in America*, pls. D 36A, 36B.

TAPESTRY. Originally hand woven with bobbins, tapestries were worked on vertical looms and used as wall hangings or furniture upholstery. In the late 19th and 20th centuries, jacquard-woven tapestries were used for furniture upholstery and wall hangings. These retained the pictorial motifs of earlier handmade tapestries and might employ as many as 24 colors in the design. See Grier, *Culture and Comfort*, pl. 27, pp. 217–18

TASSEL. A pendant ornament. Before the 20th century, usually suspended from a wood mold covered with strands of wool or silk in one or more colors. Now often merely a cluster of threads or cords, gathered together at the top.

THEATRICAL GAUZE. Cotton fabric with a lightweight, plain weave stiffened with sizing. Popular for table mats and window curtains in the years 1920–65.

TICKING. Heavy cotton in a twill weave, usually in a striped design. Used as container or covering for pillows, beds and cushions. See p. 257–59.

TISSUE. An expensive silk with rich texture; sometimes woven with gold or silver threads.

TOBACCO CLOTH. Unbleached, lightweight, plain-woven, cotton cloth used for protecting certain tobacco plants from direct sunlight during the growing process, thus producing shadegrown tobacco. Resembles the texture and weight of pure cotton muslin and can be used effectively as a substitute for it.

TOILE. From *toile imprimée,* meaning "printed cotton." Now, generally refers to copperplate-printed fabrics or those printed in the style of the 18th-century copperplate designs on either cotton or linen cloth; more correctly, those of French origin.

TOW. Short flax fibers, separated in the combing process. Can be spun and woven into coarse cloth. Usually unbleached.

TREE OF LIFE. In the Garden of Eden the tree of life yielded food that gave everlasting life (Genesis 2:9; 3:22). A popular motif in textile design since the 17th century; found in woven, printed and embroidered work.

TURKEY RED. Bright red calico dyed with madder fixed by the use of oil; a very durable color. In the 1830s this technique was a specialty of Alsatian calico printers, who kept it a closely guarded secret.

TURKEYWORK. An upholstery fabric having a knotted wool pile in bright colors with a black background. Made as covers for chairs, settees and stools. It is believed that in many instances furniture was made specifically to fit the finished covers. Used from the late 17th century to the mid-18th century. Not currently available as a commercial reproduction. See essay by Margaret Swain in Cooke, *Upholstery in America and Europe.*

TWILL. A weave in which the weft threads pass over one and then under two warp threads, thus producing a diagonal pattern. See Gallagher, *Linen Heirlooms,* fig. 2 and chap. 8.

UNION (also BRITISH UNION). Fabric often used as ground for printed designs in England today. Usually a linen-cotton combination, sometimes with a small percentage of nylon.

UTRECHT VELVET. Mohair plush with a linen foundation. Because of its durability this fabric was favored for upholstery in railway cars.

VELVET. A pile fabric produced by the use of an extra series of warps passing over wires in loops. It can be plain (left as woven), or the loops can be cut when the wires are removed. If a pattern is created by alternating areas of cut and uncut loops, the fabric is called ciselé velvet. If the pattern is woven leaving some areas without pile, it is called voided velvet. Usually wool, silk or cotton.

VELOUR. A solid-colored fabric with a coarse pile woven on both sides, usually cotton in the 19th century, now often synthetic.

VERMICELLI, VERMICULAR. A design motif consisting of an endless meandering line. Referred to in at least one 18th-century document as "worm."

VISCOSE. A particular type of rayon, distinguished by the process of manufacture.

VOILE. Fine, sheer cotton, popular for window curtains and women's clothing.

WARP. The threads stretched lengthwise on the loom, usually spun more tightly than the weft and therefore stronger.

WEBBING. Coarse, plain-woven strips of hemp or jute. Usually a natural brown color, sometimes with black or red stripes. Used as a fundamental support in spring seat upholstery.

WEFT. The threads interwoven with the warp, running cross-wise in the goods, from selvage to selvage. Also called filling.

WELTING. In the 18th century, the term for piping in upholstery and made of straight strips of fabric sewn over tightly spun linen cord. Used to strengthen seams in furniture upholstery.

WITNEY. A town in Oxfordshire, England, which has been a center of blanket manufacture since the 17th century.

WOOF. See WEFT.

WORSTED. Fabric made of long staple wool that has been combed to make the fibers lie parallel to each other when spun. The effect is silky and durable.

BIBLIOGRAPHY   In earlier editions, this listing has emphasized books and articles that are likely to be readily available in public library collections and through interlibrary loan services. Today, the body of literature devoted to textiles, upholstery and interior design is much larger. In addition, many more 19th-century works are available as inexpensive reprints. The books cited here that will be most difficult to find are the expensive catalogs of the textile collections of the Victoria and Albert Museum and the Musee de l'Impression sur Etoffes; however, these contain lavish color illustrations that will certainly be useful. An asterisk (*) identifies important works on fabric design history.

Adrosko, Rita J. *Natural Dyes and Home Dyeing*. New York: Dover, 1971.

Agius, Pauline, and Stephen Jones. *Ackermann's Regency Furniture and Interiors*. Marlborough, Wiltshire: Crowood Press, 1984.

All Sorts of Good Sufficient Cloth: Linen Making in New England, 1640–1860. North Andover, Mass.: Merrimack Valley Textile Museum, 1980.

Alswang, Hope, and Donald C. Pierce. *American Interiors, New England and the South: Period Rooms at the Brooklyn Museum*. Brooklyn, N.Y.: Brooklyn Museum, 1983.

Ayres, James. *The Shell Book of the Home in Britain*. London: Faber and Faber, 1981.

Baumgarten, Linda. "Bed Hangings in the Eighteenth Century" and "Window Curtains in the Eighteenth Century." In *Williamsburg Reproductions*. Williamsburg, Va.: The Colonial Williamsburg Foundation, 1989.

_____. "The Textile Trade in Boston, 1650–1700." In *Arts of the Anglo-American Community in the Seventeenth Century, Winterthur Conference Report 1974*, pp. 219–73. Charlottesville: University Press of Virginia, 1975.

_____. "Textiles in the Eighteenth Century." In *Williamsburg Reproductions*. Williamsburg, Va.: The Colonial Williamsburg Foundation, 1989.

Beecher, Catherine E. *A Treatise on Domestic Economy*. Boston, 1841. Reprint. New York: Source Book Press, 1970.

Beecher, Catherine E., and Harriet Beecher Stowe. *The American Woman's Home*. 1869. Reprint. Hartford, Conn.: Stowe-Day Foundation, 1975.

Beecher, Mrs. H.W. *All Around the House: or, How to Make a Home Happy.* New York: D. Appleton, 1879.

*Beer, Alice B. Trade Goods: *A Study of Indian Chintz.* Washington, D.C.: Smithsonian Institution Press, 1970.

Blackburn, Rodric H. *Cherry Hill: The History and Collections of a Van Rensselaer Family.* Albany, N.Y.: Historic Cherry Hill, 1976.

*Bredif, Josette. *Printed French Fabrics Toiles de Jouy.* New York: Rizzoli International Publications, 1989.

Brett, Katherine B. "Some Eighteenth Century French Woodblock Printed Cotton in the Royal Ontario Museum." In *Studies in Textile History.* Toronto: Royal Ontario Museum, 1977.

Brightman, Anna. "Window Curtains in Colonial Boston and Salem." *Antiques.* August 1964, pp. 184–87.

_____. *Window Treatments for Historic Houses, 1700–1850.* Preservation Leaflet Series, no. 14. Washington, D.C.: National Trust for Historic Preservation, 1968.

_____. "Woolen Window Curtains: Luxury in Colonial Boston and Salem." *Antiques,* December 1964, pp. 722–27.

British Textile Design in the Victoria and Albert Museum. Tokyo: Gakken, 1980. Vol. I, *The Middle Ages to Rococo (1200–1750).* Vol. II, *Rococo to Victorian (1750–1850).* Vol. III, *Victorian to Modern (1850–1940).*

*Bronson, J. R. *The Domestic Manufacturer's Assistant.* Reissued as *Early American Weaving and Dyeing: The Domestic Manufacturer's Assistant and Family Director in the Arts of Weaving and Dyeing.* New York: Dover, 1977.

Burnham, Harold B., and Dorothy K. Burnham. *Keep Me Warm One Night: Early Handweaving in Eastern Canada.* Toronto and Buffalo: University of Toronto Press, in cooperation with the Royal Ontario Museum, 1972.

*Carlano, Marianne, and Larry Salmon, eds. *French Textiles from the Middle Ages through the Second Empire.* Hartford, Conn.: Wadsworth Atheneum, 1985.

Caulfeild, Sophia, and Blanche C. Saward. *The Dictionary of Needlework,* 1882. Facsimile eds. New York: Arno Press, 1972; as *Encyclopedia of Victorian Needlework.* Dover, 1972 (2 vols.).

Chefs d'Oeuvre du Musée de l'Impression sur Etoffes, Mulhouse. Tokyo: Gakken, 1978. Vol. I, *Imprimis Francais 1.*

Vol. II, *Imprimis Francais II, Européens et Orientaux.* Vol. III, Dessins, *Emprientes et Papiers Peints.*

Cherol, John A. "Designed for Another Age: Decorative Arts in Newport Mansions." *Antiques* 118, no. 3, September 1980, pp. 498–501.

Church, Ella Rodman. *How to Furnish a Home.* Appleton's Home Books. New York: D. Appleton and Company, 1881.

*A Choice of Design. 1850–1980. Fabrics by Warner & Sons Limited. London: Warner & Sons, 1981.

Clabburn, Pamela. *The National Trust Book of Furnishing Textiles.* London: Viking, 1988.

**Clark, Fiona. *William Morris Wallpapers and Chintzes.* New York: St. Martin's Press, 1974.

Clinton, Elizabeth. "Regency Furnishing Designs." *Connoisseur,* June 1978, pp. 106–17.

Clouzot, Henri, and Frances Morris. *Painted and Printed Fabrics.* New York: Metropolitan Museum of Art, 1927.

Collard, Frances. "Curtains Up." *Country Life,* April 20, 1989, pp. 194–197.

Colonial Williamsburg Today, vol. 3, no. 3 [Special edition on the Governor's Palace]. Williamsburg, Va.: Colonial Williamsburg, 1981.

Cooke, Clarence. *The House Beautiful.* New York: Scribner, Armstrong and Company, 1878.

Cooke, Edward S., Jr., ed. *Upholstery in America and Europe: From the Seventeenth Century to World War I.* New York: W.W. Norton, 1987.

Cooper, Dan. *Inside Your Home.* New York: Farrar, Straus, 1946.

**Cooper, Grace Rogers. *The Copp Family Textiles.* Washington, D.C.: Smithsonian Institution Press, 1971.

Cooper, Nicholas. *The Opulent Eye: Late Victorian and Edwardian Taste in Interior Design.* London: Architectural Press, 1976.

Cornforth, John. *English Interiors 1790–1848: The Quest for Comfort.* London: Barrie and Jenkins, 1978.

_____. *The Inspiration of the Past: Country House Taste in the Twentieth Century.* New York: Viking, 1985.

_____. "Weaving in the Grand Manner." *Country Life,* July 12, 1984, pp. 95–98.

**Cummin, Hazel E. "Calamanco." Antiques 39, 1941, pp. 182–83.

*_____. "Camlet." *Antiques* 42, 1942, pp. 309–12.

*_____. "Colonial Dimities, Checked and Diapered." *Antiques* 38, 1940, pp. 111–12.

*_____. "Moreen — A Forgotten Fabric." *Antiques* 38, 1940, pp. 286–87.

*_____. "Tammies and Durants." *Antiques* 40, 1941, pp. 153–54.

*_____. "What Was Dimity in 1790?" *Antiques* 38, 1940, pp. 23–25.

Cummings, Abbott Lowell, ed. *Bed Hangings: A Treatise on Fabrics and Styles in the Curtaining of Beds, 1650–1850.* Boston: Society for the Preservation of New England Antiquities, 1961.

_____. *Rural Household Inventories.* Boston: Society for the Preservation of New England Antiquities, 1964.

d'Allemagne, Henry-René. *La Toile Imprimée et les Indiennes de Traite.* 2 vols. Paris: Gruend, 1942.

Davidson, Caroline. *Women's Worlds: The Art and Life of Mary Ellen Best 1809–1891.* New York: Crown Publishers, 1985.

Davison, Marguerite Porter. *A Handweaver's Pattern Book.* Swarthmore, Pa.: Author, 1958.

_____. *A Handweaver's Source Book.* Swarthmore, Pa.: Author, 1953.

de Gaigneron, Axelle. "Silk Makes a Comeback." *Connaissance des Arts,* no. 412, June 1986.

Des Dorelotiers aux Passementiers. Paris: Musée des Arts Décoratifs, 1973.

DeWolfe, Elsie. *The House in Good Taste.* New York: Century, 1913.

Dornsife, Samuel J. "Design Sources for Nineteenth-Century Window Hangings." In *Winterthur Portfolio,* 10. pp. 66–99. Charlottesville: University Press of Virginia, 1975.

Dow, George Francis. *The Arts and Crafts in New England, 1704–1775; Gleanings from Boston Newspapers.* Topsfield, Mass: Wayside Press, 1927.

_____. *Everyday Life in the Massachusetts Bay Colony.* Boston: Society for the Preservation of New England Antiquities, 1935.

Downing, A. J. *The Architecture of Country Houses, with Remarks on Interiors, Furniture.* New York, 1850. Reprint. New York: Dover, 1969.

Draper, Dorothy. *Decorating is Fun!* New York: Doubleday, Doran, 1939.

Dresser, Christopher. *Principles of Decorative Design.* London, 1873.

Earle, Alice Morse. *Costume of Colonial Times.* New York: Charles Scribner's Sons, 1894.

_____. *Two Centuries of Costume in America, 1620–1820.* 2 vols. New York: Macmillan, 1903.

Earnshaw, Pat. *Lace Machines and Machine Laces.* London: B. T. Batsford, 1986.

Eastlake, Charles L. *Hints on Household Taste.* London, 1868. 4th ed., 1878. Reprint. New York: Dover, 1969.

Edwards, Ralph. *English Chairs.* London: Victoria and Albert Museum and Her Majesty's Stationery Office, 1970.

Edwards, Ralph, and Percy Macquoid. *Dictionary of English Furniture.* Rev. ed. Suffolk, England: Baron Publishing, 1983.

Edwards, Ralph, and L. G. G. Ramsey. *Connoisseur Period Guides to the Houses, Decorations, Furnishing and Chattels of the Classic Periods.* 6 vols. New York: Reynal, 1957–58. 1 vol. New York: Bonanza, 1968.

English Chintz. London: Her Majesty's Stationery Office, 1955.

English Chintz: English Printed Furnishing Fabrics from Their Origins to the Present Day. Catalog of a loan exhibition at the Victoria and Albert Museum. London: Her Majesty's Stationery Office, 1960.

English Chintz: Two Centuries of Changing Taste. London: Her Majesty's Stationery Office, 1955.

Etoffes Imprimées Françaises, Musée de l'Impression sur Etoffes de Mulhouse. Catalog of an exhibition held at Kyoto, Japan, 1981.

*Fairclough, Oliver, and Emmeline Learly. *Textiles by William Morris and Morris and Company 1861–1940.* London: Thames and Hudson, 1981.

*Fagan-Affleck, Diane. *Just New from the Mills: Printed Cottons in America, Late Nineteenth and Early Twentieth Centuries.* North Andover, Mass.: Museum of American Textile History, 1987.

Fales, Martha Gandy. "A Nineteenth-Century Guide to Making Curtains." *Antiques,* March 1981, pp. 682–85.

Floud, Peter. "The Drab Style and the Designs of Daniel Goddard." *Connoisseur* 139, June 1957, pp. 234–39.

Floud, Peter, and Barbara Morris. Series of articles on chintz design. *Antiques,* March–December 1957.

Fowler, John, and John Cornforth. *English Decoration in the 18th Century.* Princeton, N.J.: Pyne Press, 1974.

*From East to West: Textiles from G. P. & J. Baker. London: G. P. & J. Baker and Victoria and Albert Museum, 1984.

Gallagher, Constance Dann. *Linen Heirlooms.* Newton Centre, Mass.: Charles T. Branford Company, 1968.

_____. *More Linen Heirlooms.* Boston: Weavers Guild, 1982.

Garrett, Elisabeth Donaghy. "The American Home, Part I: 'Centre and Circumference': The American Domestic Scene in the Age of the Enlightenment," *Antiques,* January 1983, pp. 214–25; "Part II: Lighting Devices and Practices," *Antiques,* February 1983, pp. 408–17; "Part III: The Bedchamber," *Antiques,* March 1983, pp. 612–25; "Part IV: The Dining Room," *Antiques,* October 1984, pp. 910–22.

Geer, Katherine. *Nineteenth–Century Interiors.* New York: Abrams, 1989.

Girouard, Mark. *Life in the English Country House: A Social and Architectural History.* New Haven: Yale University Press, 1978.

_____. *Sweetness and Light: The 'Queen Anne' Movement 1860–1900.* New Haven and London: Yale University Press, 1977.

_____. *The Victorian Country House.* Rev. ed. New Haven and London: Yale University Press, 1979.

Gloag, John. *Victorian Comfort.* London: A.& C.Black, 1961.

Godey, Louis. *Godey's Lady's Book.* Philadelphia, 1830–92 (various titles).

Gordon, Beverly. *Shaker Textile Arts.* Hanover, N.H., and London: University Press of New England, 1980.

Grier, Katherine C. *Culture and Comfort: People, Parlors, and Upholstery, 1850–1930.* Rochester, N.Y.: The Strong Museum, 1988.

Handler, Mimi. "Toile: Engravings by the Yard." *Early American Life,* October 1989, pp. 28–35.

Hanks, David A. *The Decorative Designs of Frank Lloyd Wright.* New York: E. P. Dutton, 1979.

Hargrove, John. *The Weaver's Draft Book and Clothier's Assistant.* 1792: Reprint with an introduction by Rita Adrosko. Worcester, Mass.: American Antiquarian Society, 1979.

Harrison, Constance Cary. *Woman's Handiwork in Modern Houses.* New York: Charles Scribner's Sons, 1881.

Hay, Susan Anderson, ed. *A World of Costume and Textiles: A Handbook of the Collection.* Providence: Museum of Art, Rhode Island School of Design, 1988.

Heckscher, Morrison. *In Quest of Comfort: The Easy Chair in America.* New York: Metropolitan Museum of Art, 1971.

Hosley, William, and Elizabeth Pratt Fox, eds. *The Great River.* Hartford, Conn: Wadsworth Atheneum, 1984.

Huette, R. *Le Livre de la Passementeric.* Paris, 1972.

Hunter, George Leland. *Decorative Textiles: An Illustrated Book on the Coverings for Furniture, Walls and Floors.* Philadelphia: J. B. Lippincott Company, 1918.

Irwin, John, and Katherine Brett. *The Origins of Chintz.* London: Her Majesty's Stationery Office, 1970.

Jackson-Stops, Gervase, and James Pipkin. *The English Country House: A Grand Tour.* Boston: Little, Brown, 1985.

Jameson, Clare. *The Potterton Book of Curtain and Drapery Designs.* Late 19th century. Reprint. Sessay, Yorkshire, England: Potterton Books, 1986.

———. *The Potterton Pictorial Treasury of Curtain and Drapery Designs.* 1750–1930. Reprint. Sessay, Yorkshire, England: Potterton Books, 1987.

———. *The Potterton Sketchfile of Elaborate Bed Drapery Designs.* Late 19th century. Reprint. Sessay, Yorkshire, England: Potterton Books, 1987.

Jobe, Brock. "The Boston Furniture Industry." In *Boston Furniture of the Eighteenth Century.* Boston: Colonial Society of Massachusetts, 1974.

Jones, Chester. *Colefax & Fowler: The Best in English Interior Decoration.* Boston: Little, Brown, 1989.

Jones, Owen. *The Grammar of Ornament.* London, 1856.

Jourdain, Margaret. "Window Curtains of the Eighteenth Century." *Country Life,* 1946, pp. 668–69.

Kaplan, Wendy. *'The Art That Is Life': The Arts & Crafts Movement in America, 1875–1920.* Boston: Museum of Fine Arts, 1987.

Katzenberg, Dena S. *The Great American Cover-Up: Counterpanes of the Eighteenth and Nineteenth Centuries.* Baltimore: Baltimore Museum of Art, 1971.

Keyser, Alan G. "Early Pennsylvania-German Traditions: Beds, Bedding, Bedsteads, and Sleep." In *Jeannette Lasan-*

sky, Pieced by Mother. Lewisburg, Pa.: Oral Traditions Project of the Union County Historical Society, 1988.

Kimball, Fiske, and Marie G. Kimball. "Jefferson's Curtains at Monticello." *Antiques* 52, no. 4, October 1947, pp. 266–68.

Kimball, Marie G. "The Original Furnishings of the White House." *Antiques* 15, 1929, pp. 481–85; 16, 1929, pp. 33–37.

_____. "Thomas Jefferson's French Furniture." *Antiques* 15, 1929, p. 123.

Klapthor, Margaret Brown. "Benjamin Latrobe and Dolley Madison Decorate the White House, 1809–1811." Contributions from the Museum of History and Technology, Bulletin 241, Paper 49. Washington, D.C.: Smithsonian Institution, 1965.

The Lady's Handbook of Fancy Needlework. London, 1880. Facsimile ed. *Late Victorian Needlework for Victorian Houses.* Watkins Glen, N.Y.: American Life Foundation, 1979.

Lancaster, Clay. *New York Interiors at the Turn of the Century.* New York: Dover, 1976.

Larsen, Jack Lenor. *Jack Lenor Larsen: 30 Years of Creative Textiles.* New York: Jack Lenor Larsen, 1981.

Lasansky, Jeannette. *Pieced by Mother: Symposium Papers.* Lewisburg, Pa.: Oral Traditions Project of the Union County Historical Society, 1988.

Lasdun, Susan. *Victorians at Home.* New York: Viking, 1981.

Le Musée de l'Impression sur Etoffes de Mulhouse. Mulhouse: Société Industrielle de Mulhouse, 1975.

Leslie, [Eliza]. *The Lady's House Book: A Manual of Domestic Economy.* Philadelphia, 1841.

Little, Francis. *Early American Textiles.* New York: Century, 1931.

Loudon, J. C. *An Encyclopaedia of Cottage, Farm and Villa Architecture and Furniture.* London: Longman, Brown, Green and Longmans, 1833.

Low, Betty-Bright, and Jacqueline Hinsley. *Sophie du Pont: A Young Lady in America.* New York: Abrams, 1987.

Lubell, Cecil. *Textile Collections of the World.* Vol. I, *United States and Canada.* Vol. II, *United Kingdom and Ireland.* Vol. III, *France.* Cincinnati: Van Nostrand Reinhold Company, 1976–77.

Mayhew, Edgar deN., and Minor Myers, Jr. *A Documentary*

History of American Interiors. New York: Charles Scribner's Sons, 1980.

Merrell, Jeannette. "Chintzes from Portugal." *Antiques,* June 1928, pp. 496–98.

Metcalf, Pauline C. "The Interiors of Ogden Codman, Jr. in Newport, Rhode Island." *Antiques* 118, no. 3, September 1980, pp. 486–97.

_____. ed. *Ogden Codman and the Decoration of Houses.* Boston: The Boston Athenaeum, David R. Godine, 1989.

Michie, Audrey. "Charleston Textile Imports, 1738–1742." *Journal of Early Southern Decorative Arts,* May 1981, pp. 21–39.

Montgomery, Florence. "Antique and Reproduction Furnishing Fabrics in Historic Houses and Period Rooms." *Antiques* 107, January 1975, pp. 164–69.

_____. "Eighteenth-Century English and American Furnishing Fashions." *Antiques,* February 1970, pp. 267–71.

_____. "Furnishing Textiles at the John Brown House, Providence, Rhode Island." *Antiques,* March 1972, pp. 496–500.

*_____. "John Holker's Mid-Eighteenth Century 'Livre d'Enchantillons.'" In *Studies in Textile History,* edited by Veronika Gervers. Toronto: Royal Ontario Museum, 1977.

*_____. *Printed Textiles: English and American Cottons and Linens, 1700–1850.* New York: Viking, 1970.

_____. "Room Furnishings as Seen in British Prints from the Lewis Walpole Library." *Antiques.* Part I: "Bed Hangings," June 1973, pp. 1068–75. Part II: "Window Curtains, Upholstery and Slip Covers," March 1974, pp. 522–33.

_____. "Stylistic Change in Printed Textiles." In *Technological Innovation and the Decorative Arts.* Winterthur Conference Report, 1973, edited by Ian M. G. Quimby and Polly Ann Earl. Charlottesville: University Press of Virginia, Henry Francis du Pont Winterthur Museum, 1974.

*_____. *Textiles in America, 1650–1870.* New York: W. W. Norton, 1984.

_____. "Upholstery and Furnishing Fabrics." In *American Furniture, The Federal Period,* edited by Charles F. Montgomery. New York: Viking, 1966.

Morland, Frank A. *Practical Decorative Upholstery: Containing Full Instructions for Cutting, Making, and Hanging All*

Kinds of Interior Upholstery Decoration. 1890. Reprinted as *The Curtain Maker's Handbook.* Edited by Martha Gandy Fales. New York: E.P. Dutton, 1979.

Morris, Barbara. *Inspiration for Design: The Influence of the Victoria & Albert Museum.* London: Victoria and Albert Museum, 1986.

*Moss, Gillian. "British Copperplate-Printed Textiles." *Antiques,* April 1990, pp. 940–51.

*_____. *Printed Textiles 1760–1860 in the Collection of the Cooper-Hewitt Museum.* New York: Smithsonian Institution Press, 1986.

Nancy Graves Cabot: In Memoriam. Sources of Design for Textiles and Decorative Arts. Boston: Museum of Fine Arts, 1973.

Noetzli, E. *Practical Drapery Cutting.* 1906. Reprint. Sessay, North Yorkshire, England: Potterton Books, 1986.

Nylander, Jane C. "Window Hangings." *Early American Life,* December 1979, p. 40.

_____. *Beds and Bed Hangings.* Slide tape. Nashville: American Association for State and Local History, 1982.

_____. "Textiles, Clothing and Needlework." In *The Great River,* edited by William Hosley and Elizabeth Pratt Fox. Hartford, Conn.: The Wadsworth Atheneum, 1985.

Nylander, Jane C., and Caroline Fuller Sloat. "White Curtains." *Early American Life,* August 1982, pp. 54–57.

Nylander, Richard C. "Documenting the Interior of Codman House: The Last Two Generations." *Old Time New England,* 62, 1981, pp. 84–102.

O'Conner, Deryn, and Hero Granger-Taylor. *Colour and the Calico Printer.* Farnham, Surrey, England: West Surrey College of Art and Design and the Quarry Bank Mill, 1982.

Palmer, F. *Practical Upholstering and the Cutting of Loose Covers.* London, 1921. Reprint. Sessay, North Yorkshire, England: Potterton Books, 1985.

Parkes, Frances Byerly. *Domestic Duties: Or Instructions to Young Married Ladies.* London: Longman, Hurst, Rees, Brown and Green, 1825. New York: J. R. J. Harper, 1829.

*Parry, Linda. *William Morris Textiles,* New York: Viking, 1983.

*_____. *Textiles of the Arts and Crafts Movement.* London: Thames & Hudson, 1988.

Passeri, Andrew, and Trent, Robert F. "Two New England

Queen Anne Easy Chairs with Original Upholstery." *Maine Antique Digest* 11, no. 4, April 1983, pp. 26A–28A.

Peterson, Harold L. *Americans at Home.* New York: Charles Scribner's Sons, 1971. Reissued as *American Interiors from Colonial Times to the Late Victorians.* New York: Charles Scribner's Sons, 1979.

Pettit, Florence H. *America's Printed and Painted Fabrics, 1600–1900.* New York: Thames and Hudson, 1982.

*Pitoiset, Gilles. *Toiles Imprimées, XVIIIe–XIXe Siècles.* Paris: Bibliotheque Forney, 1982.

Praz, Maria. *Conversation Pieces.* University Park: Pennsylvania State University, 1971.

_____. *An Illustrated History of Furnishing from the Renaissance to the Twentieth Century.* New York: Braziller, 1964. Reissued as *An Illustrated History of Interior Decorating from Pompeii to Art Nouveau.* New York: Thames and Hudson, 1982.

Quinn, Mary J. *Planning and Furnishing the Home.* New York and London: Harper & Brothers Publishers, 1914.

Robinson, Stuart. *A History of Printed Textiles.* Cambridge, Mass.: MIT Press, 1969.

Roth, Rodris. "Nineteenth-Century American Patent Furniture." In *Innovative Furniture in America from 1800 to the Present,* edited by David Hanks. New York: Horizon Press, 1981.

_____. "Seating for Anyplace: The Folding Chair." *Nineteenth Century,* 8, 1982, pp. 131–52.

Rothstein, Natalie. "Silks Imported into America in the 18th Century, An Historical Survey." In *Irene Emery Roundtable on Museum Textiles, 1975 Proceedings: Imported and Domestic Textiles in Eighteenth-Century America.* Washington, D.C.: Textile Museum, 1976.

_____. "The Warner Archive." *Bulletin de Liason du Centre International d'Etude des Textils Anciens,* 36, 1972, pp. 25–28.

_____. ed. *A Lady of Fashion: Barbara Johnson's Album of Styles and Fabrics.* New York: Thames and Hudson, 1987.

Rowe, Anne Pollard. "Crewel Embroidered Bed Hangings in Old and New England." *Bulletin of the Museum of Fine Arts, Boston,* 71, 1973, p. 365.

Rutz-Rees, Janet E. *Home Decoration: Art Needlework, and Embroidery, Painting on Silk, Satin and Velvet; Panel Paint-*

ing; and Wood Carving. Appleton's Home Books. New York: D. Appleton and Company, 1881.

Scalamandré: Preserving America's Textile Heritage 1929–1989. Philadelphia: Paley Design Center, Philadelphia College of Textiles and Science, 1989.

Schoelwer, Susan Prendergast. "Form, Function, and Meaning in the Use of Fabric Furnishings: A Philadelphia Case Study, 1700–1775." *Winterthur Portfolio,* Spring 1979, pp. 25–40.

*Schoeser, Mary, and Celia Rufey. *English and American Textiles from 1790 to the Present.* New York: Thames and Hudson, 1989.

Seale, William. *Recreating the Historic House Interior.* Nashville: American Association for State and Local History, 1979.

————. *The Tasteful Interlude: American Interiors Through the Camera's Eye, 1860–1917.* Reprint. Nashville: American Association for State and Local History, 1980.

*Slavin, Richard Edward, III. *A Century of Opulent Textiles: The Schumacher Collection.* New York: Horizon Magazine, 1989.

————. "Fabrics of Being." *Horizon* 32, no. 2, March-April 1989, pp. 49–51.

Sprague, Laura, ed. *Agreeable Situations: Society, Commerce and Art in Southern Maine, 1780–1830.* Kennebunk, Maine: Brick Store Museum, 1987.

Stickley, Gustav. *Craftsman Homes.* New York: Craftsman Publishing Company, 1909.

Storey, Joyce. *The Thames and Hudson Manual of Dyes and Fabrics.* London: Thames and Hudson, 1978.

————. *The Thames and Hudson Manual of Textile Printing.* London: Thames and Hudson, 1974.

Swan, Susan Burrows. *Plain and Fancy: American Women and Their Needlework, 1700–1850.* New York: Holt, Rinehart & Winston, 1977.

Talbot, George. *At Home: Domestic Life in the Post Centennial Era.* Madison: State Historical Society of Wisconsin, 1976.

Thornton, Peter. *Authentic Decor. The Domestic Interior: 1620–1920.* New York: Viking Penguin, 1982.

————. *Baroque and Rococo Silks.* New York: Taplinger, 1965.

_____. *Seventeenth-Century Interior Decoration in England, France and Holland.* New Haven: Yale University Press, 1978.

Tilton, John Kent. *Textiles of the Italian Renaissance: Their History and Development.* New York: Scalamandré Silks, n.d.

*Toiles de Nantes, des XVIIIe et XIXe Siècles. Mulhouse: Musée de l'Impression sur Etoffes, 1977.

Trent, Robert. "More on Sofas." *Maine Antiques Digest,* September 1988, pp. 10B–14B.

Trent, Robert, Robert Walker and Andrew Passeri. "The Franklin Easy Chair and Other Goodies." *Maine Antiques Digest* 7, no. 11, December 1979, pp. 26B-29B.

Tuchscherer, J.-M. *Etoffes Merveilleuses du Musée Historique des Tissus, Lyon.* 3 vols. Tokyo: Gakken, 1976.

*_____. *The Fabrics of Mulhouse and Alsace, 1801–1850.* Leigh-on-Sea, England: The Collectors' Book Club, 1972.

Victoria and Albert Museum. *English Printed Textiles: Large Picture Book No. 13.* London: Her Majesty's Stationery Office, 1960.

Walton, Karen M. *Golden Age of Furniture Upholstery, 1660–1840.* Leeds, England: Stable Court Exhibition Galleries, 1973.

Wass, Janice Tauer. *Weaver's Choice: Patterns in American Coverlets.* Springfield: Illinois State Museum, 1988.

Watson, Francis. "French Tapestry Chair Coverings: A Popular Fallacy Re-Examined." *Connoisseur* 148, no. 596, October 1961, pp. 166–69.

Webster, Thomas, and Frances B. Parkes, *Encyclopaedia of Domestic Economy.* New York: Harper, 1845.

Weissman, Judith Reiter, and Wendy Lavitt. *Labors of Love: America's Textiles and Needlework, 1650–1930.* New York: Alfred A. Knopf, 1987.

Westman, Annabel. "English Window Curtains in the Eighteenth Century." *Antiques,* June 1990, pp. 1406–17.

Wharton, Edith, and Ogden Codman, Jr. *The Decoration of Houses.* 1897. Reprint. New York: W. W. Norton, 1978.

Wheeler, Candace. *The Development of Embroidery in America.* New York: Harper and Brothers, 1921.

_____. *Principles of Home Decoration.* New York: Doubleday, Page and Company, 1908.

Wheeler, Gervase. *Rural Homes.* New York, 1851.

Williams, Henry T., and Mrs. C. S. Jones. *Beautiful Homes.* New York: Williams, 1878.

Winkler, Gail Caskey, and Roger W. Moss. *Victorian Interior Decoration: American Interiors 1830–1900.* New York: Henry Holt, 1987.

*Woods, Isabel B., ed. *Sanderson's 1860–1985.* London: Arthur Sanderson & Sons, 1985.

The Workwoman's Guide. London: Simpkin, Marshall, 1838. Reprint. Guilford, Conn.: Opus Publications, 1986.

Wright, Janet McNair. *The Complete Home: An Encyclopedia of Domestic Life and Affairs.* Philadelphia: Bradley, Garretson and Co., 1884.

SOURCES OF
INFORMATION

AMERICAN SOCIETY OF INTERIOR DESIGNERS. 1430 Broadway, New York, N.Y. 10018 (212) 944-9220

ART INSTITUTE OF CHICAGO. Michigan Avenue and Adams Street, Chicago, Ill. 60603 (312) 443-3600

COLONIAL WILLIAMSBURG FOUNDATION. P.O. Box C, Williamsburg, Va. 23187 (804) 229-1000

COOPER-HEWITT MUSEUM. Smithsonian Institution, 2 East 91st Street, New York, N.Y. 10028 (212) 860-6898

INTERNATIONAL LINEN PROMOTION COMMISSION. 200 Lexington Avenue, Suite 225, New York, N.Y. 10016 (212) 685-0424

METROPOLITAN MUSEUM OF ART. 82nd Street and Fifth Avenue, New York, N.Y. 10028 (212) 879-5500

MUSÉE DES ARTS DÉCORATIFS. Palais du Louvre, Pavillon de Marsan, 107-109 rue de Rivoli, 75001 Paris, France

MUSÉE DES ARTS DE LA MODE. 11 Avenue du President Wilson, 75016 Paris, France

MUSÉE DE L'IMPRESSION SUR ETOFFES. 3 rue des Bonnes-Gens, 68100 Mulhouse, France 89-45-51-20.

MUSÉE HISTORIQUE DES TISSUS. 34 rue de la Charite, 69001 Lyons, France

MUSÉE OBERKAMPF. Jouy, France

MUSEUM OF EARLY SOUTHERN DECORATIVE ARTS. Drawer F, Salem Station, Winston-Salem, N.C. 27108 (919) 721-7360

MUSEUM OF FINE ARTS. 465 Huntington Avenue, Boston, Mass. 02116 (617) 267-9300

OLD STURBRIDGE VILLAGE. 1 Old Sturbridge Village Road, Sturbridge, Mass. 01566 (508) 347-3362

PHILADELPHIA MUSEUM OF ART. 26th Street at Benjamin Franklin Parkway, Philadelphia, Pa. 19130 (215) 763-8100

ROYAL ONTARIO MUSEUM. 100 Queens Park, Toronto 5, Canada

SOCIETY FOR THE PRESERVATION OF NEW ENGLAND ANTIQUITIES. 141 Cambridge Street, Boston, Mass. 02114 (617) 227-3956

VICTORIA AND ALBERT MUSEUM. Exhibition and Cromwell Roads, London SW 7, England

THE VICTORIAN SOCIETY IN AMERICA. 219 East Sixth Street, Philadelphia, Pa. 19106 (215) 627-4252

THE WARNER ARCHIVE. Warner & Sons, 2 Anglia Way, Chapel Hill, Braintree, Essex CM7 2RS, England (0376) 21132. Direct inquiries to Mary Schoeser, archivist.

WILLIAM MORRIS SOCIETY. 420 Riverside Drive, 7D, New York, N.Y. 10025

WINTERTHUR MUSEUM AND GARDENS. Route 52, Kennett Pike, Winterthur, Del. 19735 (302) 686-8591

Preparation of *Fabrics for Historic Buildings* was greatly aided by the cooperation and assistance of Judith Straeton and Murray Douglas at Brunschwig & Fils, Cecilia Hatfield, Sheila Pollack and Adriana Bitter at Scalamandré, Richard Slavin and Margot Horsey at Schumacher, John Buscemi and Guy Evans at Classic Revivals, and a host of other individuals who provided information, loaned samples and answered questions. Valerie Wayne typed the full text of the third edition on to floppy discs in preparation for this revision, and Richard Nylander, as always, provided insight and assistance at every turn.

Fabrics for Historic Buildings was edited by Gretchen Smith and Janet Walker. Patricia Flowe and Samantha Pillar assisted in the production.

The book was designed and typeset in Berkeley Oldstyle by Robert Wiser and Marc Alain Meadows, Meadows & Wiser, Washington, D.C., and printed by the John D. Lucas Printing Company, Baltimore, Md.

ACKNOWLEDG-
MENTS

JANE C. NYLANDER, an authority on 18th- and 19th-century textiles and interiors, is director of Strawbery Banke Museum in Portsmouth, N.H. Well known as a lecturer, she was curator of textiles and ceramics at Old Sturbridge Village from 1969 to 1986 and has written widely for both popular and scholarly journals. She has taught at the University of New Hampshire, Boston University and New England College and is a member of the Visiting Committee to the Department of American Decorative Arts and Sculpture of the Museum of Fine Arts, Boston.

AUTHOR

FABRICS &
WALLPAPERS

FOR HISTORIC BUILDINGS

JANE C. NYLANDER

RICHARD C. NYLANDER

WILEY

JOHN WILEY & SONS, INC.

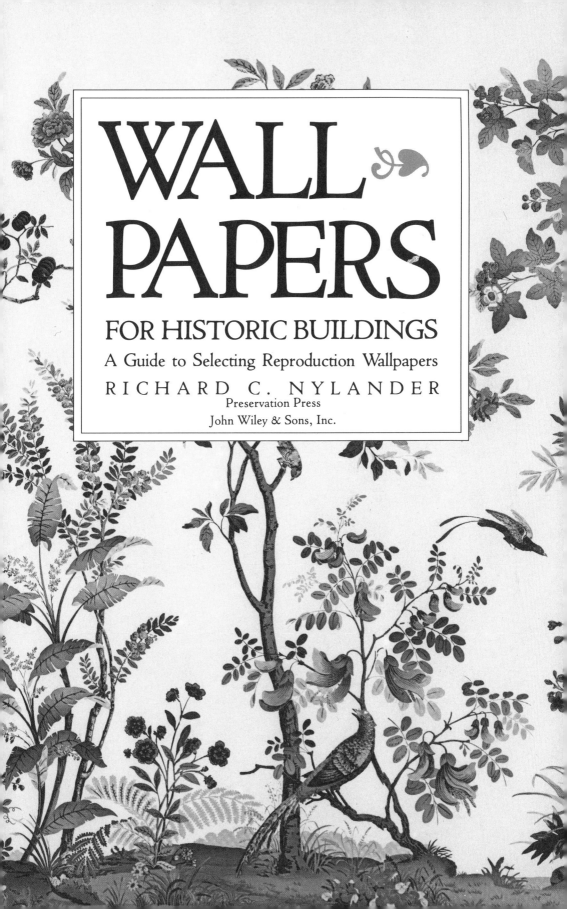

WALL PAPERS

PAPERS

FOR HISTORIC BUILDINGS

A Guide to Selecting Reproduction Wallpapers

RICHARD C. NYLANDER

Preservation Press

John Wiley & Sons, Inc.

Printed in the United States of America
   4   3   2

Library of Congress Cataloging in Publication Data

Nylander, Richard C.
   Wallpapers for historic buildings: a guide to selecting reproduction wallpapers / Richard C. Nylander. — [2nd ed.]
      p.   cm.
   Includes bibliographical references.
   ISBN 0-471-14431-2
   1. Wallpaper—Reproduction—Catalogs.   I. Title.
NK3399.H37   1992
747'.3'074—dc20   91-43269

Cover and endleaves: LA HAIE PANEL, 1815–25. Brunschwig & Fils. (See page 47.)
Title pages 2–3: DECOR CHINOIS, 1832. Zuber. (See page 92.)
Page 6: Detail of a billhead, Appleton Prentiss, Boston, 1791. (Society for the Preservation of New England Antiquities)
Pages 8–9: BOWER, c. 1910. Bradbury & Bradbury. (See page 211.)
Pages 28–29: IRIS FRIEZE, 1876, from Fenway Roomset. Bradbury & Bradbury. (See page 175.)

Designed and typeset by Meadows & Wiser, Washington, D.C.

This revised edition of Wallpapers for Historic Buildings was made possible in part by the generous support of Brunschwig & Fils, F. Schumacher & Company, Galacar & Company, and Classic Revivals.

ACKNOWLEDGMENTS

This revised edition of *Wallpapers for Historic Buildings* would not have been possible without the interest and assistance of the following people. Special thanks goes to those who provided additional information on their collections and arranged for special photography.

Bruce Bradbury, Bradbury & Bradbury; Judy Straeten, Thomas Marshall, and Murray Douglas, Brunschwig & Fils; John Burrows and Andrew Naeve, J. R. Burrows & Company; Susan Freedman, Clarence House; John Buscemi, Paula Tomaso, Guy Evans, Patrice Mauny, Tom Helm, Robert Ness, Robert Weston, Georgina Hamilton, and Suzanne Forge, Classic Revivals; Ron Tanner, Cowtan & Tout; Whitney Lewis, Bentley Brothers; Deborah Diament, A. L. Diament & Company; Frederic Galacar, Galacar & Company; Christopher Hyland, Christopher Hyland Incorporated; Kathleen Boston and Janice Rox, Katzenbach & Warren; Martha Kazelunas, Lee Jofa; Robert Carter, Mt. Diablo Handprints; Denise Vouri and Lesley Hoskins, Sanderson & Sons; Robert Bitter and Leslie Degeorges, Scalamandré; Margot Horsey, Richard Slavin and Vivian Infante, Schumacher; Lori Reagle, Thibaut; Arthur Athas and Leah Forsman, Twigs; Florence Schroeder and Wendy Schroeder, Victorian Collectibles Limited; Bernard Scott, Waterhouse Wallhangings; Tania Bobrinskoy, Zina Studios; Gisele Chalaye, Zuber; Penny Bigmore, Essex Institute; Susan Borchardt, Gunston Hall; William Flynt, Historic Deerfield; Karin Cullity, Strawbery Banke Museum; and Robert Kelly of *Wallpaper Reproduction News*.

Additional thanks go to Andrea Gilmore for researching specific reproductions, Anne Donaghy for assisting with the production of the manuscript, and David Bohl for photographing many of the samples. Margaret Pritchard provided information on the wallpapers at Colonial Williamsburg, and Julian Hudson made it possible to include photographs of the wallpapers at Prestwould. Gretchen Smith Mui provided essential editorial support.

Special thanks to Jane Nylander, for her patience, insight, and help, and to Sarah, Tom, and Tim, who lived through the preparation of another manuscript.

INTRODUCTION

WALLPAPERS
FOR HISTORIC BUILDINGS

Since its earliest documented use in England, in the Master's Lodgings at Christ College in Cambridge in 1509, wallpaper has been a popular means of enhancing interior spaces in both domestic and public buildings because it fills otherwise blank walls with a wide variety of design and color. Reproduction wallpaper can be an important element in the restoration of historic buildings.

Like carpets and textiles, wallpaper was chosen to make a room fashionable, complement its architecture, and provide a unifying background for its furnishings. Once applied to the walls, however, wallpaper became a part of the structure. Unlike carpets, textiles, and other furnishings, it could not be moved and incorporated into another decorative scheme. When wallpaper became worn or unfashionable, it no longer fulfilled its purpose and was either covered or removed. Only occasionally was a fragment kept for sentimental reasons. Thus, fewer samples of historic wallpaper survive than do examples of other decorative interior elements.

Since 1983, when the first edition of *Wallpapers for Historic Buildings* was published, the interest in wallpaper as a decorative component has steadily increased. More information is now available about historic wallpaper patterns, their designers, and the technology that produced them. Many rooms of original or early wallpapers have been professionally conserved so that they can be enjoyed for years to come. Reproduction wallpapers have been introduced into countless historic houses as an integral part of the restoration process.

Interest in reproduction wallpapers has been shared by curators, historic house administrators, interior designers, and museums with wallpaper archives as well as the manufacturers themselves. The quest for accuracy in recreating period interiors has led curators, house committees, and even some private home owners to commission custom reproduction wallpapers rather than rely on what is commercially available. Manufacturers have responded by paying more attention to accurate artwork and color matching.

The stairhall, or "saloon," at Prestwould in Clarksville, Virginia,

Hanging a custom-made reproduction wallpaper at the Hamilton House, South Berwick, Maine, in 1898. The pattern copied fragments of the 18th-century pillar and arch wallpaper found in the same hallway. The pattern "Arch" on page 45 is the current reproduction. (Society for the Preservation of New England Antiquities) provides an excellent example in one room of the various approaches to wallpaper possible in a historic building. The old photograph shows the space as it appeared around 1900. At some point after the photograph was taken, all the decorative papers in the room with the exception of the French scenic paper seen on the left wall were removed, and the walls and woodwork were painted white. Recently, the room has been restored to its former splendor. The antique scenic wallpaper has been professionally conserved. The elaborate flocked border, the only other pattern to be saved, was reproduced from a fragment. The two other designs were known only from the photograph. Research revealed that a pristine sample of the neoclassical dado was preserved in the collections of the Cooper-Hewitt Museum; it was reproduced with the museum's cooperation. No example of the sidewall pattern could be located in any wallpaper collection. Therefore the design was reproduced using the photograph for the design elements, the 1829 bill for color references, and other period wallpapers to ensure a correct approach to the design motifs.

Until the past decade, wallpaper design and its use in American buildings had not been explored as extensively as other decorative arts. The reasons are many. Foremost is that few collections of historic wallpaper samples exist. Few manufacturers had maintained a company archive in the European tradition, where samples of each pattern were retained. Major museums have not collected samples of historic wallpaper; wallpaper is not easily displayed, nor is it easily collectible unless it covers a hat box or lines a trunk. Moreover, the written records most often relied on when researching a historic house—estate inventories and probate deeds, for example—seldom document the use of wallpaper. Consequently, the importance of wallpaper in the decoration of a room had never been recognized or considered as seriously as the other elements.

This lack of interest and information changed dramatically in the 1980s both in the United States and abroad. Wallpaper finally came of age. In 1980 Catherine Lynn's *Wallpaper in America* became the first book on the subject since Nancy McClelland's study of 1924. It was followed by this author's more regional survey, *Wallpaper in New England*, in 1986. These recent publications grew out of in-depth studies of the two largest repositories of historic wallpapers in the country—the collections of the Cooper-Hewitt Museum and the Society for the Preservation of New England Antiquities. In addition to these publications, special exhibitions of this rarely seen decorative art were mounted by both museums. Wallpaper collections in England and France were brought to the attention of the American public through *Wallpapers*, Charles Oman and Jean Hamilton's 1982 survey of the Victoria and Albert Museum collec-

The "Saloon" at Prestwould, Clarksville, Virginia, c. 1900 and today. The historic photograph documents the wallpapers and border that were purchased from F. Regnault, Jr., of Richmond, Virginia, in 1831. All the wallpapers except the French scenic paper seen at the left were subsequently removed. Reproduction wallpaper patterns were copied from surviving fragments of the originals and reconstructed from the historic photograph. (Prestwould Foundation)

tion, and Odile Nouvel's *Wallpapers of France* (1981).

In her introduction to *Wallpaper in America*, Lynn refers to a promotional pamphlet written in 1880 by Clarence Cook entitled "What Shall We Do with Our Walls?" The question remains a valid one that should be considered by every property owner and restoration committee dedicated to restoring a historic building accurately. A quick survey, however, reveals that little attention had been paid to this question. During the 1950s, 1960s, and 1970s the most popular solution had been to paint the walls of an 18th- or early 19th-century house white. This approach has conveyed the false impression that before the Victorian period rooms were stark, the only color coming from elaborate draperies at the windows and oriental rugs on the floors—equally false presumptions. Lynn notes that in the late 19th century, the peak period of wallpaper production and use, white walls were considered "relics of barbarism, and almost a thing of the past." In the mid-20th century, however, white walls became almost a symbol of traditional historic decoration.

Whitewash, an easy and effective treatment for walls, was used extensively in the 18th century. Wallpaper, when first produced, was a luxury. Anyone who could afford expensive furniture and textiles would also have wanted to complement this display of wealth and taste by hanging paper on the walls of the family home. As wallpaper became increasingly available and affordable, it became the typical wall treatment. In 1850 Andrew Jackson Downing wrote in his popular and useful book *The Architecture of Country Houses*: "We confess a strong partiality for the use of paperhangings for covering the walls of cottages." Downing stressed that one advantage is "in the enhanced architectural effect which may be given to a plain room, by covering the walls with a paper of suitable style."

The use of reproduction wallpaper and the choice of a particular pattern depend on the purpose of the restoration, rehabilitation, or redecoration of the historic building. The information included here is intended to serve as a guide for curators and committees of museum houses whose aim is to convey an accurate impression of a building's former appearance or create an accurate period interpretation, for homeowners who are seeking wallpapers that are appropriate to the architectural style of a historic house or that provide a sympathetic background for a collection of antiques, and for people who wish to introduce a period look to a rehabilitation or adaptive-use project.

This book presents reproductions of historic wallpapers that are currently available. The original documents from which the designs are copied date from 1700 to 1930, and the information is organized according to historical period. A short essay introducing popular patterns and technology precedes each section. The works cited in the bibliography should be consulted for their illustrations and detailed information on the history of wallpaper design and production.

Like Downing, this author confesses a strong partiality toward the appropriate use of wallpaper in restoration and rehabilitation projects, and it is hoped that the reproduction wallpaper patterns included here will help restorers of historic buildings paper their walls in a style suitable to the purpose of the restoration.

HISTORY OF REPRODUCTION WALLPAPERS

The interest in old wallpaper patterns seems to have begun in the late 19th century and coincides with a general interest in the American past that was kindled by the Centennial Exhibition of 1876 in Philadelphia. By that time architects had already begun to study early American buildings for design inspiration. In the course of the next 20 years, local groups became increasingly concerned about the fate of buildings considered historically important to their communities. Many were saved and became the repositories for collections of artifacts. Interest in the American past also was reflected in interior decoration; imitating the historical styles of European decoration was no longer the only option. The fashionable American interior acquired a certain charm and aura of stability with the inclusion of an heirloom chair found in Grandmother's attic or a piece of old china purchased during an afternoon outing of "antiquing."

Before 1900 some historical societies and occasionally even a few private owners had commissioned custom reproductions of early papers they had found on the walls of the buildings they were restoring. In her chatty book *Old Time Wall Papers*, published in 1905, Kate Sanborn indicates that wallpaper manufacturers had responded to a demand for papers appropriate for Colonial Revival houses and that wallpapers reproducing old designs were readily available. Sanborn considered wallpaper reproductions an "expensive matter," the price per roll being six to ten dollars. Expensive they were when one realizes that the cheapest paper offered in the Sears catalog of the same year cost only three cents for a double roll. These early reproductions were not as accurate as those reproduced today. More liberties were taken with the designs, and many incorporated architectural elements or motifs from old tapestries. Today, they reflect their own time more than the period they sought to represent.

During the first half of the 20th century, better reproduction wallpapers became available and were standard offerings of many wallpaper manufacturers. Firms such as Thomas Strahan Company in Chelsea, Massachusetts, and the M. H. Birge Company in Buffalo, New York, specialized in such papers. The documents from which the designs were taken dated almost exclusively before 1850, and from the 1920s to the 1940s these so-called colonial wallpapers adorned the walls of a vast number of both privately and publicly owned historic houses.

The extensive use of reproduction papers in older houses coincided with a general use of wallpaper in most American homes in the early 20th century. In the mid-20th century the preference for unadorned, white walls in modern interiors influenced the tastes of committee members in charge of the decoration of museum houses. When the wall surfaces needed to be renewed, the reproduction wallpapers that had been hung only a generation earlier were taken down and the walls painted white. Today, the pendulum has swung back. Modern designers and homeowners are incorporating wallpaper into their decorative schemes. Museum curators are no longer content to display just a small sample of antique wallpaper in a room whose walls were once covered with it; they consider the wallpaper an integral part of the room's historic decoration and are using reproduction wallpaper in an effort to present as accurate an impression of the past as possible.

RESEARCH

Paint and wallpaper are the two elements of any previous decorative scheme that are most likely to remain in a building as evidence of the tastes of the original and subsequent occupants. The probability that wallpaper was used as a decorative finish in a building should be considered from the outset of a restoration project, not toward the end, when all evidence for its use has most likely been erased. Time should be taken to examine the structure for all evidence it may yield. Often, potentially helpful wallpaper evidence is overlooked in the rush to begin structural rehabilitation of a building. Photographs should be taken before any investigation and as work proceeds. Each wallpaper remaining on the walls should be examined to determine its age; it is not inconceivable that one may be an early paper or perhaps the original paper. No wallpaper should be removed until a target date for the restoration or redecoration has been established. This includes those wallpapers that initially appear to be "too late" even to be considered because they fall within the memory of the restorers. After all the research has been done, the decision may be made to interpret the house as it was at a fairly recent time. If the decision is made to retain an existing paper, a paper conservator should be consulted about whether cleaning and readhesion are possible. Current preservation philosophy strongly favors preserving a room of original or early wallpaper rather than removing and reproducing it.

A room whose walls have been stripped to the bare plaster is not necessarily devoid of wallpaper evidence. Plaster that has never been painted can be an indication that the walls had a decorative covering from the outset, most likely a wallpaper.

Check all surfaces of the room, including the ceiling, for wallpaper evidence. Later architectural changes may obscure an early wallpaper. Often a room was divided. Occasionally a new wall was built directly in front of an old one, thereby concealing a wealth of information. Other elements, such as door and window casings, baseboards, and mantels, often were replaced in an effort to "modernize" a room. Carpenters rarely took the time to strip the wallpaper before applying the new millwork. Cupboards may have been built in, or a Victorian picture molding may have been applied just below the ceiling. Even electrical switchplates may conceal a small fragment of early wallpaper. Often, large pieces of furniture, such as bookcases or mirrors secured to the walls, were not moved when a room was repapered.

Be sure to look for samples in more than one location in any given room. Many decorative schemes made use of more than one wallpaper pattern. In the mid-19th century, for example, fresco papers, consisting of several different elements, were designed to divide the wall into a series of framed panels. In the same period many hallways were papered with columns, capitals, bases, and friezes. In the 1880s dividing the wall surface into dado, fill, and frieze was an immensely popular procedure. During the same period, ceilings were frequently papered. The wallpapers revealed during the course of investigation may range from large samples in good condition to frustratingly incomplete bits that indicate only that wallpaper was used at one time but reveal no clues as to when it was applied or what the color or pattern may have been.

When a wallpaper sample is located, it should be documented with both color and black-and-white photographs, as color photographs have a tendency to fade. The sample's location should be noted on a sketch of the wall plan. Ideally such information is included in a historic structures report.

The thickness of a paper sample removed from the walls can be deceiving. Often it contains more than one layer. Before the invention of the wallpaper steamer, removing the existing layer of paper when a new paper was applied was not common practice; only loose or damaged portions were removed so the new paper would lie flat. The layers of a wallpaper "sandwich" can be separated by careful steaming or soaking. Ideally a paper conservator should be consulted. One sandwich separated by the author contained 27 layers of paper recording the decoration of the room from which it was removed from about 1780 until a matchboard dado was installed in the 1930s.

When wallpaper is found, a record should be kept for each sample, noting the room from which it was removed and, if part of a sandwich, its place in the sequence of layers. Small fragments should not be considered worthless. They are an important part of the sequence and may be identified fully if a larger sample of the pattern exists in another wallpaper collection or the pattern is recorded in an early photograph. Interior photographs taken in the late 19th and early 20th centuries often record the design of a wallpaper that has since been removed. Many successful reproduction wallpaper patterns have been reconstructed by carefully analyzing early photographs.

If no wallpaper samples are found in the structure itself, information may be obtained from other sources related to the site. For example, objects associated with former occupants should be studied. Extra pieces of wallpaper were used for a variety of purposes, such as sealing the backs of framed pictures, covering homemade diaries and account books, and making small boxes. One should be wary of some wallpapers found in trunks or on band boxes, however. Many small-figured designs used for trunk linings were manufactured specifically for that purpose and were not used to paper rooms. The same is true for many of the large, continuous designs found on hat boxes.

All wallpaper evidence should be coordinated with a thorough search of the documents relating to the building and its occupants. Not until all the research is reviewed can a target date for the restoration be established. Although the initial idea may be to restore a building to its original appearance, complete information about all the components of its interior finishes and furnishings may not exist. Documentation about the wallpaper, textiles, and furniture used at a later date may be more extensive. A broad research project will place the building in an architectural context within the community as well as establish the socioeconomic level of its various occupants.

Once the target date for the restoration and interpretation has been established, the wallpaper samples that have been found can then be reviewed to determine whether any were used during that time. At this point the decision is made whether the sample will be duplicated in a custom-made reproduction or whether it will be used as a guide in choosing a similar pattern available as a commercial reproduction.

If no samples of wallpaper are found in a historic building, choosing an appropriate wallpaper design depends almost entirely on research into the selected historical period. This research into secondary sources is necessary to answer general questions about wallpaper: What patterns were available? What styles were fashionable? Where was wallpaper purchased? In what rooms was it most often used? These questions, asked within the framework of the documentary research on the building and its occupants, can help determine the type of wallpaper pattern to select.

In 1787, after looking at the wallpapers available for his new house, a Boston merchant wrote, "There are so great a variety of Fashions, I am totally at a loss as to what kind to get." Today, an owner of a historic building may well have the same experience when trying to choose a pattern from the variety of reproductions available. The Boston merchant concluded that a person's choice of wallpaper "principally depends on fancy." Like today's homeowner, he was trying to choose a paper that was not only fashionable but also appealing to his taste. Those responsible for a museum restoration, however, do not have the same latitude in their selection. Their choice of a reproduction wallpaper pattern should not be subject to 20th-century taste. The reproduction wallpaper should be chosen within the bounds of the prevailing taste of the period chosen for the restoration.

WHAT TO LOOK FOR IN A REPRODUCTION

The term "documentary design" is often loosely interpreted and therefore can be misleading. Many wallpaper sample books labeled "The Colonial Collection" include designs that have no relationship to the wallpapers used during the 18th century. Rather, these designs are the small-figured patterns or stenciled designs that have become associated with the traditional "Early American" look or more recently with "American Country." Many interpretive designs are created by reworking motifs from historic documents—not necessarily wallpapers—into new patterns.

Even when a wallpaper is part of a collection licensed by a museum or preservation organization, the source of the design may be another type of object in its collection, such as a printed or woven fabric, a book endpaper, or a motif from a sampler, a quilt, or a ceramic plate. These are attractive designs created to appeal to current popular taste and complement a manufacturer's collection or line. However evocative of the past, such designs have nothing to do with historic wallpaper patterns and are not recommended for use in historic buildings being restored with an eye toward accuracy. Although it has been impossible to research each reproduction wallpaper listed here, the purpose of this book is to include only those documentary designs that are derived from wallpapers.

The manufacturers listed in this book offer two types of documentary wallpapers acceptable in restoration work: exact reproductions and adaptations. An exact or accurate reproduction faithfully follows the design, scale, and color of the original document. The artwork, or an artist's rendering of the wallpaper design, should strive to reproduce the appearance of the document when it was new, not the worn, abraded look of the antique sample. A successful adaptation achieves the overall appearance of the original wallpaper but incorporates certain changes made by the manufacturer. The design and scale may have been altered; a motif may have been reworked; a design element may have been omitted or a new one introduced; the colors may vary in intensity from the original, or the number of colors may have been reduced. Often such changes are made to make the design more appealing to the contemporary market. Other times they are necessitated by production constraints. Scalamandré refers to designs where changes in scale and composition, such as embossing and flocking, have been made because of technical limitations as "historic representations."

The question to consider with adaptations is the extent to which the design of the document can be altered or reworked before it becomes a new pattern. An adaptation should not be chosen if the scale has been substantially reduced or enlarged, if a major motif has not been included or an incongruous one introduced, or if it includes a color that had not been invented when the original paper was produced. Again, always check the documentation for a paper labeled an adaptation; as noted previously, its source may not even have been a wallpaper.

The artwork of the reproduction design also should reflect the technology that produced the original wallpaper. The most successful artwork captures the variation and modulation of a hand-blocked wallpaper and the precision of machine printing. Even today's most accurate reproductions cannot exactly duplicate the appearance of the documents they are copying. The production methods, the inks that are used, and the paper stock on which the reproduction design is printed all differ substantially from those used to create the historic document. Although some reproduction papers are printed with rollers, the majority are produced with silk screens.

The silk-screen method of printing best imitates the look of a block-printed paper. When an 18th-century design is printed with a roller, the definition of line and the opacity of pigment of the original are lost, and the overall pattern appears weak. Conversely, a late Victorian roller-printed paper reproduced today by the silk-screen process often looks more substantial than the original. The running together of thin colors, which occurred in the rapid roller-printing process of the original, can best be duplicated by machine.

Both screen- and roller-printed papers use commercially available ground papers on which the design is printed. Modern ground papers do not have the texture of 18th-century handmade paper, nor are they as thin as the cheap machine-made paper on which many late Victorian designs were printed. Modern ground papers come in standard widths. These widths are wider than those of historic papers, which usually ranged from 18 to 23 inches, depending on the date and country of origin. All-over patterns with small horizontal repeats can easily be accommodated on modern widths. Although a greater number of horizontal repeats can fit on today's wider paper, the scale remains the same. Occasionally the scale of the document design has to be adjusted slightly to fill the modern width. (Such adjustment is often necessary for papers that are pretrimmed.) The horizontal repeat of a large design often cannot be adjusted to fill a modern width. The original width, therefore, is copied, leaving a wider-than-usual margin on each side. Although these margins may appear to be a waste of paper, the manufacturer compensates by increasing the length of the roll, so that the area the paper covers meets the standard of approximately 30 square feet per roll.

The visual differences created by modern production methods are most apparent when directly comparing a sample of the historic paper with a sample of the reproduction. However, the differences become less noticeable when the reproduction paper is installed and the room receives its full complement of furniture, textiles, and pictures.

The changes brought about by modern printing methods and materials are compromises that are generally accepted in restoration wallpapers today. Many curators, however, are striving to capture the visual qualities of 18th-century handmade and hand-printed wallpapers. There is renewed interest in the art of block printing. Block-printed wallpapers from England and France are being used in and more American restorations. Colonial Williamsburg is planning to offer several of its reproduction wallpapers in block-printed as well as screen-printed versions. The colors used to print its reproductions are based on scientific pigment analysis. Others interested in historic wallpapers are pursuing sources of handmade paper so that future reproductions of early wallpapers technically will be as accurate as possible.

Custom-made Reproduction Wallpapers

Today's manufacturers produce reproduction wallpapers not only for use in historic buildings. They also sell to a contemporary market and, therefore, must consider current tastes when choosing patterns from historic documents. No manufacturer should be expected to include reproductions of every popular style from each historical period. Often a style most popular in a given period will simply not be appealing today and, thus, will not be found on the market.

Given the variety of patterns of historic wallpaper, the odds that the exact design of a wallpaper found in a particular historic building has already been reproduced are slim. Custom work may be the only means of obtaining an exact copy of a pattern needed for an accurate

Custom-made repro-
duction wallpaper
("Green Wheat" and
"Green Wheat Bor-
der"), textiles, and
carpets were needed
to re-create the origi-
nal appearance of the
master bedroom in
the Gardner-Pingree
House (1804), Salem,
Massachusetts.
(Essex Institute)

restoration project. If the wallpaper samples found in a building are
appropriate to the historical period of the restoration and if a complete
design exists, having the paper custom-reproduced may be preferable
to choosing a pattern from those commercially available. The goal of
custom work is as accurate a reproduction as possible with respect to
design, color, scale, and simulation of the original printing technique.
It cannot be stated too strongly that neither the client nor the manufacturer should "improve" the design; unclear lines and faded colors
should not be used to give the paper an "antique" look.

Most wallpaper firms will consider doing custom work, but it is
an expensive and time-consuming procedure. The client is responsible for all costs incurred, including the artwork, the cost of each
silk screen (one for each color of the design and often a blotch
screen for the ground color), and the set-up and printing expenses.
The client is responsible also for approving both the artwork before
the screens are cut and the strike-offs for final color. Custom work
usually requires the client to order a minimum number of rolls; it
may be wise to order enough to paper a room twice in case damage
occurs. Before a historic sample is sent to a manufacturer, it should
be protected from possible damage by encasing it in mylar.

It is popularly believed that a wallpaper manufacturer will happily
reproduce any sample of wallpaper found in a historic building, in-

clude the reproduction in a commercial line, and donate enough paper to paper one room of the building. In reality, the manufacturer rarely does any of these things. A firm may wish to add the reproduction to its line if the design is considered appealing by today's standards. In this case a royalty arrangement should be negotiated and confirmed by a written contract. The manufacturers may also wish to produce the design in other color combinations, called colorways. If a client approves such a proposal, he or she should obtain royalties on all colorways produced.

TODAY'S WALLPAPER REPRODUCTION MARKET

Manufacturers approach reproduction papers from different points of view. Most firms favor a particular historic period and color pallette. Some firms reproduce the exact appearance of a historic sample, including faded colors and missing design elements. They may also reproduce a printing flaw found on the original document. Other manufacturers compensate for loss of color or design defects by making the reproduction resemble the appearance of the original when it was new. Although this book includes reproduction papers of both types, current restoration practice favors the latter approach.

This book seeks to list currently available reproduction wallpapers and establish guidelines for choosing a pattern appropriate to the project at hand. Today, as in any period in the past, there is a wide range in the quality of wallpapers on the market, both in design and execution. It behooves those making the selection to familiarize themselves with the designs that were popular during the selected period as well as the printing techniques that produced them, so that they can select from the listings in this book with an educated eye.

The reproduction wallpapers available today present an almost overwhelming array of pattern and period styles. The majority of the patterns included in commercial lines are chosen because they appeal to modern taste. Many designs that copy those in European archives may never have been available to the American consumer until the present. In addition to domestically produced reproduction wallpapers, a large number of imported ones are also available. Most are printed in England or France, although some come from as far away as Australia. Such wallpapers are included only if they are available through an American distributor.

Over the past decade dozens of custom reproductions have been commissioned by museums. Many of these wallpapers are now being made available to the public through museum shops or reproduction programs. They are listed separately at the end of the appropriate chapter. Because they are not stock items, they must be custom ordered. As in all custom work, the manufacturer may stipulate a minimum amount that must be ordered. Order information and sample availability vary with each museum. Other patterns that are not listed may be also available from a variety of museums. If you see an appealing reproduction design in a museum installation, inquire about whether it can be purchased on a custom basis.

In addition to patterns ordered through museum gift shops, other custom patterns are available directly through the manufacturers. These are on a custom only or special-order basis and are so listed in the catalog under the manufacturer's name. This type of custom order means that the pattern or document color is not carried as a stock item. The screens are already made, and the order is treated as a normal custom order by the company. Terms vary with each company. Usually a minimum number of rolls or yards of border is required; the customer is also responsible for the cost of any overruns. Other costs include set-up charges and possibly surcharges for the number of colors printed. A deposit is usually required. It is always wise to order a strike-off to make sure that the colors are correct.

PERIOD INSTALLATION

Once a reproduction wallpaper has been chosen, some attention should be paid to its installation. While the basic methods of applying paper to walls have not changed, certain period practices should be noted.

Although paste has always been the most common means of attaching paper to walls, there are references to securing some early wallpapers to the walls with small tacks. Lining paper was not commonly used during the 18th and 19th centuries. However, it is recommended when hanging modern reproduction wallpaper.

Most wallpapers today, including many of the reproduction papers, are pretrimmed. Papers produced in the 18th and 19th centuries had an unprinted margin, or selvage, on each side. Usually only one selvage was cut off and the seams were overlapped when the paper was hung. Today the preferred method of hanging an untrimmed paper is to cut off both margins and butt the edges. If, for the sake of accuracy, overlapping seams are preferred, experiment first. Because of the thickness of the modern paper stock, the seam may appear more prominently than it would have originally.

Board or sheathed walls were frequently papered instead of painted. Before paper was applied, thin strips of cloth were pasted over the joints of the boards so the paper would lie flat and not split or be punctured. Plaster dados under a chair rail were often papered rather than painted the color of the woodwork. Corner posts found in early buildings were not usually covered with paper until the late 19th century.

In the 18th and early 19th centuries fireboards used to cover the fireplace opening during the summer months were often papered.

Some papers were designed with this specific purpose in mind, although many fireboards were covered with the same paper and border used in the rest of the room.

The most important consideration when installing reproduction wallpaper, particularly when attempting an accurate restoration, is the use of a border. Borders were an important part of wallpaper design and were used to some degree in every historical period discussed. Often borders were an integral part of the overall pattern; others were designed to complement the design of the sidewall. But some found in historic buildings bear no relationship to the paper with which they were used. The extent to which borders were used in a room varies. In some cases they surrounded all the architectural elements; in other cases they were used only at the ceiling level (or just below the cornice) or at both the ceiling level and above the chair rail or baseboard. Often a border at the ceiling level was wider than the one used elsewhere in the room; also, it may have been of a completely different design. The borders in different rooms of a building may have been treated differently. The location where borders were used in a room also varied during different historical periods. During the 18th century borders were commonly used to outline the architecture of a room; each wall was treated as a separate unit, so that two widths of borders appeared in each corner. With the exception of bordering the corners, this practice continued into

A reproduction wallpaper border was used to frame the wallpaper, "Tassel," and to outline the woodwork in the north parlor of the Wells-Thorn House, Deerfield, Massachusetts. (Historic Deerfield, Inc.)

the early 19th century. The use of borders only around the ceiling and chair rail was also fashionable. In the mid-19th century borders were sometimes used to divide a room into a series of panels. Late 19th-century paper hangers used borders to divide the wall into three horizontal units. These general principles should be kept in mind while investigating the structure and searching for evidence that will indicate how the room was bordered.

Locating an old photograph that illustrates how the wallpaper was installed in a room can be a great help in researching an accurate restoration; it can also create a dilemma. The photograph of the parlor of the Short House, Newbury, Massachusetts, shows the best parlor of an early 18th-century house as it looked in 1911. Samples of the paper survive and date between 1800 and 1810. However, whoever hung the paper obviously did not understand the pattern. Other photographs of the room show the cornice border applied vertically in the corners and alongside the windows and doors. It was also used to outline a dado created by hanging a floral pattern horizontally. Should this evidence be precisely duplicated in hanging the reproduction wallpaper, or should the period mistake be corrected? The final decision depends on the purpose of the restoration or rehabilitation. In some cases such mistakes have been corrected.

How to Use the Catalog

The following catalog of reproduction wallpapers is arranged by historical period from 1700 to 1930. Short essays introduce the popular styles of the particular period and precede the list of available reproductions of these styles. The essays should be amplified by consulting the various books on wallpaper in particular and interior decoration in general that are cited in the bibliography.

Borders, dados, and panels are not included with sidewall papers but are listed separately at the end of each section. Other types of wallpapers, including coordinating patterns, scenic papers, ceiling papers, embossed papers, and relief decorations, are also listed separately for that historical period, as are wallpapers available through museums and types of designs that have changed little over the years, including solid stripes and nonrepeating Chinese papers.

Individual catalog entries give the following information when it is available:

Manufacturer's catalog name for the wallpaper pattern.

Country, date, and method of manufacture of the original or document, followed by the designer and original manufacturer when known.

Source of a published photograph of the document wallpaper (see bibliography for complete titles).

The photograph of the parlor at the Short House (c. 1911) in Newbury, Massachusetts, documents wallpaper that was poorly installed 100 years earlier. (Society for the Preservation of New England Antiquities)

Width, repeat, and roll content of reproduction wallpaper (listed as "yds. per s/r [single roll]" for domestically produced papers and "yds. per roll" indicating the metric roll of European imports).

Changes, if known, made by the manufacturer in the reproduction.

Organization or museum for which the wallpaper was reproduced (see sources of information for location if none is given in entry).

Information about the document and its location.

Manufacturer's catalog number or code for the reproduction wallpaper.

Manufacturer's name for the document color or description of the document color. An additional color may occasionally be listed as a period coloring; this is a colorway produced by the manufacturer that the author has selected as being an appropriate coloring for the design. The word "series" after a manufacturer's order number indicates that all colorings are acceptable.

"Block print" at the end of an entry indicates that the reproduction wallpaper itself is block printed.

Remember that American wallpaper is priced by the single roll but sold in double- or triple-roll quantities. Make sure the room being papered is measured accurately and that the repeat of the pattern is figured into the calculations to determine the number of rolls needed. Borders are sold by the yard.

CATALOG
OF REPRODUCTION
WALLPAPERS

1700 TO 1780:
LUXURIES FOR ENGLISH
COLONISTS

The earliest reference to wallpaper in America was recorded in 1700 in the inventory of a Boston stationer. In the first half of the 18th century, painted paper hangings were found only in wealthy households in urban areas. Colonists who could afford wallpaper purchased it either from stationers or booksellers who dealt in an entire range of paper goods or from merchants as special orders. The availability and use of wallpaper increased steadily from 1750 as technology improved and demand for this new decorative commodity spread. Toward the end of the 18th century, wallpaper was purchased also from upholsterers, the equivalent of modern interior designers.

In the 18th century, wallpaper was most commonly printed with wood blocks. Occasionally, stencils were used to create large areas of color and handwork was used to create very fine lines. Individual sheets of handmade paper were pasted together to form a roll, because it was not possible to produce the continuous roll of paper we know today. Once the 12-yard roll was created, it received a ground color, which was applied with large brushes. Finally, the pattern was printed with a series of wood blocks, one for each color and unit of the design.

A roll of paper was called a "piece." This terminology, along with the use of the smaller sheets of paper to form the roll, has led to the misconception that early wallpapers were hung by pasting each separate sheet onto the wall. Although this method of application was sometimes used with the earliest "painted papers," careful examination of a large sample of l8th-century wallpaper reveals no color under the horizontal seam where the sheets are joined. Scrutiny of the design indicates that the size of the repeat (and, therefore, the size of the block used to print it) is rarely the same as the size of the individual piece of paper.

"Lambeth Saracen" (page 34), "Hogarth" (page 37), and "Hunting Scene" (page 36) are examples of the simple black-and-white woodblock prints made in England between 1690 and 1700. "Cerises" (page 33) reproduces a "domino" paper made around 1750. These early French papers are named after the group of craftsmen called

Entrance Hall of Gunston Hall, Lorton, Virginia, showing custom reproduction "Pillar and Arch," 1769. (Gunston Hall)

"dominotiers," who specialized in simple one-or two-color prints. All illustrate the types of patterns that may have been exported to the colonies early in the 18th century. Only "Hunting Scene" is documented as actually having been available in New England; it is preserved as the covers of three small almanacs dated 1725–27 in the collections of the Essex Institute, Salem, Massachusetts.

Most wallpapers used in American buildings before the Revolution were of English origin. The patterns available in the mid-18th century can be separated into several distinct types. Most expensive were the custom-made paper hangings—i.e., those made specifically to fit the walls of a new house. Notable examples of this type of wallpaper can be seen today in three rooms of the Jeremiah Lee Mansion (1768) in Marblehead, Massachusetts, and in the Van Rensselaer Hall (1768), installed in the American Wing of the Metropolitan Museum of Art. Designed to imitate walls hung with large framed oil paintings, they depict classical ruins copied from prints and are surrounded with large trompe l'œil frames. Wallpapers with repeating patterns simulating walls hung with smaller framed prints, such as "Lady Pepperrell House," were more readily available.

Pillar and arch designs were more popular in the 18th century than they are today. When hung, they formed a series of arcades. Their large repeats made them appropriate for rooms with high ceilings and for entries, the 18th-century term for staircase halls. "Gunston Hall" and "Arch" are two pillar and arch designs available as custom orders. "Gunston Hall" (page 30) was commissioned for the stair hall of the Virginia house of the same name. "Arch" is the pattern being installed in the 1898 photograph (page 10) depicting a paper hanger at work in South Berwick, Maine; the pattern was reproduced that year from fragments found in the same space during the course of restoration.

Textiles inspired many wallpaper designs available in the 18th century. For example, exotic chintzes and plate-printed fabrics provided the motifs used in "East India" and "Yellow Peacock" (page 39) respectively. "Pekin" (page 34) and "Green Lace" (page 37) imitate colorful silk brocades, while "Fiore" (page 36) and "Leopard" (page 36) copy the more expensive silk and wool damasks used for curtains, upholstery, and wallhangings in elaborate English houses.

Some of the large-scale damask-pattern wallpapers were made to look even more like their textile counterparts by means of flocking, a process in which small fragments of chopped wool or silk were spread over the paper, adhering where the design had been printed with a varnish instead of a color. Flocked papers were expensive; evidence of their use has been found primarily in parlors and best chambers. These large-scale flocked designs printed in bold colors are not as favored in today's decorative schemes as they were in the 18th century. Custom work may be the only way to obtain one for a restoration project.

BRUNSCHWIG & FILS

෯ CERISES. French, 1750–60, block print. 26³/₄" wide, 4¹/₄" repeat, 5 yds. per s/r. Document at Musée des Arts Décoratifs, Paris. No.12581.06 (brick and blue).

෯ CHINA FANCY. English, 1750–80, block print. 21¹/₂" wide, 43" drop repeat, 6 yds. per s/r. Adaptation: colors not reproduced exactly. Document at Winterthur Museum. Document color, no. 10771.06 (pink and jade on ivory), is a custom order.

෯ CHINOISERIE. French, 1770–90, block print. 24" wide, 36" repeat, 5 yds. per s/r. Reproduced for Museum of Early Southern Decorative Arts. Document in Brunschwig Archives. No. 610.06 (lacquer red and blue on parchment).

෯ FAMILY TREE. French, 1775–90, block print. Designed by Reveillon. Clouzot and Follot, pl. 6. 27" wide, 36" half-drop repeat, 5 yds. per s/r. Adaptation: colors softened and scale altered. Document in Brunschwig Archives. No.14450.06 (off-white).

෯ PEKIN. French, 1773–1800, block print. 20" wide, 14¹/₄" repeat, 6 yds. per s/r. Document at Musée des Arts Décoratifs. No.13442.06 (blue).

෯ REVE DU PAPILLON. French, 1770–85, hand painted. 27¹/₄" wide, 33³/₈" repeat, 5 yds. per s/r. Adapted from a hand-painted document at Corbit-Sharp House, Odessa, Del., a property of Winterthur Museum. No.12473.06 (yellow).

CLARENCE HOUSE

෯ COALPORT. English, 1770–90, block print. 20¹/₂" wide, 16¹/₈" repeat, 11 yds. per roll. Reproduced from a period design for a wallpaper. Document in Courtauld Archives, London. Period colorings: No.W9011/002 (blue); No.W9011/003 (green); No.W9011/004 (yellow).

CERISES, 1750–60. Brunschwig & Fils.

LAMBETH SARACEN,
1690–1700. Classic
Revivals (Hamilton-
Weston Collection).

PEKIN, 1773–1800.
Brunschwig & Fils.

ঔ TEMPLE NEWSAM. English, 1720–40, block print with flock. 21" wide, 21" repeat, 11 yds. per roll. Reproduction not flocked. Coles Traditional Collection. Period colorings: No.C238 (mustard); No.C242 (red on yellow).

CLASSIC REVIVALS

Hamilton-Weston Historic Handprint Collection

ঔ LAMBETH SARACEN. English, 1690–1700, block print. 20¼" wide, 8" repeat, 11 yds. per roll. No.8111 (black on tan).

ঔ MAYFAIR. English, 1750–80, block print. 21" wide, 21" repeat, 11 yds. per roll. No.405 (blue on white).

ঔ TWICKENHAM. English, 1755–80, block print. 20¾" wide, 18½" repeat, 11 yds. per roll. Green. Order by name.

Mauny Collection

ঔ LE CHASSEUR. French, 1770–1800, block print. 20⅞" wide, 20" repeat, 11 yds. per roll. No.198 (black and white on gray). Block print.

ঔ CONCERT CHAMPETRE. French, 1770–1800, block print. 21⅝" wide, 39½" repeat, 11 yds. per roll. No.192 (pink and gray on gray). Block print.

ঔ DANSE VILLAGEOISE. French, 1770–1800, block print. 20" wide, 21¼" repeat, 11 yds. per roll. No.175 (blue and orange on cream). Block print.

ঔ DENTELLE ET BOUQUETS. French, 1770–1800, block print. 21¼" wide, 19¼" repeat, 11 yds. per roll. No.173 (gray and white on blue-gray). Block print.

ঔ LEOPARD. French, 1760–80, block print. 20½" wide, 21½" repeat, 11 yds. per roll. No.1515 (green). Block print.

CHRISTOPHER HYLAND INCORPORATED

ঔ ARLESFORD. English, 1690–1700, block print. Wells-Cole, no. 30, p. 25. 21" wide, 24½" repeat, 11 yds. per roll. No.AB129/4 (gray, green, peach, and black).

ঔ CHINTZ. English, 1730–50, block print. 18⅝" wide, 21⅞" repeat, 11 yds. per roll. No.AB149/2 (blue on yellow).

ঔ FIORE. English, 1750–60, block print. 21" wide, 44" repeat, 11 yds. per roll. No.AB252 (black and white on blue).

ঔ HOGARTH. English, 1690–1700, block print. 15⁷⁄₁₆" wide, 18¼" repeat, 11 yds. per roll. No.AB151/2 (black on yellow).

ঔ HOLCOMBE. English, 1680–1700, block print. Teynac, Nolot, and Vivien, p. 56; Wells-Cole, no. 27, p. 24. 16⅜" wide, 21" repeat, 11 yds. per roll. No.AB144/3 (beige, blue, and black).

ঔ HUNTING SCENE. English, 1690–1710, block print. Greysmith, fig. 31, p. 46; Teynac, Nolot, and Vivien, p. 44; Wells-Cole, no. 28, p. 26. 19¾" wide, 15¾" repeat, 11 yds. per roll. No.AB146/4 (multi).

ঔ MELTON. English, 1720–40, block print. Wells-Cole, no. 31, p. 26.

right
HUNTING SCENE, 1690–1710. Christopher Hyland Incorporated.

below left
LEOPARD, 1760–80. Classic Revivals (Mauny Collection).

below right
FIORE, 1750–60. Christopher Hyland Incorporated.

top left
HOGARTH, 1690–1700.
Christopher Hyland
Incorporated.

left and top right
Original document
and artwork for
"Green Lace," a wall-
paper of 1720–40
now reproduced by
Schumacher.

$17^1/2$" wide, $28^1/2$" repeat, 11 yds. per roll. No.AB138/2 (green and white).

᧞ POMEGRANATE. English, 1750–60, block print. Wells-Cole, no. 4, p. 12. 21" wide, $20^1/2$" half-drop repeat, 11 yds. per roll. Document at Temple Newsam, Leeds, England. Reproduction not flocked. No.ZZ92006 (red on red).

COLEFAX & FOWLER

Available through Cowtan & Tout.

᧞ SUDBURY PARK. English, 1770–90, block print. Oman and Hamilton, no. 127, p. 128. $20^1/2$" wide, 3" repeat, 11 yds. per roll. No.7046/06 (gray and white).

SCHUMACHER

᧞ DAISY. English, 1770–1800, block print. Wells-Cole, no. 3, p. 10. 21" wide, $2^1/2$" repeat, 11 yds. per roll. Document at Temple Newsam, Leeds, England. No.TN02 (white on yellow).

᧞ DIAMONDS AND FLOWERS. English, 1750–70, block print with flocking. Wells-Cole, front cover. 21" wide, 3" half-drop repeat, 11 yds. per roll. Adaptation: flocking not reproduced. Document at Temple Newsam, Leeds, England. No.TN08 (rust on gray).

᧞ EVERARD. English, 1770–90, block print. $27^1/2$" wide, 11" repeat, $4^1/2$ yds. per s/r. Document at Colonial Williamsburg. No.513100 (document azure).

᧞ GREEN LACE. English, 1720–40, block print. Lynn, fig. 3-7, p. 74. $22^1/2$" wide, $20^1/2$" repeat, $5^1/2$ yds. per s/r. Document at Colonial Williamsburg. No.513060 (document emerald).

᧞ POMEGRANATE. English, 1760–70, block print with flocking. Oman and Hamilton, no. 193, p. 146; Sugden and Edmundson, pl. 30, p. 105; Wells-Cole, no. 4, p. 12. 20" wide, 20" half-drop repeat, 11 yds. per roll. Adaptation: flocking not reproduced. Document at Temple Newsam, Leeds, England. No.TN09 (red on white).

᧞ YELLOW PEACOCK. English, 1740–60, block print. Nylander, Redmond, and Sander, fig. 11-c, p. 68. 21" wide, 44" repeat, $5^1/2$ yds. per s/r. Document at Colonial Williamsburg. No.513070 (document flax).

WATERHOUSE WALLHANGINGS

᧞ CAPE COD FLORAL. English, 1770–90, block print. $20^3/4$" wide, $12^1/2$" repeat, 7 yds. per s/r. Document in Waterhouse Archives. No.209202 (charcoal on pale mustard).

᧞ CAPTAIN JOHN KENDRICK HOUSE. English, 1760–80, block print. 20" wide, 22" repeat, 7 yds. per s/r. Document in Waterhouse Archives. No.177269 (black and white on ochre). Period coloring: No.177248 (green on gray).

᧞ EAST INDIA. French, 1760–70, block print. Lynn, color pl. 20,

Original document
for "Yellow Peacock,"
a wallpaper of 1740–60
now reproduced by
Schumacher.

CAPE CODE FLORAL, 1770–90. Water-house Wallhangings.

p. 64. 20¹/₂ʺ wide, 22ʺ repeat, 7 yds. per s/r. Adaptation: colors not reproduced exactly. Document at Cooper-Hewitt Museum. No.158635 (green and orange on white).

ॐ GENERAL SAMUEL McCLELLAN. English, 1770–80, block print. 21ʺ wide, 22¹/₂ʺ repeat, 7 yds. per s/r. Document privately owned. No.155947 (gray ground).

ॐ LADY PEPPERRELL HOUSE. English, 1760–70, block print. Nylander, Redmond, and Sander, fig. 5.1, p. 52. 23ʺ wide, 42ʺ repeat, 5 yds. per s/r. Document at Society for the Preservation of New England Antiquities. No.182433 (gray on pink).

ॐ WAREHAM FLORAL. English, 1770–80, block print. 21ʺ wide, 18¹/₂ʺ repeat, 7 yds. per s/r. Document in Waterhouse Archives. No.176433 (pink ground).

CUSTOM PATTERNS FROM MUSEUMS

GUNSTON HALL

ॐ PILLAR AND ARCH. English, 1769–80, block print. Oman and Hamilton, color pl. p. 136; Sugden and Edmundson, frontispiece. 21ʺ wide plus 1³/₄ʺ border, 41¹/₄ʺ repeat, 5 yds. per s/r. Sidewall document at Victoria and Albert Museum; border document at Society for the Preservation of New England Antiquities. Black and white on light yellow.

GENERAL SAMUEL
McCLELLAN, 1770–80.
Waterhouse Wall-
hangings.

1780 TO 1840:
STYLISH IMPORTS AND
AMERICAN PATTERNS

Between 1780 and 1840 wallpaper became more commonly used in American interiors. At the same time the American consumer was confronted with a wider selection of patterns available from a greater number of sources. After the American Revolution, expanded trade opportunities enabled American merchants to import French and Chinese wallpapers directly. English wallpapers remained popular, but French imports were beginning to provide strong competition. American manufacture of wallpaper, which had been discouraged during the colonial period, was well established by 1790, especially in Boston, New York, and Philadelphia. The patterns produced by this newly founded American industry were inspired by or copied directly from imported papers; however, they were advertised as being a better buy—equal in quality and less expensive.

Because of the various sources of supply during this period, determining the origin of a paper found in the course of a restoration is often difficult. From 1714 to 1836 English wallpapers were required by law to have a stamp printed on the reverse indicating that a tax on the paper used to form the roll had been paid. This stamp usually comprises an interlace of the letters GR surmounted with a crown. Although the stamp indicates the origin of the paper, it is of little help in dating the sample. American and French papers, on the other hand, were rarely marked in any way. The earliest papers produced in America were not necessarily cruder than their European counterparts; in fact, the quality of inexpensive English and French papers was sometimes quite poor.

With the exception of the custom-made hangings imitating large framed paintings, the types of patterns described in the previous chapter continued to be popular during the 1780s and into the 1790s. The use of plain-colored papers with borders surrounding the architectural elements of the room increased. This type of wall treatment became fashionable in the mid-18th century; the preferred colors were blue and green, and the borders usually were made of papier-mâché. Manufacturers in the late 18th century offered a wider

ROBBINS HOUSE, 1810–25. Water-house Wallhangings.

43

choice of colors for the plain papers and a greater variety in the patterns and widths of printed borders.

Except when they copied an imported paper, American wallpapers from 1790 to 1820 are usually simple repeating or striped patterns, often printed in only one or two colors. These, no doubt, were the types of patterns referred to as "common papers" in one Boston manufacturer's advertisement.

Beginning in the early 19th century, the importation and use of French wallpapers increased markedly. The French manufacturers had perfected the block-printing process, and their designs and colors clearly captivated the American consumer. Until about 1870 French wallpaper styles dominated the market.

Late 18th-century and early 19th-century French papers excelled in the realistic rendering of both color and shading of flowers, fruit, drapery, lace, ribbon, marble, architectural elements, and even statuary. See, for example, "Mirage" (page 49), "La Haie Panel" (cover and endleaves), "Draperie Josephine" (page 57), "Finistere" (page 85), and "Floral Drapery Cornice" (page 79). The goal of some designs seems to have been total deception. Neoclassical designs, especially those by Reveillon, and floral patterns with arabesques seem to be as popular now as when they were first imported. They are reproduced by a number of firms. Many of these classically inspired designs were perfect complements to the new style of Federal architecture.

"Glenmoral" (page 69), "New Clarissa" (page 49), and "Wheeler House" (page 53) are reproductions of a French style of paper hanging that was popular from about 1810 until the late 1820s. The style consisted of small-figured designs, often overprinted with drapery and floral motifs and crowned by elaborate drapery borders. A similar type, called a "landscape figure," relied on the same basic formula. Vignettes of people or animals alternated with smaller floral motifs on small-figured backgrounds between stripes. An almost endless variety of motifs was plugged into this formula; see "Personnages et Oiseaux" (page 58) and "Louise" (page 72). Today, often only the stripes and small-figured grounds are copied from this style of wallpaper as these elements appeal most to modern taste. Because the principal motifs are omitted, these adaptations are unsuccessful.

"Landscape figures" should not be confused with the French scenic wallpapers often referred to as landscape papers. These continuous nonrepeating panoramas are perhaps the most widely known examples of any historic wallpapers because more examples have been preserved in historic buildings and installed in period room settings in art museums than any other type. The first scenic wallpaper, "Vue de Suisse," was produced by Zuber in 1804. Many of the titles popular during this period are available today. Most are produced by

Zuber & Cie and are still printed with the original wood blocks.

The attention given to scenic papers has often overshadowed other styles of wallpaper that were popular at the same time and used more extensively. Odile Nouvel's *Wallpapers of France, 1800–1850* presents an impressive survey of the variety of designs found in French wallpapers of the first half of the 19th century. Not all the styles illustrated actually found their way to the United States, but those that did were imitated widely by American manufacturers. Patterns composed of floral motifs, geometric designs, and medallions were popular in the 1820s and 1830s. Many French papers of the 1830s are characterized by shaded or blended backgrounds. This process, also developed by the Zuber factory, was called "irisée." These papers were referred to as "rainbow papers" in this country and are examples of a type of design that was very popular in its own day but is rarely reproduced today. A custom reproduction of an American-made rainbow paper has been installed by Historic Deerfield in a chamber of the Wells-Thorn House (page 95).

BRUNSCHWIG & FILS   WALLPAPERS

❧ ALEXANDRIA SIDEWALL. French, 1810–15, block print. 21³/₄" wide plus 4¹/₂" border, 9" repeat, 5 yds. per s/r. No. 11519.06 (clay).

❧ ANANAS. French, 1780–1800, block print. 24¹/₄" wide, 24" repeat, 6 yds. per s/r. Adaptation. Document in McClelland Collection, Brunschwig Archives. No.11606.06 (persimmon on cream).

❧ ARCH. American, c. 1787, block print and stencil. Nylander, Redmond, and Sander, fig. 9.1, p. 60, and fig. 79.2, p. 269. 21¹/₂" wide, 42¹/₄" repeat. Reproduced from an 1898 reproduction in which the background color was changed from gray to blue. Document at Hamilton House, South Berwick, Maine, a property of Society for the Preservation of New England Antiquities. No.363.6C. Custom order.

❧ AURORA. French, 1790–1800, block print. Originally printed by Reveillon. Lynn, color pl. 10, p. 57. 21" wide, 48" repeat, 6 yds. per s/r. Document at Phelps-Hatheway House, Suffield, Conn., a property of Antiquarian and Landmarks Society. No.14224.06 (green on off-white).

❧ BAGATELLE. French, 1790–1810, block print. Lynn, color pls. 4 and 5, pp. 36 and 37. 21" wide, 21" repeat, 7 yds. per s/r. Document at Cooper-Hewitt Museum. Document color, no. 12508.06 (brown), is a custom order.

❧ BOSPHORE SEMIS. French, 1790–1820, block print. 27¹/₄" wide, 19" repeat, 5 yds. per s/r. Document in McClelland Collection, Brunschwig Archives. No.11531.06 (red).

❧ BOUTONNIERE. French, 1789–1800, block print. 27" wide, 7³/₄" repeat, 5 yds. per s/r. Document at Musée des Arts Décoratifs. No.13402.06 (blue on blue).

❧ BOSQUET. French, 1798–99, block print. Originally printed by

BOUTONNIERE, 1789–1800. Brunschwig & Fils.

Jacquemart et Bénard. Greysmith, fig. 59, p. 86. 21¼" wide, 20¼" repeat, 6 yds. per s/r. Document at Musée des Arts Décoratifs, Paris. No.12642.6C (blue). Custom order.

᠔ BULFINCH SWAG SIDEWALL AND BORDER. American, 1810–20, block print. Nylander, Redmond, and Sander, fig. 29.6, p. 132. 27⁷/₁₆" wide including 5⁹/₁₆" border, 7½" repeat. Document at Society for the Preservation of New England Antiquities. No.1323.6C (blue). Custom order.

᠔ CORNFLOWER RESIST. Probably American, c. 1796, block print. Nylander, Redmond, and Sander, fig. 22.5, p. 98. 22" wide, 9¼" repeat. Document at Society for the Preservation of New England Antiquities. No.13202.6C (blue). Custom order.

᠔ CRISTAUX. French, 1827, block print. Designed by A. Merii. Nouvel, fig. 170, p. 61. 18½" wide, 9¼" repeat. Document at Musée des Arts Décoratifs. No.12599.6C (gray). Custom order.

᠔ DEBUSSY. French, 1825–35, block print. Nouvel, fig. 201, p. 66. 24" wide, 18¼" repeat, 5 yds. per s/r. Document in Brunschwig Archives. No.11579.06 (pearl gray).

᠔ DORCHESTER. Probably French, 1780–1800, block print. Nylander, Redmond, and Sander, fig. 7.3, p. 56. 21" wide, 22½" repeat, 6 yds. per s/r. Document at Society for the Preservation of New England Antiquities. No.11049.06 (rose on black).

ᘒ EXETER FAN. American, 1800–20, block print. 28¼" wide, 9½" repeat, 5 yds. per s/r. Document in Brunschwig Archives. No. 11218.6C (beige). Custom order.

ᘒ FOX AND ROOSTER. French, 1780–1800, block print. 24" wide, 21" repeat, 6 yds. per s/r. Reproduced for Museum of Early Southern Decorative Arts. Document in Brunschwig Archives. No.640.06 (rose and blue on clay beige).

ᘒ FRAMBOISE. French, 1795–1800, block print. 27" wide, 16½" repeat, 5 yds. per s/r. Document at Musée des Arts Décoratifs. Document color, no. 12602.06 (taupe on blue), is a custom order.

ᘒ GALLIER DIAMOND. French or English, 1800–20, block print. 28" wide, 13⅜" repeat, 5 yds. per s/r. Document in Brunschwig Archives. No.10410.06 (brown and green on beige).

ᘒ GEOMETRIQUE. French, 1825–35, block print. 27" wide, 4⅝" repeat, 5 yds. per s/r. Document at Musée des Arts Décoratifs. Document color, no. 12569.06 (gray), is a custom order.

ᘒ LA HAIE PANEL. French, 1815–25, block print. Nouvel, fig. 39, p. 39, and fig. 262, p. 77. 21" wide, 11½' panel. Adaptation: border motifs simplified. Document at Musée des Arts Décoratifs. No.13509.06 (forest and rose).

ᘒ IMLAY. American, c. 1794, block print. McClelland, p. 258. 20½" wide, 21½" repeat, 5 yds. per s/r. Document at Winterthur Museum. No.10862.6C (orange and blue on blue). Custom order.

ᘒ JARDINIERE. French, 1780–1800, block print. Probably printed by Reveillon. 21½" wide, 21¼" repeat. Document in Brunschwig Archives. Document color, no. 12384.06 (rose on seafoam), is a custom order.

ᘒ LITCHFIELD. French, 1800–20, block print. 27" wide, 25¼" repeat, 5 yds. per s/r. Document in McClelland Collection, Brunschwig Archives. No.13713.06 (yellow).

ᘒ LOCKLIN PLANTATION. Probably English, 1780–1810, block print. 28¼" wide, 30" repeat, 5 yds. per s/r. Adaptation: pattern slightly enlarged. Reproduced for Liberty Hall, Kenansville, N.C. Document in Brunschwig Archives. No.800.06 (lacquer and blue on beige).

ᘒ MAIZE. French, 1800–20, block print. 18½" wide plus 4¼" border, 22¾" repeat, 6 yds. per s/r. Document in McClelland Collection, Brunschwig Archives. Document color, no. 11399.06 (gray), is a custom order.

ᘒ MAYTIME. French, 1810–25, block print. 28" wide, 23⅞" repeat, 5 yds. per s/r. Adaptation: width reduced by 4" between stripes. Reproduced for the Valentine Museum, Richmond, Va. Document in Brunschwig Archives. Document color, no. 10502.06 (gray and orange on blue), is a custom order.

ᘒ MIRAGE. French, 1780–1810, block print. McClelland, p. 137. 27" wide plus 5¼" border, 18" repeat, 5 yds. per s/r. Document at

Cooper-Hewitt Museum. No.12532.06 (blue).

❧ MUGUET MOUSSELINE. French, 1800–10, block print. 20¹/₂" wide, 10¹/₄" repeat, 6 yds. per s/r. Document at Musée des Arts Décoratifs. No.13391.06 (white on pink).

❧ NEW CLARISSA. French, 1823–30, block print. 18³/₄" wide, 18¹/₄" repeat, 7 yds. per s/r. Document at Society for the Preservation of New England Antiquities. No.13332.06 (yellow on azure).

❧ ONDINE. French, 1830–35, block print. 21" wide, 26⁵/₈" repeat, 6 yds. per s/r. Document at Musée des Arts Décoratifs. No.12619.6C (gray). Custom order.

❧ OSBORNE ARCADED PANEL. American, 1800–7, block print. Originally printed by Moses Grant. Nylander, Redmond, and Sander, fig. 23.1, p. 111. Panel size: 21⁵/₈" wide, 10' 2" high. Document at Society for the Preservation of New England Antiquities. No.13294.6C (green). Custom order.

❧ OTIS DAMASK. English, c. 1796, block print. Nylander, Redmond, and Sander, fig. 22.1, p. 96. 27" wide, 5¹/₄" repeat, 5 yds. per s/r. Document at Harrison Gray Otis House, Boston, a property of Society for the Preservation of New England Antiquities. No.13263.06 (gold).

❧ PASSIFLORE. French, 1825–35, block print. Originally printed by Jacquemart et Bénard, 27³/₄" wide, 4⁵/₈" repeat, 5 yds. per s/r. Document at Musée des Arts Décoratifs. No.12547.6C (dusty mauve). Custom order.

❧ PENELOPE. American or French, 1810–25, block print. 28" wide, ⁷/₈" repeat, 5 yds. per s/r. Adaptation: slight color change. Reproduced for Liberty Hall, Kenansville, N.C. Document in Brunschwig Archives. Document color, no. 792.06 (white on blue), is a custom order.

❧ PENSEES MOUSSELINE. French, 1800–10, block print. 20⁷/₈" wide, 10¹/₄" repeat, 6 yds. per s/r. Document at Musées des Arts Décoratifs. No.13412.06 (violet on blue).

❧ POMMIER. French, 1830–40, block print. 28" wide, 18" repeat, 5 yds. per s/r. Document in McClelland Collection, Brunschwig Archives. No.11408.06 (vanilla).

❧ RAYURES MOUSSELINE. French, 1801–10, block print. 20¹/₂" wide, 10¹/₄" repeat, 6 yds. per s/r. Document at Musée des Arts Décoratifs. Period coloring: No.13452.06 (aqua on blue).

❧ REVEILLON TULIPS. French, 1790–95, block print. Originally printed by Jacquemart et Bénard. Clouzot and Follot, p. 193. 27³/₄" wide, 18⁵/₈" repeat, 5 yds. per s/r. Document in McClelland Collection, Brunschwig Archives. Period coloring: No.11593.06 (red on yellow).

❧ ROYAL DOLPHIN. English, 1817–25, block print. Designed by Robert Jones; originally printed by Frederick Crace. Greysmith, fig. 52, p. 74; Oman and Hamilton, fig. 1024, p. 353. 25³/₈" wide, 40" half-drop repeat, 5 yds. per s/r. Document at Royal Pavilion, Brighton, England. Document color, no. 13024.6 (jade), is a custom order. Period color-

left
NEW CLARISSA
and
NEW CLARISSA
FESTOON BORDERS,
1823–30.
Brunschwig & Fils.

top
MIRAGE, 1780–1810.
Brunschwig & Fils.

above
OTIS DAMASK, c. 1796.
Brunschwig & Fils.

above left
POMMIER, 1830–40.
Brunschwig & Fils.

above right
RAYURES MOUSSELINE,
1801–10. Brun-
schwig & Fils.

right
SHIRLEY PLACE
FLORAL, 1790–1810.
Brunschwig & Fils.

ings: No.13021.06 (pomegranate); No.13023.06 (mandarin yellow).

&❧ ROYAL PROMENADE PANELS. English, 1800–20, hand painted. Adaptations of hand-painted panels in entrance of Royal Pavilion, Brighton, England. Nos.13065.06, 13075.06, 13085.06, 13095.06, 13105.06, 13115.06 (all blue on pink).

&❧ ROYALTON VINE. American, 1790–1810, block print. Nylander, Redmond, and Sander, fig. 12.3, p. 71. 28" wide, 18¾" repeat. Document at Society for the Preservation of New England Antiquities. No.13192.6C (blue on aqua). Custom order.

&❧ SHIRLEY PLACE FLORAL. Chinese, 1790–1810, hand painted. Nylander, Redmond, and Sander, fig. 21.3, p. 94. 27" wide, 11½" repeat, 5 yds. per s/r. Document at Society for the Preservation of New England Antiquities. No.13240.06 (white).

&❧ SPATTERWARE. Probably English or French, 1790–1820, block print. 27" wide, 5 yds. per s/r. Document in Brunschwig Archives. No.11702.06 (blue).

&❧ LES SYLPHIDES. French, 1790–1800, block print. Originally printed by Reveillon. *Bulletin*, p. 121; Clouzot and Follot, p. 93; Lynn, color pl. 9, p. 40, and fig. 4.3, p. 95. 21" wide, 48" repeat, 6 yds. per s/r. Adaptation: not all motifs reproduced. Document at Phelps-Hatheway House, Suffield, Conn., a property of Antiquarian and Landmarks Society. No.14234.06 (green).

&❧ TALAVERA. American, 1810–25, block print. 27" wide, 25" repeat, 5 yds. per s/r. Adaptation: colors not reproduced exactly. Document in Brunschwig Archives. No.14346.06 (bisque).

&❧ TENTURE FLOTTANTE. French, c. 1812, block print. 20¾" wide, 21¼" repeat, 6 yds. per s/r. Adaptation. Document in McClelland Collection, Brunschwig Archives. No.11569.06 (gray).

&❧ TRELLIS. French, 1800–5, block print. Designed by Ebert & Buffard; printed by Jacquemart et Bénard. Nouvel, fig. 166, p. 61. 27" wide, 3½" repeat, 5 yds. per s/r. Document at Musée des Arts Décoratifs. No.12579.6C (gray). Custom order.

&❧ VOLGER HOUSE. Probably French, 1815–25, block print. Nylander, Redmond, and Sander, color pl. 16, p. 107 (pattern shown reversed). 21½" wide, 20¾" repeat. Document at Old Salem, Winston-Salem, N.C. No.367.6C. Custom order.

&❧ WHEELER HOUSE SIDEWALL. French, 1810–25, block print. 21⅜" wide, 21" repeat. Reproduced for John Wheeler House, Murfreesboro, N.C. No.12899.06 (grisaille). Custom order.

CLARENCE HOUSE

&❧ GARDEN VINE. English, 1815–25, block print. 20½" wide, 10½" repeat, 11 yds. per roll. Document in Courtauld Archives, London. No.W9007/048 (sage green).

&❧ GOTHIK FRETWORK. English, 1835–45, block print. For a similar

top
TENTURE FLOTTANTE, c. 1812.
Brunschwig & Fils.

above
TALAVERA, 1810–25. Brunschwig
& Fils.

right
LES SYLPHIDES, 1790–1800.
Brunschwig & Fils.

pattern, see Oman and Hamilton, no. 692A, color pl. p. 261. 27"
wide, 3½" repeat, 5 yds. per s/r. Document in Clarence House
Archives. No.9400/6 (red).

ঙ OAK LEAF. English, 1810–20, block print. 27" wide, 3¼" repeat,
5 yds. per s/r. Adaptation. Document in Clarence House Archives.
No.9430/3 (green).

ঙ REGENCY MEDALLION. English, 1820–30, block print. 27" wide,
5½" repeat, 5 yds. per s/r. Document in Clarence House Archives.
No.9290/1 (white).

CLASSIC REVIVALS

Hamilton-Weston Historic Handprint Collection

ঙ BEDFORD STRIPE. English, 1780–90, block print. 21" wide, 5¼"
repeat, 11 yds. per roll. No.301 (blue and tan).

ঙ BLOOMSBURY SQUARE. English, 1800–10, block print. 21" wide,
1½" repeat, 11 yds. per roll. No.507 (green and black).

above left
WHEELER HOUSE
SIDEWALL and
border, 1810–25.
Brunschwig & Fils.

above right
GOTHIK FRETWORK,
1835–45. Clarence
House.

above left
ROYAL CRESCENT,
1780–1810. Classic
Revivals (Hamilton-
Weston Collection).

above right
STRAND TEARDROP,
1790–1810. Classic
Revivals (Hamilton-
Weston Collection).

☙ COVENT GARDEN FLORAL. English, 1830–40, block print. 21"
wide, 11¼" repeat, 11 yds. per roll. No.8141 (red on yellow).

☙ FUCHSIA ST. JAMES. English, 1830–40, block print. 21" wide,
10¾" repeat, 11 yds. per roll. No.8151 (red and green on gray).

☙ KINGSTON MARKET. English, 1810–20, block print. 21" wide,
10½" repeat, 11 yds. per roll. No.8131 (blue and white).

☙ RICHMOND TRELLIS. English, 1830–40, block print. 21" wide,
7¾" repeat, 11 yds. per roll. No.8161 (green on ivory).

☙ ROYAL CRESCENT. English, 1780–1810, block print. 21" wide, 21"
repeat, 11 yds. per roll. Gray on blue. Order by name.

☙ STRAND TEARDROP. English, 1790–1810, block print. 20½" wide,
1½" repeat, 11 yds. per roll. No.8121 (blue and white).

Mauny Collection

☙ ALLEGORIES. French, 1790–1810, block print. McClelland, p. 174.
18¼" wide, 20⅞" repeat, 11 yds. per roll. No.239 (green and tan on
white). Block print.

☙ AMOUR AVEUGLE. French, 1815–25, block print. 19¼" wide,
25¼" repeat, 11 yds. per roll. No.171 (grays on gray). Block print.

☙ LES AMOURS. French, 1780–1800, block print. McClelland, p. 133.
21⅝" wide, 46" repeat, 11 yds. per roll. No.203 (multi on gray).
Block print.

☙ AMOURS ET OISEAUX. French, 1780–1800, block print. 21¼" wide,

21¼" repeat, 11 yds. per roll. No.134 (multi on yellow). Block print.

ᐩ ANANAS. French, 1780–1800, block print. 21⅝" wide, 20⅞" repeat, 11 yds. per roll. No.197 (multi on cream). Block print.

ᐩ ARC DE TRIOMPHE. French, 1780–1800, block print. 20½" wide, 19⅝" repeat, 11 yds. per roll. No.105 (tan on blue). Block print.

ᐩ LE BAL DE SCEAUX. French, 1815–25, block print. 18⅞" wide, 26¾" repeat, 11 yds. per roll. No.1512 (green on tan). Block print.

ᐩ BARABAN. French, 1800–30, block print. 21¼" wide, 5¼" repeat, 11 yds. per roll. No.161 (white on yellow). Block print.

ᐩ BLUET. French, 1835–45, block print. 19" wide, 9" repeat, 11 yds. per roll. No.223 (tan on ochre). Block print.

ᐩ BOSQUET DE LUNAN. French, 1790–1810, block print. 21¼" wide, 34½" repeat, 11 yds. per roll. No.1503 (multi on cream). Block print.

ᐩ BOUQUET ET AQUEDUC. French, 1780–1800, block print. McClelland, p. 77. 23¼" wide, 32⅝" repeat, 11 yds. per roll. No.119 (multi on white). Block print.

ᐩ BOUQUET TRANSITION. French, 1780–90, block print. Originally printed by Reveillon. Clouzot and Follot, p. 39. 23½" wide, 37" repeat, 11 yds. per roll. No.180.

ᐩ BRANCHE D'EGLANTIER. French, 1800–50, block print. 21¼" wide, 21⅝" repeat, 11 yds. per roll. No.296 (multi on dark brown). Block print.

ᐩ BRIGHTON. French, 1830–60, block print. 18⅞" wide, 5½" repeat, 11 yds. per roll. No.2014 (green on cream). Block print.

ᐩ LE CAMEE. French, 1790–1800, block print. 21¼" wide, 21¼" repeat, 11 yds. per roll. No.214 (gray and blue on gray). Block print.

ᐩ CAMPAGNE FLEURIE. French, 1800–20, block print. 21¼" wide, 21¼" repeat, 11 yds. per roll. No.186 (multi on cream). Block print.

ᐩ CENELLE. French, 1815–25, block print. 19⅞" wide, 19⅞" repeat, 11 yds. per roll. No.262 (pink and green on yellow). Block print.

ᐩ CHASSE AU CANARD. French, 1790–1800, block print. 20" wide, 21⅝" repeat, 11 yds. per roll. No.187 (mauve on yellow). Block print.

ᐩ CHAR ET COLOMBES. French, 1780–1800, block print. 21⅝" wide, 21⅝" repeat, 11 yds. per roll. No.137 (pink and white on blue). Block print.

ᐩ CHIEN COURANT. French, 1780–1800, block print. 21⅝" wide, 21⅝" repeat, 11 yds. per roll. No.189 (orange and blue on light blue). Block print.

ᐩ CLOCHETTES. French, 1780–1800, block print. 21¼" wide, 21¼" repeat, 11 yds. per roll. No.127 (multi on yellow). Block print.

ᐩ LES COLOMBES. French, 1780–1800, block print. 22" wide, 21¼" repeat, 11 yds. per roll. No.110 (blue and red on blue). Block print.

᠔᠊ COLONNADES. French, 1780–1800, block print. 21⁵/₈" wide, 21⁵/₈" repeat, 11 yds. per roll. No.114 (pinks and green on light blue). Block print.

᠔᠊ COMBAT AERIEN. French, 1780–90, block print. Olligs, vol. 1, fig. 165, p. 244. 20¹/₂" wide, 24³/₄" repeat, 11 yds. per roll. No.199. Block print.

᠔᠊ LE COQ. French, 1780–1800, block print. Olligs, vol. 1, fig. 166, p. 244. 21⁵/₈" wide, 42¹/₂" repeat, 11 yds. per roll. No.116 (multi on tan). Block print.

᠔᠊ CORBEILLE ET TREILLAGE. French, 1820–30, block print. 22" wide, 18¹/₂" repeat, 11 yds. per roll. No.174 (rust on yellow). Block print.

᠔᠊ COUPE DE PIERRE. French, 1830–50, block print. 11 yds. per roll. No.229 (gray and tan). Block print.

᠔᠊ LES CYGNES. French, 1780–1800, block print. McClelland, p. 130. 21¹/₄" wide, 21¹/₄" repeat, 11 yds. per roll. No.135 (gray and white on light gray). Block print.

᠔᠊ DAMAS CHARLES X. French, 1825–40, block print. 18¹/₂" wide, 15³/₄" repeat, 11 yds. per roll. No.297 (gray on gray). Block print.

᠔᠊ DAMAS DE MARSAN. French, 1825–40, block print. 18⁷/₈" wide, 18¹/₈" repeat, 11 yds. per roll. No.235 (cream on red). Block print.

᠔᠊ DAMAS LOUIS XV. French, 1825–40, block print. 21¹/₄" wide, 21⁵/₈" repeat, 11 yds. per roll. No.221 (ochre on yellow). Block print.

᠔᠊ DAMAS MEDAILLON LOUIS XVI. French, 1825–90, block print. 21¹/₄" wide, 13³/₈" repeat, 11 yds. per roll. No.226 (gold on gold). Block print.

᠔᠊ DAMAS RIVIERE. French, 1835–60, block print. 23⁵/₈" wide, 15³/₄" repeat, 11 yds. per roll. No.233 (cream on red). Block print.

᠔᠊ DAMAS VITRIAL. French, 1835–50, block print. 18¹/₂" wide, 20¹/₂" repeat, 11 yds. per roll. No.222 (gold on gray). Block print.

᠔᠊ DRAPERIE JOSEPHINE. French, 1810–25, block print. Nylander, Redmond, and Sander, fig. 25b, p. 117; Olligs, vol. 1, fig. 231, p. 325. 20¹/₂" wide, 15³/₈" repeat, 11 yds. per roll. Fragments and samples at Old Manse, Concord, Mass., and Society for the Preservation of New England Antiquities. No.245 (white and gray on gold). Block print.

᠔᠊ DRAPERIE MARIE LOUISE. French, 1815–25, block print. 20⁷/₈" wide, 21¹/₄" repeat, 11 yds. per roll. No.227 (blue-gray). Block print.

᠔᠊ ECUREUIL. French, 1790–1810, block print. 21¹/₄" wide, 19⁵/₈" repeat, 11 yds. per roll. No.126 (white on blue). Block print.

᠔᠊ ECUREUIL POLYCHROME. French, 1790–1810, block print. 21¹/₄" wide, 17" repeat, 11 yds. per roll. No.208 (multi on cream). Block print.

᠔᠊ ELYSEE. French, 1830–40, block print. 20¹/₂" wide, 10¹/₂" repeat, 11 yds. per roll. No.283 (gray on white). Block print.

ᔜ EMPIRE MAIS. French, 1800–20, block print. Olligs, vol. 1, fig. 227, p. 322. 18½" wide, 23¼" repeat, 11 yds. per roll. No.104. Block print.

ᔜ EMPIRE POLYCHROME. French, 1815–25, block print. 21⅝" wide, 9½" repeat, 11 yds. per roll. No.177 (multi on cream). Block print.

ᔜ ESCARGOT. French, 1830–60, block print. 18½" wide, 1¾" repeat, 11 yds. per roll. No.864 (gold on cream). Block print.

ᔜ FAUNE DANSANT. French, 1790–1810, block print. 18⅛" wide, 19" repeat, 11 yds. per roll. No.107 (black and mauve on yellow). Block print.

ᔜ FELICITE. French, 1790–1810, block print. 21¼" wide, 21¼" repeat, 11 yds. per roll. No.170 (multi on yellow). Block print.

ᔜ FEUILLE JAUNE. French, 1810–25, block print. McClelland, p. 178. 18" wide, 18⅞" repeat, 11 yds. per roll. No.1502 (yellow on rose). Block print.

ᔜ FRANKLIN. French, 1815–30, block print. 19¼" wide, 14" repeat, 11 yds. per roll. No.1510 (red, white, and blue on tan). Block print.

ᔜ LA GLORIETTE. French, 1780–1800, block print. 22½" wide, 43" repeat, 11 yds. per roll. No.133 (pinks and greens on blue). Block print.

ᔜ GRAND CHINOIS ET VASES. French, 1780–1800, block print. 21¼" wide, 42½" repeat, 11 yds. per roll. No.136 (tans). Block print.

above left
DRAPERIE JOSEPHINE, 1810–25. Classic Revivals (Mauny Collection).

above right
FAUNE DANSANT, 1790–1810. Classic Revivals (Mauny Collection).

above left
PERSONNAGES ET
OISEAUX, 1815–25.
Classic Revivals
(Mauny Collection).

above right
PLUMES DE PAON,
1790–1810. Classic
Revivals (Mauny
Collection).

ॐ GRENADE. French, 1780–1800, block print. McClelland, p. 77. 22" wide, 16¹/₈" repeat, 11 yds. per roll. No.122 (multi on white). Block print.

ॐ HORTENSIA. French, 1800–30, block print. 19¹/₄" wide, 19¹/₄" repeat, 11 yds. per roll. No.147 (green and pink on yellow). Block print.

ॐ LES IFS. French, 1790–1810, block print. 21¹/₄" wide, 9¹/₂" repeat, 11 yds. per roll. No.146 (orange and blue on buff). Block print.

ॐ LANTERNE MAGIQUE. French, 1790–1800, block print. McClelland, p. 134; Olligs, vol. 1, fig. 219, p. 317. 20¹/₈" wide, 21⁵/₈" repeat, 11 yds. per roll. No.115 (pinks and green on light blue). Block print.

ॐ LYS ET PERDRIX. French, 1780–1800, block print. McClelland, p. 138. 21¹/₄" wide, 45¹/₄" repeat, 11 yds. per roll. No.121 (pink and white on blue). Block print.

ॐ MA NORMANDIE. French, 1780–1800, block print. 20¹/₂" wide, 21¹/₄" repeat, 11 yds. per roll. No.206 (blue and orange on yellow). Block print.

ॐ MARBRE. French, 1820–40, block print. 18¹/₂" wide, 19³/₄" repeat, 11 yds. per roll. No.163 (gray on gray). Block print.

ॐ MINERVE. French, 1795–1810, block print. 21¹/₄" wide, 21¹/₄" repeat, 11 yds. per roll. No.1511 (multi). Block print.

ॐ MOIRE ANCIENNE. French, 1835–50, block print. 19⁷/₈" wide,

20$\frac{1}{2}$" repeat, 11 yds. per roll. No.270 (white on gray). Block print.

&❧ LES MOUTONS. French, 1780–1800, block print. Olligs, vol. 1, fig. 177, p. 253 (variant). 21$\frac{1}{4}$" wide, 21$\frac{1}{4}$" repeat, 11 yds. per roll. No.194 (multi on gray). Block print.

&❧ OEUILLER ET NARCISSE. French, 1790–1810, block print. 21$\frac{5}{8}$" wide, 21$\frac{5}{8}$" repeat, 11 yds. per roll. No.191 (multi on yellow). Block print.

&❧ OFFRANDE A CERES. French, 1815–30, block print. McClelland, p. 174. 17$\frac{3}{4}$" wide, 18$\frac{1}{2}$" repeat, 11 yds. per roll. No.1509 (black and white on tan). Block print.

&❧ PALMETTE. French, 1800–20, block print. 20$\frac{7}{8}$" wide, 4" repeat, 11 yds. per roll. No.100 (gray and black). Block print.

&❧ PALMIERS ET BOUQUETS. French, 1780–1800, block print. 21$\frac{1}{4}$" wide, 21$\frac{1}{4}$" repeat, 11 yds. per roll. No.145 (multi on light blue). Block print.

&❧ PAPIER FLEURETTE. French, 1810–25, block print. 18$\frac{7}{8}$" wide, 3$\frac{1}{4}$" repeat, 11 yds. per roll. No.1513 (tan). Block print.

&❧ PARASOL. French, 1790–1800, block print. 21$\frac{5}{8}$" wide, 43" repeat, 11 yds. per roll. No.168 (multi on gray). Block print.

&❧ LE PECHEUR. French, 1780–1800, block print. 19$\frac{3}{4}$" wide, 18$\frac{7}{8}$" repeat, 11 yds. per roll. No.117 (mauve on light blue). Block print.

&❧ LA PENSEE. French, 1825–35, block print. 21$\frac{1}{4}$" wide, 2$\frac{3}{8}$" repeat, 11 yds. per roll. No.202 (tan on off-white). Block print.

&❧ PERSONNAGES ET OISEAUX. French, 1815–25, block print. 19$\frac{1}{4}$" wide, 20$\frac{7}{8}$" repeat, 11 yds. per roll. No.164 (blue on gray). Block print.

&❧ PETITS PONTS CHINOIS. French, 1780–1800, block print. 22$\frac{1}{2}$" wide, 22$\frac{1}{2}$" repeat, 11 yds. per roll. No.124 (multi on off-white). Block print.

&❧ PILLEMENT. French, 1790–1810, block print. 21$\frac{5}{8}$" wide, 20$\frac{7}{8}$" repeat, 11 yds. per roll. No.156 (multi on cream). Block print.

&❧ LES PLUMES. French, 1825–40, block print. 26$\frac{3}{4}$" wide, 22$\frac{7}{8}$" repeat, 11 yds. per roll. No.225 (white on blue). Block print.

&❧ PLUMES DE PAON. French, 1790–1810, block print. 19$\frac{1}{4}$" wide, 21$\frac{1}{4}$" repeat, 11 yds. per roll. No.118 (blue and lavender on yellow). Block print.

&❧ POMETTES. French, 1780–1800, block print. 20$\frac{7}{8}$" wide, 16$\frac{1}{2}$" repeat, 11 yds. per roll. No.181 (green). Block print.

&❧ POUPETTE. French, 1815–25, block print. 18$\frac{1}{2}$" wide, 18$\frac{7}{8}$" repeat, 11 yds. per roll. No.207 (pink and green on blue). Block print.

&❧ RAYURE CYGNE. French, 1785–1800, block print. 21$\frac{5}{8}$" wide, 20" repeat, 11 yds. per roll. No.182 (tans). Block print.

&❧ RAYURE ET CORAIL. French, 1815–30, block print. 20$\frac{7}{8}$" wide, 26$\frac{3}{8}$" repeat, 11 yds. per roll. No.279. Block print.

&❧ RAYURE FEUGERE. French, 1810–25, block print. 18$\frac{1}{2}$" wide,

9½" repeat, 11 yds. per roll. No.246 (white on buff). Block print.

❧ REVEILLOND. French, 1790–1810, block print. 21¼" wide, 21⅝" repeat, 11 yds. per roll. No.228 (multi on cream). Block print.

❧ REVOLUTION. French, 1790–1810, block print. 20½" wide, 22" repeat, 11 yds. per roll. No.143 (blue on off–white). Block print.

❧ ROBESPIERRE. French, 1815–25, block print. 24" wide, 9⅞" repeat, 11 yds. per roll. No.149 (blue and orange). Also available with flocked border; No.608. Block print.

❧ ROSACE ET CANARD. French, 1790–1810, block print. 19" wide, 12⅝" repeat, 11 yds. per roll. No.101 (black on yellow). Block print.

❧ ROSE DE NOEL. French, 1780–85, block print. Probably originally printed by Reveillon. Clouzot and Follot, p. 38 (pattern shown reversed). 20½" wide, 40⅛" repeat, 11 yds. per roll. No.184 (multi on cream). Block print.

❧ ROSES FRANCE. French, 1780–1800, block print. Lynn, color pls. 4 and 5, pp. 36 and 37. 21¼" wide, 22" repeat, 11 yds. per roll. No.210 (multi on blue). Block print.

❧ ROSE LAQUE. French, 1790–1810, block print. 22¾" wide, 34¼" repeat, 11 yds. per roll. No.195 (yellow). Block print.

❧ LE SALON DE MUSIQUE. French, 1780–1800, block print. 21¼" wide, 11" repeat, 11 yds. per roll. No.292 (multi on buff). Block print.

❧ SATIN BLANC REGENCY. French, 1830–60, block print. 18⅞" wide, 8¼" repeat, 11 yds. per roll. No.244 (gold on cream). Block print.

❧ SEMIS BOSPHORE. French, 1790–1820, block print. 19⅞" wide, 19⅞" repeat, 11 yds. per roll. No.273 (green on white). Block print.

❧ SEMIS ETOILE. French, 1835–60, block print. 18½" wide, 3¼" repeat, 11 yds. per roll. No.255 (buff on gray). Block print.

❧ SEMIS PILASTRE. French, 1815–25, block print. 26¾" wide, 1⅜" repeat, 11 yds. per roll. No.285 (brick). Block print.

❧ LA STATUE. French, 1790–1810, block print. 20⅞" wide, 21¼" repeat, 11 yds. per roll. No.112 (blue and green on light blue). Block print.

❧ TEMPLE DE L'AMOUR. French, 1780–1800, block print. 22⅞" wide, 21¼" repeat, 11 yds. per roll. No.132 (mauve and black on light blue). Block print.

❧ TENTURE FLOTANTE. French, 1812–40, block print. 26¾" wide, 23⅝" repeat, 11 yds. per roll. No.220 (gray). Block print.

❧ LES TULIPES. French, 1790–95, block print. Originally printed by Jacquemart et Bénard. Clouzot and Follot, p. 23. 21⅝" wide, 21¼" repeat, 11 yds. per roll. No.190 (multi on gray). Block print.

❧ VASE ET BOUQUET. French, 1790–1810, block print. 21¼" wide, 21¼" repeat, 11 yds. per roll. No.106 (multi on gray). Block print.

Silvergate Collection

&❧ MISTLETOE. English, 1780–90, block print. 21" wide, 7⅞" repeat, 11 yds. per roll. Document at Rosehill House, Ironbridge, England. No.CS053. Block print.

&❧ NEWMAN HOUSE. English, 1780–90, block print. 21" wide, 11 yds. per roll. Document at Newman House, Dublin, Ireland. No.AS081. Block print.

COLE & SON

Available through Clarence House as custom order only.

&❧ CHINESE TRELLIS. English, 1830–60, block print. Oman and Hamilton, no. 265, p. 159. 21" wide, 11 yds. per roll. Coles Book. No.98846 (gold on white). Block print.

&❧ CLANDON. English, 1810–20, block print with flocking. Oman and Hamilton, no. 128, p. 128. 21" wide, 11 yds. per roll. Adaptation: flocking not reproduced. Coles Book. No.98880 (red). Block print.

&❧ FLOWER SPRAY. English, 1790–1810, block print. 21" wide, 10½" repeat, 11 yds. per roll. Coles Book. No.98883 (tan on white). Block print.

&❧ HADDON HALL. English, 1780–1810, block print. 21" wide, 13" repeat, 11 yds. per roll. Coles Book. No.98840 (brown on white). Block print.

&❧ WHICKHAM. English, 1780–1800, block print. 21" wide, 30" repeat, 11 yds. per roll. Coles Book. No.98831 (green on blue). Block print.

COLEFAX & FOWLER

Available through Cowtan & Tout.

&❧ ALBANY DAMASK. English, 1800–10, block print. 20½" wide, 5½" repeat, 11 yds. per roll. No.7073-03 (taupe); No.7073-04 (yellow).

&❧ BERKELEY SPRIG. English, 1780–1800, block print. Oman and Hamilton, no. 126, p. 127, and endpapers. 20¾" wide, 11¾" repeat, 11 yds. per roll. No.7010/01 (navy blue); No.7010/03 (blue on off-white).

&❧ CAMROSE. English, 1800–20, block print. 20½" wide, 3" repeat, 11 yds. per roll. No.7107-4 (yellow).

&❧ HUNTINGTON. English, 1790–1815, block print. 20½" wide, 6" repeat, 11 yds. per roll. No.7025/6 (green); No.7025/11 (blue).

&❧ SACKVILLE. English, 1800–10, block print. 20½" wide, 2½" repeat, 11 yds. per roll. No.7071-03 (stone); No.7071-07 (yellow); No.7071-08 (red).

COWTAN & TOUT

&❧ BRAMDEAN. English, 1790–1815, block print. 20½" wide, 3½" repeat, 11 yds. per roll. No.8020-04 (beige and blue).

A. L. Diament & Company

❧ LES ABEILLES. French, 1825–35, block print. 27″ wide, 26³⁄₄″ half-drop repeat, 5 yds. per roll. No.151-10 (green, rose, and tan on blue).

❧ DECOR LOUIS XVI CABLE DOVES. French, 1785–95, block print. 21¹⁄₂″ wide, 50¹⁄₂″ repeat. Multi on beige.

❧ HERMITAGE SIDEWALL. French, 1830–50, block print. 21³⁄₄″ wide, 18¹⁄₂″ repeat, 6 yds. per s/r. No.111-03 (green and copper).

❧ LE JOUEUR DE FLUTE. French, 1780–1800, block print. 19¹⁄₄″ wide, 21″ repeat. No.175-04 (buff on ochre).

❧ MENTON. French, 1815–25, block print. 27″ wide, 18¹⁄₂″ repeat, 5 yds. per s/r. No.80211-07 (gray).

Galacar & Company

❧ LA FALAISE. French, 1799, block print. Originally printed by Jacquemart et Bénard. 27¹⁄₄″ wide, 13¹⁄₄″ repeat, 5 yds. per s/r. Document at Musée des Arts Décoratifs. No.GP-2801 (blues and greens).

❧ FIGARO. French, 1805, block print. Originally printed by Jacquemart et Bénard. 27¹⁄₂″ wide, 27¹⁄₂″ repeat, 5 yds. per s/r. Document at Musée des Arts Décoratifs. No.GP-3101 (greens and orange).

❧ FINISTERE. French, 1798, block print. Originally printed by Jacquemart et Bénard. 25″ wide, 25¹⁄₄″ half-drop repeat, 5 yds. per s/r. Document at Musée des Arts Décoratifs. No.GP-1701 (document colors on white).

Christoper Hyland Incorporated

❧ AMBOISE. English, 1835–50, block or machine print. 20¹⁄₂″ wide, 20¹⁄₂″ repeat, 11 yd. per roll. No.ZZCHC03 (multi on creme).

❧ BLOIS. English, 1800–20, block print. 20¹⁄₂″ wide, 3¹⁄₂″ repeat, 11 yds. per roll. No.ZZCHB01 (white on tan).

❧ BOUQUET TRANSITION. French, 1780–90, block print. Originally printed by Reveillon. Clouzot and Follot, p. 39. 23¹⁄₂″ wide, 37″ repeat, 11 yds. per roll. No.MN180. Block print.

❧ BRANCHE D'EGLANTIER. French, 1800–50, block print. 21¹⁄₂″ wide, 21¹⁄₂″ repeat, 11 yds. per roll. No.MN296. Block print.

❧ CHAUMONT. French, 1820–40, block print. 20¹⁄₂″ wide, 3¹⁄₂″ repeat, 11 yds. per roll. No.ZZCHEO2 (blue ground).

❧ CHENONCEAU. English or French, 1810–40, block print. 20¹⁄₂″ wide, 4¹⁄₂″ repeat, 11 yds. per roll. No.ZZCHF series.

❧ CHINON. French, 1815–20, block print. 20¹⁄₂″ wide, 5¹⁄₃″ repeat, 11 yds. per roll. No.ZZCHA10 (blue ground).

❧ DUFOUR. French, 1805–20, block print. 21″ wide, 34⁵⁄₈″ repeat, 11 yds. per roll. No.ZZ0404 (creme).

❧ HYDRANGEA. French, 1815–25, block print. 18⁷⁄₈″ wide, 9³⁄₈″ repeat, 11 yds. per roll. No.ZZ1103 (gray and white).

❧ LILY. French, 1810–25, block print. 21″ wide, 14⁵⁄₈″ repeat, 11

above left
LE JOUEUR DE FLUTE,
1780–1800.
A. L. Diament &
Company.

above right
MISTLETOE, 1780–90.
Classic Revivals (Sil-
vergate Collection).

left
AMBOISE, 1835–50.
Christopher Hyland
Incorporated.

top left

REVEILLON, 1785–1800. Christopher Hyland Incorporated.

top right

LILY, 1810–25. Christopher Hyland Incorporated.

yds. per roll. No.ZZ0704 (blue base, multi).

᠀ OAK GARLAND. English, 1790–1800, block print. Greysmith, fig. 48, p. 70; Wells-Cole, no. 10, p. 14. 21″ wide, 18⅝″ repeat, 11 yds. per roll. Document at Temple Newsam, Leeds, England. No.ZZ94007 (gold on pink).

᠀ REVEILLON. French, 1785–1800, block print. 21″ wide, 21¾″ repeat, 11 yds. per roll. No.ZZ0205 (blue base).

᠀ ROBESPIERRE. French, 1815–25, block print. 25½″ wide, 9½″ repeat, 11 yds. per roll. No.MN149. Block print.

᠀ ST. JAMES PLACE. English, 1790–1810, block print. 21″ wide, 5″ repeat, 11 yds. per roll. No.ZZ1301 (rust red, black, and white).

᠀ TRIANON. French, 1810–20, block print. 21″ wide, 21″ repeat, 11 yds. per roll. No.ZZ061 (ivory, steel gray, and red).

᠀ VALENCAY. English, 1800–30, block print. 20½″ wide, 3¾″ repeat, 11 yds. per roll. No.ZZCHD02 (terra cotta and white).

KATZENBACH & WARREN

᠀ MARBLE ASHLAR. French, 1800–50, block print. 27″ wide, 32¼″ half-drop repeat, 4½ yds. per s/r. Adaptation. Document at The Athenaeum of Philadelphia. No.AE1024 (sienna).

SCALAMANDRE

᠀ BLAKESLEE HOUSE. American or French, 1830–40, block print. 27⅛″ wide, 22″ repeat, 5 yds. per s/r. Historic representation. Reproduced for Old Economy Village, Ambridge, Pa. No.WP8820 (white and brown on blue). Special order.

❧ THE CEDARS. French, 1833, block print. Designed by A. Merii. Nouvel, fig. 13, p. 35. 18½" wide, 18½" repeat, 8 yds. per s/r. Reproduced from an English copy of the French pattern. Reproduced for Bliss Nash Davis House, Danville, Vt. No.WP81221-001 (pearl gray on ivory). Special order.

❧ CHESTERFIELD. American, 1800–20, block print. 28½" wide, 6⅞" repeat, 5 yds. per s/r. Reproduced for Hayes Tavern, Brattleboro, Vt. No.WP8640 (brown and white on tan). Special order.

❧ CHLOE. French, 1810–30, block print. Printed by Dufour et Leroy. Guibert, fig. 459, p. 68. 27" wide, 19" repeat, 5 yds. per s/r. Adaptation: floral motifs omitted. Document at Bibliothèque Forney, Paris. No.WP81402-001 (multi peaches on emerald).

❧ CHRISTOPHER MURPHY HOUSE. Probably American, 1820–30, block print. 27" wide, 13½" repeat. Historic Savannah Foundation. No.WP81125 (green and white on yellow). Special order.

❧ DERBY HOUSE. American, 1810–25, block print. 26¾" wide, 8¾" repeat, 5 yds. per s/r. Document at Shelburne Museum, Shelburne, Vt. No.WP8931 (yellow and green on white). Special order.

❧ FARRINGTON HOUSE. American, 1815–30, block print. 28" wide, 10" repeat, 5 yds. per s/r. Adaptation. Old Deerfield Collection. No.8902 (white and green on light blue). Special order.

❧ 48 LAURENS STREET. English, 1800–10, block print. 27" wide, 36" repeat, 5 yds. per s/r. Adaptation. Historic Charleston Reproductions. No.WP81274 (blue ground). Special order.

❧ HAYES TAVERN. French or English, 1810–25, block print. 28½" wide, 8" repeat, 5 yds. per s/r. Reproduced for Hayes Tavern, Brattleboro, Vt. No.WP8642 (blue and white on gray). Special order.

❧ MIDDLETON'S PLANTATION PARLOR. French or American, 1830–50, block print. 21" wide, 21" half-drop repeat, 7 yds. per s/r. See borders (page 80) for companion frieze and base border. Reproduced for Middleton's Plantation, Edisto Island, S.C. No. WP81416-001 (aquas and mahogany on pearl gray). Special order.

❧ MONIQUE. French, 1820–30, block print. Guibert, fig. 228, p. 29. 27" wide, 27" repeat, 5 yds. per s/r. Historic representation. Reproduced from a period design for a wallpaper; scale enlarged. Document at Bibliothèque Forney, Paris. No.WP81396-001 (multi roses and lilacs on ivory).

❧ MUIR'S MEDALLION. French or American, 1825–35, block print. 27" wide, 15" repeat, 5 yds. per s/r. Historic representation. Old Deerfield Collection. No.WP8913 (blue on gold). Special order.

❧ NANCY. French, 1800–15, block print. Guibert, fig. 583, p. 89. 21" wide, 21" repeat, 5 yds. per s/r. Adaptation: sprig motif omitted.

right
MONIQUE, 1820–30.
Scalamandré.

right and above
MIDDLETON'S
PLANTATION PARLOR
and frieze, 1830–50.
Scalamandré.

Document at Bibliothèque Forney, Paris. No.WP81397-001 (multi terragons and lilacs on nude).

❧ PRESTWOULD SALOON SIDE PAPER. French, 1820–30, block print. 18¾" wide, 19½" repeat, 7 yds. per s/r. Historic representation. Reproduced from a photograph for Prestwould, Clarksville, Va., operated by Prestwould Foundation. No.WP81502-001 (multi greens on pearl gray). Special order.

❧ PRINCESS LACE. American, 1810–25, block print. 27½" wide, 20" repeat. Old Deerfield Collection. No.WP8905 (cream on beige). Special order.

SCHUMACHER

❧ BERNARDSTON. American, 1790–1810, block print. Document at Colonial Williamsburg. 20" wide, 18¾" repeat. No.513080 (document gold).

❧ BLUEBELLS. English, 1790–1820, block print. 21" wide, 9" half-drop repeat, 11 yds. per roll. Document at Temple Newsam, Leeds, England. No.TN04 (blue on white).

❧ CARNATION. English, 1820–40, block print. Wells-Cole, no. 17, p. 18. 21" wide, 15" half-drop repeat, 11 yds. per roll. Document at Temple Newsam, Leeds, England. No.TN06 (blue on buff).

❧ FLORALESQUE. French, 1835–50, block print. 27" wide, 12⅞" repeat, 4½ yds. per s/r. Document in Schumacher Archive. No.505244 (pumice).

❧ FOX GRAPE. English or French, 1780–1810, block print. 27" wide, 18" repeat, 4½ yds. per s/r. Document at Colonial Williamsburg. No.513050 (document ivory).

❧ GWENDOLYN SWAG. French, 1835–60, block print. 20½" wide, 25¼" repeat, 5½ yds. per s/r. Document in Hobe Erwin Collection, Schumacher Archive. No.506185 (opal).

❧ HOBE BLOCK. American or French, 1815–30, block print. 19" wide, 18¼" repeat, 6 yds. per s/r. Document in Hobe Erwin Collection, Schumacher Archive. No.506234 (delft).

❧ LONG GALLERY. English, c. 1827, block print. Sugden and Edmundson, pl. 31. 20" wide, 40" half-drop repeat, 11 yds. per roll. Document at Temple Newsam, Leeds, England. No.TN10 (red).

❧ LONG GALLERY. English, c. 1827, block print. Wells-Cole, no. 8, p. 13. 21" wide, 42" repeat, 11 yds. per roll. Document at Temple Newsam, Leeds, England. No.TN12 (green).

❧ OAK GARLAND. English, c. 1796, block print. Greysmith, fig. 48, p. 70; Wells-Cole, no. 10, p. 14. 21" wide, 18½" half-drop repeat, 11 yds. per roll. Document at Temple Newsam, Leeds, England. No.TN05 (gold on pink).

❧ PARLOR PORTIERES. French, 1815–20, block print. 27" wide, 19" repeat, 4½ yds. per s/r. Document in Schumacher Archive. No.505274 (document moss).

❧ PENNYWEATHER BLOCKS. French, 1825–35, block print. 18" wide, 15¾" repeat, 6 yds. per s/r. Document in Hobe Erwin Collection, Schumacher Archive. No.506121 (cafe au lait).

❧ REDOUBTE'S WREATH. French, 1820–35, block print. 27" wide, 19" repeat, 4½ yds. per s/r. Reproduced from a period design for a wall-paper. Document in Schumacher Archive. No.512890 (aqua).

❧ STENCIL SQUARE. American, 1815–25, block print. Nylander, Red-mond, and Sander, fig. 30.1, p. 133. 19¼" wide, 19" repeat, 5½ yds. per s/r. Document at Colonial Williamsburg. No.513040 (document indigo).

THE TWIGS

❧ BIRDS OF PARADISE. French, 1780–1810, block print. Originally printed by Jacquemart et Bénard. McClelland, p. 244. 18½" wide plus 7½" border, 37" half-drop repeat, 5 yds. per s/r. Adaptation. Repro-duced for Gore Place, Waltham, Mass. No.6504 (multi on meringue).

❧ BRIGHTON LATTICE. English, 1830–40, block print. 27¼" wide, 14" repeat, 5 yds. per s/r. No.7501 (green on meringue).

❧ CAPRICCIO. French, 1800–20, block print. 25" wide plus 2¾" bor-der, 10" repeat, 5 yds. per s/r. No.4509 (coral and green on white).

❧ CHENONCEAUX. French, 1780–1800, block print. 21" wide plus 3" border, 21" half-drop repeat, 5 yds. per s/r. No.6492 (documentary on bone).

❧ DRAPERY SIDEWALL. French, 1810–25, block print. 27½" wide, 23½" repeat, 5 yds. per s/r. No.5501 (gray); No.5502 (taupe).

❧ DUTTON HOUSE. American, 1810–25, block print. 27" wide, 5" re-peat, 5 yds. per s/r. No.A2210/007 (white on custard).

❧ FAUX MARBRE. English, 1820–40, block print. 27" wide, 36" re-peat, 5 yds. per s/r. No.66250/002 (cream).

❧ FOLSOM TAVERN. French, 1835–45, block print. 27" wide, 12" re-peat. Custom order.

❧ GLENMORAL SIDEWALL. French, 1810–20, block print. 19" wide plus 4¾" border, 2½" repeat, 6 yds. per s/r. No.63600/004 (green and salmon); No.63600/007 (green and gold).

❧ JAFFREY ROOM. French, 1780–90, block print. 22½" wide, 42½" half-drop repeat. Document at Museum of Fine Arts, Boston, Mass. No.4010 (multi on melon).

❧ LA NANCY. French, 1810–20, block print. 19¼" wide, 22½" half-drop repeat. No.A2290/004 (coral and green on white).

❧ LA NANCY FILLER. French, 1810–20, block print. 19¼" wide, 23" repeat. No.FA229/004 (green and kraft on white).

❧ ORLEANS. French, 1815–20, block print. 26½" wide, 26¼" re-peat, 5 yds. per s/r. No.6511 (multi).

ঌ OSIER. French, 1830–40, block print. 24¼" wide plus 1¾" border, 3" repeat, 5 yds. per s/r. No.63100/001 (tan on custard).

ঌ PINGREE HOUSE. French, 1800–15, block print. 27" wide, 24" repeat, 5 yds. per s/r. No.A1220/009 (camel on meringue).

ঌ RED ANCHOR. French, 1830–40, block print. Guibert, fig. 234, p. 30. 19" wide, 18" one third–drop repeat. Reproduced from a period design for a wallpaper. No.99800/003 (burgundy and cerulean blue on almost white).

WATERHOUSE WALLHANGINGS

ঌ BREWSTER FLORAL. Probably American, 1800–20, block print. 20½" wide, 15½" repeat, 7 yds. per s/r. Document in Waterhouse Archives. No.194635 (slate blue on white).

ঌ CHATHAM LACE. Probably American, 1825–35, block print. 20" wide, 9½" repeat, 7 yds. per s/r. Document in Waterhouse Archives. No.190312 (blue). Period colorings: No.190335 (pink); No.190519 (gray); No.190518 (yellow).

ঌ CHRISTMAS ROSE. Probably American, 1790–1810, block print. 24" wide, 2½" repeat, 6 yds. per s/r. Document in Waterhouse Archives. Document color not reproduced. Period coloring: No.161258 (green on light blue).

ঌ COYLE HOUSE. American, 1822–28, block print. Lynn, figs. 12-19

above left
Original document for "Stencil Square," 1815–25, a wallpaper reproduced by Schumacher.

above right
GLENMORAL SIDEWALL with border, 1810–20. The Twigs.

69

and 12-20, p. 283. 26½" wide, 5 yds. per s/r. Document at Old Sturbridge Village, Sturbridge, Mass., and the Coyle House, Natchez, Miss. No.168190 (pink and white on yellow). Period coloring: No.168579 (green and orange on light green).

☙ DANDELION STRIPE. American, 1810–25, block print. 18" wide, 7 yds. per s/r. Document in Waterhouse Archives. No.128512 (blue and orange). Period colorings: No.128622 (mustard); No.128518 (yellow).

☙ DEVIL PAPER. French, 1820–40, block print. 26½" wide, 5 yds. per s/r. Document at Gore Place, Waltham, Mass. No.138576 (black on white). Special order.

☙ EAGLE HILL. English, 1790–1810, block print. 26" wide, 4½" repeat, 5 yds. per s/r. Adaptation: color not reproduced exactly. Document in Waterhouse Archives. No.106335 (gray on white).

☙ EDGARTOWN. American, 1800–15, block print. 23¾" wide, 9½" repeat, 6 yds. per s/r. Document in Waterhouse Archives. No.163618 (brown ground).

☙ ENOCH FRYE. Probably American, 1790–1810, block print. Nylander, Redmond, and Sander, fig. 30.2, p. 134 (variant). 24" wide, 9½" repeat, 7 yds. per s/r. Document in Waterhouse Archives. Additional sample at Society for the Preservation of New England Antiquities. No.112815 (ochre on gray-green). Period coloring: No.112496 (white on blue).

☙ FRENCH TASSEL. French or American, 1810–25, block print. 21½" wide, 15½" repeat, 7 yds. per s/r. Document in Waterhouse Archives; additional sample at Society for the Preservation of New England Antiquities. No.123437 (blue ground).

☙ THE GAZEBO. French, 1790–1800, block print. 20½" wide, 22" repeat, 7 yds. per s/r. Document in Waterhouse Archives. No.186613 (red and blue on gray). Period coloring: No.186444 (pink and green on blue).

☙ GENERAL JOHN WALKER. American, 1790–1810, block print. 20½" wide, 5½" repeat, 7 yds. per s/r. Document in Waterhouse Archives. No.188437 (white and black on blue).

☙ GENERAL THAYER. American, 1780–1810, block print. 19" wide, 7 yds. per s/r. Reproduced for Sylvanus Thayer House, Braintree, Mass. Document at Sylvanus Thayer House; additional sample at Society for the Preservation of New England Antiquities. No.117840 (red ground).

☙ GORE PLACE. French, 1780–1810, block print. 18¾" wide, 19" repeat, 7 yds. per s/r. Document at Gore Place, Waltham, Mass. No.139506 (multi on beige).

☙ GOVERNOR BADGER. American or French, 1815–30, block print. 18" wide, 19" repeat, 7 yds. per s/r. Document in Waterhouse Archives. No.113426 (red on brown). Period coloring: No.113496 (orange on blue).

❧ LOUISE. French or American, 1810–30, block print. 27" wide, 18¹/₂" repeat, 5 yds. per s/r. Document in Waterhouse Archives. No.141447 (pink and green on ochre). Period coloring: No.141581 (green on gray).

❧ MARY LYON. French or American, 1810–20, block print. 28" wide, 5 yds. per s/r. Document in Waterhouse Archives. No.136632 (pink). Special order.

❧ MEDALLION. French, 1820–30, block print. 28¹/₄" wide, 7" repeat, 5 yds. per s/r. Document in Waterhouse Archives. No.104613 (yellow on gray).

❧ NORWELL STRIPE. American, 1810–20, block print. 26" wide, 5¹/₂" repeat, 5 yds. per s/r. Document in Waterhouse Archives. No.108463 (rust on tan).

❧ NYE HOMESTEAD. American, 1790–1810, block print. 26¹/₂" wide, 5 yds. per s/r. Document in Waterhouse Archives. No.118496 (white on blue).

❧ OLD OAKEN BUCKET. American or French, 1810–25, block print. 28" wide, 18" repeat, 5 yd. per s/r. Document in Waterhouse Archives. No.197437 (white on blue).

❧ PARKER HILL. American, 1825–35, block print. 19" wide, 18¹/₂" repeat. Document in Waterhouse Archives. Period coloring: No.114650 (tan ground).

❧ LE PECHEUR. French, 1790–1810, block print. 18³/₄" wide, 18³/₄" repeat, 7 yds. per s/r. Document in Waterhouse Archives. No.175206 (blue and orange on white).

❧ PLYMOUTH STENCIL. American, 1815–35, block print. 20" wide, 9¹/₂" repeat, 7 yds. per s/r. Document in Waterhouse Archives. No.191613 (blue on light gray).

❧ POMEGRANATE. American, 1780–1800, block print. 28" wide, 10³/₄" repeat, 5 yds. per s/r. Document in Waterhouse Archives. No.208496 (white on blue).

❧ REVEILLON. French, 1785–1810, block print. 27¹/₄" wide, 44¹/₂" repeat, 5 yds. per s/r. Document in Waterhouse Archives. No.195707 (multi on white).

❧ ROBBINS HOUSE. American, 1810–25, block print. 27¹/₂" wide, 9¹/₄" repeat, 5 yds. per s/r. Document in Waterhouse Archives. No.213840 (gray and blue).

❧ SALEM STRIPE. Probably American, 1790–1815, block print. 26¹/₂" wide, 5 yds. per s/r. Document in Waterhouse Archives. No.169437 (white on blue).

❧ STRAWBERY BANKE STENCIL. American, 1815–25, block print. 24¹/₄" wide, 21" repeat, 7 yds. per s/r. Document at Strawbery Banke Museum, Portsmouth, N.H. No.145158 (blue on mustard).

❧ STRAWBERRY STRIPE. French or American, 1810–25, block print.

above left
RED ANCHOR,
1830–40. The Twigs.

above right
LE PECHEUR,
1790–1810. Water-
house Wallhangings.

right
LOUISE, 1810–30.
Waterhouse Wall-
hangings.

above left
REVEILLON,
1785–1810. Water-
house Wallhangings.

above right
STRAWBERRY STRIPE,
1810–25. Water-
house Wallhangings

left
POMEGRANATE,
1780–1800. Water-
house Wallhangings.

24" wide, 9¹/₄" repeat, 6 yds. per s/r. Document in Waterhouse Archives. No.143447 (mustard).

ॐ WHEAT DAMASK. American, 1810–25, block print. 24" wide, 24" repeat, 7 yds. per s/r. Document in Waterhouse Archives. No.154621 (white on mustard).

BORDERS

An asterisk (*) at the end of an entry indicates that the border was designed to go with a sidewall listed in the previous section.

LOUIS W. BOWEN

ॐ VERSAILLES BORDERS (architectural elements). French, 1800–25, block prints. Charcoal tones, gray, and white.

GUILLOCHE. 3¹/₂" wide, 9" repeat. No.87004-A.
DOUBLE GREEK WAVE. 3" wide, 9¹/₄" repeat. No.87004-B.
EGG AND DART. 4⁷/₁₆" wide, 9" repeat. No.87004-C.
COLUMN. 3¹/₄" wide, 16³/₄" repeat. No.87004-D.
SPIRAL. 5¹/₄" wide, 36" repeat. No.87004-E.
LEAF AND SPIRAL. 2¹/₂" wide, 17³/₄" repeat. No.87004-F.
CORNICE. 12¹/₂" wide, 19" repeat. No.87004-G.

BRUNSCHWIG & FILS

ॐ ACANTHUS. French, 1805–20, block print. 8¹/₂" wide, 8³/₄" repeat. Document in Brunschwig Archives. No.14441.06 (red and saffron).

ॐ ALEXANDRIA BORDER. French, 1810–15, block print. 13¹/₂" wide, 18³/₄" repeat. Document in McClelland Collection, Brunschwig Archives. No.11529.06 (sand on clay).

ॐ BOSPHORE BORDER. French, 1810–25, block print. 9³/₄" wide, 18¹/₈" repeat. Document in McClelland Collection, Brunschwig Archives. No.11541.06 (red and green).

ॐ BOSPHORE TASSEL BORDER. French, 1810–25, block print. 3³/₄" wide, 18¹/₈" repeat. Document in McClelland Collection, Brunschwig Archives. No.11551.06 (red and green).

ॐ BRAINTREE ACORN BORDER. American, 1800–10, block print. Nylander, Redmond, and Sander, fig. 14.2, p. 76. 2" wide, 1¹/₈" repeat. Document at Society for the Preservation of New England Antiquities. No.11076.6C. Custom order (minimum 300 yards).

ॐ ENTRELACS ET PIROUETTES. French, 1810–20, block print. 2³/₄" wide, 3¹/₂" repeat. No.11850.06 (multi on gray). Block print.

ॐ MARGUERITE BORDER. French, 1810–25, block print. 4¹/₂" wide, 10¹/₂" repeat. Document in McClelland Collection, Brunschwig Archives. No.14439.06 (black).

ॐ NEW CLARISSA FESTOON BORDER. French, 1825–30, block print. Nouvel, fig. 423, p. 100. Top: 10¹/₂" wide; bottom: 7¹/₂" wide; 18⁷/₈" repeat. Adaptation: motifs simplified. Document at Society for the Preservation of New England Antiquities. No.13342.06 (yellow on azure).*

❧ OTIS GARLAND BORDERS. English or French, c. 1796, block print. Nylander, Redmond, and Sander, fig 22.1, p. 96. Top: 5⅜" wide; bottom: 2¹¹/₁₆" wide; 21" repeat. Document at Harrison Gray Otis House, Boston, a property of Society for the Preservation of New England Antiquities. No.13283.06 (gold on gray).

❧ PATCHWORK BORDER. French, 1800–20, block print. Lynn, p. 131. 4⅝" wide, 4⅝" repeat. Document at Cooper-Hewitt Museum. No.12442.06 (multi with pink and sky blue).

❧ PEONY SCROLL BORDER. English or French, 1790–1810, block print. 4¾" wide, 9⅛" repeat. Document at Society for the Preservation of New England Antiquities. No.13323.06 (banana).

❧ POMPEIAN BORDER. French, c. 1795, block print. 7½" wide, 38½" repeat. Adaptation: complete repeat not reproduced. Document at Society for the Preservation of New England Antiquities. No. 13359.06 (black and orange).

❧ PORTSMOUTH DAISY BORDER. Probably French, c. 1807, block print

above
POMPEIAN BORDER, C. 1795. Brunschwig & Fils.

left
OTIS GARLAND BORDERS, c. 1796. Brunschwig & Fils.

left
PEONY SCROLL BORDER, 1790–1810. Brunschwig & Fils.

with flocking. Nylander, Redmond, and Sander, color pl. 11, p. 106. 5¹/₂" wide, 20" repeat. Adaptation: reproduction not flocked. Document at Rundlet-May House, Portsmouth, N.H., a property of Society for the Preservation of New England Antiquities. No.11086.6C (terra cotta). Custom order (minimum 150 yards).

❧ NEW SALEM FEATHER BORDER. American, 1790–1810, block print. 2³/₈" wide, 10" repeat. Document at Society for the Preservation of New England Antiquities. Period coloring: No.13279.06 (taupe and blue).

❧ SUDBURY PINEAPPLE BORDER. American, 1790–1810, block print. Nylander, Redmond, and Sander, fig. 14.1, p. 75. 3³/₄" wide, 20" repeat. Document at Society for the Preservation of New England Antiquities. No.11066.6C (terra cotta). Custom order (minimum 150 yards).

❧ WHEELER HOUSE BORDER. French, 1810–25, block print. 20¹/₄" wide plus two 3" borders, 27³/₄" repeat. Reproduced for John Wheeler House, Murfreesboro, N.C. No.12889.06 (gray and brown). Custom order.*

CLARENCE HOUSE

❧ BORDURE DIRECTOIRE. French, 1820–40, block print. 4¹/₂" wide, 9" repeat. No.F30 (orange and yellow).

CLASSIC REVIVALS

Hamilton-Weston Collection

❧ ANTHEMION BORDER. English, 1800–20, block print. 1⁵/₈" wide, 1³/₄" repeat. No.BD11 (black on green).

❧ EMBROIDERY BORDER. English, 1800–10, block print. 1⁵/₈" wide, 5¹/₂" repeat. No.BD22 (rose on white).

❧ GUILLOCHE BORDER. English, 1790–1810, block print. 1⁵/₈" wide, 1¹/₂" repeat. No.BD42 (black and white on ochre).

❧ PEARL BORDER. English, 1790–1810, block print. 1¹/₄" wide, ¹/₂" repeat. No.BD31 (green and brown).

Mauny Collection

❧ ACANTHE ET TORSADE. French, 1810–40, block print. Top: 9¹/₄" wide; bottom: 4¹/₂" wide; 5" repeat. No.638C (grays); No.638G (orange and gray). Block print.

❧ AMOUR AVEUGLE. French, 1820–30, block print. Top: 11³/₄" wide; bottom: 7¹/₂" wide. No.611B (pink, green, and gray). Block print.

❧ AMOUR AVEUGLE. French, 1810–25, block print. 1³/₈" wide. No.554F (rose on gray); No.554H (black on pink); No.554Q (black on yellow). Block print.

❧ BORDURE ANTIQUE. French, 1820–40, block print. 2¹/₂" wide. No.568B (blue and gray); No.568D (green and yellow); No.568F (rust and yellow). Block print.

வ LES BELIERS. French, 1810–25, block print. 15½" wide. No.632A (gray and pink). Block print.

வ BORDURE SAINT CLOUD. French, 1810–30, block print. 1½" wide. No.5002B (green and gray); No.5002D (red and green); No.5002P (dark green and yellow). Block print.

வ BOSPHORE. French, 1810–25, block print. 9¾" wide. No.637A (red and green); No.637D (blue). Block print.

வ CHEVREFEUILLE. French, 1790–1810, block print. 4⅞" wide. No.2604D (multi on blue); 2604E (multi on white). Block print.

வ LES DEUX PIGEONS. French, 1790–1810, block print. 12½" wide. No.617E (light green on gray). Block print.

வ DIRECTOIRE RINCEAUX. French, 1800–25, block print. 3" wide. No.511A (black and white on green). Block print.

வ DRAPERIE ET GLAND. French, 1800–15, block print. 18¾" wide. No.625A (gray). Block print.

வ ETRUSQUE. French, 1790–1810, block print. 3⅛" wide. No.512F (brown and rust on tan). Block print.

வ FABLE. French, 1800–30, block print. 9" wide. No.603G (green on yellow). Block print.

வ FEUILLES ET GRAPPES. French, 1800–15, block print. 4¾" wide. No.526A (blue and tan on black). Block print.

வ FLEURETTE. French, 1810–15, block print. Top: 8½" wide; bottom: 4¾" wide. No.1507E (blue, green, and gray). Block print.

வ FLOREAL. French, 1800–30, block print. 3⅞" wide. No.565D (rose, green, and gray). Block print.

வ GISORS. French, 1815–40, block print. 3½" wide. No.544D (pink on gray); No.544F (grays); No.544G (tans). Block print.

வ GREQUE. French, 1825–40, block print. 2" wide. No.506K (brown and orange); No.506L (grays). Block print.

வ GUIRLANDE ET TULLE. French, 1800–20, block print. 21" wide, 21½" repeat. No.639A (blue and orange). Block print.

வ LES LIONS. French, 1800–20, block print. 5½" wide. No.612C (gray on gray); No.612D (gray on yellow); No.612G (lavender on yellow). Block print.

வ LOSANGE ET GREQUE. French, 1790–1815, block print. 3⅜" wide. No.509B (orange and gray on black). Block print.

வ MALMAISON. French, 1790–1810, block print. 9" wide. No.601A (brown on orange); No.601B (gray on brown); 601D (gray on yellow). Block print.

வ PANIER. French, 1810–20, block print. Top: 13½" wide; bottom: 2" wide. No.629C (green and orange); No.629N (yellow and lavender). Block print.

வ PERLES ET FILLETS. French, 1800–40, block print. 1⅜" wide. No.5020 (gray). Block print.

❧ POINTE YACKS. French, 1800–15, block print. 4³/₄" wide. No.558D (green, black, and mauve). Block print.

❧ REGENCY. French, 1810–25, block print. Top: 12" wide; bottom: 6¹/₂" wide. No.621 (red and green). Block print.

❧ ROMANTIQUE. French, 1800–15, block print. 4¹/₂" wide. No.2606D (blue and peach on yellow). Block print.

❧ ROSACES ET FEUILLES. French, 1815–25, block print. 5" wide. No.530. Block print.

❧ SALOME. French, 1790–1810, block print. 4³/₄" wide. No.574C (yellow and blue on black); 574F (pink and green on light blue). Block print.

❧ TORE. French, 1800–40, block print. 1⁵/₈" wide. No.559H (grays). Block print.

A. L. DIAMENT & COMPANY

❧ HERMITAGE LION BORDER. French, 1830–50, block print. 9³/₄" wide, 21¹/₂" repeat. No.110-03 (green and copper).

KATZENBACH & WARREN

❧ ACANTHUS FRIEZE. French, 1800–40, block print. 8¹/₂" wide, 3¹/₄" repeat. Document at The Athenaeum of Philadelphia. No.AE 1004B (gray and gold). Period coloring: No.AE1005B (gray).

❧ EGG AND DART BORDER. French, 1800–20, block print. 2¹/₂" wide, 1¹/₂" repeat. Document at The Athenaeum of Philadelphia. No.AE1014B (gold). Period coloring: No.AE1015B (gray).

❧ FLORAL DRAPERY CORNICE. French, 1810–20, block print. 20³/₄" wide, 21" repeat. Document at The Athenaeum of Philadelphia. No.AE1181B (blue). Period coloring: No.AE1183B (green).

LEE JOFA

❧ JOSEPHINE BORDER. French, 1800–20, block print. 12" wide, 20¹/₄" repeat. Document in a museum archive. No.P902154 (blue mist and brick).

❧ NAPOLEON BORDER. French, 1790–1815, block print. 7 ¹/₄" wide, 13" repeat. Document in a museum archive. Document color not reproduced. Period coloring: No.P902003 (red and green).

SCALAMANDRE

❧ CHARLESTON FRIEZE. French, 1800–25, block print. 6¹/₂" wide, 18" repeat. Reproduced for Historic Charleston Reproductions. No. WB81268-001 (light peach, pinks, and teal on sorrel). Special order.

❧ CHLOE BORDER. French, 1810–20, block print. Designed by Xavier Mader; originally printed by Dufour. Guibert, fig. 341, p. 48. 12" wide, 18" repeat. Adaptation. Document at Bibliothèque Forney, Paris. No.WB81403-001 (multi peaches on emerald).

❧ CLASSICAL BORDER. French, 1810–25, block print. 14³/₄" wide,

above
SALOME, 1790–1810.
Classic Revivals
(Mauny Collection).

left
FLORAL DRAPERY
CORNICE, 1810–20.
Katzenbach & Warren.

left
CHLOE BORDER,
1810–20. Scalamandré.

19" repeat. Historic representation. Reproduced for Rosehill, Geneva, N.Y. No.WB81205-001 (blues, tans, browns, and rust on smoke blue). Period coloring: No.WB81205-004 (olives, golds, and teal on smoke).

➚ CONSTANTINE DADO. French, 1835–50, block print. 27½" wide, 21" repeat, 5 yds. per s/r. Historic representation. Reproduced from a period design for a wallpaper. Document in Scalamandré Archive. No.WP81462-001 (multi on plum).

➚ 48 LAURENS STREET FRET. Probably English, 1800–10, block print. 1³/₈" wide, ³/₄" repeat. Historic representation. Reproduced for Historic Charleston Reproductions. No.WB81275-001 (grays and midnight blue on deep blue).

➚ LINDENWALD BALUSTRADE. French, 1830, block print. Originally printed by Jacquemart et Bénard. Lynn, fig. 10-2, p. 232; McClelland, p. 169; Nouvel, fig. 346, p. 89. 19" wide, 5¹³/₁₆" repeat. Reproduced

LINDENWALD
BALUSTRADE, 1830.
Scalamandré.

for Martin Van Buren National Historic Site, Kinderhook, N.Y. Additional sample at Cooper-Hewitt Museum. No.WP81338-001 (grays, greens, and black on marble white).

᠍ MEZZA MAJOLICA. French, 1800–20, block print. 10" wide, 9" repeat. Historic representation. No.WB81494-1 (gold and redwood on ivory).

᠍ MIDDLETON'S PLANTATION BASEBOARD. French or American, 1830–50, block print. 5¼" wide, 21" repeat. Companion border to "Middleton's Plantation Parlor" wallpaper. Adaptation. Reproduced for Middleton's Plantation, Edisto Island, S.C. No.WB81426-001 (aquas and mahogany on pearl gray). Special order.*

᠍ MIDDLETON'S PLANTATION FRIEZE. French or American, 1830–50, block print. 10½" wide, 42" repeat. Companion frieze to "Middleton's Plantation Parlor" wallpaper. Reproduced for Middleton's Plantation, Edisto Island, S.C. No.WB81415-001 (aquas and mahogany on pearl gray). Special order.*

᠍ PRESTWOULD DRAWING ROOM TOP BORDER. French, 1820–35, block print. 10½" wide, 18¾" repeat. Reproduced for Prestwould, Clarksville, Va., operated by Prestwould Foundation. No.WB81505-001 (bronze and slate on cranberry).

᠍ PRESTWOULD SALOON DADO. French, 1810–35, block print. De-

opposite
AURORA, 1790–1800.
Brunschwig & Fils.
Page 45.

MINERVE, 1795–1810.
Classic Revivals
(Mauny Collection).
Page 58.

LA FALAISE, 1799.
Galacar & Company.
Page 62.

right
FIGARO, 1805.
Galacar & Company.
Page 62.

opposite
FINISTERE, 1798.
Galacar & Company.
Page 62.

top
PRESTWOULD SALOON
TOP BORDER, 1810–35.
Scalamandré.
Page 89.

above
PRESTWOULD SALOON
DADO, 1810–35.
Scalamandré.
Page 80.

BERNARDSTON and
BERNARDSTON
BORDER, 1790–1810.
Schumacher. Pages 67
and 89.

FOX GRAPE, 1780–
1810. Schumacher.
Page 67.

signed by Xavier Mader; originally printed by Dufour. Guibert, color pl. 2; Lynn, fig. 9-20, p. 214, and color pl. 41, p. 241; Nouvel, fig. 457, p. 107. 22" wide, 43¹/₄" repeat. Reproduced for Prestwould, Clarksville, Va., operated by Prestwould Foundation. Document at Cooper-Hewitt Museum. No.WB81504-002 (royal and gold on gray).

෨ PRESTWOULD SALOON TOP BORDER. French, 1820–35, block print with flocking. 9¹/₈" wide, 18³/₄" repeat. Reproduced for Prestwould, Clarksville, Va., operated by Prestwould Foundation. No.WB81508-001 (teals and taupe). Also available unflocked; No.WP81508A.

෨ STROBEL FRIEZE. French, 1810–30, block print. 6¹/₄" wide, 18" repeat. Historic representation. Reproduced for Historic Charleston Reproductions. No.WB81271-001 (grays, yellow, and browns on dark teal).

SCHUMACHER

෨ BERNARDSTON BORDER. Possibly American, 1790–1810, block print. Nylander, Redmond, and Sander, color pl. 8, p. 105. 2¹/₄" wide, 12³/₈" repeat. Document at Colonial Williamsburg. No.513230 (document gold).

෨ CORNUCOPIA SCROLL BORDER. French, 1810–25, block print. 8¹/₂" wide, 13¹/₂" repeat. No.509501 (sepia).

෨ LANETTE'S LILAC BORDER. French, 1815–25, block print. Nouvel, fig. 263, p. 77. 13⁵/₈" wide, 21" repeat. No.509510 (document).

෨ LAUREL BOUQUET BORDER. French, 1835–50, block print. 13¹/₂" wide, 12" repeat. Document in Schumacher Archive. No.505312 (lake and sand).

෨ LONG GALLERY BORDER. English, c. 1827, block print. 2¹/₂" wide. Document at Temple Newsam, Leeds, England. No.TN11 (green).

෨ PARLOR PORTIERE BASE. French, 1815–20, block print. 13" wide, 13¹/₂" repeat. Document in Schumacher Archive. No.505344 (document moss).*

෨ PARLOR PORTIERE BORDER. French, 1815–20, block print. 15" wide, 13¹/₂" repeat. Document in Schumacher Archive. No.505334 (document moss).*

RICHARD E. THIBAUT

෨ BOXWOOD BORDER. Possibly French, 1830–40, block print. 6" wide, 18¹/₂" repeat. Historic Homes of America Collection, produced in collaboration with the National Preservation Institute. Document at Boxwood, Yanceyville, N.C. No.839-T-790059 (multi).

THE TWIGS

෨ ACANTHUS BORDER. French, 1790–1810, block print. 2¹/₄" wide, 10" repeat. No.6716 (gray).

෨ ARCHITECTURAL BORDER. French, 1800–10, block print. 9¹/₄" wide, 20³/₄" repeat. No.6721 (gray and beige); No.6725 (gold and green).

THE MONUMENTS OF PARIS, 1814. The Twigs.

ᔰ CONCORD BORDER. American, 1811–17, block print. Originally printed by Moses Grant, Jr., & Company, Boston. Nylander, Redmond, and Sander, fig. 1-12, p. 13. 5¹/₂″ wide, 5¹/₂″ repeat. Adaptation: original color not reproduced. Period coloring: No.6604 (Pompeiian red and white).

ᔰ ERECHTHEUM DADO. English, 1790–1815, block print. 21¹/₄″ wide plus 4³/₄″ border, 42¹/₂″ repeat. No.66150/001 (green); No. 66150/002 (gray on cream).

ᔰ FEDERAL BORDER. French, 1800–10, block print. 2¹/₂″ wide, 21⁵/₈″ repeat. No.67300/005 (red).

ᔰ FLEURETTE FRIEZE. French, 1810–15, block print. 9″ wide, 19″ repeat. No.A1650/009 (coral and green).

ᔰ GLENMORAL BORDER. French, 1810–20, block print. 19″ wide, 18³/₄″ repeat. No.63700/004 (green and salmon); No.63700/007 (green and gold).*

ᔰ L'ENFANT BORDER. French, 1800–10, block print. 2″ wide, 8⁵/₈″ repeat. Period colorings: No.67400/002 (beige); No.67400/004 (navy); No.67400/005 (gray); No.67400/006 (terra cotta); No.67400/007 (coral).

ᔰ MALMAISON. French, 1810–25, block print. 21¹/₈″ wide, 21¹/₈″ repeat. No.66500/004 (blue).

ᔰ LA NANCY FRIEZE AND BASE BORDER. French, 1810–20, block print. Frieze: 13¹/₂″; bottom: 5¹/₄″; 19¹/₄″ repeat. No.A2310/004 (coral and green on white).*

ᔰ PINGREE HOUSE BORDER. French, 1800–10, block print. 6″ wide, 19¹/₂″ repeat. No.A1230/009 (camel on meringue).*

ᔰ VENDOME BORDER. French, 1800–10, block print. 2¹/₂″ wide, 10″ repeat. No.67000/001 (rose and gray).

WATERHOUSE WALLHANGINGS

❧ ROBBINS HOUSE BORDER. English or French, 1790–1810, block print. Nylander, Redmond, and Sander, color pl. 8, p. 105. 2¼" wide, 2¼" repeat. Document in Waterhouse Archives; additional samples at Society for the Preservation of New England Antiquities and the Essex Institute. No.215634 (multi on dark brown).

SCALAMANDRE

PLAIN PAPERS

Plain papers that approximate the popular colors of the late 18th and early 19th centuries include the following ground papers. All are 30" wide. No.WG115-000 (pink); No.WG119-000 (Pompeiian red); No.WG357-000 (pastel citron); No.WG396-000 (empire blue); No.WG410-000 (sage); No.WG513-000 (soft yellow); No.WG524-000 (sunflower); No.WG536-000 (peach); No.WG1852-000 (blue sky).

THE TWIGS

SCENIC WALLPAPERS

❧ THE MONUMENTS OF PARIS. French, 1814, block print in 80 colors from 2,062 blocks. Designed by Dufour et Leroy after designs by Jean Broc. Greysmith, fig. 69, p. 96; Lynn, color pl. 34, p. 173, and fig. 9-14, p. 210; McClelland, p. 337; Oman and Hamilton, color pl. p. 274 and pp. 286–87. Total width: 48'; total height: 8½'; 17"–28" per panel; 22 panels per set. Reproduced in cooperation with Metropolitan Museum of Art, New York; installed in American Wing. No.MP-22 (full set); No.MP-11 (half set).

ZUBER

❧ LES COURSES DE CHEVAUX (THE RACES). French, 1837, block print. Designed by Jean-Julien Deltil. McClelland, p. 293. Total width: 50'

LES VUES DE L'AMERIQUE DU NORD (detail, "Military Review at West Point"), 1834. Zuber.

4"; total height: 12' 10"; 18⁷/₈" per panel; 32 panels per set. Block printed in 18 colors from 767 wood blocks.

ॐ DECOR CHINOIS. French, 1832, block print. Designed by Eugene Ehrmann and Hermann Zipelius. Greysmith, color pl. 13, p. 99; Lynn, color pl. 35, pp. 174–75; Nylander, Redmond, and Sander, color pl. 37, p. 162; fig. 52-a, p. 206; Teynac, Nolot, and Vivien, p. 69. Total width: 17' 6"; total height: 12' 10"; 21" per panel; 10 panels per set. Block printed in 57 colors from 387 wood blocks.

ॐ L'HINDOUSTAN. French, 1808, block print. Designed by Antoine Pierre Mongin. *Bulletin*, color pl. 13, no. 1. Total width: 43' 11¹/₂"; total height: 12' 10"; 26³/₈" per panel; 20 panels per set. Block printed in 85 colors from 1,265 wood blocks.

ॐ LES LOINTAINS (CLASSIC LANDSCAPE). French, 1822, block print. Designed by Antoine Pierre Mongin. Total width: 10' 6"; total height: 12' 10"; 21" per panel; 6 panels per set. Printed in 11 colors from 149 wood blocks.

ॐ LE PAYSAGE A CHASSES (LANDSCAPE OF THE CHASE). French, 1832, block print. Designed by Jean-Julien Deltil. McClelland, pp. 169–70. Total width: 49' 4"; total height: 12' 10"; 18¹/₂" per panel; 32 panels per set. Block printed in 142 colors from 1,253 wood blocks.

ॐ PSYCHE. French, 1816, block print. Designed by Mery Joseph

Blondel and Louis Lafitte; originally printed by Dufour. Clouzot and Follot, p. 166; McClelland, pp. 283–86; Oman and Hamilton, no. 1040, p. 358. Four scenes: "Psyche au bain," 85" wide by 72" high (4 panels); "Psyche aux enfers," 21¼" wide by 72" high (single panel); "Psyche recueille par un pecheur," 42½" wide by 72" high (2 panels); and "Hymen de Psyche et de Cupidon," 21¼" wide by 72" high (single panel). Block printed en grisaille (shades of gray).

ॐ LES VUES DE L'AMERIQUE DU NORD (SCENIC AMERICA). French, 1834, block print. Designed by Jean-Julien Deltil. *Bulletin*, color pl. 14, no. 4; Clouzot and Follot, p. 190; Lynn, color pl. 33, p. 172; fig. 9-8, p. 193; McClelland, p. 387; Teynac, Nolot, and Vivien, p. 116. Total width: 49' 4"; total height: 12' 10"; 18½" per panel; 32 panels per set. Block printed in 223 colors from 1,690 wood blocks.

ॐ LES VUES DE SUISSE. French, 1804, block print. Designed by Antoine Pierre Mongin. Guibert, fig. 695, p. 105; Teynac, Nolot, and Vivien, p. 108. Total width: 36' 2"; total height: 12' 10"; 27½" per panel; 16 panels per set. Block printed in 95 colors from 1,024 wood blocks. This was the first scenic wallpaper.

Zuber also prints a wide variety of wallpapers and borders. The company prefers that inquiries concerning these additional patterns be made directly to its New York showroom.

ESSEX INSTITUTE

CUSTOM PATTERNS FROM MUSEUMS

All patterns were reproduced for the Gardner-Pingree House, Salem, Mass. Documents are at Essex Institute. For color illustrations, see Dean Lahikainen, "The Gardner-Pingree House, Salem, Massachusetts," *Antiques*, March 1990, pp. 718–29.

ॐ DERBY BLOCK. American, 1800–10, block print. 21" wide, 5½" repeat, 7 yds. per roll. No.GP 101 (green, black, and white).

ॐ GARDNER BLOCK. American, 1800–15, block print. 21" wide, 11" repeat, 7 yds. per roll. No.GP 102 (gray, green, blue, black, and white).

ॐ GREEN WHEAT. English, 1800–10, block print. 21" wide, 5½" repeat, 7 yds. per roll. No.GP 103 (greens, black, gray, and white on light green).

ॐ GREEN WHEAT BORDER. English, 1800–10, block print. 3⅞" wide, 11¾" repeat. No.GP 104 (greens, brown, gold, and gray on white).

ॐ ORANGE TWIG. English, 1800–10, block print. 20⅛" wide, 20½" repeat, 7 yds. per roll. No.GP 105 (orange, red, blue, and green on light blue).

HISTORIC DEERFIELD

ॐ BURRINGTON HOUSE. American, c. 1818, block print. 21" wide, 31½" repeat, 7 yds. per s/r. Reproduced for E. H. Williams House,

Deerfield, Mass. Document at Burrington House, Charlemont, Mass. No.145102 (green, dark green, and black on light blue).

❧ CELESTIAL SWAG. American, 1810–25, block print. 21³/₄" wide, 5³/₄" repeat, 7 yds. per s/r. Reproduced for E. H. Williams House, Deerfield, Mass. Document at Historic Deerfield. No.145094 (green, black, white, and pink on blue-gray).

❧ E. H. WILLIAMS FLORAL. American, 1815–25, block print. 21⁵/₈" wide, 10¹/₄" repeat, 7 yds. per s/r. Reproduced for E. H. Williams House, Deerfield, Mass. Document at Historic Deerfield. No.145093 (greens, red, and pink on tan).

❧ FLORAL STRIPE. American, 1810–25, block print. 19⁵/₈" wide, 11³/₄" repeat, 7 yds. per s/r. Reproduced for E. H. Williams House, Deerfield, Mass. Document at Historic Deerfield. No.145103 (red on white).

❧ HOIT HOUSE. American, 1810–25, block print. 18¹/₂" wide, 9¹/₄" repeat, 7 yds. per s/r. Reproduced for E. H. Williams House, Deerfield, Mass. Document at Historic Deerfield. No.145105 (gray on light gray).

❧ PARSONAGE. American, 1815–30, block print. 19¹/₄" wide, 2³/₈" repeat, 7 yds. per s/r. Reproduced for E. H. Williams House and Wells-Thorn House, Deerfield, Mass. Document at Historic Deerfield. No.145061 (burgundy on ochre or blue on white).

❧ SPRIGS. American, 1810–25, block print. 19" wide, 2¹/₂" repeat, 7 yds. per s/r. Reproduced for E. H. Williams House, Deerfield, Mass. Document at Historic Deerfield. No.145104 (dark blue and white on blue).

❧ SWAN AND URN. American, 1810–25, block print. 21¹/₂" wide, 19" repeat, 7 yds. per s/r. Reproduced for E. H. Williams House, Deerfield, Mass. Document at Historic Deerfield. No.145095 (brown, ocher, and white on beige).

❧ TASSEL. American, 1790–1810, block print. 21¹/₄" wide plus 1³/₄" border, 20³/₄" repeat, 7 yds. per s/r. Reproduced for Wells-Thorn House, Deerfield, Mass. Document at Historic Deerfield. No.145053 (green, black, and white on gray).

POCUMTUCK VALLEY MEMORIAL ASSOCIATION

❧ P.V.M.A. GEOMETRIC. American, 1825–35, block print. 19¹/₄" wide, 7¹/₄" repeat, 7 yds. per s/r. Reproduced for E. H. Williams House, Deerfield, Mass. Document at Pocumtuck Valley Memorial Association. Yellow and white on gray.

❧ P.V.M.A. RAINBOW. American, 1830–40, block print. 19" wide, 19¹/₈" repeat, 7 yds. per s/r. Reproduced for Wells-Thorn House, Deerfield, Mass. Document at Pocumtuck Valley Memorial Association. Blue, yellow, and white on ungrounded paper.

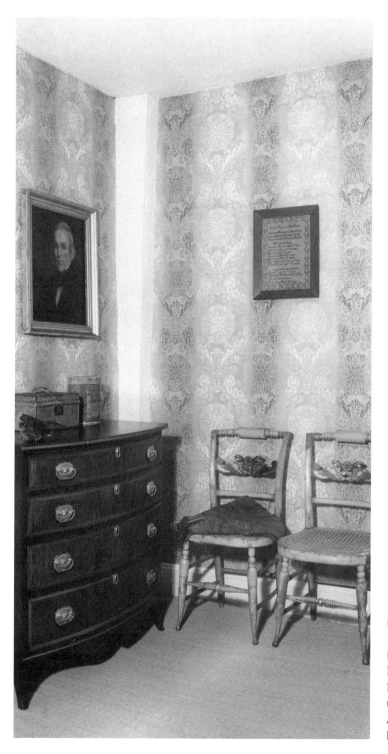

P.V.M.A. RAINBOW,
1830–40, as installed
in the Wells-Thorn
House, Deerfield,
Massachusetts. Pocum-
tuck Valley Memorial
Association. (Historic
Deerfield Inc.)

above left
RIDER-WOOD CHAMBER, 1810–25. Strawbery Banke Museum.

above right
RIDER-WOOD HALL, 1810–25. Strawbery Banke Museum.

right
RIDER-WOOD PARLOR, 1815–30. Strawbery Banke Museum.

SOCIETY FOR THE PRESERVATION OF NEW ENGLAND ANTIQUITIES

᠍᠍ SARAH ORNE JEWETT HOUSE—GUEST ROOM PAPER. French, 1829, block print. Probably printed by Zuber. See Nouvel, fig. 180, p. 63, for variant. 18^1/$_2$" wide, 18^1/$_2$" repeat, 7 yds. per roll. Reproduced from a photograph for Sarah Orne Jewett House, South Berwick, Maine, a property of Society for the Preservation of New England Antiquities. Gray on gray.

JACOB WENDELL, 1811–17. Strawbery Banke Museum.

STRAWBERY BANKE MUSEUM

ঌ JACOB WENDELL. American, 1811–17, block print. Originally printed by Moses Grant, Jr., & Company, Boston. 21¼" wide, 20¼" repeat, 7 yds. per roll. Reproduced for Chase House, Portsmouth, N.H. Document at Strawbery Banke Museum. Rose and mustard.

ঌ RIDER-WOOD HALL. American, 1810–25, block print. 18³⁄₈" wide, 18³⁄₈" repeat, 7 yds. per roll. Reproduced for Rider-Wood House, Portsmouth, N.H. Document at Strawbery Banke Museum. Brown and tan on tan.

ঌ RIDER-WOOD CHAMBER. American, 1810–25, block print. 19" wide, 3" repeat, 7 yds. per roll. Reproduced for Rider-Wood House, Portsmouth, N.H. Document at Strawbery Banke Museum; additional sample at Society for the Preservation of New England Antiquities. Dark blue and white on blue.

ঌ RIDER-WOOD PARLOR. American, 1815–30, block print. Nylander, Redmond, and Sander, fig. 33.2, p. 139. 19½" wide, 2³⁄₈" repeat, 7 yds. per roll. Reproduced for Rider-Wood House, Portsmouth, N.H. Document at Strawbery Banke Museum; additional sample at Society for the Preservation of New England Antiquities. Brown and white on rose.

1840 TO 1870:
REVIVAL STYLES AND
MACHINE PRINTING

The changes brought on by the Industrial Revolution were clearly evident in the wallpaper industry after 1840. The Four-driner machine, invented in 1799, and other similar machines enabled manufacturers to produce continuous rolls of paper. The use of continuous paper increased steadily in American wallpaper production after 1830. American manufacturers also began experimenting with cylinder printing soon after 1839, when the firm of C.,H. & E. Potter of Darwen, Lancashire, developed the first successful machine to print from rollers with raised surfaces. The output of early machine production was very uneven, and the number of colors was limited to only a few. Block printing continued to be the preferred method for printing high quality wallpapers.

Once perfected, machine production of wallpaper had an impact on the product itself as well as on the appearance of American interiors. The colors used in machine printing were thinner than those used in block printing, thus giving the design a different visual effect. The circumference of the printing roller restricted the size of the repeat. Paper width became standardized. The machine enabled manufacturers to produce larger quantities of wallpaper, making it less expensive and more within the reach of the general population. The latest styles were as readily available to consumers in rural country stores as they were in the large wallpaper warehouses in urban areas.

During this period an increasing number of books and magazines on how to decorate and manage the home were published. They promoted the use of wallpaper and began to suggest the appropriateness of specific types of patterns for certain rooms. For example, papers imitating stone, such as "Whidden Marble" (page 131) and "Thomas Sulley Ashlar" (page 112), were recommended for hallways. More elaborate schemes for the same space could be created by the paper hanger from the numerous available sets of columns, capitols, cornices, and marble papers.

The mid-19th century marked the beginning of an age of revival styles. Wallpaper manufacturers were quick to create designs that would be compatible with any style or whim of fashion. The two

FLOREAL, 1865–75. Zina Studios.

most prevalent styles during the period 1840–70 were the Gothic Revival and the Rococo Revival. Andrew Jackson Downing, a great promoter of the Gothic style in architecture, approved of wallpaper as an appropriate treatment for the walls. However, he preferred rococo florals, Elizabethan strapwork (small pieces of wood applied decoratively to walls), and even papers in imitation wood grain to Gothic Revival papers with designs imitating pointed pinnacles and carved stone arches. Evidence suggests that the latter were used to lend an air of fashion in redecorating an older home.

Bold scrolls and combinations of flowers and scrolls epitomize Rococo Revival papers. These were produced in an endless variety of design and quality, making them affordable for use in almost any building. A representative example is "Rebecca" (page 124). Striped papers and those with small repeating patterns often incorporated Gothic or rococo elements.

French imports continued to set the style throughout this period. However, by the early 1870s a reaction was building against these elaborate and over-ornamented designs that had been so popular. In the previous decade, English designers had begun to criticize French wallpapers for their flamboyant naturalism and trompe l'œil patterns. These reformers advocated two-dimensional, stylized designs as a more "honest" approach to the decoration of flat walls. These contrasting principles of design are illustrated by comparing "Roses Pompon" (page 121), an illusionistic French wallpaper, and "Isis" (page 125), a stylized design in the neo-Grec taste.

Late 20th-century infatuation with lush all-over patterning has revived many of the elaborate and illusionistic wallpaper patterns of the mid-19th century. Not all the designs favored during the mid-19th century, however, hold the same appeal. This is especially true of the inexpensive, almost ubiquitous one- and two-color wallpapers printed on ungrounded paper stock that were advertised by one Boston manufacturer as "Good-looking and Tasty as well as Cheap."

WALLPAPERS

BRADBURY & BRADBURY

☙ CARPENTER GOTHIC. American, 1860–70, machine print. 27" wide, 19" repeat, 5 yds. per s/r. Reproduced for Lathrop House, Redwood City, Calif. Code CGW. Crimson and vert on buff. Special order.

☙ FLEUR DE LYS. English, 1840–50, block print. Designed by Augustus W. N. Pugin. 27" wide, 7" repeat, 5 yds. per s/r. Adaptation: one-fourth scale. Document at Victoria and Albert Museum. Code FLW. Gold on buff. Special order.

BRUNSCHWIG & FILS

☙ ASHENDON. English, 1855, block print. Originally printed by Holmes and Aubert. 20¼" wide, 11¾" repeat, 11 yds. per roll. Reproduced from a gouache design. Document privately owned. No.14701.06 (red).

❧ CHALFONT. English, 1844, block print. Originally printed by William Cooper Boyle. 20¹/₂" wide, 20¹/₂" repeat, 11 yds. per roll. Reproduced from a gouache design. Document privately owned. No.14735.06 (pink and blue).

❧ COOMBE. English, 1855, block print. Originally printed by Holmes and Aubert. 21¹/₂" wide, 18¹/₂" repeat, 11 yds. per roll. Adaptation: satin finish in stripe not reproduced. Document privately owned. No.14775.06 (shell and cream).

❧ CRESHAM. English, 1854, block print. 20¹/₂" wide, 10¹/₄" repeat, 11 yds. per roll. Adaptation: background stripe not reproduced. Document privately owned. No.14741.06 (red and mauve).

❧ ELVIRE SIDEWALL. French, 1840–60, block print. Greysmith, fig. 89, p. 120. 27" wide, 3¹/₂" repeat, 5 yds. per s/r. Adaptation: colors softened. No.10260.06 (red and blue). Period coloring: No.10262.06 (blue and brown).

❧ LATIMER. English, 1846, block print. Originally printed by Henry Noel Turner & Company. 20¹/₂" wide, 11⅜" repeat, 11 yds. per roll. Reproduced from a gouache design. Document privately owned. Document color not reproduced. Period coloring: No.14682.06 (blue).

❧ MARLOW. English, 1857, block print. Originally printed by Henry Noel Turner & Company. 20¹/₂" wide, 8" repeat, 11 yds. per roll. Adaptation: not all motifs reproduced. Document privately owned. Document color not reproduced. Period coloring: No.14720.06 (stone).

❧ MIGNONNE. French, 1850–60, block print. Nouvel, fig. 222, p. 69. 24" wide, 24" repeat, 5 yds. per s/r. Document at Musée des Arts Décoratifs. No.12639.06 (gray).

❧ MONCEAU. French, 1855–60, block print. 17³/₄" wide, 21¹/₂" repeat, 7 yds. per s/r. Adaptation. Document at Musée des Arts Décoratifs. No.12677.06 (aubergine).

❧ OAKLEY. English, 1856, block print. Originally printed by C. E. & J. G. Potter. 20¹/₂" wide, 10¹/₄" repeat, 11 yds. per roll. Adaptation: spacing between motifs slightly enlarged. Design derived from a gouache design. Document privately owned. No.14664.06 (green).

❧ ROSES POMPON. French, 1850–65, block print. Greysmith, fig. 71, p. 100; Nouvel, fig. 217, p. 68. 20¹/₄" wide, 23¹/₄" repeat, 6 yds. per s/r. Document at Musée des Arts Décoratifs. No.13468.06 (taupe).

❧ SOPHIE. English, 1840–70, block print. Oman and Hamilton, fig. 318, p. 167. 24" wide, 15¹/₂" repeat, 5 yds. per s/r. Adaptation: pin dot ground not reproduced. Document in Brunschwig Archives. Document color not reproduced. Period coloring: No.12322.06 (blues).

❧ TAFT SIDEWALL. American, 1850–70, block or machine print.

above left
OAKLEY, 1856. Brun-
schwig & Fils.

above right
MIGNONNE, 1850–60.
Brunschwig & Fils.

right
DEMSCENE, 1850–70.
Classic Revivals
(Authentic Interiors
Collection).

102

18¹/₂" wide, 6¹/₈" repeat. Reproduced for William Howard Taft National Historic Site, Cincinnati. No.365.6C. Custom order.

❧ TRING. English, 1849, block print. Originally printed by Casper Melchior Schick. 20¹/₂" wide, 23¹/₂" repeat, 11 yds. per roll. Adaptation: colors changed slightly; background floral stripe not reproduced. Document privately owned. No.14792.06 (blue).

❧ WENDOVER. English, 1845, block print. Originally printed by Henry Noel Turner & Company. 20¹/₂" wide, 16¹/₂" repeat, 11 yds. per roll. Reproduced from a gouache design. Document privately owned. No.14715.06 (pink).

CLARENCE HOUSE

❧ GRAN CRU. English, 1850–60, machine print. 20¹/₂" wide, 5¹/₄" repeat, 11 yds. per roll. Document in Courtauld Archives, London. No.W9001/003 (green).

❧ PARLIAMENT HOUSE. English, 1850–60, block print. 27" wide, 14¹/₂" repeat, 5 yds. per s/r. Document in Clarence House Archives. No.9460/4 (red).

CLASSIC REVIVALS

Authentic Interiors Collection

❧ BIANCA. English, 1850–60, block print. 21" wide, 16" repeat, 11 yds. per roll. Price Collection. No.W-203-2A (black on green).

❧ DEMSCENE. English, 1850–70, machine print. 21¹/₂" wide, 21¹/₂" repeat, 11 yds. per roll. Archival Collection. No.W-208-2A (blue and tan).

❧ JUNIPER HALL. English, 1850–65, block print. 20¹/₂" wide, 15¹/₄" repeat, 11 yds. per roll. Archival Collection. No.W-204-4A (light gray on gray).

❧ LACE. Possibly American, 1840–60, block print. 28" wide, 18¹/₂" repeat, 11 yds. per roll. Archival Collection. No.W-157-1A (gray on white).

❧ SKINNER FLORAL. English or French, 1845–60, block print. 20¹/₂" wide, 15¹/₂" repeat, 11 yds. per roll. Archival Collection. No.W-199-4A (brown and green).

Mauny Collection

❧ CAPITON CORDE. French, 1845–75, block print. 18¹/₂" wide, 6¹/₄" repeat, 11 yds. per roll. No.218 (blue on gray). Block print.

❧ CAPITON RUBAN. French, 1845–70, block print. 18¹/₂" wide, 10⁵/₈" repeat, 11 yds. per roll. No.219 (gray on tan). Block print.

❧ CHEVREFEUILLE. French, 1860–80, block print. 18¹/₂" wide, 22⁵/₈" repeat, 11 yds. per roll. No.287 (multi on white). Block print.

❧ DAMAS AUGUSTE COMPTE. French, 1845–60, block print. 18⁷/₈" wide, 26³/₄" repeat, 11 yds. per roll. No.234 (taupe on tan). Block print.

❧ DAMAS LOUIS XIV. French, 1840–50, block print. 21⅝" wide, 20½" repeat, 11 yds. per roll. No.269 (gold on buff). Block print.

❧ DAMAS SAINT LOUIS. French, 1840–70, block print. 18½" wide, 4¾" repeat, 11 yds. per roll. No.150. Block print.

❧ DAMAS VERSAILLES. French, 1840–60, block print. 21¼" wide, 23⅝" repeat, 11 yds. per roll. No.274 (brown and tan). Block print.

❧ DAMAS VOLUTE. French, 1845–60, block print. 19¼" wide, 19¼" repeat, 11 yds. per roll. No.232 (gold on gold). Block print.

❧ DRAPERIE VICTORIA. French, 1840–60, block print. Olligs, vol. 1, fig. 230, p. 324. 26⅜" wide, 21⅝" repeat, 11 yds. per roll. No.241 (cream on rose). Block print.

❧ FLEURS COUPEES. French, 1860–80, block print. 20⅞" wide, 20⅞" repeat, 11 yds. per roll. No.128 (pinks on gray). Block print.

❧ GRAND CAPITON. French, 1845–60, block print. 18½" wide, 9⅞" repeat, 11 yds. per roll. No.277 (tans). Block print.

❧ HOUBLON. French, 1840–60, block print. 18½" wide, 16½" repeat, 11 yds. per roll. No.123 (grays). Block print.

❧ PAQUERETTES. French, 1860–70, block print. 18½" wide, 9⅞" repeat, 11 yds. per roll. No.238 (gray on cream). Block print.

❧ LES PAVOTS. French, 1850–70, block print. 18½" wide, 24⅜" repeat, 11 yds. per roll. No.290 (red and green on white). Block print.

❧ PETITES FLEURS. French, 1840–60, block print. 20½" wide, 23¼"

JUNIPER HALL, 1850–65. Classic Revivals (Authentic Interiors Collection).

above left
CAPITON CORDE,
1845–75. Classic
Revivals (Mauny
Collection).

above right
LES PAVOTS, 1850–70.
Classic Revivals
(Mauny Collection).

left
SKINNER FLORAL,
1845–60. Classic
Revivals (Authentic
Interiors Collection).

105

repeat, 11 yds. per roll. No.200 (blue on taupe). Also available with pin dot ground. Block print.

ᔕ PETITES MAISONS. French, 1850–70, block print. 21⅝" wide, 2⅝" repeat, 11 yds. per roll. No.165 (brown and green on pink). Block print.

ᔕ PETIT SEMIS. French, 1840–60, block print. 21¼" wide, 12¼" repeat, 11 yds. per roll. No.151 (multi on cream). Also available with pin dot ground. Block print.

ᔕ RAYURES BOURGOURAIS. French, 1860–70, block print. 19¾" wide, 11 yds. per roll. No.854 (gold on cream). Block print.

ᔕ LES ROSES. French, 1850–70, block print. 21⅝" wide, 21¼" repeat, 11 yds. per roll. No.153 (multi on white). Block print.

ᔕ SEMIS MUGUET. French, 1850–70, block print. 18½" wide, 4¾" repeat, 11 yds. per roll. No.263 (white on gold). Block print.

ᔕ SEMIS POULETTE. French, 1840–60, block print. 18½" wide, 1⅜" repeat, 11 yds. per roll. No.857 (gold on cream). Block print.

ᔕ VELOURS DE GENES. French, 1830–50, block print. 19¼" wide, 16½" repeat, 11 yds. per roll. No.205 (gray on blue). Block print.

ᔕ VIZELLE. French, 1840–60, block print. 18⅞" wide, 9½" repeat, 11 yds. per roll. No.2012 (rust and yellow on cream). Block print.

Silvergate Collection

ᔕ BEECH LEAF. English, c. 1840, block print. 21" wide, 10½" repeat, 11 yds. per roll. Document at Oxburgh Hall, Norfolk, England. No.CS013. Block print.

ᔕ BURGES SNAIL. English, 1860–70, block print. Designed by William Burges. 21" wide, 10½" repeat, 11 yds. per roll. Document in collection of Royal Institute of British Architects, London. No.CS293. Block print.

ᔕ CHIRK. English, c. 1860, block print. Designed by J. G. Crace. 21" wide, 42" drop repeat, 11 yds. per roll. Document at Chirk Castle, Wales. No.AS 26 1. Block print.

ᔕ HANBURY HALL. English, 1840–60, block print. 20¾" wide, 15" repeat, 11 yds. per roll. Order by name. Block print.

ᔕ OXBOROUGH FLEUR DE LIS. English, 1850–60, block print. 16¼" wide, 8⅜" repeat, 11 yds. per roll. Document at Oxburgh Hall, Norfolk, England. No.BS102. Block print.

ᔕ TABLEY FLOCK. English, 1850–60, block print. 21" wide, 51¾" repeat, 11 yds. per roll. Document at Tabley Hall, England. No.AS251. Block print.

COLE & SON

Available through Clarence House as custom orders only.

ᔕ BUTTERFIELD TILE. English, 1860–70, block print. 21" wide, 11 yds. per roll. Coles Book. No.98859 (tan and brown). Block print.

ᔕ CHINESE FRET. English, 1850–60, block print. 21" wide, 11 yds.

per roll. Coles Book. No.98849 (white on green). Block print.

ᕈ CRACE DIAPER. English, c. 1848, block print. Designed by Augustus W. N. Pugin for J. G. Crace. Oman and Hamilton, no. 1116, p. 403. 21″ wide, 11 yds. per roll. Coles Book. No.98855 (light olive on white). Block print.

ᕈ CRACE TILE. English, 1850–60, block print. Originally printed by J. G. Crace. 21″ wide, 10¹/₂″ repeat, 11 yds. per roll. Coles Book. No.98860 (terra cotta and brown). Block print.

ᕈ GOTHIC LILY. English, c. 1850, block print. Designed by Augustus W. N. Pugin for J. G. Crace. 21″ wide, 16″ repeat, 11 yds. per roll. No.98862 (white ground). Period coloring: Coles Book. No.98863 (brown ground). Block print.

ᕈ NOWTON COURT. English, 1840–50, block print with flocking. Oman and Hamilton, no. 533, p. 204. 21″ wide, 10¹/₂″ repeat, 11 yds. per roll. Adaptation: flocking not reproduced. Coles Book. No.98866 (rose and brown). Block print.

ᕈ QUATREFOIL. English, 1850–60, block print, 21″ wide, 11 yds. per roll. Coles Book. No.98853 (tan on white). Block print.

ᕈ SMALL GOTHIC SCREEN. English, 1840–60, block print. 21″ wide, 7″ repeat, 11 yds. per roll. No.98851 (brown on red). Period coloring: Coles Book. No.98852 (brown on blue). Block print.

ᕈ STRAWBERRY. English, c. 1850, block print. 21″ wide, 15″ repeat, 11 yds. per roll. Coles Book. No.98864 (white ground). Block print.

ᕈ VAUGHAN DESIGN. English, 1860–70, block print. 21″ wide, 5″ repeat, 11 yds. per roll. Coles Book. No.OEW166 (gold and brown). Block print.

COWTAN & TOUT

ᕈ EUGENIE. American or French, 1840–60, block print. 27″ wide, 21″ repeat, 5 yds. per s/r. No.16033 (green and beige).

ᕈ FERN TRELLIS. English, 1860–70, block print. 21″ wide, 21″ repeat, 11 yds. per roll. No.20530 (greens). Block print.

ᕈ FUSCIA. English, 1860–70, block print. 21″ wide, 21″ repeat, 11 yds. per roll. No.20100 (multi with gold stripe). Block print.

ᕈ MAGIQUE. French, 1840–60, block print. 25″ wide, 26¹/₂″ repeat, 5 yds. per s/r. No.13027 (blue). Period colorings: No.13026 (green); No.13025 (red).

ᕈ ROSE AND LABURNUM. English, 1850–80, block print. 24″ wide, 30″ repeat, 5 yds. per s/r. No.97301-02 (red and lilac on figured ground).

ᕈ SEA CORAL. English or American, 1840–60, block print. 26″ wide, 4″ repeat, 5 yds. per s/r. Period colorings: No.60360 (green); No.60220 (brown).

ᕈ WOOD TRELLIS. English, 1850–80, block print. 27″ wide, 9″ repeat, 5 yds. per s/r. No.94001 (green and tan).

above left
BURGES SNAIL,
1860–70. Classic
Revivals (Silvergate
Collection).

above right
REGENCE, 1840–60.
A. L. Diament &
Company.

right
EUGENIE, 1840–60.
Cowtan & Tout.

A. L. DIAMENT & COMPANY

❧ REGENCE. French, 1840–60, block print. 18¾" wide plus 4" and 1½" borders, 43¼" half-drop repeat. No.137-03 (dark green on cream).

GALACAR & COMPANY

❧ LA DAUPHINE. French, 1869, block print. Originally printed by Desfossé et Karth. 27" wide, 35½" half-drop repeat, 5 yds. per s/r. Document at Musée des Arts Décoratifs. No.GP-1301 (document colors on white).

❧ PASSERELLE. French, 1869, block print. Originally printed by Desfossé et Karth. 27½" wide, 54" repeat, 5 yds. per s/r. Document at Musée des Arts Décoratifs. No.GP-2002 (greens with cinnabar).

❧ LA TOSCA. French, 1869, block print. Originally printed by Desfossé et Karth. 27" wide, 35½" half-drop repeat, 5 yds. per s/r. Document at Musée des Arts Décoratifs. No.GP-1401 (document colors on white).

CHRISTOPHER HYLAND INCORPORATED

❧ ANDOVER. English, 1850–70, block print. 21" wide, 6½" repeat, 11 yds. per roll. No.WTGAAND (creme, blue, and white).

❧ ASHLAR MARBLE BLOCKS. English or French, 1840–60, block print.

above left
FUSCIA and FUSCIA CROWN, 1860–70. Cowtan & Tout.

above right
SEA CORAL, 1840–60. Cowtan & Tout.

18" wide, 21" repeat, 11 yds. per roll. No.AB111/4B (gray, light gray, and dark gray).

෴ BELLINI. English, 1860–90, block print. 21" wide, 7" repeat, 11 yds. per roll. No.WTSTBL.

෴ BRANDILLES. English, 1860–80, block print. 20" wide, 12" repeat, 11 yds. per roll. No.WTBR01 (brown, dark brown, gold, and maroon).

෴ ENFIELD. English, 1840–60, block print. 21" wide, 38¹/₂" repeat, 11 yds. per roll. No.WTGAENF (white, silver, and gray).

෴ FLORAL BOUQUET. English, 1840–70, block print. 21" wide, 10" repeat, 11 yds. per roll. No.AB143/9 (white, gray, green, and pink).

෴ IMPERIUM. English, 1865–90, block print. 18¹/₂" wide, 18¹/₂" repeat, 11 yds. per roll. No.AB407. Can be custom colored. Minimum order 10 rolls.

෴ KIRBY. English, 1840–70, block print. 21" wide, 15⅛" repeat, 11 yds. per roll. No.AB116/4 (putty, beige, and red).

෴ MANCHESTER. English, 1865–75, block print. 21" wide, 14" repeat, 11 yds. per roll. No.WTGAMAN (gold on gray).

෴ NAPOLIAN. English, 1850–80, block print. 18" wide, 21" repeat, 11 yds. per roll. No.WTN101 (forest, black, gold, and rust).

෴ OSBOURNE HOUSE. English, 1840–60, block print. 21" wide, 11 yds. per roll. No.AB153/9 (pink and purple on white ground).

෴ OSCAR. English, 1850–70, block print. 18¹/₂" wide, 11 yds. per roll. No.WTOSCAR (green, tan, and putty).

෴ OWEN JONES. English, 1855–80, block print. 20¹/₂" wide, 8¹/₂" half-drop repeat, 11 yds. per roll. No.ZZBLX. Period colorings.

෴ PUGIN SHREWSBURY. English, c. 1850, block print. 21" wide, 18¹/₂" repeat, 11 yds. per roll. No.WTC5B.

෴ PUGIN TRELLIS. English, c. 1850, block print. 21" wide, 7" repeat, 11 yds. per roll. No.WTHTR5. Block print.

෴ RIALTO. English or French, 1845–65, block print. 21" wide, 21¹/₄" repeat, 11 yds. per roll. No.ZZ1203 (olive green and burgundy).

෴ SOMMES. English, 1840–60, block print. 21" wide, 21" repeat, 11 yds. per roll. No.WTGASOM01 (French yellow). Block print.

෴ STONE BLOCK. English, 1840–60, block print. 21" wide, 11 yds. per roll. No.AB180/3.

෴ TRIAD. English, 1851, block print. Designed by Augustus W. N. Pugin. Oman and Hamilton, no. 1125, p. 405. 21" wide, 31¹/₂" repeat, 11 yds. per roll. No.WTCTD1 (red on creme).

෴ VERNON. English, 1850–75, block print. 21" wide, 7¹/₂" repeat, 11 yds. per roll. No.WTGAVER (tan and light blue).

KATZENBACH & WARREN

෴ CORDED SATIN. French, 1840–60, block print. 20¹/₂" wide, 25¹/₄" repeat, 6 yds. per s/r. Document at The Athenaeum of Philadelphia. No.AE1241 (gray and mauve). Period colorings: No.AE1242 (gray

FLORAL BOUQUET, 1840–70. Christopher Hyland Incorporated.

OSCAR, 1850–70. Christopher Hyland Incorporated.

above left

THOMAS SULLEY ASHLAR, 1840–50. Katzenbach & Warren.

above right

LINCOLN'S PARLOR, 1850–60. Mt. Diablo Handprints.

and blue); No.AE1243 (gold); No.AE1245 (beige and green).

ઈ THOMAS SULLEY ASHLAR. English or American, 1840–50, block print. 20½" wide, 18" repeat, 6 yds. per s/r. Document at The Athenaeum of Philadelphia. No.AE1083 (tan and green). Period coloring: No.AE1082 (tan and red).

LEE JOFA

ઈ BOWOOD DAMASK. French, 1840–60, block print. 26¾" wide, 13½" repeat, 5 yds. per s/r. Document in a museum archive. Original color not reproduced. Period colorings: No.P902102 (taupe); No.P902103 (pale gray).

ઈ REBECCA. French, 1840–60, block print. 27" wide, 20" repeat, 5 yds. per s/r. Document in a museum archive. No.P902200 (dove).

ઈ HOLLYHOCK MINOR. French, 1840–50, block print. 24" wide plus 3½" border, 23½" repeat, 5 yds. per s/r. Adaptation. No.P9394-0 (ivory). Period coloring: No.P9395-0 (light green).

MT. DIABLO HANDPRINTS

Order by name unless pattern number is listed.

ઈ BARBER HOUSE FOLIAGE WITH BORDER. American or French, 1850–60, block print. 19" wide, 11⅛" repeat. Reproduced for Eliel Barber House, Bloomington, Ill. Dark gray on light gray.

&❧ CARR HOUSE FLORAL. Canadian or American, c. 1860, machine print. 21" wide, 11⅞" repeat. Reproduced for Richard Carr House, Canada. Gold and pale blues on gray.

&❧ THE CEVERA. French or American, 1850–60, block or machine print. 18½" wide, 22" repeat. Copy of a c. 1930 reproduction by Thomas Strahan Company, Chelsea, Mass. Mauves and greens on cream.

&❧ CHINESE LATTICE. American, 1840–60, machine print. 19" wide, 6¼" repeat. Reproduced for Santa Cruz Mission Adobe, operated by California Department of Parks and Recreation. No.SCW-001 (documentary blue and gray on eggshell).

&❧ EDSEL STRIPE. American, 1860–90, block or machine print. 18½" wide, 1⅛" repeat. Reproduced for Henry Ford Museum & Greenfield Village, Dearborn, Mich. Ultramarine blue, yellow, gray, and black.

&❧ FARNSWORTH FLORAL. American, 1850–70, machine print. 18¾" wide, 20½" repeat. Reproduced for Farnsworth Museum, Rockland, Maine. Gray, green, and chocolate on cream.

&❧ GREVENBERG LATTICE. American, c. 1860, machine print. 27½" wide, 4⅛" repeat. Reproduced for Grevenberg House, Franklin, La. Document at Chicago Historical Society. Maroon and blue on parchment.

&❧ GREVENBERG SCENIC. American, 1860–70, machine print. 18⅞" wide, 19½" repeat. Reproduced for Grevenberg House, Franklin, La. Document at Chicago Historical Society. Gray, green, and umber on off-white.

&❧ HENRY FORD PANEL STRIPE. American, 1860–70, block or machine print. 19⅝" wide, 3¼" repeat. Reproduced for Henry Ford Museum & Greenfield Village, Dearborn, Mich. Burnt orange, white, and grays.

&❧ LINCOLN'S BEDROOM. French, 1850–60, block print. 19" wide, 21½" repeat. Reproduced for Lincoln Home National Historic Site, Springfield, Ill. Ultramarine blue, white, and browns.

&❧ LINCOLN'S PARLOR. French, 1850–60, block print. 18½" wide, 20¼" repeat. Reproduced for Lincoln Home National Historic Site, Springfield, Ill. Document at Society for Preservation of New England Antiquities. No.LPW-001 (document taupes and gold on cream).

&❧ NETZLEY-YENDER STRIPE. American, 1850–60, machine print. 18¾" wide, 9¼" repeat. Reproduced for Netzley-Yender House, Lisle, Ill. Maroon, aqua, and cream.

&❧ WIDOW CLARKE STRIPE. French or American, 1850–60, block or machine print. 18½" wide, 18⅝" repeat. Reproduced for Widow Clarke House, Chicago, Ill., a property of Chicago Architecture Foundation. Document at Chicago Historical Society. Gray and blue on bone.

ම WIDOW CLARKE VERTICAL STRIPE WITH OVERLAY. American, 1850–60, machine print. 18" wide, 19$^{1}/_{2}$" repeat. Adaptation. Reproduced for Widow Clarke House, Chicago, Ill., a property of Chicago Architecture Foundation. Gray and green on bone.

ම WIDOW CLARKE WALLPAPER. American, 1850–60, machine print. 18" wide, 18" repeat. Reproduced for Widow Clarke House, Chicago, Ill., a property of Chicago Architecture Foundation. Blue-grays on bone.

ම WILLIAM TAFT DIAMOND WALL. American, 1840–70, machine print. 21" wide, 1$^{3}/_{8}$" repeat. Reproduced for William Howard Taft National Historic Site, Cincinnati. Red and cream on gray-green.

ම WILLIAM TAFT TILE. American, 1860–80, machine print. 18$^{1}/_{2}$" wide, 9$^{1}/_{2}$" repeat. Reproduced for William Taft National Historic Site, Cincinnati. Red and cream on gray-green.

ARTHUR SANDERSON & SONS

ම AVON. English, 1850–1900, block print. 20$^{1}/_{4}$" wide, 24" repeat, 11 yds. per roll. Document in Sanderson Archives. Period colorings: No.WR 7512-1 (alabaster); No.WR 7512-4 (ocean blue).

ම BOWERY. English, 1850–1920, block print. 20$^{1}/_{4}$" wide, 21" repeat, 11 yds. per roll. Adaptation. Document in Sanderson Archives. Period coloring: No.WR 7450-2 (bottle, jade, and tartan green on parchment).

ම COLERIDGE. English, c. 1870, block print. Designed by Owen Jones. 20$^{1}/_{4}$" wide, 3$^{1}/_{4}$" repeat, 11 yds. per roll. Document in Sanderson Archives. Period coloring: No.WH 7371-1 (copper on bottle).

ම OKEFORD. English, 1860–70, block print. Originally printed by Jeffrey & Company. 20$^{1}/_{4}$" wide, 5$^{1}/_{4}$" repeat, 11 yds. per roll. Document in Sanderson Archives. Period colorings: No.WH 7372-1 (grisaille on cream); No.WH 7372-4 (red on garnet).

ම SAVILLE. English, 1860–80, block print. Originally printed by Jeffrey & Company. 20$^{1}/_{4}$" wide, 12" repeat, 11 yds. per roll. Document in Sanderson Archives. Period coloring: No.WH 7374-1 (cypress green and rose on white).

SCALAMANDRE

ම BUCCLEUCH MANSION. American, 1850–70, block or machine print. 18$^{1}/_{2}$" wide, 6$^{7}/_{16}$" repeat, 8 yds. per s/r. Reproduced for Buccleuch Mansion, New Brunswick, N.J. No.WP81413. Special order.

ම THE CEDARS—FRONT HALL AND PARLOR. French or American, 1840–50, block print. 18$^{3}/_{4}$" wide, 18$^{1}/_{2}$" repeat, 8 yds. per s/r. Reproduced for Bliss Nash Davis House, Danville, Vt. No.WP81474. Special order.

ම EASTMAN. French or American, 1840–50, block or machine print. 23$^{5}/_{8}$" wide, 20$^{3}/_{8}$" repeat, 6 yds. per s/r. Reproduced for George Eastman Birthplace, now at Genesee County Museum, Mumford, N.Y. No.WP81188-001 (green, brown, off-white, and French blue blotch).

❧ FLEUR GOTHIQUE. French, 1840–50, block print. 21" wide, 21" repeat, 7 yds. per s/r. Historic representation. Reproduced from a period design for a wallpaper. Document in Scalamandré Archive. No.WP81463-001 (oyster and silver on ecru).

❧ GENEVIEVE. French, 1840–60, block print. Guibert, fig. 44, p. 6. 27" wide, 24" repeat, 5 yds. per s/r. Historic representation: design slightly reduced. Document at Bibliothèque Forney, Paris. No.WP81401-001 (grays and yellows on ecru and blue).

❧ INGE-STONEHAM HOUSE. English or German, 1860–70, block print with embossing. 18¾" wide, 19" repeat, 8 yds. per s/r. Historic representation. Reproduced for Inge-Stoneham House, Round Top, Tex. No.WP81411. Special order.

❧ INGE-STONEHAM HOUSE GUEST BEDROOM. French, 1860–70, block print. 18½" wide, 16" repeat, 8 yds. per s/r. Historic representation. Reproduced for Inge-Stoneham House, Round Top, Tex. No.WP81412. Special order.

❧ INGE-STONEHAM HOUSE PARLOR. English or German, 1860–70, block print. 18¾" wide, 19" repeat, 8 yds. per s/r. Historic representation. Reproduced for Inge-Stoneham House, Round Top, Tex. No.WP81410. Special order.

❧ JACQUELINE. French, 1860–70, block print. Guibert, fig. 763, p. 117 and pl. 5. 27" wide, 27" repeat, 5 yds. per s/r. Historic representation: scale enlarged. Document at Bibliothèque Forney, Paris. No.WP81394-001 (multi lilac on cream).

❧ KELTON HOUSE RESTORATION. French, 1855–75, machine print. 18½" wide, 19½" repeat, 7 yds. per s/r. Reproduced for Kelton House, Columbus, Ohio. Document at Cooper-Hewitt Museum. No.WP81202-001 (brown, beiges, green, yellow, red, and cocoa). Special order.

❧ LINDENWALD GEOMETRIC. American, 1840–50, machine print. 18" wide, 2" repeat, 8 yds. per s/r. Reproduced for Martin Van Buren National Historic Site, Kinderhook, N.Y. No.WP88031-001 (gold, green, and white on beige). Special order.

❧ LINDENWALD—NORTHWEST BEDROOM. American or French, c. 1840, block print. 18½" wide, 12" repeat, 8 yds. per s/r. Reproduced for Martin Van Buren National Historic Site, Kinderhook, N.Y. No.WP81342-001 (pinks, blues, and grays on polar white). Special order.

❧ LINDENWALD NURSERY. American or French, c. 1850, block print. 27" wide, 10⅝" repeat, 8 yds. per s/r. Reproduced for Martin Van Buren National Historic Site, Kinderhook, N.Y. No.WP81341-001 (mauves, greens, gold, and gray-violet on straw). Special order.

❧ LINDENWALD PARLOR AND DINING ROOM. American or French,

above left
INGE-STONEHAM
HOUSE GUEST
BEDROOM, 1860–70.
Scalamandré.

above right
THE CEDARS—FRONT
HALL AND PARLOR,
1840–50.
Scalamandré.

right
EASTMAN, 1840–50.
Scalamandré.

c. 1840, block print. 18⅝" wide, 9¾" repeat, 8 yds. per s/r. Reproduced for Martin Van Buren National Historic Site, Kinderhook, N.Y. No.WP81339-001 (gray and metallic gold on ecru embossed texture). Special order.

ॐ LINDENWALD—SERVANTS' DINING ROOM. American, c. 1840, block print. 19" wide, 4¾" repeat, 8 yds. per s/r. Reproduced for Martin Van Buren National Historic Site, Kinderhook, N.Y. No.WP81373-001 (white, tangerine, violet, and browns on straw). Special order.

ॐ LINDENWALD—SOUTHEAST BEDROOM. American or French, c. 1840, block print. 18⅜" wide, 1¼" repeat, 8 yds. per s/r. Reproduced for Martin Van Buren National Historic Site, Kinderhook, N.Y. No.WP81344-001 (green on chalk white). Special order.

ॐ LINDENWALD—SOUTHWEST BEDROOM. American or French, c. 1840, block print. 19" wide, 4¾" repeat, 8 yds. per s/r. Reproduced for Martin Van Buren National Historic Site, Kinderhook, N.Y. No.WP81345-001 (white and pistachio on mushroom). Special order.

ॐ LINDENWALD—STRIPE. American, c. 1850, machine print. 18" wide, 8 yds. per s/r. Reproduced for Martin Van Buren National Historic Site, Kinderhook, N.Y. No.WP88030-001 (tans and roses on off-white). Special order.

ॐ LORENZO STUDY. American or French, 1860–70, block or machine print. 18½" wide, 25¼" repeat, 8 yds. per s/r. Reproduced for

above left
JACQUELINE, 1860–70. Scalamandré.

above right
LINDENWALD PARLOR AND DINING ROOM, c. 1840. Scalamandré.

Lorenzo, Cazenovia, N.Y. No.WP81167-001 (grays, browns, gold, silver, black, and wine). Special order.

❧ LOCUST GROVE FLOWER. English, 1850–60, block print. 18¾" wide, 1⅞" repeat, 8 yds. per s/r. Reproduced for Young-Morse Historic Site, Poughkeepsie, N.Y. No.WP81227-001 (medium gray on polished white). Special order.

❧ MARGOT. French, 1850–60, machine print. Guibert, fig. 51, p. 7. 27" wide, 9¾" repeat, 5 yds. per s/r. Adaptation: floral motifs omitted. Document at Bibliothèque Forney, Paris. No.WP81395-001 (multi cream).

❧ PITTSON HOUSE. American or English, 1840–50, block print. 28" wide, 22" repeat, 5 yds. per s/r. Reproduced for Old Economy Village, Ambridge, Pa. No.WP8788 (white and black on gray). Special order.

❧ POTERLET ARCADE. French, 1840–60, block print. 27" wide, 3" repeat, 5 yds. per s/r. Historic representation. Reproduced from a period design for a wallpaper. Document in Scalamandré Archive. No.WP81459-001 (grays on plum).

❧ RUSSIAN BISHOP'S HOUSE—DINING ROOM. French or English, 1850–60, block print. 21" wide, 21" repeat, 7 yds. per s/r. Reproduced for Russian Bishop's House, Sitka National Historical Park, Sitka, Alaska. No.WP81368. Special order.

❧ RUSSIAN BISHOP'S HOUSE—LAYMAN'S ROOM. English or American, 1850–60, machine print. 21" wide, 8⅜" repeat, 7 yds. per s/r. Reproduced for Russian Bishop's House, Sitka National Historical Park, Sitka, Alaska. No.WP81363-001 (indigo on chalk white). Special order.

❧ RUSSIAN BISHOP'S HOUSE—RECEPTION ROOM. Probably American, 1850–60, block or machine print. 21" wide, 18¾" repeat, 7 yds. per s/r. Reproduced for Russian Bishop's House, Sitka National Historical Park, Sitka, Alaska. No.WP81366-001 (off-white, green, and maroon on warm gray). Special order.

❧ RUSSIAN BISHOP'S HOUSE—STUDY. American, 1850–60, machine print. 21" wide, 10½" repeat, 7 yds. per s/r. Reproduced for Russian Bishop's House, Sitka National Historical Park, Sitka, Alaska. No.WP81371-001 (green and burgundy on coated white). Special order.

❧ STANTON HOUSE—BACK BEDROOM. American, 1850–60, block or machine print. 19" wide, 3⅛" repeat, 8 yds. per s/r. Reproduced for Elizabeth Cady Stanton House, Seneca Falls, N.Y. No.WP81331-001 (beige and golds on polar white). Special order.

❧ STANTON HOUSE—DINING ROOM. American, c. 1846, machine print. 18" wide, 9¾" repeat, 8 yds. per s/r. Reproduced for Elizabeth Cady Stanton House, Seneca Falls, N.Y. No.WP81329-001 (brick, mustard, and green on ivory). Special order.

❧ STANTON HOUSE—DOUBLE PARLOR. American, c. 1846, block or

RUSSIAN BISHOP'S HOUSE—RECEPTION ROOM, 1850–60. Scalamandré.

RUSSIAN BISHOP'S HOUSE—STUDY, 1850–60. Scalamandré.

STANTON HOUSE—
STAIR HALL, c. 1850.
Scalamandré.

machine print. 18″ wide, 10⅝″ repeat, 8 yds. per s/r. Reproduced for Elizabeth Cady Stanton House, Seneca Falls, N.Y. No.WP81327-001 (Wedgewood and light emerald on polar white). Special order.

❧ STANTON HOUSE—FRONT BEDROOM. American, c. 1846, block or machine print. 18″ wide, 10¾″ repeat, 8 yds. per s/r. Reproduced for Elizabeth Cady Stanton House, Seneca Falls, N.Y. No.WP81330-001 (gray, kelly green, and brick on polar white). Special order.

❧ STANTON HOUSE—STAIR HALL. American, c. 1850, block print. 18″ wide, 20″ repeat, 8 yds. per s/r. Reproduced for Elizabeth Cady Stanton House, Seneca Falls, N.Y. No.WP81328-001 (smoke and kelly green on polar white). Special order.

❧ TOOMBS HOUSE. English or French, 1850–70, block print. 18½″ wide, 9¼″ repeat, 8 yds. per s/r. Reproduced for General Robert Toombs House, Washington, Ga. No.WP81246-001 (grays and metallic gold on haze blue).

❧ WIDOW CLARKE HOUSE. Probably American, 1840–50, machine print. 19″ wide, 18¾″ repeat, 8 yds. per s/r. Historic representation. Reproduced for Widow Clarke House, Chicago, Ill., a property of Chicago Architecture Foundation. No.WP81231-001 (white and off-white on polished white). Special order.

opposite

ROSES POMPON,
1850–65. Brunschwig
& Fils. Page 101.

❧ WAYNE HOUSE. American, 1830–50, block print. 28″ wide, 10″ repeat, 5 yds. per s/r. Reproduced for Old Economy Village, Ambridge, Pa. No.WP8821 (brown, blue, and green on tan). Special order.

120

opposite
HANBURY HALL, 1840–
60. Classic Revivals
(Silvergate Collection).
Page 106.

left
LA DAUPHINE with dado
and frieze, 1869.
Galacar & Company.
Page 109.

ANTEBELLUM BLOCKS,
1845–55. Schumacher.
Page 129.

REBECCA, 1840–60.
Lee Jofa. Page 112.

NEO-GREC FLORAL
VINE, 1865–75.
Schumacher.
Page 129.

ISIS, 1865–75. Water-
house Wallhangings.
Page 130.

SMALL ACANTHUS,
1880–1910. Clarence
House. Page 147.

IRIS TAPESTRY, 1880–
1900. Katzenbach &
Warren. Page 156.

ALHAMBRA, 1880–1900. Katzenbach & Warren. Page 156.

SCHUMACHER

❧ ANTEBELLUM BLOCKS. American, 1845–55, block print. 27" wide, 24¼" repeat, 4½ yds. per s/r. Document in Schumacher Archive. No.512930 (document).

❧ CABBAGE ROSE. French, 1850–70, block print. 20½" wide, 25¼" repeat, 5½ yds. per s/r. Document in Hobe Erwin Collection, Schumacher Archive. No.506191 (antique); No.506194 (spring pink).

❧ FLOWERS AND BERRIES. English, 1840–60, block print. Wells-Cole, no. 18, p. 19. 21" wide, 15" half-drop repeat, 11 yds. per roll. Document at Temple Newsam, Leeds, England. No.TN03 (green).

❧ MONCEAU. French, 1860–70, block print. 54" wide, 36" repeat, 4½ yds. per s/r. Document in Schumacher Archive. No.509313 (coral and seafoam).

❧ MOSS ROSE STRIPE. English or French, 1850–70, block print. 20½" wide, 22¼" repeat, 5½ yds. per s/r. Document in Hobe Erwin Collection, Schumacher Archive. No.506204 (tea rose).

❧ NEO-GREC FLORAL VINE. American, 1865–75, block print. 27" wide, 19" repeat, 4½ yds. per s/r. Document in Schumacher Archive. No.512870 (document).

RICHARD E. THIBAUT

❧ ACORN HALL. English or German, 1860–70, block print. 28" wide, 22" repeat, 4½ yds. per s/r. Adaptation: embossing not reproduced. Historic Homes of America Collection, produced in collaboration with National Preservation Institute. Document at Acorn Hall, Morristown, N.J. No.839-T-7933 (gold on white).

❧ SALEM PAISLEY. American, 1860–80, machine print. 27" wide, 13½" repeat, 4½ yds. per s/r. Historic Homes of America Collection, produced in collaboration with National Preservation Institute. Document at Essex Institute. No.839-T-7925 (multi on white).

❧ TRIMBLE STRIPE. American, 1850–70, machine print. 27" wide, 12⅝" repeat, 4½ yds. per s/r. Historic Homes of America Collection, produced in collaboration with National Preservation Institute. Document at Trimble House, Washington, Ark. No.839-T-7984 (green and brown).

❧ WHIDDEN MARBLE. American, 1865–75, machine print. 27" wide, 12⅝" repeat, 4½ yds. per s/r. Historic Homes of America Collection, produced in collaboration with National Preservation Institute. Document at Whidden House, East Boston, Mass. No.839-T-7909 (taupe and pale green).

THE TWIGS

❧ EMBROIDERED NET. American or French, 1830–60, block print. 27" wide, 25¼" repeat, 5 yds. per s/r. No.A2720/008 (morning glory).

opposite
FRUIT, 1864. Arthur Sanderson & Sons. Page 202.

ॐ GALLOP CLUB. French, 1860–80, machine print. Guibert, fig. 946, p. 139. 21³/₄" wide plus 5³/₈" border, 21¹/₂" repeat, 5 yds. per s/r. No.65400/001 (multi on white).

ॐ LILY OF THE VALLEY. French, 1840–60, block print. 25¹/₂" wide, 3¹/₂" repeat, 5 yds. per s/r. No.A1010/009 (blue on bone).

ॐ PANIER DES ROSES SIDEWALL. French, 1850–70, block print. 19" wide, 36³/₄" half-drop repeat. No.65200/001 (blue ribbon on white).

ॐ ROSES AND RIBBONS. French, 1840–60, block print. 27" wide, 32" half-drop repeat, 5 yds. per s/r. No.98500/001 (pink, cream, and green on clear yellow).

ॐ WOODROSE. French, 1860–70, block print. 27⁷/₈" wide, 9³/₈" repeat, 5 yds. per s/r. No.67000/003 (coral on off-white).

WATERHOUSE WALLHANGINGS

ॐ BELLE EPOCH. English or German, 1860–70, machine print. 27" wide, 12" repeat, 5 yds. per s/r. Document in Waterhouse Archives. No.183613 (gold on gray). Period coloring: No.183610 (gold on white).

ॐ BISSELL HOUSE. Probably English, 1850–60, machine print. 26¹/₂" wide, 5 yds. per s/r. Document at Bissell House, St. Louis, Mo. No.134467 (gold on white).

ॐ CRYSTAL PALACE. English, 1860–70. 27" wide, 26¹/₄" repeat, 5 yds. per s/r. Adaptation: design derived from a published design. Document in Waterhouse Archives. No.220635 (multi on white).

ॐ GALLIER HOUSE. French, 1840–50, block print. 18¹/₂" wide, 28¹/₂" repeat. Document in Waterhouse Archives. Multi on white. Order by name.

ॐ THE GRIFFEN. English or German, 1860–75, block print. 27¹/₄" wide, 22¹/₂" repeat, 5 yds per s/r. Adaptation: colors altered slightly. Document in Waterhouse Archives. No.221438 (terra cotta). Period coloring: No.221469 (light blue).

ॐ ISIS. English, 1865–75, machine print. 27" wide, 24¹/₂" repeat, 5 yds. per s/r. Document in Waterhouse Archives. No.178443 (green and red on blue). Period coloring: No.178700 (blue and red on tan).

ॐ NEW ENGLAND FLORAL. 1850–70, French, probably a block print. 18¹/₂" wide, 18³/₄" repeat, 7 yds. per s/r. Document in Waterhouse Archives. No.203489 (multi on ivory).

ॐ TRELLIS. American or French, 1860–70, machine print. 21" wide, 11" repeat, 7 yds. per s/r. Document in Waterhouse Archives. No.181335 (pink and green on white).

ॐ VICTORIAN FLORAL. German or English, 1860–70, machine print. 27" wide, 8¹/₂" repeat, 5 yds. per s/r. Document in Waterhouse Archives. No.179613 (gold on light gray). Period coloring: No.179610 (gold on white).

above left
MONCEAU, 1860–70.
Schumacher.

above right
WHIDDEN MARBLE,
1865–75. Richard E.
Thibaut.

left
GALLOP CLUB,
1860–80. The Twigs.

131

GALLIER HOUSE,
1840–50. Waterhouse
Wallhangings.

THE GRIFFEN,
1860–75. Water-
house Wallhangings.

NEW ENGLAND FLORAL, 1850–70. Waterhouse Wallhangings.

GRIFFON, 1860–80. Zina Studios.

ZINA STUDIOS

Order by pattern name.

🔊 FLOREAL. English or French, 1865–75, block print. 19″ wide, 12″ repeat. Reproduced for Chateau-sur-Mer, Newport, R.I., a property of Preservation Society of Newport County/Newport Mansions. Pink, green, and gold.

🔊 GRIFFON. English, 1860–80, block print. Lynn, color pl. 88, p. 351. 23″ wide, 24″ repeat. Reproduced for Chateau-sur-Mer, Newport, R.I., a property of Preservation Society of Newport County/Newport Mansions. Red and gold on brown.

BORDERS

An asterisk (*) indicates a border designed specifically to go with a sidewall listed in the previous section.

BRUNSCHWIG & FILS

🔊 CERES BORDER. French, 1850–70, block print. 5″ wide, 18¹/₂″ repeat. Period colorings: No.13830.06 (white); No.13832.06 (blue); No.13838.06 (gray). Block print.

🔊 CHARTRIDGE BORDER. English, 1844, block print. Originally printed by John Todd Merrick & Company. 6¹/₂″ wide, 24″ repeat. Reproduced from a gouache design. Document privately owned. No.14802.06 (cornflower and leaf green).

🔊 ELVIRE BORDER NO.1. French, 1840–60, block print. Greysmith, fig. 89, p. 120. 13″ wide, 18³/₄″ repeat. Adaptation: colors softened. No.10276.06 (coral and blue). Period coloring: No.10279.06 (brown and blue).

🔊 ELVIRE BORDER NO.2. French, 1840–60, block print. Greysmith, fig. 89, p. 120. 5³/₈″ wide, 18³/₄″ repeat. No.10286.06 (coral and blue). Period coloring: No.10289.06 (brown and blue).

🔊 KENNWORTH BORDER. English, 1856, block print. Originally printed by Heywood, Higgenbottom, Smith & Company. 6″ wide, 18″ repeat. Adaptation: design derived from striped wallpaper. Document privately owned. No.14752.06 (blue).

🔊 TAFT BORDER. American, 1850–70, block or machine print. 9¹/₄″ wide, 18¹/₂″ repeat. Reproduced for William Howard Taft National Historic Site, Cincinnati. No.366.6C. Custom order.*

🔊 TIPPERARY BORDER. French, 1840–60, block print. 4¹/₂″ wide, 21³/₄″ repeat. Adaptation: colors not reproduced exactly. Document in Brunschwig Archives. No.14318.06 (stone green).

🔊 VOLUBILIS BORDER. French, 1863–70, block print. 5″ wide, 20″ repeat. Document at Musée des Arts Décoratifs. No.13524.06 (coral and blue on light green).

🔊 VOLUBILIS CORNER. French, 1863–70, block print. 14⁵/₈″ wide each side. Document at Musée des Arts Décoratifs. No.13514.06 (coral and blue on light green).

CHARTRIDGE BORDER, 1844. Brunschwig & Fils.

TIPPERARY BORDER, 1840–60. Brunschwig & Fils.

VOLUBILIS BORDER and corner, 1863–70. Brunschwig & Fils.

෨ WALTON BORDER. English, 1857, block print. Originally printed by William Cooke. 3″ wide, 8″ repeat. Adaptation: design derived from striped wallpaper. Document privately owned. Document color not reproduced. Period coloring: No.14761.06 (red).

CLASSIC REVIVALS

Mauny Collection

෨ BORDURE ET ANGLE SAINT BRIAC. French, 1840–60, block print. Border: 1″ wide; corner: 6¹/₂″ each side. No.5004 (series). Block print.

෨ BORDURE SAINT CAST. French, 1840–60, block print. 1¹/₂″ wide. No.5003 (series). Block print.

෨ DRAPERIE ET ROSES. French, 1840–60, block print. Top: 13¹/₄″ wide; bottom: 5³/₄″ wide. No.619J (red and gold). Block print.

෨ GROSSE CORDE. French, 1840–60, block print. 2¹/₈″ wide. No.570D (green); No.570G (red); No.570H (blue). Block print.

෨ RESTAURATION. French, 1850–70, block print. Top: 7³/₄″ wide; bottom: 2¹/₂″ wide. No.626F (blue and gray); No.626I (green and gray); No.626K (mauve and gray). Block print.

ᔥ ROSE MOUSSE. French, 1840–60, block print. 3$^1/_2$" wide. No.546F (pink and white). Block print.

ᔥ RUBAN FLEURI. French, 1860–75, block print. Border: 3" wide; corner: 7$^1/_2$" each side. No.2617A (blue and rose). Block print.

COWTAN & TOUT

ᔥ DOG ON WOOD AND IVY STRIPS. English, 1850–80, block print. 8" wide, 25" repeat. No.572 (green and brown).*

ᔥ FUCHSIA CROWN. English, 1860–70, block print. No.CT-20101 (multi with gold stripe). Block print.*

ᔥ ROSE AND PANSEY BORDER. English, 1860–80, block print. 5" wide, 21" repeat. No.140 (multi).

ᔥ SOLANGE BORDER. French, 1835–60, block print. 12$^1/_2$" wide, 14" repeat. No.168-01 (taupe).

ᔥ SPRING FLOWERS BORDER. English, 1860–70, block print. 5" wide, 21" repeat. No.190 (white); No.191 (black). Block print.

A. L. DIAMENT & COMPANY

ᔥ ROSE BORDER. French, 1850–60, block print. 10$^3/_4$" wide, 23$^3/_4$" repeat. No.150-20 (rose and green on aubergine).

ᔥ SWAG AND TASSEL. French, 1860–75, block print. 11" wide, 9" repeat. No.158-04 (gold).

GALACAR & COMPANY

ᔥ LA DAUPHINE DADO. French, 1869, block print. Originally printed by Desfossé et Karth. 16$^1/_2$" wide, 27" repeat, 5 yds. per s/r. Document at Musée des Arts Décoratifs. No.GP-1301 (greens on white).*

ᔥ LA DAUPHINE FRIEZE. French, 1869, block print. Originally printed by Desfossé et Karth. 16$^1/_2$" wide, 27" repeat, 5 yds. per s/r. Document at Musée des Arts Décoratifs. No.GP-1301 (greens on white).*

CHRISTOPHER HYLAND INCORPORATED

ᔥ CLASSICAL COLUMN—CAPITAL AND BASE. English or French, 1840–60, block print. 12$^1/_2$" wide. No.AB107/5 (gray, light gray, and dark gray).

ᔥ CLASSICAL COLUMN—SHAFT. English or French, 1840–60, block print. 8$^7/_8$" wide. No.AB108/5 (gray, light gray, and dark gray).

ᔥ CLASSICAL CORNICE. English or French, 1840-60, block print. 9" wide, 4$^1/_2$" repeat. No.AB110/6B (gray, light gray, and dark gray).

ᔥ STAFFORD BORDER. English, 1850–70, block print. 10" wide, 10$^1/_2$" repeat. No.WTGASTAB (cream, sienna, light blue, and black).

ᔥ OWEN JONES BORDER. English, 1855–70, block print. 4$^5/_8$" wide, 5" repeat. No.ZZBLJ (period colorings).

KATZENBACH & WARREN

❧ BRAIDED CORD BORDER. French, 1850–60, block print. 3" wide, 9¼" repeat. Document at The Athenaeum of Philadelphia. No.AE1074B (green and gold).

❧ ROCOCO BORDER. French, 1850–60, block print. 7½" wide, 18⅜" repeat. Document at The Athenaeum of Philadelphia. Adaptation: flocking not reproduced. No.AE1112B (multi and tan).

❧ ROSE AND RIBBON BORDER. French, 1850–60, block print. 3¾" wide, 12" repeat. Adaptation: created to accompany "Rose and Ribbon Corner." No.AE1043B (blue and pink). Period coloring: No.AE1042B (yellow and purple).

❧ ROSE AND RIBBON CORNER. French, 1850–60, block print. 20½" wide. Document at The Athenaeum of Philadelphia. No.AE1033B (blue and pink). Period coloring: No.AE1032B (yellow and purple).

❧ SATIN DRAPERY FRIEZE. French, 1840–60, block print. Originally printed by Desfossé et Karth. 10¼" wide (including top and bottom borders), 18" repeat. Document at The Athenaeum of Philadelphia. No.AE1231B (gray and mauve). Period colorings: No.AE1232 (gray and blue); No.AE1233B (gold); No.AE1235B (beige and green).

MT. DIABLO HANDPRINTS

Order by name unless a pattern number is listed.

❧ DIAMOND STRIPE BORDER. French or American, 1860–70, block print. 3" wide, 6½" repeat. Reproduced for Henry Ford Museum & Greenfield Village, Dearborn, Mich. Gold, black, and green on ochre.

❧ SANDRA'S BORDER. American, 1840–60, machine print. 3" wide, 21" repeat. Reproduced for Santa Cruz Mission Adobe, operated by California Department of Parks and Recreation. No.SCB-001 (documentary red and greens).

❧ SANTA CRUZ DADO. American, 1840–60, block or machine print. 21" wide, 19¼" repeat. Reproduced for Santa Cruz Mission Adobe, operated by California Department of Parks and Recreation. No.SCD-001 (documentary orange, blue, and green on clear yellow).

❧ WILLIAM TAFT FRIEZE. American, 1840–70, machine print. 5⅜" wide, 4¾" repeat. Reproduced for William Howard Taft National Historic Site, Cincinnati. Red, gray, gold, and black.

ARTHUR SANDERSON & SONS

❧ BUCKINGHAM ROSE BORDER. English, 1840–70, block print. 5¼" wide, 21" repeat. Document in Sanderson Archives. No.SP 12162 (roses on cream). Block print.

❧ WINDSOR ROSE BORDER. English, 1840–70, block print. 10½" wide, 22" repeat. Document in Sanderson Archives. No.SP 12159 (roses on white). Block print.

ROCOCO BORDER, 1850–60. Katzenbach & Warren.

LINDENWALD—HALL BORDER, c. 1840. Scalamandré.

LINDENWALD— NORTHEAST BEDROOM BORDER, c. 1840. Scalamandré.

LINDENWALD— NORTHEAST PARLOR BORDER, c. 1850. Scalamandré.

LINDENWALD— SOUTHEAST BEDROOM BORDER, c. 1840. Scalamandré.

SCALAMANDRÉ

☙ CATALDO MISSION BORDER. French or American, 1850–60, block print with flocking. 4⅞" wide, 8¼" repeat. Historic representation. Reproduced for Old Mission, Cataldo, Idaho. No.WB600-001 (rose, brown, and terra cotta). Special order.

☙ LINDENWALD—HALL BORDER. French or English, c. 1840, block print. 2¾" wide, 9¼" repeat. Reproduced for Martin Van Buren National Historic Site, Kinderhook, N.Y. No.WB81348-001 (olive, greens, and black flock on polar white). Special order.

☙ LINDENWALD—NORTHEAST BEDROOM BORDER. French, c. 1840, block print. 4½" wide, 10 5/8" repeat. Reproduced for Martin Van Buren National Historic Site, Kinderhook, N.Y. No.WB81346-001 (grays, roses, teals, and brown on polar white). Special order.

☙ LINDENWALD—NORTHEAST PARLOR BORDER. French or English, c. 1850, block print. 4" wide, 18¾" repeat. Reproduced for Martin Van Buren National Historic Site, Kinderhook, N.Y. No.WB81350-001 (grays, mustard, and turquoise on marble white). Special order.

☙ LINDENWALD—PARLOR AND DINING ROOM BORDER. French, c. 1840, block print. 2⅜" wide, 4¾" repeat. Reproduced for Martin Van Buren National Historic Site, Kinderhook, N.Y. No.WB81349-001 (maroon and black flock with metallic gold on ecru embossed texture). Special order.

☙ LINDENWALD—ROSE BORDER. French or English, 1840–60, block print. 4½" wide, 18¾" repeat. Reproduced for Martin Van Buren National Historic Site, Kinderhook, N.Y. No.WB81409-001 (multi lilac on chalk white).

☙ LINDENWALD—SOUTHEAST BEDROOM BORDER. French, c. 1840, block print. 4½" wide, 9½" repeat. Reproduced for Martin Van Buren National Historic Site, Kinderhook, N.Y. No.WB81351-001 (grays, black, and green on marble white). Special order.

☙ LOCUST GROVE BORDER. English, 1850–60, block print. 4¾" wide, ⅜" repeat. Reproduced for Young-Morse Historic Site, Poughkeepsie, N.Y No.WB81228-001 (metallic gold, slate gray, and charcoal on pebble gray). Special order.

☙ RUSSIAN BISHOP'S HOUSE—GUEST ROOM BORDER. French, 1850–60, block print. 2¼" wide, 18" repeat. Reproduced for Russian Bishop's House, Sitka National Historical Park, Sitka, Alaska. No.WB81370-001 (rusts, greens, and browns on black). Special order.

☙ RUSSIAN BISHOP'S HOUSE—LAYMAN'S ROOM BORDER. French, 1850–60, block print. 3½" wide, 20¼" repeat. Reproduced for Russian Bishop's House, Sitka National Historical Park, Sitka, Alaska. No.WB81364-001 (roses, golds, green, and black on coated white). Special order.

☙ RUSSIAN BISHOP'S HOUSE—RECEPTION ROOM BORDER. French, 1850–60, block print. 1¾" wide, 10½" repeat. Reproduced for Russian Bishop's House, Sitka National Historical Park, Sitka, Alaska. No.WB81367-001 (roses, greens, and black on warm gray). Special order.

☙ RUSSIAN BISHOP'S HOUSE—STUDY BORDER. English or French, 1850–60, block print. 1¼" wide, ¾" repeat. Reproduced for Russian Bishop's House, Sitka National Historical Park, Sitka,

Alaska. No.WB81372-001 (roses and greens on coated white). Special order.

SCHUMACHER

❧ BAROQUE BORDER. French, 1850–70, block print. 3¼" wide, 4¾" repeat. Document in Dornsife Collection, Victorian Society in America. No.5703A (mulberry and spruce).

❧ BAROQUE CORNER. French, 1850–70, block print. Document in Dornsife Collection, Victorian Society in America. No.5704A (mulberry and spruce).

❧ BRAID BORDER. French, 1840–70, block print. 3¼" wide, 1½" repeat. Document in Dornsife Collection, Victorian Society in America. No.5706A (document brown and blue).

❧ ROCOCO CARTOUCHE. American, 1850–60, machine print. 9½" wide, 9½" repeat. Document, a reproduction of c. 1905, in Schumacher Archive. No.512953 (document).

❧ ROCOCO LEAF BORDER. American, 1850–60, machine print. 3¾" wide, 6¹⁵⁄₁₆" repeat. Document, a reproduction of c. 1905, in Schumacher Archive. No.512963 (document).

❧ ROCOCO ROSES. American, 1850–60, machine print. 7" wide, 7 ³⁄₈" repeat. Document, a reproduction of c. 1905, in Schumacher Archive. No.512973 (document).

❧ ROPE BORDER. English or American, 1850–60, block print. 1⁵⁄₁₆" wide, 8" repeat. Document in Dornsife Collection, Victorian Society in America. No.5707A (document cerise and green).

THE TWIGS

❧ PANIER DES ROSES BORDER. French, 1850–70, block print. 8" wide, 18³⁄₈" repeat. No.65250/001 (blue swag on white).

WATERHOUSE WALLHANGINGS

❧ ARENENBURG FRIEZE. French, 1860–75, block print. 10½" wide, 9" repeat. Document privately owned. Document coloring: special order. Period colorings: No.225540 (red and gold); No.225476 (green and gold).

❧ GREEK REVIVAL BORDER. English or French, 1860–75, block print. 3" wide, 18" repeat. Adaptation: flocking not reproduced. Document at New Bedford Glass Museum, New Bedford, Mass. No.226525 (gold on black).

ZINA STUDIOS

Order by pattern name.

❧ GREEN ANIMALS BORDER. English or French, 1865–80, block print. 8" wide, 9" repeat. Reproduced for Green Animals, Portsmouth, R.I., a property of Preservation Society of Newport County/Newport Mansions. Greens and golds.

ZUBER

🙞 ELDORADO. French, 1848, block print. Designed by Eugene Ehrmann, Joseph Fuchs, and Hermann Zipelius. *Bulletin*, color pl. 15, no. 4, and p. 159; McClelland, p. 305; Oman and Hamilton, fig. 616, p. 222; Teynac, Nolot, and Vivien, p. 114. Total width: 42'; total height: 12'10"; 21" per panel; 24 panels per set. Block printed in 192 colors from 1,554 wood blocks.

🙞 LA GUERRE D'INDEPENDENCE. French, 1852–53, figures painted over Deltil's "Scenic America." *Bulletin*, color pl. 14, no. 3; McClelland, p. 199. Total width: 49'4"; total height: 13'; 18½" per panel; 32 panels per set. Block printed in 223 colors from 1,690 wood blocks.

🙞 ISOLA BELLA. French, 1842, block print. Designed by Eugene Ehrmann and Hermann Zipelius. *Bulletin*, color pl. 16; Lynn, fig. 9-26, p. 220. Total width: 27'9"; total height: 12'10"; 18½" per panel; 18 panels per set. Block printed in 85 colors from 742 wood blocks.

🙞 LE JARDIN JAPONAIS. French, 1861, block print. Designed by Victor Poterlet. Total width: 17'3½"; total height: 12'10"; 20¾" per panel; 10 panels per set. Block printed in 72 colors from 417 wood blocks.

Zuber also prints a wide variety of wallpapers and borders. The company prefers that inquiries concerning these additional patterns be made directly to its New York showroom.

SCENIC WALLPAPERS

above
LE JARDIN JAPONAIS (detail), 1861. Zuber.

1870 TO 1900: PATTERN EVERYWHERE

In the United States the late 19th century was unparalled in the manufacture and use of wallpaper. Most residential rooms were papered, including kitchens, closets, attic staircases, and even privies. Ceilings covered with one or more patterns also were fashionable.

Wallpaper was no longer considered only a finish; it became an essential part of a room's overall design. As a result, wallpaper design became a highly regarded branch of the decorative arts. Wallpaper patterns no longer had to imitate other materials such as draped fabric or stone. Indeed, papering a room was likened to bringing art into the home. Books on decorating and pamphlets produced by wallpaper companies promoted the stylized patterns and palettes favored by the English design theorists. As a result, England replaced France and once again became the source for fashionable wallpaper designs.

During this period, many English wallpaper manufacturers hired well-known designers and artists to create a succession of new patterns. One of the most well-known and influential English designers was William Morris, whose patterns of stylized flowers and foliage have remained popular to this day. Some have never gone out of production, and many of those available today are still printed from the original wood blocks. Because wallpapers designed by Morris were expensive, they were not used as extensively in this country as one might expect. His approach to design, however, was widely imitated, and most Americans had to settle for an inexpensive imitation "Morris paper."

Dividing a wall surface into three horizontal units—frieze, fill, and dado—was a popular wall treatment in the 1870s and 1880s. Coordinating borders marked the division between the different but compatible patterns. See, for example, "Chrysanthemum" frieze, fill, dado, and dado border (page 182). Toward the end of the century the dado and dado border were eliminated. However, the wide frieze designed to echo the pattern of the sidewall remained a popular and lucrative offering of the wallpaper manufacturers into the 20th cen-

BROAD MEADOWS, 1880–90. Waterhouse Wallhangings.

tury. See, for examples, the patterns "Mary Dailey Crook" (page 186) or "Emperor" (page 189). Ceilings also could be papered with one or more different patterns separated by a judicious use of borders. Often the ceiling paper was designed en suite with the sidewall and wide frieze.

The interest in Japanese design is evident in wallpapers produced during the 1880s. The asymmetrical designs and exotic motifs of patterns in the "Anglo-Japanese" style are direct contrasts to the wallpapers being imported from Japan at the same time; see, for example, "Oriental Garden" (page 168) and "Alhambra" (page 127). Expensive Japanese "leather" papers emulated the stylized English designs and were embossed and highlighted with gilding.

As their name indicates, the Japanese imports were intended to imitate leather. They were only one of several wallcoverings classified as relief decoration and widely used in late 19th-century interiors. Others included Anaglypta and Lincrusta. Both are available today, and many of the patterns are produced from the original rollers. Lincrusta Walton, developed in 1877 by Frederick Walton, the inventor of linoleum, is a composition material whose design is impressed with rollers. Anaglypta is a less substantial copy made from embossed paper. Both receive their decorative coloring after they are applied to the wall.

The elegant effects of many other English and American wallpapers made during the late 19th century were produced by embossing. Because of the expense involved, few firms replicate embossing on reproduction wallpapers. Textured (rather than embossed) wallpapers popular from the 1880s into the 1920s include ingrain and oatmeal papers. Both are considered unsuitable wallcoverings today because of their insubstantial quality and their rough, unwashable surfaces.

By the 1890s designers had stopped emphasizing the use of artistic wallpaper in "tasteful" interiors. Manufacturers catering to the middle-class market returned to producing patterns with floral and scroll motifs, such as "Rococo Rose" (page 188) and "Fortino" (page 189), rendered in a much less stylized manner. Those responsible for decorating interiors for wealthier clients, on the other hand, once again sought wallpaper patterns that imitated more costly textiles. In addition to creating new patterns, many companies reissued the damask and moiré patterns that had been popular a generation earlier. Because of the popularity of damask-patterned wallpapers during this period, most of the reproductions available today are listed in this section rather than in previous sections. Some, however, may be appropriate for earlier restoration projects. If the restoration of an earlier interior requires a wallpaper with a damask pattern, further research should be done on the patterns listed to determine which may be the most appropriate.

The 1980s witnessed an overwhelming interest in Victorian design. As a result a new decorating style called Victorian Revival emerged. Interiors promoted as being decorated in this style are quite diverse. Those that feature floral chintzes, lace curtains, pale colors, and white wicker or stripped furniture—an eclectic combination of English country house and the age of golden oak—would both astonish and confuse our Victorian ancestors. On the other hand, interiors that feature rich combinations of both color and pattern in correct proportion would receive their hearty approval because they are created with a full understanding of Victorian design vocabulary and color theory. The room sets offered by Bradbury & Bradbury are excellent examples of Victorian Revival as it relates to wall decoration. Some of the designs are exact copies of period wallpapers; others copy alternative approaches to Victorian wall decoration, such as stenciling or fresco. Some patterns are derived from published designs that were available to Victorian designers, and others have been developed by contemporary designers to coordinate with them. Like the best revival design in any period, these patterns do not slavishly replicate the past but take the appealing elements from historical designs and combine them in new ways in an attempt to evoke the decorative spirit of an era.

BRADBURY & BRADBURY

WALLPAPERS

᪥ CHILD'S GARDEN. American Victorian Revival, 1980. Designed by S. J. Bauer in the style of a nursery paper by Walter Crane. 27" wide, 27" repeat, 5 yds. per s/r. Code GDW (2 period colorings).

᪥ KNIGHTSBRIDGE DAMASK. American Victorian Revival, 1980. Designed by S. J. Bauer in the style of William Morris. 27" wide, 27" repeat, 5 yds. per s/r. Code KDW.

BRUNSCHWIG & FILS

᪥ FLOWERING TREE. English, 1880–1900, block print. 23½" wide, 39½" repeat, 6 yds. per s/r. Adaptation: scale slightly reduced. Document in Brunschwig Archives. No.11307.06 (indigo and rose).

᪥ FORET FOLIAGE. French, 1890-1900, block print. 21" wide, 24¾" repeat, 11 yds. per s/r. Document privately owned. No.13534.06 (green); No.13538.06 (brown).

᪥ FUCHSIA TRELLIS. French or English, 1870–85, block print. 18½" wide, 23" repeat, 7 yds. per s/r. Document at Cooper-Hewitt Museum. No.12514.06 (pistachio).

᪥ JAPANESQUE. American, 1870–90, machine print. 24½" wide, 15¾" half-drop repeat, 5 yds. per s/r. Document at Cooper-Hewitt Museum. No.12496.6C (gold on light brown). Custom order.

᪥ MAREIKO. French or English, 1870–1900, machine print. 27"

above left
WOODBURY MOIRE,
1890–1915.
Brunschwig & Fils.

above right
FUCHSIA TRELLIS,
1870–85.
Brunschwig & Fils.

wide, 23½" repeat, 5 yds. per s/r. Adaptation: width increased and compatable motif added. Document at Cooper-Hewitt Museum. No.12487.06 (aubergine).

෯ WOODBURY MOIRE. American, 1890–1915, machine print. 28" wide, 13¾" repeat, 5 yds. per s/r. Document at Society for the Preservation of New England Antiquities. Document color, no. 13214.6C (avocado), is a special order. Period colorings: No.13210.06 (sand); No.13213.06 (yellow).

J. R. BURROWS & COMPANY

Order by pattern name and color. All patterns can be custom colored.
෯ ALDAM. English, 1884–95, block print. Designed by Aldam Heaton. 21" wide, 21" repeat, 6 yds. per s/r. Document privately owned. Deep cream. Period coloring: celadon on buff. Also available block printed as a special order.
෯ HEATON. English, 1884–95, block print. Designed by Aldam Heaton. 21" wide, 42" half-drop repeat, 6 yds. per s/r. Document privately owned. Terra cotta on deep cream. Period coloring: celadon on buff. Pattern is made up of two widths of paper, marked A and B; both must be ordered to complete design.
෯ PERSIS. English, 1880–90, block print. 21" wide, 21" repeat, 6 yds. per s/r. Document in Burrows Archive. Sage green. Period colorings:

terra cotta; cream on buff.

❧ SUMMER STREET DAMASK. English, 1880–95, block print. 21" wide, 36" repeat, 6 yds. per s/r. Document privately owned. Terra cotta. Period colorings: celadon on buff; cream on buff.

CLARENCE HOUSE

❧ CANONBURY. English, 1890–1910, block print. 21" wide, 21" repeat, 11 yds. per roll. Coles Traditional Collection. No.C260 (gold); No.C264 (blue).

❧ FLORENTINE DIAPER. English, 1880–1900, block print. 21" wide, 10¹/₂" repeat, 11 yds. per roll. Coles Traditional Collection. No.C202 (old rose). Block print.

❧ MILLIKEN. English, 1880–1900, block print. Designed by Henry H. Mott, originally printed by H. Scott Richmond & Company. Nylander, Redmond, and Sander, front cover and p. 251. 21" wide, 21" repeat, 11 yds. per roll. Coles Traditional Collection. No.C227 (green); No.C229 (white); No.C230 (gold). Block print.

❧ SAVOY. English, 1870–90, block print. 20¹/₂" wide, 5¹/₄" repeat, 11 yds. per roll. Document in Courtauld Archives, London. No.W9005 (series).

❧ SMALL ACANTHUS. English, 1880–1910, block print. 21" wide, 24" repeat, 11 yds. per roll. Coles Traditional Collection. Period color-

above left
HEATON, 1884–95.
J. R. Burrows &
Company.

above right
PERSIS, 1880–90.
J. R. Burrows &
Company.

above left
CANONBURY,
1890–1910.
Clarence House.

above right
MILLIKEN,
1880–1900.
Clarence House.

right
SUMMER STREET
DAMASK, 1880–95.
J. R. Burrows &
Company.

VALLIERE MINOR, 1890–1910. Clarence House.

ings: No.C217 (parchment); No.C221 (raspberry); No.C220 (green). Block print.

ᴥ VALLIERE MINOR. English, 1890–1910, block print. 21" wide, 14" repeat, 11 yds. per roll. Coles Traditional Collection. No.C213 (green); No.C214 (salmon). Block print.

CLASSIC REVIVALS

Authentic Interiors Collection

ᴥ CHARLOTTE. English, 1880–90, machine print. 21" wide, 18" repeat, 11 yds. per roll. Price Collection. No.W-169-4B (ochre and olive).

ᴥ TRACCY. English, 1880–90, machine print. 21" wide, 20" repeat, 11 yds. per roll. Archival Collection. No.W-205-3A (light green on tan).

Mauny Collection

ᴥ BOUQUET ET GRANDE RAYURE. French, 1890–1930, block print. 21¼" wide, 44" repeat, 11 yds. per roll. Possibly a reproduction of an 18th-century design. No.140 (pinks and green on blue stripe). Block print.

ᴥ DAMAS CHOISEUL. French, 1870–90, block print. 18⅛" wide, 26" repeat, 11 yds. per roll. No.111-I (ochre on ochre). Block print.

ᴥ DAMAS ESPAGNOL. French, 1890–1920, block print. 18½" wide, 21¼" repeat, 11 yds. per roll. No.111-B (white on gray). Block print.

இ DAMAS FLAMAND. French, 1890–1920, block print. 18" wide, 20$^{1}/_{2}$" repeat, 11 yds. per roll. No.111-C (rust on orange). Block print.

இ DAMAS LA CAGE. French, 1890–1920, block print. 18$^{1}/_{2}$" wide, 21$^{3}/_{4}$" repeat, 11 yds. per roll. No.111-D (green and gold on white). Block print.

இ DAMAS LE NID. French, 1880–1920, block print. 18$^{1}/_{2}$" wide, 22$^{3}/_{4}$" repeat, 11 yds. per roll. No.111-E (white on green). Block print.

இ DAMAS PALMETTE. French, 1870–80, block print. 18$^{1}/_{2}$" wide, 8$^{5}/_{8}$" repeat, 11 yds. per roll. No.252 (buff on white). Block print.

இ DAMAS ROCOCO. French, 1870–1920, block print. 18$^{1}/_{2}$" wide, 19$^{5}/_{8}$" repeat, 11 yds. per roll. No.111-G (white on tan). Block print.

இ DAMAS ROYAL. French, 1890–1920, block print. 22" wide, 37$^{3}/_{8}$" repeat, 11 yds. per roll. No.111-A (rust on off-white). Block print.

இ DAMAS UTRECH. French, 1890–1920, block print. 18$^{7}/_{8}$" wide, 34$^{1}/_{4}$" repeat, 11 yds. per roll. No.111-F (beige on white). Block print.

இ PLUMES ET POMMES. French, 1890–1920, block print. 19$^{1}/_{4}$" wide (2 widths required for the complete horizontal repeat), 24$^{3}/_{4}$" repeat, 11 yds. per roll. No.160 (multi on light blue). Block print.

இ SEMIS PLUMETS. French, 1890–1920, block print. 18$^{1}/_{2}$" wide, 5$^{1}/_{8}$" repeat, 11 yds. per roll. No.261 (yellow on blue). Block print.

St. James Collection

இ FERN FILLER. English, 1892, machine print. Originally printed by Allan, Cockshut and Company. 28" wide, 11" repeat, 11 yds. per roll. No.FF1 (sage); No.FF6 (olive); No.FF11 (rose); No.FF13 (turquoise).

இ IRIS FILLER. English, 1885–1900, machine print. 21" wide, 18" repeat, 11 yds. per roll. No.IF6 (olive).

இ LARGE CHRYSANTHEMUM FILLER. English, 1890–1900, machine print. 21" wide, 21" repeat, 11 yds. per roll. No.YF14 (old gold).

இ PEONY FILLER. English, 1890–1900, machine print. 21" wide, 21" repeat, 11 yds. per roll. No.NF4 (deep red); No.NF7 (pink).

இ ROSE BOUQUET FILLER. English, 1890–1900, machine print. 21" wide, 16" repeat, 11 yds. per roll. No.QF7 (pink).

இ ROSEBUD FILLER. English, 1892, machine print. Originally printed by Allan, Cockshut and Company. 28" wide, 21" repeat, 11 yds. per roll. No.RF1 (sage); No.RF5 (gray buff); No.RF10 (sienna); No.RF12 (pink olive).

Silvergate Collection

இ BROCKHAMPTON SNOWFLAKE. English, c. 1870, block print. 21" wide, 10$^{3}/_{8}$" repeat, 11 yds. per roll. Document at Brockhampton House, Worcestershire, England. No.AS031. Block print.

இ BROCKHAMPTON TRELLIS. English, c. 1870, block print. 21" wide, 3$^{7}/_{8}$" repeat, 11 yds. per roll. Document at Brockhampton House, Worcestershire, England. No.BS022. Block print.

இ BURGES BLOCK. English, c. 1875, block print. Probably designed by William Burges. 21″ wide, 14″ repeat. Document at Knightshayes Court, Devon, England. No.AS141. Block print.

❧ BURGES BUTTERFLY. English, c. 1870. Designed by William Burges. 21″ wide, 5¼″ repeat, 11 yds. per roll. Adaptation: design derived from a sketch for a wallpaper. Document in collection of Royal Institute of British Architects, London. No.CS153. Block print.

❧ EASTLAKE PLAIN HORSE. English, 1872. Designed by Charles Locke Eastlake. 21″ wide, 4¼″ repeat, 11 yds. per roll. Adaptation: design derived from a published design in Eastlake, 1872 ed. No.AS181. Block print.

❧ EASTLAKE SHADOW HORSE. English, 1872. Designed by Charles Locke Eastlake. 21″ wide, 4¼″ repeat, 11 yds. per roll. Adaptation: design derived from a published design in Eastlake, 1872 ed. No.BS192. Block print.

❧ EASTLAKE PLAIN SPRIG. English, 1872. Designed by Charles Locke Eastlake. 21″ wide, 3½″ repeat, 11 yds. per roll. Adaptation: design derived from a published design in Eastlake, 1872 ed. No.AS201. Block print.

❧ EASTLAKE SHADOW SPRIG. English, 1872. Designed by Charles Locke Eastlake. Lynn, fig. 16-9, p. 378. 21″ wide, 3½″ repeat, 11 yds. per roll. Adaptation: design derived from a published design in Eastlake, 1872 ed. No.BS212. Block print.

❧ EASTLAKE PLAIN STAR. English, 1872, block print. Designed by Charles Locke Eastlake. 21″ wide, 3½″ repeat, 11 yds. per roll. Adaptation: design derived from a published design in Eastlake, 1872 ed. No.AS161. Block print.

❧ EASTLAKE SHADOW STAR. English, 1872. Designed by Charles Locke Eastlake. 21″ wide, 3½″ repeat, 11 yds. per roll. Adaptation: design derived from a published design in Eastlake, 1872 ed. No.BS172. Block print.

❧ LAKE DISTRICT ORIGINAL. English, 1880–90, block print. 21″ wide, 18″ repeat, 11 yds. per roll. Document at Townend House, Windermere, England. No.AS091. Block print.

❧ OXBOROUGH TRELLIS. English, 1870–80, block print. 21″ wide, 13¹³⁄₁₆″ repeat, 11 yds. per roll. Document at Oxburgh Hall, Norfolk, England. No.DS064. Block print.

COLE & SON

Available through Clarence House as custom orders only.

❧ ACANTHUS. English, 1870–90, block print. 21″ wide, 46″ repeat, 11 yds. per roll. Coles Book. No.98874 (red). Block print.

❧ AUDLEY END. English, 1890–1900, block print. 21″ wide, 17″ repeat, 11 yds. per roll. Coles Book. No.98870 (terra cotta). Block print.

❧ BEATRIX DESIGN. English, 1880–90, block print. 21″ wide, 21″ repeat, 11 yds. per roll. Adaptation. Coles Book. No.OEW143 (tan).

above left
OXBOROUGH TRELLIS,
1870–80. Classic
Revivals (Silvergate
Collection).

above right
CADORA, 1870–1910.
Cowtan & Tout.

Period coloring: No.OEW144 (brown). Block print.

☙ CELTIC. English, 1890, block print. 21″ wide, 8″ repeat, 11 yds. per roll. Coles Book. No.98885 (blue on green). Period coloring: No.98886 (brown on gold). Block print.

☙ LARGE ADAMS. English, 1890–1900, block print. 21″ wide, 24″ repeat, 11 yds. per roll. Coles Book. No.98816 (white on blue). Block print.

☙ POPPY. English, 1880–1900, block print. 21″ wide, 17″ repeat, 11 yds. per roll. Coles Book. No.98887 (pink and brown). Block print.

☙ ROYSTON. English, 1890–1900, block print. 21″ wide, 28″ repeat, 11 yds. per roll. Coles Book. No.PR15013 (green ground). Block print.

COWTAN & TOUT

☙ AMBERLY. English, 1880–1910, block print. 20½″ wide, 77″ repeat, 11 yds. per roll. No.21065 (blue). Block print.

☙ BURLINGTON. English, 1880–1900, block print. 21″ wide, 23″ repeat, 11 yds. per roll. No.20576 (hickory). Block print.

☙ CADORA. English, 1870–1910, block print. 21″ wide, 17″ repeat, 11 yds. per roll. No.20583 (buff); No.20584 (hunter green). Block print.

☙ GERANIUM. English, 1890–1910, block print. 21″ wide, 16½″ repeat, 11 yds. per roll. No.20580 (reds and greens on white). Block print.

HUMMINGBIRD. English, 1890–1900, block print. 21" wide, 19½" repeat, 11 yds. per roll. No.20500 (multi on white). Block print.

MARLBOROUGH. English, 1880–1900, block print. 20½" wide, 24" repeat, 11 yds. per roll. No.7075-08 (gray). Block print.

ROSE BOUQUET. English, 1890–1910, block print. 21" wide, 12" repeat, 11 yds. per roll. No.20540 (red on white). Block print.

SWEET PEA. English, 1890–1910, block print. 21" wide, 15" repeat, 11 yds. per roll. No.20570 (multi/stripe). Block print.

WESTERN BIRDS. English, 1870–90, block print. 21" wide, 20" repeat, 11 yds. per roll. No.27120 (multi on white). Block print.

WILD ROSE TRELLIS. English, 1880–1900, block print. 21" wide, 15½" repeat, 11 yds. per roll. No.20202 (reds). Block print.

WILLOW LEAVES. English, 1880–1900, block print. 24" wide, 21" repeat, 5 yds. per s/r. No.25087 (cream and gray); No.25088 (cream and green).

A. L. DIAMENT & COMPANY

ESCARPALETTE. French, 1880–90, block print. 19" wide, 41" half-drop repeat. No.176-02 (taupe on French blue).

CHINAMAN IN SWING. French, 1890–1900, block print. 27" wide, 30½" repeat, 5 yds. per s/r. Adapted from an 18th-century design; scale enlarged. No.80264-19 (beige).

above left
GERANIUM,
1890–1910. Cowtan
& Tout.

above right
WESTERN BIRDS,
1870–90. Cowtan &
Tout.

above left

BAMBOO JASMINE, 1870–80. Christopher Hyland Incorporated.

above right

AESTHETIC GARDEN, 1880–90. Katzenbach & Warren.

CHRISTOPHER HYLAND INCORPORATED

δ➤ BAMBOO JASMINE. English, 1870–80, block print. 21" wide, 23¾" repeat, 11 yds. per roll. No.WTCBJ2 (beige, green, and light blue).

δ➤ BODLEY. English, 1870–90, block print. 21" wide, 10½" repeat, 11 yds. per roll. No.WTCBO7 (greens).

δ➤ BOKHARA. English, 1880–1900, block print. 21" wide, 24⅛" repeat, 11 yds. per roll. No.ZZ93013 (crimson red).

δ➤ BUCCA CLARENCE. English, 1870–80, block print. 21" wide, 10¼" repeat, 11 yds. per roll. No.WTOCL5 (gray on white).

δ➤ CORN. English, 1897, block print. Designed by Archibald Knox. 21" wide, 24⅛" repeat, 11 yds. per roll. No.AB123/3 (yellow and blue).

δ➤ GENOESE. English, 1877, block print. Designed by George Gilbert Scott II; printed by Watts & Company. Nylander, Redmond, and Sander, color pl. 44, p. 164, and fig. 60-B, p. 222; Oman and Hamilton, no. 1136, p. 411. 21" wide, 35¾" repeat, 11 yds. per roll. No.WTHGN3 (blue-greens). Block print

δ➤ LACE SUNFLOWER. English, 1880–90, block print. 21" wide, 20½" repeat, 11 yds. per roll. No.WTOSF5 (white on tan).

δ➤ LENNEL. English, 1870–90, block print. 20" wide, 12½" half-drop repeat, 11 yds. per roll. No.ZZBL402 (black on rust).

δ➤ LITTLE VILLANDRY. English, 1880–90, block print. 21" wide,

23¹/₄″ repeat, 11 yds. per roll. No.ZZ91004 (mustard beige).

🔖 MACKINTOSH STRIPE. English, 1890–1900, block print. 21″ wide. 11 yds. per roll. No.AB207.2 (blue ground).

🔖 MAGNOLIA. English, 1897, block print. Designed by Archibald Knox. 21″ wide, 22¹/₂″ repeat, 11 yds. per roll. No.AB125/5.

🔖 MALMESBURY. English, 1880–90, block print. 20³/₄″ wide, 63″ repeat, 11 yds. per roll. No.WTHML1 (green on creme). Block print.

🔖 NIMUE. English, 1880–1900, block print. 22″ wide, 19″ repeat, 11 yds. per roll. No.WTNIMUE.

🔖 OAKLEAF. English, 1870–90, block print. 21″ wide, 15″ repeat, 11 yds. per roll. No.WTCOA8 (blue).

🔖 OLD ENGLISH. English, 1880–90, block print. 21″ wide, 59¹/₂″ repeat, 11 yds. per roll. No.WTSTOE3 (gray on white).

🔖 PEAR. English, 1880–90, block print. 21″ wide, 35″ repeat (two widths required for the complete horizontal repeat), 11 yds. per roll. No.WTHPR.

🔖 RAVENNA. English, 1880–90, block print. 21″ wide, 27″ repeat, 11 yds. per roll. No.WTHRV5 (blue and white).

🔖 ROCK MAPLE HOUSE DAMASK. English, 1880–90, block print. 21″ wide, 21″ repeat, 11 yds. per roll. No.AB179/2A (creme, beige, and white).

🔖 ROSE. English, 1880–90, block print. 21″ wide, 28″ repeat, 11 yds. per roll. No.WTHRS3 (tan and red). Block print.

🔖 ROSE AND CORONET. English, 1875–90, block print. 21″ wide, 17³/₄″ repeat, 11 yds. per roll. No.WTHRC2 (rose and blue).

🔖 ROSY BUDS. English, 1897, block print. Designed by Archibald Knox. 21″ wide, 25″ repeat, 11 yds. per roll. No.AB117/4AB (aquamarine).

🔖 TEA ROSE. English, 1897, block print. Designed by Archibald Knox. 21″ wide, 22¹/₂″ repeat, 11 yds. per roll. No.AB124/3 (blue and green).

🔖 TRELLIS. English, 1875–85, block print. 21″ wide, 7″ repeat, 11 yds. per roll. No.WTSTTE.

🔖 VENETIAN. English, 1880–90, block print. 21″ wide, 47¹/₂″ drop repeat, 11 yds. per roll. No.WTHVT1 (green).

🔖 VERSAILLES. English, 1880–1900, block print. 21″ wide, 41¹/₂″ repeat, 11 yds. per roll. No.ZZ0106. Period colorings.

🔖 VIOLA. English, 1870–80, block print. 20¹/₂″ wide, 15″ repeat, 11 yds. per roll. No.41002 (multi on blue-gray); No.41005 (multi on beige).

KATZENBACH & WARREN

🔖 AESTHETIC GARDEN. American, 1880–90, machine print. 27″ wide, 12⁵/₈″ repeat, 4¹/₂ yds. per s/r. Document at The Athenaeum of Philadelphia. No.AE1163 (terra cotta and gold). Period coloring: No.AE1161 (olive and gold).

ॐ ALHAMBRA. American, 1880–1900, machine print. 27" wide, 25¹/₄" repeat, 4¹/₂ yds. per s/r. Document at The Athenaeum of Philadelphia. No.AE1141 (tan and maroon).

ॐ BIRDS & BOUGHS. French, 1875–80, block print. 27" wide, 25¹/₄" repeat, 4¹/₂ yds. per s/r. Document at The Athenaeum of Philadelphia. No.AE1104 (blue ground). Period coloring: No.AE1101 (green and tan).

ॐ BYZANTIUM. American, 1880–1900, machine print. 27" wide, 5³/₈" repeat, 4¹/₂ yds. per s/r. Document at The Athenaeum of Philadelphia. No.AE1151 (olive and maroon).

ॐ GRAND DAMASK. French, 1880–90, block print. 20¹/₂" wide, 24¹/₄" repeat, 6 yds. per s/r. Adaptation: design slightly enlarged; flocking not reproduced. Document at The Athenaeum of Philadelphia. No.AE1063 (red). Period colorings: No.AE1062 (gold); No.AE1065 (green).

ॐ IRIS TAPESTRY. French, 1880–1900, block print. 20¹/₂" wide, 25¹/₄" drop repeat, 6 yds. per s/r. Adaptation: embossing not reproduced. Document at The Athenaeum of Philadelphia. No.AE1123 (multi).

ॐ NOSEGAYS. French, 1870–90. 27" wide, 25¹/₄" repeat, 4¹/₂ yds. per s/r. Adaptation. No.AE1053 (blue and pink).

LEE JOFA

ॐ COLETTE. French, 1880–90, block print. 27" wide, 36" repeat, 5 yds. per s/r. Reproduced from a period design for a wallpaper. No.P912003 (dove).

ॐ MARGARET CLAIRE. French, 1875–90. 27" wide, 27⁵/₈" repeat, 5 yds. per s/r. Created as a companion to a document border. No.912105 (silver).

ॐ RIBBON AND TRAIL TRELLIS. American or English, 1880–1900, machine print. 27" wide, 15⁵/₈" repeat, 5 yds. per s/r. No.P779003 (cream).

MT. DIABLO HANDPRINTS

Order by name unless pattern number is listed.

ॐ ANGLO-JAPANESE COLLAGE WALL. American, 1880–90, machine print. 18³/₄" wide, 19³/₄" repeat. Reproduced for Fallon Hotel, Columbia, Calif., operated by California Department of Parks and Recreation. Greens, blues, maroon, and gold.

ॐ BIBLIO DAMASK. American, 1890–1910, machine print. 18" wide, 17³/₄" repeat. Reproduced for Byers-Evans House, Denver, Colo., a property operated by Colorado Historical Society. No.BDW-001 (document browns and greens on chestnut).

ॐ BILLINGS ACANTHUS. American, 1890–1900, machine print. 18" wide, 16" repeat. Reproduced for Billings Farm & Museum, Wood-

above left
GRAND DAMASK,
1880–90. Katzenbach
& Warren.

above right
Original document
for "Colette," a
wallpaper of 1880–90
reproduced by
Lee Jofa.

left
BILLINGS ACANTHUS,
1880–90. Mt. Diablo
Handprints.

above left
GRIFFITHS FLORAL,
1880–90. Mt. Diablo
Handprints.

above right
KATHERINE'S BED-
ROOM, 1890–1910.
Mt. Diablo Hand-
prints.

right
NOUVEAU ROSE,
1890–1910.
Mt. Diablo Hand-
prints.

stock, Vt. No.BAW-001 (document custard on camel).

&❧ BILLINGS BEDROOM WALL. American, 1890–1900, machine print. 17³/₄" wide, 15¹/₂" repeat. Reproduced for Billings Farm & Museum, Woodstock, Vt. Gold, copper, mica, and light greens.

&❧ CAMPBELL HOUSE DAMASK. American, 1870–90, block or machine print. 24" wide, 12" repeat. Reproduced for Campbell House Foundation, St. Louis, Mo. Chocolate on pale blue.

&❧ FALLON'S FOLLEY. American, 1880–1900, machine print. 18" wide, 15³/₄" repeat. Reproduced for Fallon Hotel, Columbia, Calif., operated by California Department of Parks and Recreation. Brown, burgundy, and yellow on tan.

&❧ GREENFIELD ANGLO-JAPANESE. American, 1880–90, machine print. 18¹/₂" wide, 16³/₈" repeat. Reproduced for Henry Ford Museum & Greenfield Village, Dearborn, Mich. Olives and gray.

&❧ GRIFFITHS FLORAL. American, 1880–1900, machine print. 20" wide, 18" repeat. Reproduced for Alan Griffiths House, San Francisco, Calif. No.GFW-001 (document lilac, sage, dove gray, and gold).

&❧ KATHERINE'S BEDROOM. American, 1890–1910, machine print. 21" wide, 12" repeat. Reproduced for Byers-Evans House, Denver, Colo., a property of Colorado Historical Society. No.KBW-001 (document rose and green on pale cream).

&❧ McFADDEN-WARD FLORAL. American, 1890–1900, machine print. 18" wide, 24" repeat. Reproduced for McFadden-Ward House, Beaumont, Tex. No.MFW-001 (document buttercream on custard).

&❧ NAVARRE. American, 1880–1900, machine print. 18" wide, 19" repeat. Reproduced for Navarre Hotel, Columbia, Calif. Butternut and gold on eggshell.

&❧ NOUVEAU ROSE. American, 1890–1910, machine print. 18" wide, 12¹/₂" repeat. Reproduced for Byers-Evans House, Denver, Colo., a property of Colorado Historical Society. No.NRW-001 (document pink and green on mica).

&❧ OGLESBY DAMASK. English or American, 1870–80, block or machine print. 22¹/₂" wide, 8³/₄" repeat. Reproduced for Governor Oglesby Mansion, Decatur, Ill. Chinese red, maroon, and gold on umber.

&❧ PLAZA HOTEL WALLPAPER AND BORDER. American, 1880–1900, machine print. 18" wide plus 6" border, 12" repeat. Reproduced for Plaza Hotel Saloon, San Juan Bautista, Calif. Burnt orange and cream.

&❧ POPPY. American, 1890–1910, machine print. 18¹/₈" wide, 16" repeat. Reproduced for Byers-Evans House, Denver, Colo., a property of Colorado Historical Society. Reds and greens.

&❧ RENAISSANCE DAMASK. American, 1890–1900. 27" wide, 25⁵/₈" repeat. Adaptation: scaled-down version of "Whittier Damask" (see page 160). Tusk on robin's egg.

&❧ ROUND TILE. American, 1880–90, machine print. 17⁵/₈" wide, 6¹/₄" repeat. Reproduced for Byers-Evans House, Denver, Colo., a property of Colorado Historical Society. Blue and umber on cream.

ᐦ SQUARE TILE. American, 1880–90, machine print. 18³⁄₈" wide, 6¹⁄₄" repeat. Reproduced for Byers-Evans House, Denver, Colo., a property of Colorado Historical Society. Blues and gray on camel.

ᐦ TEXARKANA FLORAL STRIE. American, 1890–1900, machine print. 21" wide, 18" repeat. Reproduced for Texarkana Museums and Historical Society, Texarkana, Tex. No.TFS-001 (document red, greens, and tans).

ᐦ TOTEM WALL. American, 1880–1900, machine print. 19¹⁄₂" wide, 12¹⁄₂" repeat. Reproduced for Henry Ford Museum & Greenfield Village, Dearborn, Mich. Red, olive, and robin's egg on tan.

ᐦ WHITTIER DAMASK. American, 1890–1900. 22¹⁄₂" wide, 31" repeat. Adapted from a wall stencil. Reproduced for Whittier Museum, San Francisco, a property of California Historical Society. Pumpkin on chestnut.

ᐦ WILD WEST. American, 1875–90, machine print. 21" wide, 18" repeat. Reproduced for Buffalo Bill Historical Center, Cody, Wyo. Browns.

ARTHUR SANDERSON & SONS

ᐦ BEAUMONT. English, 1890–1910, machine print. Originally printed by Jeffrey & Company. 20¹⁄₄" wide, 15¹⁄₂" repeat, 11 yds. per roll. Document in Sanderson Archives. Period coloring: No.WH 7378-4 (chalk on khaki).

ᐦ BUCKINGHAM. English, 1880–1900, machine print. Originally printed by Jeffrey & Company. 20¹⁄₄" wide, 10¹⁄₂" repeat, 11 yds. per roll. Document in Sanderson Archives. Period colorings: No.WR 7517-3 (sage); No.WR 7517-4 (terra cotta).

ᐦ GLOUCESTER. English, 1890–1920, block print. Originally printed by Chas. Knowles & Company. 20¹⁄₄" wide, 14" repeat, 11 yds. per roll. Document in Sanderson Archives. Period coloring: No.WR 7513-2 (cameo blue and coral).

ᐦ GROSVENOR. English, 1890–1910, block print. 20¹⁄₄" wide, 23³⁄₄" repeat, 11 yds. per roll. Document in Sanderson Archives. Period colorings: No.WR 7376-1 (sage on green); No.7376-5 (Medici crimson on red); No.7376-6 (satinwood on cream).

ᐦ IN MY GARDEN. English, 1870–1920, block print. Originally printed by William Woollams & Company. 20¹⁄₄" wide, 24" repeat, 11 yds. per roll. Adaptation. Document in Sanderson Archives. Period coloring: No.WR 7451-1 (pinks and moss green on white).

ᐦ LANSDOWNE. English, 1870–1920, block print. Originally printed by William Woollams & Company. 20¹⁄₄" wide, 21" repeat, 11 yds. per roll. Adaptation. Document in Sanderson Archives. Period coloring: No.WR 7346-3 (gray, azure, and blues on yellow).

ᐦ SOMERVILLE. English, 1870–1920, block print. Originally printed

above left
TEXARKANA FLORAL STRIE, 1890–1900. Mt. Diablo Handprints.

above right
IN MY GARDEN, 1870–1920. Arthur Sanderson & Sons.

left
WILD WEST, 1875–90. Mt. Diablo Handprints.

by William Woollams & Company. 20¼" wide, 21" repeat, 11 yds. per roll. Adaptation. Document in Sanderson Archives. Period coloring: No.WR 7349-1 (pink, lavender, and green on white).

❧ THE TRAIL. English, 1880–90, block print. 21" wide, 14¾" repeat, 11 yds. per roll. Document in Sanderson Archives. Period colorings: No.WH 7373-1 (slate green on oyster); No.WH 7373-2 (flaxen on cream).

❧ WESTMORELAND. English, 1880–1900, block print. 20¼" wide, 21" repeat, 11 yds. per roll. Document in Sanderson Archives. Period coloring: No.WR 7518-3 (pearl).

❧ YORK. English, 1880–1900, block print. 20¼" wide, 14" repeat, 11 yds. per roll. Document in Sanderson Archives. Period coloring: No.WR 7520-3 (green baize).

SCALAMANDRE

❧ ACORN HALL DINING ROOM. American, 1890–1900, machine print with embossing. 28" wide, 18¾" repeat, 5 yds. per roll. Historic representation. Reproduced for Acorn Hall, Morristown, N.J. No.WP81068-001 (metallic gold, mustard, cream, burgundy, and black). Special order.

❧ ACORN HALL LIBRARY. English or American, 1880–90, machine print. 24" wide, 12" repeat. Historic representation. Reproduced for Acorn Hall, Morristown, N.J. No.WP81067-001 (metallic golds on burgundy). Special order.

❧ BILTMORE. American, 1880–90, machine print. Nylander, Redmond, and Sander, cover and fig. 72-a, p. 251. 21⅛" wide, 21⅛" repeat, 7 yds. per s/r. Reproduced for Biltmore, Asheville, N.C. No. WP81171. Special order.

❧ CHATEAU-SUR-MER. French, 1870–80, block print with embossing. 28½" wide, 17½" repeat, 5 yds. per s/r. Historic representation: embossing not reproduced. Reproduced for Chateau-sur-Mer, Newport, R.I., a property of Preservation Society of Newport County/ Newport Mansions. Additional sample at Cooper-Hewitt Museum. Document color, no. WP81490-999, is a special order.

❧ CAPTAIN EDWARD PENNIMAN HOUSE—CAPTAIN'S BEDROOM. American, c. 1870, machine print. 18" wide, 18" repeat, 8 yds. per s/r. Reproduced for Capt. Edward Penniman House, Eastham, Mass., a property operated by National Park Service. No.WP81385-001 (taupes, greens, and golds on warm gray). Special order.

❧ FAIRFIELD PLANTATION PAPER. English or American, 1870–80, machine print. 27" wide, 18" repeat, 5 yds. per s/r. Historic representation. Reproduced for Historic Charleston Reproductions, Charleston, S. C. No.WP81273-001 (grays and beige on pebble gray).

❧ GLENDALE—GUEST BEDROOM. American, 1890–1900, machine print with embossing. 20" wide, 12" repeat, 7 yds. per s/r. Historic representation. Reproduced for Glendale Historical Society, Glendale, Calif. No.WP81292-001 (metallic on restoration base). Special order.

❧ GLENDALE—PARLOR/DINING ROOM. American, 1890–1900, machine print. 18¹/₈" wide, 18³/₈" repeat, 8 yds. per s/r. Reproduced for Glendale Historical Society, Glendale, Calif. No.WP81290-001 (silver and deep rose on old rose). Special order.

❧ GOODWIN PARLOR FLORAL. American or English, 1880–90, block print. 18⁵/₈" wide, 21" repeat, 8 yds. per s/r. Historic representation. Reproduced from a photograph for Wadsworth Athenaeum, Hartford, Conn. No.WP81469. Special order.

❧ GRANT KOHRS RANCH. American, 1890–1900, machine print. 18¹/₂" wide, 19⁷/₈" repeat, 8 yds. per s/r. Historic representation. Reproduced for Grant Kohrs Ranch National Historic Site, Deer Lodge, Mont. No.WP81309-001 (ivory, gray-green, metallic gold, and peach blotch). Special order.

❧ HIRSCHFELD HOUSE—DOWNSTAIRS MAIN HALL. American, 1890–1910, machine print. 18" wide, 19" repeat, 8 yds. per s/r. Reproduced for Hirschfeld House, Austin, Tex. No.WP81 192-1 (maroon and brown on beige). Special order.

❧ THE MOLLY BROWN HOUSE. American, 1890–1900, machine print. 18⁵/₈" wide, 18⁵/₈" repeat, 8 yds. per s/r. Historic representation. Re-

above left
THE TRAIL, 1880–90. Arthur Sanderson & Sons.

above right
GLENDALE—PARLOR/ DINING ROOM, 1890– 1900. Scalamandré.

above left
GOODWIN PARLOR
FLORAL, 1880–90.
Scalamandré.

above right
PHOENIX WALLS,
1890–1910. Scala-
mandré.

right
SAGAMORE HILL
LIBRARY FIELD PAPER,
1890–1900. Scala-
mandré.

produced for Molly Brown House, Denver Colo. No.WP81229-001 (blue, black, rust, and red on citron). Special order.

‎❧ MONTEZUMA FLORAL. American, 1890–1900, machine print. 36" wide, 18³/₄" repeat, 4 yds. per s/r. Historic representation. Reproduced for Villa Montezuma, San Diego, Calif. No.WP 81132-001 (creams, tan, dusty rose, plum, seafoam, and antique metallic gold blotch). Special order.

‎❧ PARSONAGE. American, 1880–90, machine print. 18³/₄" wide, 6 ¹/₄" repeat, 8 yds. per s/r. Reproduced for the Parsonage, Peru, Vt. No.WP81414. Special order.

‎❧ PHOENIX TILE. American, 1890–1910, machine print. 27" wide, 6" repeat, 5 yds. per s/r. Reproduced for Rosson House, Phoenix, Ariz. No.WP81152 (blue and white). Special order.

‎❧ PHOENIX WALLS. American, 1890–1910, machine print. 20¹/₂" wide, 22¹/₈" repeat, 7 yds. per s/r. Historic representation. Reproduced for Rosson House, Phoenix, Ariz. No.WP81150-001 (greens, aqua, turquoise, chamois, wine, and black on horse-carriage brown). Special order.

‎❧ ROSSON DINING ROOM. American, 1890–1910, machine print. 36" wide, 15¹/₂" repeat, 4 yds. per s/r. Historic representation. Reproduced for Rosson House, Phoenix, Ariz. No.WP81151-001 (gray, chamois, metallic gold, and taupe). Special order.

‎❧ ROSSON NURSERY. American, 1890–1900, machine print. 25" wide, 15¹/₂" repeat, 6 yds. per s/r. Historic representation. Reproduced for Rosson House, Phoenix, Ariz. No.WP81185 (pink and blue on beige). Special order.

‎❧ ROSSON TILE. American, 1890–1910, machine print. 25" wide, 6¹/₈" repeat, 6 yds. per s/r. Historic representation. Reproduced for Rosson House, Phoenix, Ariz. No.WP81155-001 (blues, greige, and white on ivory).

‎❧ ROSSON WALLS. American, 1890–1910, machine print. 48" wide, 7³/₄" repeat, 3 yds. per s/r. Reproduced for Rosson House, Phoenix, Ariz. No.WP81163-001 (pinks, peach, celery, rose, silver, and dusty rose).

‎❧ SAGAMORE HILL LIBRARY FIELD PAPER. American, 1890–1900, machine embossed. 27" wide, 18¹/₄" repeat, 8 yds. per s/r. Historic representation. Reproduced for Sagamore Hill, Oyster Bay, N.Y. No.WP81259-001 (browns, grays, olive, metallic gold, and copper blotch). Special order.

‎❧ THOMAS WOLFE MEMORIAL DINING ROOM. American, 1890–1910, machine print. 24¹/₂" wide, 15⁷/₈" repeat, 6 yds. per s/r. Reproduced for Thomas Wolfe Memorial, Asheville, N.C. No.WP81197-001 (light green, off-white, beige, silver, plum, and deep maroon). Special order.

‎❧ THOMAS WOLFE MEMORIAL HALL WALLS. American, 1890–1910,

above left

WETMORE LEAVES,
1875–90.
Scalamandré.

above right
Original document
for "Ogden's Floral,"
a wallpaper of 1890–
1900 reproduced by
Schumacher.

machine print. 27½" wide, 15¾" repeat, 6 yds. per s/r. Reproduced for Thomas Wolfe Memorial, Asheville, N.C. No.WP81198-001 (gold, olive, and silver).

ℬ WETMORE LEAVES. English, 1875–80, block print. Lynn, color pl. 86, p. 349. 21¾" wide, 21" repeat, 7 yds. per s/r. Historic representation. Reproduced for Chateau-sur-Mer, Newport, R.I., a property operated by Preservation Society of Newport County/Newport Mansions. No.WP81495. Special order.

SCHUMACHER

ℬ CHINTZ. English, 1870–90, block print. Sugden and Edmundson, p. 105; Wells-Cole, no. 15, p. 18. 30" wide, 33" repeat, 11 yds. per s/r. Document at Temple Newsam, Leeds, England. No.TN01 (multi on tan).

ℬ CONSTANTINE. French, 1870–90, block or machine print. 27" wide, 13" repeat, 4½ yds. per s/r. Adaptation: pattern enlarged. Document in Hobe Erwin Collection, Schumacher Archive. No.508405 (delft).

ℬ CONTINENTAL DAMASK. English or French, 1880–1900, block or machine print. 20½" wide, 18¾" repeat, 5½ yds. per s/r. Document in Hobe Erwin Collection, Schumacher Archive. No.506210 (birch).

ℬ ESTATE VINE. American, 1890–1900, machine print. 27" wide, 25½" half-drop repeat, 4½ yds. per s/r. Document in Hobe Erwin Collection, Schumacher Archive. No.508520 (document teal).

left
NEW HARMONY,
1893–1910.
Richard E. Thibaut.

ॐ OGDEN'S FLORAL. American, 1890–1900, machine print. 27" wide, 25¼" repeat, 4½ yds. per s/r. Document in Schumacher Archive. No.512850 (document tan).

ॐ STORKS AND THRUSHES. English, 1875–90, block print. Sugden and Edmundson, pl. 65, p. 104; Wells-Cole, no. 14, pp. 16–17. 30" wide, 36" repeat, 11 yds. per roll. Document at Temple Newsam, Leeds, England. No.TN07 (blue on ivory).

RICHARD E. THIBAUT

ॐ ALLEN ROSE. American, 1880–1900, machine print. 28" wide, 22" repeat, 4½ yds. per s/r. Adaptation: number of colors reduced from 16 to 10; width of pattern increased. Historic Homes of America Collection, produced in collaboration with National Preservation Institute. Document at Candace Allen House, Providence, R.I. No.839-T6523 (multi on white).

ॐ LEESBURG. American, 1890–1920, machine print. 27" wide, 12⅝" repeat, 4½ yds. per s/r. Historic Homes of America Collection, produced in collaboration with National Preservation Institute. Document at Carrier House, Leesburg, Va. No.839-T-7968 (yellow and blue).

ॐ NEW HARMONY. American, 1893–1910, machine print. 28" wide, 7⅜" repeat, 4½ yds. per s/r. Historic Homes of America Collection, produced in collaboration with National Preservation Institute. Doc-

ORIENTAL GARDEN,
1880–90. Richard E.
Thibaut.

ument at Schnee-Eliot House, New Harmony, Ind. No.839-T-7972
(red and ochre). Period coloring: No.839-T-7974 (blue and rust).

ঔ ORIENTAL GARDEN. American, 1880–90, machine print. 27″ wide,
19″ repeat, 4¹/₂ yds. per s/r. Historic Homes of America Collection,
produced in collaboration with National Preservation Institute. Document at Prater's Jewelry Store, Humbolt, Neb. No.839-T-7929 (tan
and olive).

ঔ THE HERMITAGE. American, 1890–1915, machine print. 27″ wide,
13¹/₂″ repeat, 4¹/₂ yds. per s/r. Historic Homes of America Collection, produced in collaboration with National Preservation Institute.
Document at Hermitage, Ho-Ho-Kus, N.Y. No.839-T-7992 (tan, gold,
and burnt orange).

ঔ THE WILLOWS. American, 1890–1910, machine print. 27″ wide,
19″ repeat, 4¹/₂ yds. per s/r. Historic Homes of America Collection,
produced in collaboration with National Preservation Institute. Document at the Willows, Morristown, N.J. No.839-T-7964 (copper). Period colorings: No.839-T-7965 (burgundy); No.839-T-7966 (silver);
No.839-T-7967 (rose).

VICTORIAN COLLECTIBLES LIMITED

All documents are in the Brillion Collection. Samples from the same
collection are at the Cooper-Hewitt Museum. Selected samples are
also at the Victoria and Albert Museum.

ॐ VICTORIAN STRIPE. American, 1890–1910, machine print. 27" wide, 2" repeat, 5 yds. per s/r. No.45-001 (green, ivory, and silver on putty).

WATERHOUSE WALLHANGINGS

ॐ BROAD MEADOWS. English or American, 1880–90, machine print. 21" wide, 14" repeat, 7 yds. per s/r. Document in Waterhouse Archives. No.212548 (light and dark green on cream).

ॐ BRODSWORTH. English or American, 1880–1910, machine print. 27" wide, 30" repeat, 5 yds. per s/r. Document in Waterhouse Archives. No.187540 (red on red).

ॐ CHINESE POPPY. English, 1870–80, machine print. 18½" wide, 18½" repeat, 7 yds. per s/r. Document in Waterhouse Archives. Document color, red on beige, is a special order.

ॐ FLOWERS AND FRUIT. American, 1880–1920, machine print. 18" wide, 15¾" repeat, 7 yds. per s/r. Document in Waterhouse Archives. No.205540 (red on red). Period colorings: No.205431 (white on pale green); No.205252 (white on yellow); No.205467 (beige on white).

ॐ MOSES-KENT HOUSE. English, 1870–1900, block print. 27" wide, 20" repeat, 5 yds. per s/r. Adaptation: original printed on burlap. Document privately owned. Document color, green, is a special order.

ॐ NORWICH. American, 1880–1920, block print. 27" wide, 23" repeat, 5 yds. per s/r. Reproduced for Longfellow National Historic Site, Cambridge, Mass. No.201449 (mustard on yellow).

ॐ PILLEMENT. French, 1890–1910, block print. 28" wide, 44" repeat, 5 yds. per s/r. Reproduces an 18th-century design. Document in Waterhouse Archives. No.100635 (multi on white).

ॐ QUINCY LACE. English or American, 1890–1900, machine print. 20½" wide, 18" repeat, 7 yds. per s/r. Document in Waterhouse Archives. No.180163 (yellow). Period colorings (series).

ॐ WAYSIDE FLORAL. American, 1870–90, machine print. 25" wide, 15¾" repeat, 5 yds. per s/r. Document at the Wayside, Concord, Mass., a property operated by Minute Man National Historical Park. No.142635 (white on beige).

ZINA STUDIOS

Order by pattern name.

ॐ KINGSCOTE LEAVES. American, 1890–1910, machine print. 18" wide, 19⅛" repeat. Reproduced for Kingscote, Newport, R.I., a property of Preservation Society of Newport County/Newport Mansions. Blues.

ॐ ROSE TRELLIS. English, 1890–1910, block print. 18⅝" wide, 21½" drop repeat. Reproduced for Kingscote, Newport, R.I., a property of Preservation Society of Newport County/Newport Mansions. Pinks, green, and gray on beige.

right
NORWICH,
1880–1920. Water-
house Wallhangings.

bottom left
WAYSIDE FLORAL,
1870–90. Water-
house Wallhangings.

bottom right
KINGSCOTE LEAVES,
1890–1910. Zina
Studios.

Coordinating wallpaper patterns include two or more designs that were intended to be used together. The sidewall is called the fill and the top border is called the frieze. Patterns are grouped in the following combinations under each manufacturer: roomsets; fills, friezes, dados, and borders; fills, friezes, and ceiling papers; and fills and friezes.

COORDINATING
WALLPAPER
PATTERNS

BRADBURY & BRADBURY

Bradbury & Bradbury roomsets include coordinated fills, friezes, dados, borders, and ceiling patterns. Elements may be purchased separately.

Aesthetic Movement Roomset

🔊 CHERRY BLOSSOM. English, 1878, block print. Designed by Lewis F. Day. 27" wide, 13½" repeat, 5 yds. per s/r. Code CBW (4 period colorings).

🔊 EMELITA'S FRIEZE. American, 1880–90, machine print. 15½" wide plus 3" borders, 21½" repeat. Code EMF (4 period colorings).

🔊 ICE BLOSSOM CEILING. American, 1870–90, machine print. 27" wide, 27" repeat, 5 yds. per s/r. Code ICC (4 period colorings).

🔊 ORIENTAL BROCADE PANEL. American, 1870–90. 28½" wide, 27" high. Adapted from a stencil design. Code OBP (2 period colorings).

EMELITA'S FRIEZE,
1880–90, from
Aesthetic Movement
Roomset. Bradbury
& Bradbury.

Detail from Anglo-
Japanese Roomset
ceiling, 1870–80.
Bradbury & Brad-
bury.

ICE BLOSSOM CEILING,
1870–90, from
Aesthetic Movement
Roomset. Bradbury
& Bradbury.

❧ PENELOPE BORDER. American Victorian Revival, 1980. Designed by Burt Kallander. 6″ wide, 9″ repeat. Code PEB (4 period colorings).

❧ PENELOPE CORNER BLOCK. American, 1870–90. 20″ by 24″. Adapted from a stencil design. Code PET (4 period colorings).

❧ WESTWIND ENRICHMENT. American, 1870–90, machine print. 27″ wide, 6³/₄″ repeat. Code WWE (8 period colorings).

Anglo-Japanese Roomset

❧ CLAIRE'S WILLOW. English, 1870–80. 27″ wide, 13¹/₂″ repeat, 5 yds. per s/r. Adaptation of a Morris background. Code CWW (13 period colorings).

❧ EASTLAKE COMBINATION ORNAMENT. American, 1870–80. 6″ wide, 9″ repeat. Adapted from an anonymous published design. Code ECB (5 period colorings).

❧ EASTLAKE DADO. English, 1870–80, machine print. Designed by Christopher Dresser. 26″ wide, 3″ repeat. Adapted from a published design. Reproduced for Camron-Stanford House, Oakland, Calif. Code ELD (5 period colorings).

❧ EASTLAKE FRIEZE. English, 1870–80, machine print. Based on a design by Christopher Dresser. Greysmith, fig. 105, p. 146; Lynn, color pl. 92, p. 435. 18″ plus borders, 12″ repeat. Adaptation. Reproduced for Camron-Stanford House, Oakland, Calif. Document at Cooper-Hewitt Museum. Code ELF (5 period colorings).

❧ IVY BLOCK ENRICHMENT. American Victorian Revival, 1980. Designed by S. J. Bauer. 27″ wide, 3″ repeat. Code IBE (5 period colorings).

❧ JAPANESE LATTICE. English, 1878, block print. 27″ wide, 2¹/₂″ repeat, 5 yds. per s/r. Code JLW (4 period colorings).

❧ SUNBURST CEILING. American, 1880–1900, machine print. 27″ wide, 9″ repeat, 5 yds. per s/r. Code SBC (5 period colorings).

❧ SUNFLOWER CORNER BLOCK. American Victorian Revival, 1980. Designed by S. J. Bauer. 21″ wide, 21″ high. Code SFT (5 period colorings).

❧ SUNFLOWER PANEL. American Victorian Revival, 1980. Designed by S. J. Bauer. 18″ wide, 36″ high. Code SFP (2 period colorings).

❧ SUNFLOWER ROSETTE. American Victorian Revival, 1980. Designed by S. J. Bauer. 18″ diamater. Code SFR (3 period colorings).

❧ VALENCIA PANEL. American Victorian Revival, 1980. Designed by S. J. Bauer. Panel size: 27″ wide, 12″ high. Code VLP (4 period colorings).

In the Dresser Tradition I

❧ ALGERNON. American Victorian Revival, 1980. Designed by Burt Kallander. 27″ wide, 13¹/₂″ repeat, 5 yds per s/r. Code AGW (4 period colorings).

❧ BACHELOR'S BUTTON. English, 1862. Designed by Christopher

Dresser. 27" wide, 7½" repeat, 5 yds. per s/r. Adapted from a published design. Code BBW (4 period colorings).

❧ DRESSER CEILING. English, 1875. Designed by Christopher Dresser. Adapted from a published design. 27" wide, 8" repeat, 5 yds. per s/r. Code DSC (4 period colorings).

❧ FALLON BORDER. American, 1880–90, machine print. 10½" wide, 27" repeat. Code FAB (4 period colorings).

❧ FALLON CORNER BLOCK. American, 1880–90, machine print. 18¼" wide, 18¼" high. Code FAT (4 period colorings).

❧ PINSTRIPE BORDER. English, 1870–80. Designed by Christopher Dresser. 1" or 3" wide, depending on how it is cut. Code PNB (5 period colorings).

❧ PINSTRIPE CORNER TURN. English, 1870–80. Designed by Christopher Dresser. 5½" wide, 5½" high. Adapted from a published design. Code PNT (4 period colorings).

❧ QUENTIN BORDER. English, 1870–80. Designed by Christopher Dresser. 6¾" wide, 3½" repeat. Adapted from a published design. Code QUB (4 period colorings).

❧ RANDOM STAR CEILING. English, 1870–80. Designed by Christopher Dresser. 27" wide, 27" repeat, 5 yds. per s/r. Adapted from a published design. Code RSC (light blue or midnight blue).

❧ STAR TRELLIS ENRICHMENT. English, 1870–80. Designed by Owen Jones. 27" wide, 2¼" repeat. Adapted from a published design. Code STE (9 period colorings).

❧ WATKINS GLEN FRIEZE. English or American, 1875–90, machine print. Based on a design by Christopher Dresser. 18" wide, 18¼" repeat. Code WGF (4 period colorings).

In the Dresser Tradition II

❧ LILY. American, 1875–80. *In Pursuit of Beauty*, fig. 3.2, p. 70. 27" wide, 10¾" repeat, 5 yds. per s/r. Adaptation of a sketch for a wall treatment by P. B. Wight. Document at Burnham Architectural Library, Chicago. Code LYW (4 period colorings).

❧ PINSTRIPE BORDER (see above).

❧ PINSTRIPE CORNER TURN (see above).

❧ PLAZA CEILING. American, 1880–1900, machine print. 27" wide, 9" repeat. 5 yds. per s/r. Reproduced for Plaza Hotel Saloon, San Juan Bautista, Calif. Code PLC (4 period colorings).

❧ RANDOM STAR CEILING (see above).

❧ ROLAND. English, 1875. Designed by Christopher Dresser. 27" wide, 10¾" repeat, 5 yds. per s/r. Adapted from a published design. Code RLW (4 period colorings).

❧ VICTORY FRIEZE. English, 1875–90. Designed by Christopher Dresser. 18" wide, 26" repeat. Adapted from a published design. Code VIF (4 period colorings).

❧ WESTWIND ENRICHMENT (see page 173).

Fenway Roomset

❧ FIDDLEHEAD DADO. American Victorian Revival, 1980. Designed by Carmen Reid. 27″ wide, 9″ repeat. Code FHD (4 period colorings).

❧ GOSSAMER CEILING. American Victorian Revival, 1980. Designed by S. J. Bauer. 27″ wide, 27″ repeat, 5 yds. per s/r. Code GSC (5 period colorings).

❧ IRIS FRIEZE. English, 1876, block print. Designed by Walter Crane. 18″ wide plus one 6″ and one 3″ border, 9″ repeat. Adaptation. Code IRF (4 period colorings).

❧ MOTH BORDER. American Victorian Revival, 1980. Designed by S. J. Bauer. 4″ wide, 6³⁄₄″ repeat. Code MOB (3 period colorings).

❧ NEPTUNE. American Victorian Revival, c. 1980. 27″ wide, 13¹⁄₂″ repeat, 5 yds. per s/r. Code NPW (4 period colorings).

❧ RAINDROP ENRICHMENT. American Victorian Revival, 1980. Designed by S. J. Bauer. 27″ wide, 1¹⁄₂″ repeat. Code RDE (4 period colorings).

❧ SERPENTINE. Adapted from traditional Japanese wood block. 27″ wide, 6³⁄₄″ repeat, 5 yds. per s/r. Code SPW (4 period colorings).

❧ SPIRAL CORNER BLOCK. American Victorian Revival, 1980. Designed by S. J. Bauer. Each block 6″ by 6″. Code SPT (3 period colorings).

above left
LILY, 1875–80, from Dresser Tradition II Roomset. Bradbury & Bradbury.

above right
VICTORY FRIEZE, 1875–90, from Dresser Tradition II Roomset. Bradbury & Bradbury.

In the Morris Tradition

❧ ACANTHUS BORDER. English, 1875–90. 9" wide, 13¹/₂" repeat. Adapted from stencil designs by Morris & Company. Code ACB (5 period colorings).

❧ ASTER CORNER BLOCK. American Victorian Revival, 1980. Designed by S. J. Bauer. Each block 3" by 3". Code AST (4 period colorings).

❧ BIRD AND ANEMONE (see page 202 under Wallpapers by William Morris and Morris & Company).

❧ CHEQUERBOARD. American Victorian Revival, 1980. Designed by S. J. Bauer. 27" wide, 3" repeat, 5 yds. per s/r. Code CQW (4 period colorings).

❧ CHEVRON BORDER. English or American, 1875–90, block print. 1" wide, 3" repeat. Code CVB (2 period colorings).

❧ CLAIRE'S WILLOW (see page 173).

❧ CLEMENTINA. English, 1883, block print. Adapted from William Morris's "Christchurch." 27" wide, 13¹/₂" repeat, 5 yds. per s/r. Code CLW (4 period colorings).

❧ KELMSCOTT FRIEZE. English, 1875–90. 18" wide, 27" repeat. Adapted from stencil designs by Morris & Company. Code KSF (5 period colorings).

❧ KENSINGTON CEILING. American Victorian Revival, 1980. Designed by S. J. Bauer. 27" wide, 13¹/₂" repeat, 5 yds. per s/r. Code KNC (5 period colorings).

❧ LEAF BORDER. English, 1875–90. 3" wide, 6³/₄" repeat. Adapted from stencil designs by Morris & Company. Code LEB (3 period colorings).

❧ MARIGOLD (see page 204 under Wallpapers by William Morris and Morris & Company).

❧ POMEGRANATE PANELS. American Victorian Revival, 1980. Designed by S. J. Bauer. 27" wide, 27" repeat. Code PGP (5 period colorings).

❧ RASPBERRY BRAMBLE. American Victorian Revival, 1980. Designed by Bruce Bradbury. 27" wide, 17" repeat, 5 yds. per s/r. Code RBW (4 period colorings).

❧ ROSE CORNER BLOCK. American Victorian Revival, 1980. Designed by S. J. Bauer. Each block 9" by 9". Code RST (3 period colorings).

❧ WALDEN. English, 1875–90. Adapted from a design by William Morris. 27" wide, 13¹/₂" repeat, 5 yds. per s/r. Code WAW (5 period colorings).

❧ WILLOW (see page 205 under Wallpapers by William Morris and Morris & Company).

Neo-Grec Roomset

❧ ANTHEMION WALL FILL. English, 1880–90. Designed by George and Maurice Ashdown Audsley. 27" wide, 9" repeat, 5 yds. per s/r. Adapted from a published design. Code AFW (5 period colorings).

🔊 BAYBERRY FRET BORDER. English, 1880–90. Designed by Owen Jones. 5¹/₂" wide, 8" repeat. Adapted from a published design. Pattern Code BFB (5 period colorings).

🔊 CHAIN BORDER. American Victorian Revival, 1980. Designed by S. J. Bauer. 1" wide, 2¹/₄" repeat. Code CHB (4 period colorings).

🔊 LAUREL BORDER. English, 1880–90. Designed by Owen Jones. 3" wide, 2¹/₄" repeat. Adapted from a published design. Code LRB (4 period colorings).

🔊 NEO-GREC CORNER BLOCK. English, 1880–90. Designed by George and Maurice Ashdown Audsley. 8" wide, 8" high. Adapted from a published design. Code NGC (5 period colorings).

🔊 NEO-GREC CORNER FAN. English, 1880–90. Designed by George and Maurice Ashdown Audsley. 24" wide, 24" high. Adapted from a published design. Code NGT (5 period colorings).

🔊 NEO-GREC MAIDENS. English, 1880–90. Designed by Walter Crane. Each block 18" by 18". Adapted from a published design. Code NGM (5 period colorings).

🔊 NEO-GREC DADO. English, 1880–90. Designed by George and Maurice Ashdown Audsley, 27" wide, 13¹/₂" repeat. Adapted from a published design. Code NGD (5 period colorings).

🔊 NEO-GREC FRET BORDER. English, 1880–90. Designed by George and Maurice Ashdown Audsley. 9" wide, 4" repeat. Adapted from a published design. Code NGB (5 period colorings).

🔊 NEO-GREC FRIEZE. English, 1880–90. Designed by George and Maurice Ashdown Audsley. 14" wide plus 4" border, 13¹/₂" repeat. Adapted from a published design. Code NGF (5 period colorings).

Detail from Neo-Grec Roomset ceiling, 1880–90. Bradbury & Bradbury.

177

DEER AND RABBIT
FRIEZE, 1887, from
Woodland Roomset.
Bradbury & Bradbury.

🐦 STAR TRELLIS ENRICHMENT (see page 174).

🐦 SWYRE CROSS CEILING. English, 1880–90. Designed by Bruce Talbert. 27″ wide, 2″ repeat. 5 yds. per s/r. Adapted from a published design. Code SWC (5 period colorings).

🐦 WAVE BORDER. English, 1870–80. Designed by Owen Jones. 3″ wide, 3½″ repeat. Adapted from a published design. Code WVB (4 period colorings).

Woodland Roomset

🐦 ASTER BORDER. English or American, 1880–90, block print. 3″ wide, 9″ repeat. Code ASB (4 period colorings).

🐦 ASTER CORNER BLOCK (see page 176).

🐦 BLOSSOM AND BLOCK. American Victorian Revival, 1980. Designed by S. J. Bauer. 27″ wide, 6¾″ repeat, 5 yds. per s/r. Code BKW (4 period colorings).

🐦 CRAB APPLE. American Victorian Revival, 1980. Designed by S. J. Bauer. 27″ wide, 13½″ repeat, 5 yds. per s/r. Code SRW (4 period colorings).

🐦 DAISY CORNER BLOCK. American Victorian Revival, 1980. Each block 6″ by 6″. Code DST (3 period colorings).

🐦 DEER AND RABBIT FRIEZE. English, 1887. Designed by Walter Crane; originally printed by Jeffrey & Company. 18″ plus 6″ border, 19″ repeat. Minor changes in design. Document at Victoria and Albert Museum. Code DRF (4 period colorings).

🐦 MORRIS CEILING (see page 201 under Wallpapers by William Morris and Morris & Company).

🐦 ROSE BORDER. English, 1880–90. Designed by George and Maurice Ashdown Audsley. 6″ wide, 13″ repeat. Adapted from a stencil design. Code ROB (4 period colorings).

❧ SWEET BRIAR (see page 246 under Wallpapers by William Morris and Morris & Company).

❧ WOODLAND BORDER. 1880–1900, block print. 6″ wide, 6½″ repeat. Code WOB (4 period colorings).

Additional Patterns

The following group includes a fill, a frieze, and a ceiling pattern.

❧ SEASHELL WALL. American, 1880–1900, machine print. 27″ wide, 27″ one third–drop repeat, 5 yds. per s/r. Code SHW. Special order.

❧ SEASHELL FRIEZE. American, 1880–1900, machine print. 18″ wide plus 7½″ border, 19″ repeat. Code SHF. Special order.

❧ STARFISH CEILING. American, 1880–1900, machine print. 27″ wide, 27″ repeat, 5 yds. per s/r. Code SFC. Special order.

CLASSIC REVIVALS

Authentic Interiors Collection

The following group includes a fill, a frieze, a dado, and a border.

❧ ARCADIA FILL. English, 1880–90, machine print. 21″ wide, 18″ repeat, 11 yds. per s/r. Archival Collection. No.W-191-5A (yellow and brown).

❧ ROSAL FRIEZE. English, 1880–90, machine print. 5″ wide, 16½″ repeat. Archival Collection. No.F-194-6A (yellow and brown).

❧ MANWEL BORDER. English, 1880–90, machine print. 5″ wide, 12″ repeat. Archival Collection. No.B-192-6A (yellow and brown).

❧ JASMIN DADO. English, 1880–90, machine print. 24″ wide, 20½″ repeat. Archival Collection. No.D-193-6A (yellow and brown).

The following group includes a fill, a frieze, and a dado.

❧ KLARA FILL. English, 1870–80, machine print. Murphy, no. 12, p. 16. 20¾″ wide, 22¾″ repeat, 11 yds. per roll. Price Collection. No.W-180-1A (deep olive).

❧ BAGHA FRIEZE. English, 1870–80, machine print. Murphy, no. 12, p. 16. 6¾″ wide, 20¾″ repeat. Price Collection. No.F-179-5A (deep olive).

❧ BENARES DADO. English, 1870–80, machine print. 26″ wide, 21″ repeat, 11 yds. per roll. Price Collection. No.D-178-5A (deep olive).

The following group includes a fill and a frieze.

❧ OWEN FILL. English, 1880–90, machine print. Murphy, no. 18, p. 22. 21″ wide, 15″ repeat, 11 yds. per roll. Price Collection. No.W-166-1A (tan).

❧ ISIS FRIEZE. English, 1880–90, machine print. Murphy, no. 18, p. 22. 7″ wide, 15″ repeat. Price Collection. No.F-167-2A (tan).

St. James Collection

The following group includes a fill, a frieze, a dado, and a border.

❧ CHRYSANTHEMUM DADO. English, 1892, machine print. Originally

KLARA FILL, BAGHA
FRIEZE, and BENARES
DADO, 1870–80.
Classic Revivals
(Authentic Interiors
Collection).

printed by Allan, Cockshut and Company. 21" wide, 16½" repeat, 11 yds. per roll. No.CD5 (gray buff); No.CD6 (olive); No.CD9 (citron); No.CD10 (sienna); No.CD12 (pink olive); No.CD16 (drab olive); No.CD18 (slate); No.CD23 (acid green); No.CD26 (khaki); No.CD27 (vivid green).

❧ CHRYSANTHEMUM DADO BORDER. English, 1892, machine print. Originally printed by Allan, Cockshut and Company. 5¼" wide, 10 ½" repeat. No.CB5 (gray buff); No.CB6 (olive); No.CB9 (citron); No.CB10 (sienna); No.CB12 (pink olive); No.CB16 (drab olive); No.CB18 (slate); No.CB23 (acid green); No.CB26 (khaki); No.CB27 (vivid green).

❧ CHRYSANTHEMUM FILLER. English, 1892, machine print. Originally printed by Allan, Cockshut and Company. 28" wide, 21" repeat, 11 yds. per roll. No.CF6 (olive); No.CF12 (pink olive); No.CF18 (slate); No.CF27 (vivid green); No.CF28 (ginger).

❧ CHRYSANTHEMUM FRIEZE. English, 1892, machine print. Originally printed by Allan, Cockshut and Company. 10¾" wide, 12" repeat. No.CZ1 (sage); No.CZ5 (gray buff); No.CZ6 (olive); No.CZ8 (teal); No.CZ10 (sienna); No.CZ11 (rose); No.CZ12 (pink olive); No.CZ16 (drab olive); No.CZ18 (slate); No.CZ23 (acid green); No.CZ26 (khaki).

The following group includes fills and friezes.

❧ BURWOOD FILLER. English, 1892, machine print. Originally printed by Allan, Cockshut and Company. 21" wide, 16" repeat, 11 yds. per roll. No.BF1 (sage); No.BF11 (rose); No.BF13 (turquoise); No.BF14 (old gold); No.BF19 (burnt sienna).

❧ BURWOOD FRIEZE. English, 1892, machine print. Originally printed by Allan, Cockshut and Company. 10" wide, 21" repeat. No.BZ1 (sage); No.BZ11 (rose); No.BZ13 (turquoise); No.BZ14 (old gold); No.BZ19 (burnt sienna).

❧ POMEGRANATE FILLER. English, 1892, machine print. Originally printed by Allan, Cockshut and Company. 28" wide, 18" repeat, 11 yds. per roll. No.GF1 (sage); No.GF7 (pink); No.GF27 (vivid green); No.GF28 (ginger).

❧ POMEGRANATE FRIEZE. English, 1892, machine print. Originally printed by Allan, Cockshut and Company. 10" wide. No.GZ1 (sage); No.GZ7 (pink); No.GZ9 (citron).

❧ POPPY FILLER. English, 1892, machine print. Originally printed by Allan, Cockshut and Company. 28" wide, 18" repeat, 11 yds. per roll. No.PF2 (olive rust); No.PF3 (pink blue); No.PF4 (deep red); No.PF14 (old gold); No.PF18 (slate).

❧ POPPY FRIEZE. English, 1892, machine print. Originally printed by Allan, Cockshut and Company. 16½" wide. No.PZ2 (olive rust); No.PZ3 (pink blue); No.PZ4 (deep red); No.PZ5 (gray buff); No.PZ28 (ginger).

CHRYSANTHEMUM FRIEZE, with filler, dado border and dado, 1892. Classic Revivals (St. James Collection).

POPPY FRIEZE, 1892. Classic Revivals (St. James Collection).

POMEGRANATE FRIEZE, 1892. Classic Revivals (St. James Collection).

MT. DIABLO HANDPRINTS

Order by name unless a pattern number is listed. The following group includes a fill, a frieze, a dado, and two borders.

᪉ MARSH CREEK WALL. English, 1870–80, block or machine print. 21″ wide, 18″ repeat. Reproduced for Raheen, Kew, Victoria, Australia. No.MCW-001 (document blues, greens, and gold).

᪉ MARSH CREEK KINGFISHER DADO/ FRIEZE. English, 1870–80, block or machine print. 28″ wide, 24″ repeat. Reproduced for Raheen, Kew, Victoria, Australia. No.MCK-001 (document blues, greens, pink, and gold).

᪉ MARSH CREEK FISH DADO. English, 1870–80, block or machine print. 10³/₄″ wide, 22³/₄″ repeat. Reproduced for Raheen, Kew, Victoria, Australia. No.MCF-001 (document greens, khaki, and gold).

᪉ MARSH CREEK FLORAL BORDER. English, 1870–80, block or machine print. 5¹/₄″ wide, 10³/₄″ repeat. Reproduced for Raheen, Kew, Victoria, Australia. No.MCD-001 (document greens, yellow, and red).

᪉ MARSH CREEK LILY PAD BORDER. English, 1870–80, block or machine print. 3³/₄″ wide, 21″ repeat. Reproduced for Raheen, Kew, Victoria, Australia. No.MCL-001 (document greens, blues, and ochre). The following group includes fills and friezes.

᪉ BARNUM WALL. American, c. 1893, machine print. 18″ wide, 7⁷/₈″ repeat. Reproduced for Barnum Museum, Bridgeport, Conn. Reds, green, and tans.

᪉ BARNUM FRIEZE. American, c. 1893, machine print. 18″ wide, 12″

repeat. Reproduced for Barnum Museum, Bridgeport, Conn. Reds, green, and tans.

❧ BILLINGS PARLOR WALL. American, 1890–1900, machine print. 18" wide, 12½" repeat. Reproduced for Billings Farm & Museum, Woodstock, Vt. Rose, burgundy, and gold on tan.

❧ BILLINGS PARLOR FRIEZE. American, 1890–1900, machine print. 9½" wide, 12½" repeat. Reproduced for Billings Farm & Museum, Woodstock, Vt. Rose, burgundy, and gold on tan.

❧ ETRUSCAN MOSAIC. American, 1880–1900, machine print. 18" wide, 18¾" repeat. Reproduced for Fallon Hotel, Columbia, Calif., a property operated by California Department of Parks and Recreation. Copper, metallic blue, umber, and gray-green on deep ochre.

❧ ETRUSCAN MOSAIC FRIEZE. American, 1880–1900, machine print. 21¼" wide, 18¾" repeat. Reproduced for Fallon Hotel, Columbia, Calif., a property operated by California Department of Parks and Recreation. Copper, metallic blue, umber, and gray-green on deep ochre.

❧ FALLON FLORAL WALL. American, 1880–1900, machine print. 18½" wide, 15½" repeat. Reproduced for Fallon Hotel, Columbia, Calif., a property operated by California Department of Parks and Recreation. Gold and mica on cream.

❧ FALLON FLORAL FRIEZE. American, 1880–1900, machine print. 18½" wide, 15¾" repeat. Reproduced for Fallon Hotel, Columbia, Calif., a property operated by California Department of Parks and Recreation. Gold and mica on cream.

❧ KLINE CREEK FARM WALL. American, c. 1889, machine print. 18⅞" wide, 12½" repeat. Reproduced for Kline Creek Farmhouse, Dupage, Ill. Mica, gold, and lavender on cream.

❧ KLINE CREEK FARM BORDER. American, c. 1889, machine print. 9¾" wide, 12½" repeat. Reproduced for Kline Creek Farmhouse, Dupage, Ill. Mica, gold, and lavender on cream.

VICTORIAN COLLECTIBLES LIMITED

All documents are in the Brillion Collection. Samples from the same collection are at the Cooper-Hewitt Museum, and selected samples are at the Victoria and Albert Museum. The following groups include a fill, a frieze, and a ceiling paper. Some of the ceiling patterns are interchangeable.

❧ DAYLE. American, 1890–1910, machine print. Originally printed by Standard Wall Paper Company. 27" wide, 18¾" repeat, 5 yds. per s/r. No.21-001 (burgundy, gold, and bisque on butternut).

❧ DAYLE BORDER. American, 1890–1910, machine print. 9" wide, 15¾" repeat. No.21-061 (burgundy, gold, and bisque on butternut).

❧ DAYLE CEILING. American, 1890–1910, machine print. 24" wide,

MARSH CREEK WALL, with borders, frieze, and dado, 1870–80. Mt. Diablo Handprints.

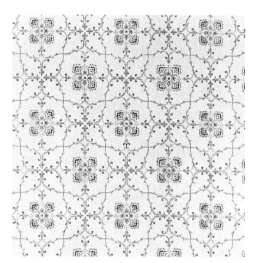

above left
DAYLE CEILING,
1890–1910. Victorian
Collectibles Limited.

above right
MARY DAILEY CROOK
and border,
1890–1910. Victorian
Collectibles Limited.

12¹/₂" repeat, 5 yds. per s/r. No.21-031 (blue and gold on amber crackle).

ð♥ HERALDIC. American, 1890–1910, machine print. Originally printed by Standard Wall Paper Company. 18" wide, 15¹/₂" repeat, 5 yds. per s/r. No.40-001 (burgundy, rose, green, and golds on brown). Period coloring: No.40-003 (black, brown, terra cotta, gold, and copper on beige weave).

ð♥ HERALDIC BORDER. American, 1890–1910, machine print. 18" wide, 18" repeat. No.40-051 (burgundy, rose, green, and golds on brown). Period coloring: No.40-053 (black, brown, terra cotta, gold, and copper on beige weave).

ð♥ HERALDIC BORDER (narrow). American, 1890–1910, machine print. 9" wide, 8" repeat. Half-scale adaptation of preceding pattern. No.40-061 (burgundy, rose, green, and golds on brown). Period coloring: No.40-063 (black, brown, terra cotta, gold, and copper on beige weave).

ð♥ HERALDIC CEILING. American, 1890–1910, machine print. 24" wide, 18" repeat, 5 yds. per s/r. No.40-031 (golds and brown on burgundy). Period colorings: No.40-032 (golds and brown on ivory); No.40-033 (green and golds on off-white).

ð♥ MARY DAILEY CROOK. American, 1890–1910, machine print. 24" wide, 15¹/₂" repeat, 5 yds. per s/r. No.25-001 (mauve, green, ivory, and navy on Victorian blue). Period colorings: No.25-002 (rose, gold, and cream on pink); No.25-003 (toasts, greens, and gold on beige).

ᥟ MARY DAILEY CROOK BORDER. American, 1890–1910, machine print. Originally printed by S. A. Maxwell & Company. 18" wide, 18³/₄" repeat. No.25-055 (mauve, green, ivory, and navy on Victorian blue). Period colorings: No.25-052 (rose, gold, and cream on pink); No.25-053 (toasts, greens, and gold on beige).

ᥟ MARY DAILEY CROOK CEILING. American, 1890–1910, machine print. Originally printed by Standard Wall Paper Company. 18¹/₂" wide plus two 2¹/₂" borders, 18³/₄" repeat, 5 yds. per s/r. No.25-031 (mauve, green, gold, and blue on ivory). Period colorings: No.25-032 (rose, gold, and cream on ivory); No.25-033 (toasts, green, and gold on off-white).

ᥟ MILLARD. American, 1890–1910, machine print. 24" wide, 10" repeat, 5 yds. per s/r. No.24-001 (burgundy, white, and gold on gray). Period coloring: No.24-003 (brown and greens on green crackle).

ᥟ MILLARD BORDER. American, 1890–1910, machine print. 18" wide, 18¹/₂" repeat. No.24-051 (burgundy, white, and gold on gray). Period coloring: No.24-053 (brown and greens on green crackle).

ᥟ MILLARD BORDER (narrow). American, 1890–1910, machine print. 9" wide, 18¹/₂" repeat. Half-scale adaptation of preceding pattern. No.24-061 (burgundy, white, and gold on gray). Period coloring: No.24-063 (brown and greens on green crackle).

ᥟ MILLARD CEILING. American, 1890–1910, machine print. Originally printed by S. A. Maxwell & Company. 24" wide, 12¹/₂" repeat, 5 yds. per s/r. No.24-031 (burgundy, gray, and gold on white).

ᥟ ROCOCO ROSE. American, 1890–1910, machine print. Originally printed by S. A. Maxwell & Company. 24" wide plus 2¹/₂" border, 12¹/₂" repeat, 5 yds. per s/r. No.31-001 (cream, green, and gold on beige).

ᥟ ROCOCO ROSE BORDER. American, 1890–1910, machine print. Originally printed by S. A. Maxwell & Company. 18" wide, 16" repeat. No.31-051 (cream, green, and gold on beige).

ᥟ ROCOCO ROSE BORDER (narrow). American, 1890–1910, machine print. 9" wide, 8" repeat. Half-scale adaptation of preceding pattern. No.31-061 (cream, green, and gold on beige).

ᥟ ROCOCO ROSE CEILING. American, 1890–1910, machine print. Originally printed by S. A. Maxwell & Company. 24" wide plus 3" border, 12" repeat, 5 yds. per s/r. No.31-031 (gold, cream, and green on ivory).

ᥟ VICTORIAN TEA ROSE. American, 1890–1910, machine print. 24" wide, 15³/₄" repeat, 5 yds. per s/r. No.42-001 (rose, burgundy, tan, and silver on pink). Period colorings: No.42-002 (rose, burgundy, tan, and silver on beige); No.42-003 (rose, burgundy, tan, and silver on Victorian gold).

above left
MILLARD and border, 1890–1910. Victorian Collectibles Limited.

above right
ROCOCO ROSE and border. 1890–1910. Victorian Collectibles Limited.

❧ VICTORIAN TEA ROSE BORDER. American, 1890–1910, machine print. 18″ wide, 19″ repeat. No.42-051 (rose, burgundy, tan, silver, and pink on beige). Period coloring: No.42-003 (rose, burgundy, tan, silver, and pink on Victorian gold).

❧ VICTORIAN TEA ROSE BORDER (narrow). American, 1890–1910, machine print. 18″ wide, 19″ repeat. Half-scale adaptation of preceding pattern. No.42-061 (rose, burgundy, tan, silver, and pink on beige). Period coloring: No.42-063 (rose, burgundy, tan, silver, and pink on Victorian gold).

❧ VICTORIAN TEA ROSE CEILING. American, 1890–1910, machine print. 25″ wide, 12″ repeat, 5 yds. per s/r. No.42-035 (gold, pink, silver, and green on beige). Period coloring: No.42-032 (gold, pink, silver, and green on white).

The following group includes fills and friezes.

❧ EMPEROR. American, 1890–1910, machine print. 24″ wide, 18½″ repeat, 5 yds. per s/r. No.19-001 (dark green and gold on pumpkin). Period coloring: No.19-004 (greens on green crackle).

❧ EMPEROR BORDER. American, 1890–1910, machine print. 18″ wide, 16″ repeat. No.19-051 (dark green and gold on pumpkin). Period coloring: No.19-054 (greens on green crackle).

❧ EMPEROR BORDER (narrow). American, 1890–1910, machine print. 9″ wide, 16″ repeat. Half-scale adaptation of preceding pattern.

No.19-061 (dark green and gold on pumpkin). Period coloring: No.19-064 (greens on green crackle).

꙰ FORTINO. American, 1890–1910, machine print. 27" wide, 18³/₄" repeat, 5 yds. per s/r. No.20-001 (green, gold, and cream on sage).

꙰ FORTINO BORDER. American, 1890–1910, machine print. Originally printed by Janeway & Company. 18" wide, 15³/₄" repeat. No.20-051 (green, gold, and cream on sage).

꙰ REGAL MEDALLION. American, 1890–1915, machine print. 24" wide, 26¹/₂" repeat, 5 yds. per s/r. No.15-001 (burgundy on beige). Period coloring: No.15-006 (burgundy and green on beige).

꙰ REGAL MEDALLION BORDER. American, 1890–1915, machine print. 18" wide, 19" repeat. No.15-051 (burgundy on beige). Period coloring: No.15-056 (burgundy and green on beige).

above left
EMPEROR and border, 1890–1910. Victorian Collectibles Limited.

above right
FORTINO and border, 1890–1910. Victorian Collectibles Limited.

ZINA STUDIOS

Order by pattern name. The following group includes a fill, a freize, and a border.

꙰ PASSION FLOWER. English, 1875–85, machine print. Lynn, color pl. 89, p. 352, and dust jacket. 21¹/₂" wide, 19⁷/₈" repeat, 5 yds. per s/r. Reproduced for Camron-Stanford House, Oakland, Calif. Document at Cooper-Hewitt Museum. Turquoise and orange on cream.

꙰ PASSION FLOWER BORDER. English, 1875–85, machine print. 3³/₄" wide, 5" repeat. Document at Cooper-Hewitt Museum. Turquoise on cream.

ॐ PASSION FLOWER FRIEZE. English, 1875–85, machine print. Lynn, color pl. 89, p. 352, and dust jacket. 21" wide, 5" repeat. Reproduced for Camron-Stanford House, Oakland, Calif. Document at Cooper-Hewitt Museum. Turquoise and orange on cream.

BORDERS, DADOS, AND PANELS

BRADBURY & BRADBURY

ॐ PEACOCK FRIEZE. English, 1889, block print. Designed by Walter Crane; originally printed by Jeffrey & Company. 21³/₄" wide, 21³/₄" repeat. Design derived from a printed advertisement. Document at Victoria and Albert Museum. Code PKF. Special order.

ॐ PERSIA BORDERS. French, 1870–80. 10" wide, 18" repeat. Design derived from a published design by Racinet. Code PSB. Special order.

ॐ VERMILLION STAR FRIEZE. American, 1890-1900. 18" wide, 9¹/₂" repeat. Reproduced from a photograph for Clay County Historical Society, Vermillion, S.D. Code VSF. Special order.

J. R. BURROWS & COMPANY

Order by pattern name and color.

ॐ CHAUNCY FRIEZE. American, 1885–95, machine print. 18" wide, 22¹/₄" repeat. Document privately owned. Brown on brown. Can be printed on oatmeal paper as special order.

ॐ PERSIS FRIEZE. American Victorian Revival. 9¹/₂" wide, 20" repeat. Designed to complement "Persis" sidewall (page 146). Period colorings: sage green; terra cotta; celadon on buff.

CLASSIC REVIVALS

Authentic Interiors Collection

ॐ BETTINGTON FRIEZE. English, 1880–90, machine print. Murphy, no. 23 (5th frieze from top), p. 28. 5¹/₄" wide, 15" repeat. Archival Collection. No.F-197-10A (multi).

ॐ SWALLOW FRIEZE. English, 1880–90, block or machine print. 10¹/₂" wide, 20¹/₂" repeat. Archival Collection. No.F-170-11A (blue).

ॐ TESSA FRIEZE. English, 1870–80, machine print. 8¹/₂" wide, 16" repeat. Price Collection. No.F-202-2A.

St. James Collection

ॐ DAISY FRIEZE. English, 1890–1900, machine print. 12" wide. No.DZ28 (ginger).

ॐ GALLICA FRIEZE. English, 1892, machine print. Originally printed by Allan, Cockshut and Company. 7" wide. No.AZ2 (rust olive); No.AZ3 (pink blue); No.AZ4 (deep red); No.AZ18 (slate); No.AZ27 (vivid green).

ॐ GOTHIC BORDER. Australian, 1890–1900. 7¹/₂" wide. Reproduced from a stencil design. No.GB22 (terra cotta).

PASSION FLOWER,
1875–85.
Zina Studios.

CHAUNCEY FRIEZE,
1885–95.
J. R. Burrows &
Company.

SWALLOW FRIEZE,
1880–90. Classic
Revivals (Authentic
Interiors Collection).

DAISY FRIEZE, 1880–90. Classic Revivals (St. James Collection).

GALLICA FRIEZE, 1892. Classic Revivals (St. James Collection).

WHISTLER DADO BORDER, 1892. Classic Revivals (St. James Collection).

RIBBONS AND BOWS BORDER, 1890–1920. Cowtan & Tout.

ॐ HAWTHORN DADO. English, 1892, machine print. Originally printed by Allan, Cockshut and Company. 21″ wide, 5½″ repeat, 11 yds. per roll. No.HD15 (china blue); No.HD16 (drab olive); No.HD17 (salmon); No.HD22 (terra cotta).

ॐ HAWTHORN DADO BORDER. English, 1892, machine print. Originally printed by Allan, Cockshut and Company. 4½″ wide, 5½″ repeat. No.HB15 (china blue); No.HB16 (drab olive); No.HB17 (salmon); No.HB22 (terra cotta).

ॐ JAPANESE DADO. English, 1890–1900, machine print. 28″ wide, 18″ repeat, 11 yds. per roll. No.SD6 (olive); No.SD28 (ginger).

ॐ JAPANESE DADO BORDER. English, 1892, machine print. Originally printed by Allan, Cockshut and Company. 4⅞″ wide. No.SB6 (olive); No.SB28 (ginger).

ॐ JUNIPER HALL DADO. English, 1885–1900, machine print. 26″ wide, 19″ repeat, 11 yds. per roll. No.JD2 (olive rust); No.JD13 (turquoise).

ॐ JUNIPER HALL DADO BORDER. English, 1885–1900, machine print.

4¹/₄" wide, 2³/₈" repeat. No.JB2 (olive rust); No.JB13 (turquoise).

❧ LOUISA BORDER. English, 1892, machine print. Originally printed by Allan, Cockshut and Company. 5" wide, 12" repeat. No.LB13 (turquoise); No.LB15 (china blue); No.LB19 (burnt sienna); No.LB20 (eau de Nil); No.LB21 (antique blue); No.LB22 (terra cotta).

❧ MATHER BORDER. English, 1885–1900, machine print. 4¹/₂" wide, No.MB6 (olive).

❧ MENINGOORT DADO. English, 1885–1900, machine print. 21" wide, 11 yds. per roll. No.MD14 (old gold).

❧ PRIMROSE FRIEZE. English, 1885–1900, machine print. 7" wide. No.EZ3 (pink blue); No.EZ10 (sienna); No.EZ17 (salmon).

❧ QUEENSCLIFF. English, 1890–1900, machine print. 10" wide. No.QZ1 (sage).

❧ WHISTLER DADO. English, 1892, machine print. Originally printed by Allan, Cockshut and Company. 28" wide, 18" repeat, 11 yds. per roll. No.WD1 (sage); No.WD2 (olive rust); No.WD8 (teal).

❧ WHISTLER DADO BORDER. English, 1892, machine print. Originally printed by Allan, Cockshut and Company. 4⁷/₈" wide. No.WB1 (sage); No.WB2 (olive rust); No.WB8 (teal).

COWTAN & TOUT

❧ HAWTHORNE BORDER. English, 1890–1910, block print. 4" wide, 21" repeat. No.133 (multi). Block print.

❧ MYRTLE BORDER. English, 1890–1910, block print. 5" wide, 7¹/₄" repeat. No.181 (pink). Block print.

❧ RIBBONS AND BOWS BORDER. English, 1890–1920, block print. 5" wide, 24" repeat. No.128 (green); No.128-1 (rose). Block print.

❧ RIBBONS AND BOWS BORDER. English, 1890–1920, block print. 5" wide, 21" repeat. No.132 (pink); No.132-1 (blue). Block print.

❧ SWEET PEA BORDER. English, 1890–1920, block print. 5" wide, 21" repeat. No.134 (multi). Block print.

CHRISTOPHER HYLAND INCORPORATED

❧ ETIENNE. French, 1870–1900, block print. 18¹/₂" wide, 10" repeat. No.AB170/5 (gold, brown, and green).

❧ LOGRIS. English, 1880–90, block print. 7" wide, 6" repeat. Sold only in 11-yard rolls. No.WTLB101 (rust, creme, mint, and forest).

❧ OLEANDER TRELLIS. English, 1870–90, block print. 18³/₄" wide, 18" repeat. No.AB161/20 (multi on document original colors).

❧ POIMA. English or French, 1890–1910, block print. 21" wide, 23¹/₂" repeat. No.AB101/10A (multi).

LEE JOFA

❧ COLETTE BORDER. French, 1880–90, block print. 13³/₈" wide, 36" repeat. Design derived from a period design for a wallpaper. No.P912023 (dove).

ᕥ MARGARET CLAIRE BORDER. French, 1875–90, block print. 13½" wide, 27" repeat. Adaptation: flocking not reproduced. No.P912124 (silver).

ᕥ PETIT MARGARET BORDER. French, 1875–90, block print. 5" wide, 27" repeat. Adaptation: scale reduced. No.P912154 (silver).

Mt. Diablo Handprints

ᕥ FALLON FRIEZE. American, 1880–1900, machine print. 19" wide, 20⅞" repeat. Reproduced for Fallon Hotel, Columbia, Calif., operated by California Department of Parks and Recreation. Golds and silver on gray.

ᕥ FLORAL GARLAND FRIEZE. American, 1880–90, machine print. 17" wide, 16" repeat. Reproduced for Woodland Opera House, Woodland, Calif. Pinks, greens, taupe, and cream.

ᕥ FLORAL SCENIC BORDER. American, 1880–90, machine print. 6¼" wide, 16¼" repeat. Reproduced for Henry Ford Museum & Greenfield Village, Dearborn, Mich. Burgundy, blue, and greens.

ᕥ GOLD LEAF FLORAL BORDER. American, 1880–90, machine print. 7½" wide, 21¾" repeat. Reproduced for Fallon Hotel, Columbia, Calif., operated by California Department of Parks and Recreation.

ᕥ GROS POINT FRIEZE. American, 1880–1900, machine print. 9½" wide, 21" repeat. Reproduced for Fallon Hotel, Columbia, Calif., operated by California Department of Parks and Recreation. Blues, green, drab, and maroon.

ᕥ OGLESBY "ARABIC" FRIEZE. English or American, 1870–80, block or machine print. 21" wide, 20" repeat. Reproduced for Governor Oglesby Mansion, Decatur, Ill. Chinese red, maroon, and gold on umber.

ᕥ WOODLAND OPERA FRIEZE. American, 1890–1900, machine print. 19" wide, 19" repeat. Reproduced for Woodland Opera House, Woodland, Calif. Roses and gold.

Scalamandre

ᕥ BYERS-EVANS PARLOR FRIEZE. American, 1890–1915, machine print. 18" wide, 21⅞" repeat. Reproduced for Byers-Evans House, Denver, Colo. No.WB81465. Special order.

ᕥ GRANT KOHRS RANCH—DINING ROOM BORDER. American, 1890–1900, machine print. 18" wide, 24" repeat. Historic representation. Reproduced for Grant Kohrs Ranch National Historic Site, Deer Lodge, Mont. No.WB81264-001 (oatmeal and metallic silver on smoke).

ᕥ GRANT KOHRS RANCH FRIEZE. American, 1890–1900, machine print. 18" wide, 24" repeat. Historic representation. Reproduced for Grant Kohrs Ranch National Historic Site, Deer Lodge, Mont. No.WB81263-001 (cinnamon, slate, topaz, and metallic gold). Special order.

GRANT KOHRS RANCH
FRIEZE, 1890–1900.
Scalamandré.

SAGAMORE HILL
LIBRARY FRIEZE, 1890–
1900. Scalamandré.

❧ MONTEZUMA DADO. English or American, 1890–1900, machine print. 36" wide, 20⅝" repeat. Historic representation. Reproduced for Villa Montezuma, San Diego, Calif. No.WB81131-001 (multi). Special order.

❧ MONTEZUMA FLORAL BORDER. American, 1890–1900, machine print. 7¼" wide, 15¹¹/₁₆" repeat. Historic representation. Reproduced for Villa Montezuma, San Diego, Calif. No.WB81130 (multi on bronze). Special order.

❧ PHOENIX FRIEZE. American, 1890–1910, machine print. 18" wide, 22⅛" repeat. Historic representation. Reproduced for Rosson House, Phoenix, Ariz. No.WB81161 (multi on brown). Special order.

❧ ROSE SWAG BORDER. American, 1890–1900, machine print. 18" wide, 14" repeat. Adaptation. Central City Collection. No.WB81142-001 (green and pink on yellow). Special order.

❧ ROSSON HOUSE FRIEZE. American, c. 1900, machine print. 17" wide, 9⅜" repeat. Reproduced for Rosson House, Phoenix, Ariz. No.WB81147-001 (pinks, peach, celery, rose, silver, and dusty rose blotch).

❧ SAGAMORE HILL LIBRARY FRIEZE. American, 1890–1900, machine print. 9½" wide, 18³/₁₆" repeat. Historic representation. Design reconstructed from photographs. Reproduced for Sagamore Hill, Oyster Bay, N.Y. No.WB81258-001 (browns, gray, olive, metallic gold, and copper blotch). Special order.

❧ SAVANNAH HOUSE BORDER. American, 1890–1900, machine print. 18⅛" wide, 19" repeat. Savannah Collection. Document at Werms House, Savannah, Ga. No.WB81087 (brown and rust on beige). Special order.

MAY TREE FRIEZE,
1896. Victorian Col-
lectibles Limited.

GRIFFON BORDER,
1875. Zina Studios.

SCHUMACHER

᪐ CHRYSANTHEMUM BORDER. English or American, 1890–1900, machine print. 9" wide, 10" repeat. Document at Whitworth Art Gallery,
Manchester, England. Period coloring: No.5702B (mulberry and
spruce).

᪐ DAUPHIN BORDER. American, 1890–1910, machine print. 22" wide,
23" repeat. Document in Schumacher Archive. No.512680 (aqua).

VICTORIAN COLLECTIBLES LIMITED

᪐ BENSON BORDER. American, 1890–1910, machine print. 9" wide,
16" repeat. No.26-061 (gold and brown on brown).

᪐ LIBERTY FLOWER BORDER. American, 1890–1910, machine print. 6"
wide, 29¾" repeat. No.35-061 (cream, burgundy, and gold on buff).

᪐ MAY TREE FRIEZE. English, 1896, block print. Designed by
Walter Crane for Jeffrey & Company. Oman and Hamilton, color

196

pl. p. 321; Teynac, Nolot, and Vivien, color pl. p. 159. 21½" wide, 36" repeat. No.36-051 (greens, blues, black, terra cotta, and cream on putty).

&❧ OPERA SCROLL BORDER. American, 1890–1910, machine print. Originally printed by S. A. Maxwell & Company. 18" wide, 15½" repeat. No.33-051 (greens, gold, and white on beige).

WATERHOUSE WALLHANGINGS

&❧ SAMANTHA. American, 1890–1920, machine print. 13½" wide, 9½" repeat. Document in Waterhouse Archive. Period coloring: No.228328 (brown and blue).

ZINA STUDIOS

Order by pattern name.

&❧ GRIFFON BORDER. English, 1875, block print. Designed by William Burges. Lynn, color pls. 87–88, pp. 250–51. 11¾" wide, 21" repeat. Reproduced for Chateau-sur-Mer, Newport, R.I., a property of Preservation Society of Newport County/Newport Mansions. Document at Cooper-Hewitt Museum. Blue and white.

&❧ THE WILLOWS. American, 1890–1910, machine print. 19⅞" wide, 18⅝" repeat. Reproduced for the Willows, operated by Morris County (N.J.) Park Commission. Red and terra cotta.

For additional ceiling papers, see listings under coordinated patterns (pages 171–88).

CEILING PAPERS, CEILING BORDERS, AND CORNERS

BRADBURY & BRADBURY

&❧ MOSSWOOD BORDERS. American, 1870–80. Two 7" and two 4" borders per sheet, 7" repeat. Design derived from a sketch for a ceiling treatment by P. B. Wight. Document at Burnham Architectural Library, Chicago. Code MWB (3 period colorings).

&❧ MOSSWOOD ROSETTE. American, 1870–80. Panel 24" by 24". Design derived from a sketch for a ceiling treatment by P. B. Wight. Document at Burnham Architectural Library, Chicago. Code MWR (3 period colorings).

J. R. BURROWS & COMPANY

Order by pattern name and color. All patterns can be custom colored.

&❧ PERSIS CEILING. American Victorian Revival. 21" wide, 21" repeat, 6 yds. per s/r. Design based on motifs in "Persis" wallpaper (page 146). Period coloring: gold on buff.

&❧ ALDAM CEILING. American Victorian Revival. Block printed with custom stencils in neoclassical manner of Aldam Heaton. Deep cream with blue.

CLASSIC REVIVALS

Authentic Interiors Collection

❧ BURGIS. English, 1880–90, machine print. 21" wide, 21" repeat, 11 yds. per roll. Archival Collection. No.C-201-1A (silver on beige).

St. James Collection

❧ MOSAIC CEILING. English, 1890–1900, machine print. 21" wide, 11 yds. per roll. No.MC9 (citron).

❧ SWALLOW CEILING. English, 1890–1900, machine print. 18" wide, 18⅞" repeat, 11 yds. per roll. No.SC12 (pink olive).

❧ VICTORIAN CEILING. English, 1892, machine print. Originally printed by Allan, Cockshut and Company. 21" wide, 10½" repeat, 11 yds. per roll. No.VC1 (sage); No.VC5 (gray buff); No.VC10 (sienna); No.VC14 (old gold); No.VC17 (salmon); No.VC29 (mauve); No.VC30 (lustre).

MT. DIABLO HANDPRINTS

Order by name unless pattern number is listed.

❧ BILLINGS CEILING. American, 1880–1900, machine print. 18¼" wide, 12¼" repeat. Reproduced for Billings Farm & Museum, Woodstock, Vt. Copper, gold, peach, and ochre on buff.

❧ CHAMPAGNE CEILING. American, 1880–1900, machine print. 18" wide, 15¾" repeat. Reproduced for Fallon Hotel, Columbia, Calif., operated by California Department of Parks and Recreation. Gold, silver, and copper on cream.

❧ CRACKED ICE CEILING. American, 1880–90, machine print. 27" wide, 6¾" repeat. Reproduced for Alameda Historical Society, Alameda, Calif. Dark umber and gold on ochre.

❧ FALLON CEILING. American, 1880–1900, machine print. 19½" wide, 19" repeat. Reproduced for Fallon Hotel, Columbia, Calif., operated by California Department of Parks and Recreation. Green, gold, mica, and yellow on pink.

❧ RAVEL CEILING. American, 1890–1910, machine print. 18" wide, 18½" repeat. Reproduced for Byers-Evans House, Denver, Colo., a property of Colorado Historical Society. No.RVC-001 (document yellow and umber on kraft).

❧ SUNBURST CEILING. American, 1880–1900, machine print. 19" wide, 13" repeat. Reproduced for Fallon Hotel, Columbia, Calif., a property of California Department of Parks and Recreation. Gold, mica, pine, and blue on cream.

SCALAMANDRE

❧ MONTEZUMA CEILING. American, 1890–1900, machine print. 35½" wide, 15¹³⁄₁₆" repeat, 4 yds. per s/r. Document at Villa Montezuma, San Diego, Calif. No.WP81127-1 (green and metallic on terra cotta). Special order.

☙ THOMAS WOLFE MEMORIAL HALL CEILING. American, 1880–1900, machine print. 27″ wide, 5⅝″ repeat, 5 yds. per s/r. Reproduced for Thomas Wolfe Memorial, Asheville, N.C. No.WP81199-001 (taupe and off-white). Special order.

☙ WERMS HOUSE DIAMOND. American, 1870–80, machine print. 48″ wide, 6″ repeat, 3 yds. per s/r. Adaptation. Savannah Collection. Document at Werms House, Savannah, Ga. No.WP81112 (green and ecru on beige). Special order.

above left
SWALLOW CEILING, 1890–1900. Classic Revivals (St. James Collection).

VICTORIAN COLLECTIBLES LIMITED

☙ LIBERTY BIRD CORNER. American, 1890–1910, machine print. 18″ each side. Order with "Liberty Bird 18″ Ceiling Set." No.1886B1 (golds, burgundy, cream, and blue on buff).

☙ ROCOCO BOWS. American, 1890–1920, machine print. 25″ wide, 12″ repeat, 5 yds. per s/r. No.43-031 (brown on ivory).

above right
LIBERTY BIRD CORNER, 1890–1910. Victorian Collectibles Limited.

SCALAMANDRE

☙ TEKKO FIRST CLASS. Austria (now produced in Switzerland), 1890–1900, machine embossed. 31½″ wide, 3½″ repeat, 5 yds. per s/r. No.TB7-124 (champagne).

☙ TEKKO FIRST CLASS. Austria (now produced in Switzerland), 1890–1900, machine embossed. 31½″ wide, 6½″ repeat, 5 yds. per s/r. No.TB8-127 (sand).

EMBOSSED PAPERS

ॐ TEKKO FIRST CLASS. Austria (now produced in Switzerland), 1890–1900, machine embossed. 31$^{1}/_{2}$" wide, 24" repeat, 5 yds. per s/r. No.TC2-173 (jade).

ॐ TEKKO FIRST CLASS. Austria (now produced in Switzerland), 1890–1900, machine embossed. 31$^{1}/_{2}$" wide, 4$^{1}/_{2}$" repeat, 5 yds. per s/r. No.TC3-174 (gold).

ॐ TEKKO FIRST CLASS. Austria (now produced in Switzerland), 1890–1900, machine embossed. 31$^{1}/_{2}$" wide, 5 yds. per s/r. No.TD1-174 (gold).

ॐ TEKKO FIRST CLASS. Austria (now produced in Switzerland), 1890–1900, machine embossed. 31$^{1}/_{2}$" wide, 22" half-drop repeat, 5 yds. per s/r. No.TD2-175 (cognac).

ॐ TEKKO FIRST CLASS. Austria (now produced in Switzerland), 1890–1900, machine embossed. 31$^{1}/_{2}$" wide, 10$^{1}/_{2}$" repeat, 5 yds. per s/r. No.TD3-152 (lavender-blue).

ॐ TEKKO FIRST CLASS. Austria (now produced in Switzerland), 1890–1900, machine embossed. 31$^{1}/_{2}$" wide, 8$^{3}/_{4}$" repeat, 5 yds. per s/r. No.TD7-154 (corn).

ॐ TEKKO FIRST CLASS. Austria (now produced in Switzerland), 1890–1900, machine embossed. 31$^{1}/_{2}$" wide, 28" half-drop repeat, 5 yds. per s/r. No.TE1-123 (cream).

ॐ TEKKO FIRST CLASS. Austria (now produced in Switzerland), 1890–1900, machine embossed. 31$^{1}/_{2}$" wide, 17" half-drop repeat, 5 yds. per s/r. No.TE6-124 (champagne).

ॐ TEKKO FIRST CLASS. Austria (now produced in Switzerland), 1890–1900, machine embossed. 31$^{1}/_{2}$" wide, 25$^{1}/_{2}$" half-drop repeat, 5 yds. per s/r. No.TF7-174 (gold).

RELIEF DECORATIONS—LINCRUSTA AND LINCRUSTA BORDERS

CROWN DECORATIVE PRODUCTS

Crown Decorative Products are available through Bentley Brothers, Classic Ceilings, and Mile Hi Crown. Product comes unfinished and must be painted.

ॐ ANNE FRIEZE. English, 1890–1910, impressed composition. 10$^{1}/_{2}$" wide, 21" repeat. No.RD 1947.

ॐ BYZANTINE. English, 1895–1910, impressed composition. 20$^{1}/_{2}$" wide, 2$^{1}/_{10}$" repeat, 11 yds. per roll. No.RD 1954.

ॐ EMPIRE FRIEZE. English, 1890–1910, impressed composition. 10$^{7}/_{8}$" wide, 21" repeat. No.RD 1957.

ॐ ITALIAN RENAISSANCE. English, 1895–1910, impressed composition. 20$^{1}/_{2}$" wide, 40" repeat, 11 yds. per roll. No.RD 1952.

WALLPAPERS BY WILLIAM MORRIS AND MORRIS & COMPANY

BRADBURY & BRADBURY

Bradbury & Bradbury's reproductions of William Morris patterns are reduced in scale by 13 percent. They are screen printed in period colorings.

෪ BIRD AND ANEMONE. English, 1882, block print. Clark, no. 16, p. 72; Oman and Hamilton, no. 1065, p. 377. 27" wide, 22" repeat, 5 yds. per s/r. Document at Victoria and Albert Museum. Code BAW (8 period colorings).

෪ MARIGOLD. English, 1875, block print. Clark, no. 16, p. 27; Lynn, no. 16-5, p. 371. 27" wide, 9" repeat, 5 yds. per s/r. Document at Victoria and Albert Museum. Code MAW (8 period colorings).

෪ MORRIS CEILING. English, 1888, block print. Oman and Hamilton, no. 1065, p. 375. 27" wide, 13½" repeat, 5 yds. per s/r. Design based on Morris's "Borage Ceiling" (page 202). Document at Victoria and Albert Museum. Code MOC (4 period colorings).

ARTHUR SANDERSON & SONS

Unless otherwise noted, the patterns listed in this section were designed by William Morris. Morris & Company's wallpapers were originally printed by Jeffrey & Company. The original wood blocks are now owned by Arthur Sanderson & Sons, and the following patterns are printed from them. Other Morris patterns printed from the original blocks are available as special orders with a minimum of six rolls of 11 yards each.

෪ ACORN. English, 1879, block print. Clark, no. 26, p. 34; Oman and Hamilton, no. 1065, p. 373. 21" wide, 19" repeat, 11 yds. per s/r.

above left
ITALIAN RENAISSANCE, 1895–1910. Crown Decorative Products.

top right
EMPIRE FRIEZE , 1890–1910. Crown Decorative Products.

above right
ANNE FRIEZE , 1890–1910. Crown Decorative Products.

Page from the *William Morris Log Book*, 1864–c. 1896, illustrating DAISY and FRUIT, both from 1864 and now printed by Arthur Sanderson & Sons.

Document in Sanderson Archives. No.114 (green). Block print.

ॐ BIRD AND ANEMONE. English, 1882, block print. Clark, no. 16, p. 72; Oman and Hamilton, no. 1065, p. 377. 21″ wide, 20½″ repeat, 11 yds. per roll. Document in Sanderson Archives. No.143 (red); No.144 (yellow). Block print.

ॐ BORAGE CEILING. English, 1888, block print. Oman and Hamilton, no. 1065, p. 375. 21″ wide, 20″ repeat, 11 yds. per roll. Document in Sanderson Archives. No.142190 (yellow on cream); No.479 (white). Block print.

ॐ CHRYSANTHEMUM. English, 1877, block print. Clark, no. 22, p. 31; Greysmith, fig. 100, p. 137; Oman and Hamilton, no. 1065, p. 373. 21″ wide, 21″ repeat, 11 yds. per roll. Document in Sanderson Archives. No.118 (green). Block print.

ॐ DAISY. English, designed in 1862, first printed in 1864, block print. Clark, no. 1, p. 19; Lynn, color pl. 81, p. 345; Sugden and Edmundson, color pl. 110; Teynac, Nolot, and Vivian, color pl. p. 150. 21″ wide, 14″ repeat, 11 yds. per roll. Document in Sanderson Archives. No.1 (dark green); No.75 (light green). Block print.

ॐ FRUIT (also POMEGRANATE). English, designed in 1862, first printed in 1864, block print. Clark, no. 2, p. 20; Oman and Hamilton, no. 1067, p. 381; Sugden and Edmundson, color pl. 11. 21″ wide, 21″ repeat, 11 yds. per roll. Document in Sanderson Archives. No.4 (dark green); No.5 (cream). Block print.

ॐ GOLDEN LILY. English, 1899, block print. Designed by John Henry Dearle. Oman and Hamilton, no. 1076, p. 385. 21″ wide, 17½″ repeat, 11 yds. per roll. Document in Sanderson Archives. No.346 (multicolor). Block print.

ॐ GRANVILLE. English, 1895, block print. Designed by John Henry Dearle. Oman and Hamilton, no. 1066, p. 378. 21" wide, 19³/₄" repeat, 11 yds. per roll. Document in Sanderson Archives. No.325 (blue and green). Block print.

ॐ HONEYSUCKLE. English, 1883, block print. Designed by May Morris. Oman and Hamilton, no. 1065, p. 373. 21" wide, 21" repeat, 11 yds. per roll. Document in Sanderson Archives. No.147 (green); No.263 (light). Block print.

ॐ INDIAN. English, 1868–70, block print. Clark, no. 5, p. 21; Oman and Hamilton, no. 1066, p. 380. 21" wide, 26¹/₂" repeat, 11 yds. per roll. Document in Sanderson Archives. No.14 (light blue); No.32 (green; No.470 (red). Block print.

ॐ IRIS. English, 1888, block print. Designed by John Henry Dearle. Oman and Hamilton, no. 1066, p. 377. 21" wide, 16¹/₂" repeat, 11 yds. per roll. Document in Sanderson Archives. No.224 (green). Block print.

ॐ LARKSPUR. English, 1874, block print. Clark, no. 11, p. 23; Oman and Hamilton, no. 1065, p. 372. 21" wide, 14" repeat, 11 yds. per roll. Document in Sanderson Archives. No.30 (yellow); No.64 (green); No.160 (salmon). Block print.

ॐ LOOP TRAIL. English, 1877, block print. Designed by Kate Faulkner. Oman and Hamilton, no. 1066, p. 380. 21" wide, 11 yds.

below left
GOLDEN LILY, 1899.
Arthur Sanderson
& Sons.

below right
GRANVILLE, 1895.
Arthur Sanderson
& Sons.

LARKSPUR, 1874.
Arthur Sanderson &
Sons.

per roll. Document in Sanderson Archives. No.94 (blue); No.95 (yellow); No.169 (red). Block print.

ᐧᕈ MALLOW. English, 1879, block print. Designed by Kate Faulkner. Oman and Hamilton, no. 1066, p. 380. 21ʺ wide, 12ʺ repeat, 11 yds. per roll. Document in Sanderson Archives. No.107 (yellow); No.140 (red); No.145 (green); No.159 (salmon). Block print.

ᐧᕈ MARIGOLD. English, 1875, block print. Clark, no. 16, p. 27; Lynn, fig. 16-5, p. 371. 21" wide, 10½" repeat, 11 yds. per roll. Document in Sanderson Archives. No.39 (dark); No.532 (olive). Block print.

POPPY. English, 1881, block print. Clark, no. 27, p. 35; Oman and Hamilton, no. 1065, p. 373. 21" wide, 16¼" repeat, 11 yds. per roll. Document in Sanderson Archives. No.440 (red); No.531 (brown). Block print.

SUNFLOWER. English, 1879, block print. Clark, no. 25, p. 33; Oman and Hamilton, no. 1065, p. 373. 21" wide, 18" repeat, 11 yds. per roll. Document in Sanderson Archives. No.274 (green); No.530 (white). Block print.

TRELLIS. English, designed in 1862, first produced in 1864, block print. Clark, no. 3, p. 21; Oman and Hamilton, color pl., p. 363; Sugden and Edmondson, color pl. 109. 21" wide, 21" repeat, 11 yds. per roll. Document in Sanderson Archives. No.7 (green); No.157 (cream). Block print.

VINE. English, 1874, block print. Clark, no. 14, p. 26; Nylander, Redmond, and Sander, fig. 68.1, p. 241; Oman and Hamilton, no. 1065, p. 372. 21" wide, 21" repeat, 11 yds. per roll. Document in Sanderson Archives. No.45 (black). Block print.

WILLOW. English, 1874, block print. Clark, no. 17, p. 27; Oman and Hamilton, no. 1065, p. 372. 21" wide, 17½" repeat, 11 yds. per roll. Document in Sanderson Archives. No.66 (sage); No.67 (green). Block print.

WILLOW BOUGH. English, 1887, block print. Clark, no. 35, p. 41; Oman and Hamilton, no. 1065, p. 374; Sugden and Edmondson, color pl. 114. 21" wide, 18" repeat, 11 yds. per roll. Document in Sanderson Archives. No.210 (green); No.229 (blue). Block print.

The following Morris designs have been transferred to rollers and are printed by machine.

ACORN. English, 1879, block print. Clark, no. 26, p. 34; Oman and Hamilton, no. 1065, p. 373. 21" wide, 18" repeat, 11 yds. per roll. Document in Sanderson Archives. Period coloring: No.WM 7422-2 (nutmeg on tan).

CHRISTCHURCH. English, 1882, block print. Clark, no. 30, p. 37; Greysmith, fig. 101, p. 141; Oman and Hamilton, no. 1066, p. 380. 21" wide, 10½" repeat, 11 yds. per roll. Document in Sanderson Archives. Period coloring: No.WM 7423-3 (blue on white).

CHRYSANTHEMUM. English, 1877, block print. Clark, no. 22, p. 31; Greysmith, fig. 100, p. 137; Oman and Hamilton, no. 1065, p. 373. 21" wide, 21" repeat, 11 yds. per s/r. Document in Sanderson Archives. Period coloring: No.WM 7612 (series).

FOLIAGE. English, 1899, block print. Designed by John Henry Dearle. Oman and Hamilton, no. 1076, p. 387. 21" wide, 24" repeat, 11 yds. per roll. Document in Sanderson Archives. Period colorings:

No.WM 7424-1 (moss green and khaki on green); No.WM 7424-3 (charcoal and taupe on black).

᠙ HONEYSUCKLE. English, 1883, block print. Designed by May Morris. Oman and Hamilton, no. 1065, p. 373. 21″ wide, 21″ repeat, 11 yds. per roll. Document in Sanderson Archives. Period coloring: No.WM 7611 (series).

᠙ SPRAY. English, c. 1871, block print. Produced by Morris & Company. Clark, no. 8, p. 22; Oman and Hamilton, no. 1067, p. 382. 21″ wide, 19³/₄″ repeat, 11 yds. per roll. Document in Sanderson Archives. Period coloring: No.WH 7367-4 (cafe-au-lait on oyster).

᠙ VINE. English, 1873, block print. Clark, no. 14, p. 26; Nylander, Redmond, and Sander, fig. 68.1, p. 241; Oman and Hamilton, no. 1065, p. 372. 21″ wide, 21″ repeat, 11 yds. per roll. Document in Sanderson Archives. Period coloring: No.WM 7613-3 (maroon and green on midnight ground).

᠙ WILLOW BOUGH. English, 1887, block print. Clark, no. 35, p. 41; Oman and Hamilton, no. 1065, p. 374; Sugden and Edmondson, color pl. 114. 21″ wide, 18″ repeat, 11 yds. per roll. Document in Sanderson Archives. No.WM 7614-1 (greens and tan on parchment ground).

SCALAMANDRE

The patterns listed here are screen-printed reproductions of designs by William Morris and Morris & Company.

᠙ BORAGE. English, 1888, block print. Oman and Hamilton, no. 1065, p. 375. 20⁷/₈″ wide, 20⁷/₈″ repeat, 7 yds. per s/r. Reproduced for North American Branch of William Morris Society. No.WP81240 (pearlized white). Special order.

᠙ MORRIS CEILING. English, 1883, block print. Original pattern name was "The Wreath." Oman and Hamilton, no. 1065, p. 374. 21″ wide, 21″ repeat, 7 yds. per s/r. Reproduced for North American Branch of William Morris Society. No.WP81236-001 (greens, rose, yellow, and beige on snow white).

᠙ MORRIS IRIS. English, 1888, block print. Original pattern name was "Iris," designed by John Henry Dearle. Oman and Hamilton, no. 1066, p. 377. 21″ wide, 17¹/₂″ repeat, 7 yds. per s/r. Reproduced for North American Branch of William Morris Society. No.WP81239-001 (greens, multi, and blue blotch). Special order.

᠙ MYRTLE. English, 1899, block print. Clark, no. 49, p. 52. 22″ wide, 33³/₄″ repeat, 7 yds. per s/r. Reproduced for North American Branch of William Morris Society. No.WP81237-001 (multi greens, blues, pinks, and yellows).

᠙ PIMPERNEL. English, 1876, block print. Clark, no. 19, p. 29; Greysmith, color pl. 22, p. 134; Lynn, color pl. 83, p. 346; Oman and Hamilton, no. 1065, p. 372. 21¹/₂″ wide, 16¹³/₁₆″ repeat, 7 yds. per s/r. Reproduced for North American Branch of William Morris Society.

PIMPERNEL, 1876. Scalamandré.

No.WP81226-001 (multi greens, aqua, gold, and forest-green blotch).

ᏋᎦ WALLFLOWER. English, 1890, block print. Clark, no. 39, p. 45; Oman and Hamilton, no. 1065, p. 375. 21" wide, 14¹/₂" repeat, 7 yds. per s/r. Reproduced for North American Branch of William Morris Society. No.WP81233-001 (terra cotta, brick, and salmon on ivory).

SOCIETY FOR THE PRESERVATION OF NEW ENGLAND ANTIQUITIES

ᏋᎦ JEWETT HOUSE LITHOGRAPH. American, 1880–1920, roller print. Originally printed by Frederick Beck & Company, New York. Nylander, Redmond, and Sander, fig. 65.1. p. 233. 20¹/₂" wide, 15¹/₂" repeat, 7 yds. per roll. Reproduced for Sarah Orne Jewett House, South Berwick, Maine. Document at Society for Preservation of New England Antiquities. Blue and tan.

CUSTOM PATTERNS FROM MUSEUMS

1900 TO 1930:
CHANGING TASTES IN
A NEW CENTURY

The opinions about wallpaper formed during the 1890s had an effect on its use in the 20th-century interior. "The wallpaper is killing me; one of us must go"—Oscar Wilde's reputed last words in 1900 echoed the disdain for wallpapers held by many taste makers. In *The Decoration of Houses*, published in 1897, Edith Wharton and Ogden Codman pronounced wallpaper "inferior as a wall-decoration" and stated emphatically, "These hangings have, in fact, little to recommend them."

Wallpaper manufacturers, however, disagreed. The 1899 brochure of a Worcester, Massachusetts, company claimed that "the decorative possibilities of the new WALL PAPERS are almost boundless." Manufacturers began to produce wallpaper sample books, often twice a year, so that their latest offerings could be distributed nationwide to an eager public. Brochures and pamphlets promoted repapering rooms as an integral part of spring cleaning. Mail-order houses followed the lead of the larger manufacturers. The wallpaper sample books produced by Sears, Roebuck & Company and others present an enormous array of patterns that were available to enhance middle-class homes. They also reveal how inexpensive it was to paper a room. In 1905 one could purchase wallpaper for a room 11 feet by 11 feet, including borders and the ceiling paper, for only 26 cents.

Many wallpaper styles developed in the 1890s remained fashionable into the first decades of the 20th century (consult the previous chapter for appropriate listings). This is especially true of the sidewalls and their wide companion friezes. Many friezes became even wider during this period; their designs filled the entire 18-or 21-inch width of the printing stock. The concept of the wooded forest depicted in Walter Crane's "May Tree Frieze" (page 196) was widely copied. Such friezes were used in combination with painted walls or walls covered with plain papers or wide striped wallpapers.

Floral borders, often incorporating ribbons, enjoyed a renaissance in the years preceding World War I. Note the similarities among

Strawberry Hill Room at Beauport,Gloucester, Massachusetts. The paper installed here is the document on which Brunschwig & Fils's "Beauport Promenade" is based. (Society for the Preservation of New England Antiquities)

"Rosedale" (page 239), "Rose and Ribbon Frieze" (page 237), and "Aurelia" (page 236). Narrower borders were used to form panels on walls papered with plain-colored papers, often of the ingrain or oatmeal type, or wallpapers with small repeating patterns.

Although some block printing was still done in America, most block-printed wallpapers used during this time were imported from England or France. "Beauport Promenade" (page 227) exemplifies the exotic appearance of many of these imports. Other imported patterns were more traditional. Many reproduced 18th-century fabric designs. Others like "Adam" (page 217) and "Dorset" (page 228) were based on late 18th-century neoclassical styles; the inspiration for the design, however, was 18th-century architectural decoration, not 18th-century wallpaper design.

Some elaborate floral designs of the 1850s that had not lost their appeal were still available. William Morris's wallpapers were still considered appropriate and were often used in 20th-century interiors. Most new designs offered by Morris & Company were designed by John Henry Dearle, who became the firm's artistic director after Morris's death in 1896.

The designs advertised as "novelty" papers perhaps hold the most appeal for late 20th-century taste. The term encompasses a wide variety of pattern types and styles: Arts and Crafts—for example, "Accomack" and "Accomack Border" (page 222); tapestry papers—for example, "Gobelin's Forest" (page 232); and Native American motifs—for example, "New Harmony" (page 167). The most appealing of this group to contemporary consumers are the Art Nouveau patterns, listed here and in the previous chapter, which may be more popular today than in their own time. A small interest in Art Nouveau patterns existed; however, Art Nouveau never evolved into a major wallpaper style. In his book *Home Furnishing* (1913) George Leland Hunter dismissed the style saying, "Its sinuous stems and parabolic curves have long since uncoiled themselves into nothingness."

As noted in the introduction, the interest in early wallpapers began to develop in the early 20th century. Scenic wallpapers enjoyed a new round of popularity, and the Zuber factory reissued many of its earlier patterns. In the early 19th century, when they were first imported, they were used only in best parlors, but now these colorful panoramas were considered appropriate for dining rooms and front halls.

In 1924 Nancy McClelland published *Historic Wall-Papers*. In contrast to previous articles, which discussed the "romance" of early wallpapers, this book provided the most accurate information about historic wallpapers available before 1930 and was the standard work on the subject for the next 56 years. McClelland's work as a decorator as well as her writings influenced what was considered appropriate for historic and traditional interiors. She collected wallpaper samples and later had many designs reproduced for sale. She also distributed the block-printed wallpapers made in France by André Mauny, which included many reproductions of 18th-century designs made by his predecessor Robert Caillard.

Modernists took another view. Because the purpose of wallpaper was decorative, not functional, they dismissed it as superfluous. Beginning in the 1930s plain-colored walls and textures became the prevalent treatment for stylish interiors. Having few good examples to emulate, the general public became almost afraid to apply bold patterns to walls. Today this attitude has changed, and colorful patterns are once again returning to the walls of domestic interiors.

BRADBURY & BRADBURY   WALLPAPERS

❧ BOWER. English, c. 1910, block print. 27″ wide, 13½″ repeat, 5 yds. per s/r. Code BOW (2 period colorings).

❧ BRIAR ROSE. English, 1901, block print. Designed by C. F. A. Voysey. Oman and Hamilton, no. 1242, p. 443. 27″ wide, 9″ repeat, 5 yds per s/r. Adaptation. Document at Victoria and Albert Museum. Code BRW (2 period colorings).

❧ HONEYSUCKLE. English, 1900–20, block print. 27″ wide, 15½″ repeat, 5 yds. per s/r. Code HSW (2 period colorings).

❧ ORCHARD. English, c. 1900, block print. Adaptation of "The Fairyland" by C. F. A. Voysey. Oman and Hamilton, no. 1260, p. 445. 27″ wide, 13½″ repeat, 5 yds. per s/r. Code ORW (2 period colorings).

❧ ROSAMUND. English, 1900–20, block print. Designed by Walter Crane. 27″ wide, 18″ half-drop repeat, 5 yds. per s/r. Code RMW (2 period colorings).

❧ THISTLE. English, 1900–20, block print. 17″ wide, 21″ repeat, 5 yds. per s/r. Code THW (2 period colorings).

BRUNSCHWIG & FILS

❧ APPLEDORE. French, 1920–30, block print. 20″ wide, 21″ half-drop repeat, 6 yds. per s/r. Document in Brunschwig Archives. No.13828.06 (cream ground).

❧ ART NOUVEAU TULIP. American, 1900–20, machine print. 24¼″ wide, 15¾″ repeat. Reproduced for Odessa Historical Society, Odessa, Tex. No.343.6C. Custom order.

❧ BEAUPORT PROMENADE. English, 1907, block print. 18¼″ wide, 34″ repeat, 7 yds. per s/r. Adaptation: design slightly enlarged. Document at Beauport, Gloucester, Mass., a property of Society for the Preservation of New England Antiquities. No.13369.06 (black).

❧ CANDIDE. French, 1900–20, block print. 21″ wide, 40¼″ repeat. Document in McClelland Collection, Brunschwig Archives. No. 11500.6C. Custom order.

above left
ORCHARD, c. 1900.
Bradbury & Bradbury.

above right
HONEYSUCKLE,
1900–20. Bradbury
& Bradbury.

right
ROSAMUND,
1900–20. Bradbury
& Bradbury.

ॐ TOBACCO LEAF STRIPE. American, 1900–20, machine print. 27″ wide, 19″ repeat. Reproduced for Odessa Historical Society, Odessa, Tex. No.340.6C. Custom order.

ॐ TULIP STRIPE AND BORDER. American, 1900–10, machine print. 22¾″ wide plus 4″ border. Reproduced for Odessa Historical Society, Odessa, Tex. No.7885.6C. Custom order.

CLARENCE HOUSE

ॐ BELVEDERE. English, 1900–20, block print. 21″ wide, 16″ repeat, 11 yds. per s/r. Coles Traditional Collection. No.C253 (rose); No.C254 (cream); No.C255 (blue).

ॐ DORSET. English, 1900–15, block print. 21″ wide, 18″ repeat, 11 yds. per s/r. Coles Traditional Collection. Period colorings: No.C223 (yellow); No.C224 (green); No.C226 (gold).

ॐ SWANS. American or English, 1920–30, machine print. 27″ wide, 9″ repeat, 5 yds. per s/r. No.9180/1 (brown); No.9180/3 (green); No.9180/4 (silver).

CLASSIC REVIVALS

Authentic Interiors Collection

ॐ AUSTIN. English, 1920–30, machine print. 20½″ wide, 20½″ repeat. Archival Collection. No.T-209-3A (tan).

above left
THISTLE, 1900–20.
Bradbury & Bradbury.

above right
APPLEDORE, 1920–30.
Brunschwig & Fils.

above left
BELVEDERE, 1900–20.
Clarence House.

above right
MODERNE CHINOIS,
1920–30. Classic
Revivals (Mauny
Collection).

Mauny Collection

❧ BOUQUET CHINOIS. French, 1910–30, block print. 17¼" wide, 19" repeat, 11 yds. per roll. No.201 (blues on gray). Block print.

❧ CAMPANULES. French, 1900–30, block print. 19¾" wide, 10¾" repeat, 11 yds. per roll. Possibly reproduces an earlier design. No.294. Block print.

❧ CACTUS. French, 1900–30, block print. 21¼" wide, 29" repeat, 11 yds. per roll. No.172 (red, gold, and yellow on blue). Block print.

❧ FLEURETTE. French, 1900–30, block print. 18½" wide, 15¾" repeat, 11 yds. per roll. No.237 (gray on cream). Block print.

❧ GRAND PILLEMENT. French, 1900–20, block print. 21⅝" wide, 21⅝" repeat, 11 yds. per roll. Possibly reproduces an earlier design. No.204 (multi on white). Block print.

❧ GUIRLAND FLEURIE. French, 1900–30, block print. 21¼" wide, 20" repeat, 11 yds. per roll. No.130 (green and orange). Block print.

❧ INDIEN. French, 1920–30, block print. 18½" wide, 13" repeat, 11 yds. per roll. No.120 (brown and green on white). Block print.

❧ JARDIN DE MOSSOEL. French, 1915–30, block print. 18½" wide, 37½" repeat, 11 yds. per roll. No.1500 (multi on black). Block print.

❧ LE MARMOURER. French, 1920–30, block print. 21⅝" wide, 19¼" repeat, 11 yds. per roll. No.209 (multi on cream). Block print.

❧ MODERNE CHINOIS. French, 1920–30, block print. 19¼" wide,

36$\frac{1}{2}$" repeat, 11 yds. per roll. No.157 (brown and green on tan). Block print.

❧ MONTGOLFIER. French, 1920–30, block print. 24$\frac{3}{4}$" wide, 19$\frac{3}{4}$" repeat, 11 yds. per roll. Possibly reproduces an earlier design. No.280 (red on white). Block print.

❧ MOSAIQUE. French, 1920–30, block print. 23$\frac{5}{8}$" wide, 23$\frac{5}{8}$" repeat, 11 yds. per roll. No.282 (gold and blue). Block print.

❧ PAGODE. French, 1920–30, block print. 27$\frac{1}{2}$" wide, 11 yds. per roll. No.185 (multi on blue). Block print.

❧ PALMETTE VIRGINIE. French, 1920–30, block print. 18$\frac{1}{2}$" wide, 24$\frac{3}{8}$" repeat, 11 yds. per roll. No.240 (gray on buff). Block print.

❧ PETIT MARTIN DE MONSIEUR MEAN. French, 1920–30, block print. 20$\frac{7}{8}$" wide, 20$\frac{7}{8}$" repeat, 11 yds. per roll. No.196 (multi on blue). Block print.

❧ PRIMEVERES. French, 1920–30, block print. 21$\frac{1}{4}$" wide, 40$\frac{1}{4}$" repeat, 11 yds. per roll. No.158 (rust and yellow on cream). Block print.

❧ PROMENADE CHINOISE. French, 1920–30, block print. 26$\frac{3}{8}$" wide, 29$\frac{1}{4}$" repeat, 11 yds. per roll. Possibly reproduces an earlier design. No.216 (multi on cream). Block print.

❧ P. DU ROY. French, 1920–30, block print. 21$\frac{1}{4}$" wide, 7$\frac{1}{8}$" repeat, 11 yds. per roll. No.281 (gold on white). Block print.

❧ ROSACE TOURANTE. French, 1920–30, block print. 20$\frac{1}{2}$" wide, 19$\frac{5}{8}$" repeat, 11 yds. per roll. No.102 (mauve on light blue). Block print.

❧ RUBANS ET FLEURS. French, 1920–30, block print. 21$\frac{5}{8}$" wide, 20$\frac{7}{8}$" repeat, 11 yds. per roll. Possibly reproduces an earlier design. No.298 (multi on cream). Block print.

❧ RUBAN ET PETIT RAYURE. French, 1900–30, block print. 20$\frac{7}{8}$" wide, 20$\frac{7}{8}$" repeat, 11 yds. per roll. No.144 (multi on yellow). Block print.

❧ RUBANS ET RAISINS. French, 1900–30, block print. 24" wide, 32$\frac{1}{4}$" repeat, 11 yds. per roll. No.131 (multi on light yellow). Block print.

❧ SEMIS COQUILLE. French, 1900–30, block print. 18$\frac{1}{2}$" wide, 5$\frac{1}{8}$" repeat, 11 yds. per roll. No.258 (buff on cream). Block print.

❧ SEMIS PLUMES. French, 1900–20, block print. 18$\frac{1}{2}$" wide, 5$\frac{1}{4}$" repeat, 11 yds. per roll. No.254 (gold on off-white). Block print.

❧ TREILLAGE. French, 1920–30, block print. 18$\frac{1}{2}$" wide, 7$\frac{1}{8}$" repeat, 11 yds. per roll. No.148 (gray on light gray). Block print.

❧ VOLUBILIS. French, 1920–30, block print. 22" wide, 10$\frac{3}{4}$" repeat, 11 yds. per roll. No.284 (lavender and black on tan). Block print.

Silvergate Collection

❧ SWEETPEA. English, 1900–20, block print. 21" wide, 21" repeat, 11 yds. per roll. Document at Achnacloich House, Argylshire, England. No.FS046. Block print.

ॐ TOWNEND. English, 1900–10, block print. 21" wide, 18" repeat, 11 yds. per roll. Document at Townend House, Windermere District, England. No.ES285. Block print.

COWTAN & TOUT

ॐ ADAM. English, 1900–10, block print. 21" wide plus 5" border, 22" repeat, 5 yds. per s/r. No.13690 (platinum and white).

ॐ LILAC TIME. American or English, 1910–30, machine print. 27" wide, 20" repeat, 5 yds. per s/r. No.20159-13 (periwinkle and white).

ॐ MISSENDEN MINOR. English, 1900–20, block print. 21" wide, 10" repeat, 11 yds. per s/r. No.20544 (beige). Block print.

ॐ WINDSOR ROSE. English or American, 1900–20, machine print. 27" wide, 36" repeat, 5 yds. per s/r. Adaptation. No.82000 (multi on off-white). Period coloring: No.821000-07 (antique).

CHRISTOPHER HYLAND INCORPORATED

ॐ AMOUR ET AGEON. French, 1920–30, block print. 23$\frac{1}{2}$" wide, 25" repeat, 11 yds. per s/r. No.MN5839 (violet). Block print.

ॐ ART DECO ABSTRACT. English or French, 1925–30, block print. 21" wide, 22$\frac{1}{2}$" repeat, 11 yds. per s/r. No.AB157/1 (lavender on gray).

ॐ ART DECO FANS. French, 1925–30, block print. 21" wide, 11 yds. per s/r. No.AB159/1 (peach).

ॐ NINEVEH. English, 1900–30, block or machine print. 18" wide, 11 yds. per s/r. No.ABNIN (rustic red and old gold).

ॐ OPIN. English or French, 1900–30, block print. 21" wide, 11 yds. per s/r. No.ABOPIN (black and gold).

ॐ PARIS, 1930. French, 1930, block print. 20$\frac{1}{4}$" wide, 22" repeat, 11 yds. per s/r. No.AB157/1B (peach and beige).

ॐ PERROQUETS. French, 1920–30, block print. 19$\frac{1}{2}$" wide, 24" repeat, 11 yds. per s/r. No.MN5801 (green). Block print.

ॐ PASTORALE. French, 1920–30, block print. 21$\frac{1}{2}$" wide, 24" repeat, 11 yds. per s/r. No.MN2008 (pale blue). Block print.

MT. DIABLO HANDPRINTS

Order by name unless a pattern number is listed.

ॐ DRUMMOND MEDALLION STRIPE. American, c. 1910, machine print. 18" wide, 15" repeat. Reproduced for Drummond Home, Hominy, Okla. Maroon and gold on cream.

ॐ DRUMMOND SEISMIC STRIPE. American, c. 1910, machine print. 18$\frac{3}{4}$" wide, 15$\frac{3}{8}$" repeat. Reproduced for Drummond Home, Hominy, Okla. Umber, gold, and custard on eggshell.

ॐ HUMMINGBIRD LATTICE. French, 1900–10, block print. 18$\frac{3}{4}$" wide, 23$\frac{3}{4}$" repeat. Reproduced for Kearney Mansion, Fresno, Calif. No.HBW-001 (document greens, creams, and roses on buff).

above left
ADAM, 1900–10.
Cowtan and Tout.

above right
ART DECO ABSTRACT,
1925–30. Christopher
Hyland Incorporated.

left
ART DECO FANS,
1920–30. Christopher
Hyland Incorporated.

above left
PASSION FLOWER,
1900–10. Mt. Diablo
Handprints.

above right
HUMMINGBIRD
LATTICE, 1900–10.
Mt. Diablo Hand-
prints.

right
ROSE LATTICE,
1900–10. Mt. Diablo
Handprints.

ॐ PASSION FLOWER. French, 1900–10, block print. 21¹/₂" wide, 21" repeat. Reproduced for Kearney Mansion, Fresno, Calif. No.PFW-001 (document greens and mauve on light green).

ॐ ROSE LATTICE. French, 1900–10, block print. 20¹/₂" wide, 19" repeat. Reproduced for Kearney Mansion, Fresno, Calif. No.RLW-001 (document white, pinks, and greens).

ARTHUR SANDERSON & SONS

ॐ LINCOLN. English, 1900–20, machine print. 20¹/₄" wide, 3" repeat, 11 yds. per roll. Adaptation: embossing not reproduced. Document in Sanderson Archives. Period coloring: No.WR 7516-4 (linen).

ॐ ROSE AND PEONY. English, 1917, machine print. 20¹/₄" wide, 21" repeat, 11 yds. per roll. Document in Sanderson Archives. Period colorings: No.WR 359-8 (rose and tan); No.WR 359-19 (pink and blue).

ॐ ROWAN. English, 1901, block print. Designed by C. F. A. Voysey. 20¹/₄" wide, 18" repeat, 11 yds. per roll. Document in Sanderson Archives. Period colorings: No.WH 7370-3 (fawn on oyster); No.WH 7370-4 (olivewood on black).

ॐ THE MANDERIN. English, 1920–30, machine print. 20¹/₄" wide, 20¹/₂" repeat, 11 yds. per roll. Document in Sanderson Archives. Period coloring: No.WH 7368-1 (Ming blue on white).

left
ROSE AND PEONY, 1917. Arthur Sanderson & Sons.

above
ROWAN, 1901. Arthur Sanderson & Sons.

❧ QUADRILLE. English, 1900–15, block print. 20¼" wide, 4½" repeat, 11 yds. per roll. Document in Sanderson Archives. Period coloring: No.WH 7366-5 (malachite on khaki).

❧ WARWICK. English, 1890–1900, block print. 20¼" wide, 24" repeat, 11 yds. per roll. Document in Sanderson Archives. Period colorings: No.WR 7514-2 (pale yellow); No.WR 7514-3 (gray).

SCALAMANDRE

❧ BARTON HOUSE. American, 1900–20, machine print. 47½" wide, 18¾" repeat, 3 yds. per s/r. Historic representation. Reproduced for Barton House, Lubbock, Tex. No.WP81104 (brown). Special order.

❧ BARTON HOUSE RESTORATION. American, 1900–10, machine print. 36⅜" wide, 22" repeat, 4 yds. per s/r. Reproduced for Barton House, Lubbock, Tex. No.WP 81116-001 (beige and gold tones). Special order.

❧ BARTON HOUSE RESTORATION. American, 1900–10, machine print. 27" wide, 26" repeat. Reproduced for Barton House, Lubbock, Tex. No.WP 81126 (red and green on metallic ground). Special order.

❧ BARTON HOUSE RESTORATION BEDROOM. American, 1900–10, machine print. 27" wide, 15½" repeat, 5 yds. per s/r. Reproduced for Barton House, Lubbock, Tex. No.WP81110 (pink and green on white). Special order.

❧ BARTON HOUSE RESTORATION HALL WALLS. American, 1900–10, machine print. 46¾" wide, 18¾" repeat, 3 yds. per s/r. Reproduced for Barton House. No.WP81105 (beige and brown). Special order.

❧ BARTON LILY. American, 1900–10, machine print. 45" wide, 22" repeat, 3 yds. per s/r. Reproduced for Barton House, Lubbock, Tex. No.WP81115 (pink and green on brown). Special order.

❧ FRANKLIN D. ROOSEVELT'S HOME—BIRTH ROOM–MORNING ROOM. American, c. 1916, machine print. Originally printed by Thomas Strahan Company. 23" wide, 6¹/₁₆" repeat, 6 yds. per s/r. Historic representation. Reproduced for Home of Franklin D. Roosevelt National Historic Site, Hyde Park, N.Y. No.WP81315-001 (ginger, tan, and white on straw). Special order.

❧ FRANKLIN D. ROOSEVELT'S HOME—BEDROOM. American, c. 1916, machine print. 18½" wide, 9½" repeat, 8 yds. per s/r. Reproduced for Home of Franklin D. Roosevelt National Historic Site, Hyde Park, N.Y. No.WP81319-001 (ecru on sand). Special order.

❧ FRANKLIN D. ROOSEVELT'S HOME—BOYHOOD ROOM. American, c. 1916, machine print. 21" wide, 20¾" repeat, 7 yds. per s/r. Reproduced for Home of Franklin D. Roosevelt National Historic Site, Hyde Park, N.Y. No.WP81316-001 (pale multi and white on antique white). Special order.

❧ FRANKLIN D. ROOSEVELT'S HOME—CHINTZ ROOM. American, c. 1916, machine print. 20½" wide, 21" repeat, 7 yds. per s/r. Reproduced for Home of Franklin D. Roosevelt National Historic Site, Hyde Park, N.Y. No.WP81318-001 (multi and metallic gold on ivory). Special order.

ઈ FRANKLIN D. ROOSEVELT'S HOME—PINK ROOM. American or English, c. 1916, block print. 21" wide, 17³/₈" repeat, 7 yds. per s/r. Reproduced for Home of Franklin D. Roosevelt National Historic Site, Hyde Park, N.Y. No.WP81317-001 (rose, pinks, gray, and greens on antique white). Special order.

ઈ GLENRIDGE HALL. American, 1929, machine print. 18" wide, 8" repeat, 8 yds. per s/r. Reproduced for Glenridge Hall, Atlanta, Ga. No.WP81391-1 (rust on cream). Special order.

ઈ GREEN LEAVES BOUQUET. English, 1900–30, machine print. 27" wide, 27" repeat, 5 yds. per s/r. Adaptation: moiré background added. No.WP81393-001 (multi on Persian rose).

ઈ PEARCE-MᴄALLISTER COTTAGE. American, 1920–30, machine print. 28³/₈" wide, 5 yds. per s/r. No.WP81384-001 (caramel and sand on special cream). Special order.

ઈ SAVANNAH TULIP. American, 1900–15, machine print. 27³/₈" wide, 18¹/₂" repeat, 5 yds. per s/r. Reproduced for Historic Savannah Foundation, Savannah, Ga. Document at John Barlow House, Savannah, Ga. No.WP81092 (brown on bisque). Special order.

ઈ SCHREINER ROSE. American, 1900–10, machine print. 19" wide,

above left
FRANKLIN D. ROOSEVELT'S HOME— CHINTZ ROOM, c. 1916. Scalamandré.

above right
BARTON HOUSE, 1900– 20. Scalamandré.

221

above left
SAVANNAH TULIP,
1900–15.
Scalamandré.

above right
ACCOMACK and
border, 1904–20.
Richard E. Thibaut.

19″ repeat, 8 yds. per s/r. Reproduced for Schreiner Mansion, Kerrville, Tex. No.WP81235-001 (ivory, yellows, old rose, greens, and olive blotch). Special order.

ᕦ SCHREINER STRIPE. American, 1900–10, machine print. 18″ wide, 15³/₈″ repeat, 8 yds. per s/r. Reproduced for Schreiner Mansion, Kerrville, Tex. No.WP81244-001 (ivory, yellow, taupe, gold metallic, and beige blotch). Special order.

ᕦ SORRELL-WEED HOUSE. Probably American, 1900–10, machine print. 48″ wide, 22¹/₂″ repeat, 3 yds. per s/r. Reproduced for Historic Savannah Foundation, Savannah, Ga. Document at Sorrell-Weed House, Savannah, Ga. No.WP81119-001 (celadon and white). Special order.

ᕦ STANROD MANSION FOYER. American, 1900–10, machine print. 36″ wide, 18³/₄″ repeat, 4 yds. per s/r. Reproduced for Stanrod Mansion, Pocatello, Idaho. No.WP81079. Special order.

ᕦ TELLER'S THISTLE. American, 1900–10, machine print. 48″ wide, 20″ repeat, 3 yds. per s/r. Reproduced for Lake House, Central City, Colo. No.WP81145-1 (birch color ground). Special order.

SCHUMACHER

ᕦ GOBELIN'S FOREST. American, 1900–10, machine print. 27″ wide, 25¹/₄″ repeat, 4¹/₂ yds. per s/r. Document in Schumacher Archive.

Adaptation: pattern enlarged 25 percent. No.512830 (forest green).

꙰ GREEN LEAVES LACE STRIPE. American, 1900–15, machine print. 27" wide, 25$\frac{1}{4}$" half-drop repeat, 4$\frac{1}{2}$ yds. per s/r. Reproduced for Historic Natchez Foundation. No.504742 (green house).

꙰ GREEN LEAVES OAK. American, 1900–15, machine print. 27" wide, 25$\frac{1}{4}$" repeat, 4$\frac{1}{2}$ yds. per s/r. Reproduced for Historic Natchez Foundation. No.504670 (forest).

꙰ RICHMOND PRIMAVERA. American, 1900–10, machine print. 27" wide, 25$\frac{1}{4}$" repeat, 4$\frac{1}{2}$ yds. per s/r. Adaptation. Reproduced for Historic Natchez Foundation. No.504763 (cranberry and green).

꙰ SPLATTER TEXTURE. American, 1900–20, machine print. 20$\frac{1}{2}$" wide, 12$\frac{1}{2}$" repeat, 5$\frac{1}{2}$ yds. per s/r. Document in Hobe Erwin Collection, Schumacher Archive. No.506165 (coco).

RICHARD E. THIBAUT

꙰ ACCOMACK. American, 1904–20, machine print. 27" wide, 6$\frac{1}{4}$" repeat, 4$\frac{1}{2}$ yds. per s/r. Historic Homes of America Collection, produced in collaboration with National Preservation Institute. Document at Harmanson House, Onancock, Va. No.839-T-7976 (rust and ochre on ivory).

꙰ ANDOVER. American, 1920–30, machine print. 20$\frac{1}{2}$" wide, 19" repeat, 5$\frac{1}{2}$ yds. per s/r. No.839-T-7660 (pale orange).

꙰ ELIZABETH. American, 1920–30, machine print. 20$\frac{1}{2}$" wide, 19" repeat, 5$\frac{1}{2}$ yds. per s/r. Historic Homes of America Collection, produced in collaboration with National Preservation Institute. Document at Clarence Wilson House, Gastonia, N.C. No.839-T-7955 (multi on gray).

꙰ LORENZO. American, 1910–30, machine print. 20$\frac{1}{2}$" wide, 25$\frac{1}{4}$" repeat, 4$\frac{1}{2}$ yds. per s/r. Historic Homes of America Collection, produced in collaboration with National Preservation Institute. Document at Lorenzo, Cazenovia, N.Y. No.839-T-7941 (multi on gray).

꙰ NEWTON. American, 1900–20, machine print. 27" wide, 12$\frac{5}{8}$" repeat, 5 yds. per s/r. No.839-T-274 (beige).

VICTORIAN COLLECTIBLES LIMITED

All documents are in the Brillion Collection. Samples from the same collection are at the Cooper-Hewitt Museum, and selected samples are also at the Victoria and Albert Museum.

꙰ HERRINGBONE. American, 1900–20, machine print. 27" wide, 36" repeat, 5 yds. per s/r. No.49-001 (brown on brown). Period coloring: No.49-004 (white mica on filagree cream).

꙰ ORCHARD HALL. American, 1900–20, machine print. Originally printed by S. A. Maxwell & Company. 24" wide, 19" repeat, 5 yds.

above left
ORCHARD HALL,
1900–20. Victorian
Collectibles Limited.

above right
WELLINGTON HOUSE,
1900–10. Water-
house Wallhangings

per s/r. No.18-001 (sage and gold on gold string). Period coloring: No.18-003 (brown, gold, and green on straw string).

ᘐ PETITE FLEURS. American, 1900–20, machine print. 28" wide, 29¹/₂" repeat, 5 yds. per s/r. No.40-001 (brown and gold on brown).

WATERHOUSE WALLHANGINGS

ᘐ GEORGETOWN FLORAL. American, 1900–20, machine print. 20¹/₂" wide, 19" repeat, 7 yds. per s/r. Document in Waterhouse Archives. No.192519 (gray-green ground).

ᘐ JARDIN CHINOIS. Probably American, 1915–25, machine print. 22" wide, 21" repeat, 7 yds. per s/r. Document color unknown. Period colorings: No.172519 (gray on white); No.172810 (beige on Chinese red).

ᘐ WELLINGTON HOUSE. American, 1900–10, machine print. 21" wide, 18³/₄" repeat, 5 yds. per s/r. Document in Waterhouse Archives. No.198513 (gold and white on gold). Period coloring: No.198635 (white and gold on ivory).

ZINA STUDIOS

Order by pattern name.

ᘐ OLD GREENWICH. American, 1900–30, machine print. 24" wide, 4" repeat. Green and yellow on gray.

CHATEAU-SUR-MER,
1870–80. Scalamandré.
Page 162.

LION AND DOVE
FRIEZE, 1900. Brad-
bury & Bradbury.
Page 235.

BEAUPORT PROMENADE,
1907. Brunschwig &
Fils. Page 211.

DORSET, 1900–15.
Clarence House.
Page 213.

top
TULIP FRIEZE, 1903.
Arthur Sanderson &
Sons. Page 246.

above
STUPA BORDER,
c. 1905. Schumacher.
Page 238.

right
APPLEDORE, 1920–30.
Brunschwig & Fils.
Page 211.

opposite
FRANKLIN ROOSEVELT'S
HOME—PINK ROOM,
c. 1916. Scalamandré.
Page 221.

The following groups include a fill and a frieze.

CLASSIC REVIVALS

St. James Collection

➤ BELLEVUE HOMESTEAD FILLER. English, 1900–10, machine print. 21" wide, 11 yds. per roll. Reproduced by National Trust of Queensland for Bellevue Homestead, Coominya, Queensland, Australia. No.VF4 (deep red); No.VF7 (pink); No.VF21 (antique blue).

➤ BELLEVUE HOMESTEAD FRIEZE. English, 1900–10, machine print. 16" wide. Reproduced by National Trust of Queensland for Bellevue Homestead, Coominya, Queensland, Australia. No.VZ4 (deep red); No.VZ7 (pink); No.VZ21 (antique blue).

MT. DIABLO HANDPRINTS

Order by name unless pattern number is listed.

➤ DRUMMOND STRIPE. American, c. 1910, machine print. 18⅞" wide. Reproduced for Drummond Home, Hominy, Okla. Raspberry and mauve.

➤ DRUMMOND PANEL. American, c. 1910, machine print. 24¾" wide, 22" repeat. Reproduced for Drummond Home, Hominy, Okla. Raspberry, mauve, and cream.

VICTORIAN COLLECTIBLES LIMITED

All documents are in the Brillion Collection. Samples from the same collection are at the Cooper-Hewitt Museum, and selected samples are also at the Victoria and Albert Museum.

➤ BRILLION TULIP. American, 1900–20, machine print. Originally printed by Standard Wall Paper Company. 24" wide, 16¼" repeat, 5 yds. per s/r. Adaptation: document color not reproduced exactly. No.22-001 (green, gold, and brown on gold crespi). Period colorings: No.22-002 (browns and pearl on beige weave); No.22-005 (greens, terra cotta, and gold on beige).

➤ BRILLION TULIP BORDER. American, 1900–20, machine print. Originally printed by Standard Wall Paper Company. 18" wide, 19" repeat. Adaptation: document color not reproduced exactly. No.22-051 (green, gold, and brown on gold crespi). Period colorings: No.22-052 (browns and pearl on beige weave). No.22-055 (greens, terra cotta, and gold on beige).

➤ IVY. American, 1910–20, machine print. 29" wide, 12½" repeat, 5 yds. per s/r. Adaptation. No.39-001 (gold on cream).

➤ IVY BORDER. American, 1910–20, machine print. 10½" wide, 19" repeat. Adaptation. No.39-051 (gold on cream).

➤ LACEY ROSE. American, 1900–20, machine print. Originally printed by Gledhill Wall Paper Company. 18" wide plus three 2" borders, 19" repeat, 5 yds. per s/r. No.38-001 (tan, pinks, golds, and

COORDINATING
WALLPAPER
PATTERNS

opposite
GOBELIN'S FOREST,
1900–10. Schumacher.
Page 222.

greens on cream). Period coloring: No.38-002 (pinks, golds, and greens on cream).

☙ LACEY ROSE BORDER. American, 1900–20, machine print. Originally printed by Gledhill Wall Paper Company. 18″ wide, 19″ repeat. No.38-051 (tan, pinks, golds, and greens on cream). Period coloring: No.38-052 (pinks, golds, and greens on cream).

☙ LACEY ROSE BORDER (narrow). American, 1900–20, machine print. 9″ wide, 9¹⁄₂″ repeat. Half-scale adaptation of preceding pattern. No.38-061 (tan, pinks, golds, and greens on cream). Period coloring: No.38-062 (pinks, golds, and greens on cream).

☙ NOUVEAU FLEUR. American, 1910–30, machine print. 23″ wide, 9¹⁄₂″ repeat, 5 yds. per s/r. No.37-001 (mint plaid on ivory). Period coloring: No.37-002 (beige plaid on beige weave).

☙ NOUVEAU FLEUR BORDER. American, 1910–30, machine print. 9″ wide, 19″ repeat. No.37-061 (pale pinks, blues, and green on ivory). Period coloring: No.37-062 (greens, brown, gold, and dark mauve on beige weave).

☙ URN. American, 1900–20, machine print. 27″ wide, 18³⁄₄″ repeat, 5 yds. per s/r. No.27-001 (gold, and brown on brown).

☙ URN BORDER. American, 1900–20, machine print. 18″ wide, 16″ repeat. No.27-051 (gold and brown on brown).

below left
BELLEVUE HOMESTEAD FRIEZE, 1900–10. Classic Revivals (St. James Collection).

bottom left
BELLEVUE HOMESTEAD FILLER, 1900–10. Classic Revivals (St. James Collection).

below right
LACEY ROSE and border, 1900–20. Victorian Collectibles Limited.

BRADBURY & BRADBURY   BORDERS

ॐ LION AND DOVE FRIEZE. English, 1900, block print. Designed by
Walter Crane; originally printed by Jeffrey & Company. 26½″ wide,
46″ repeat. Document at Victoria and Albert Museum. Code LDF.
Special order.

BRUNSCHWIG & FILS

ॐ AURELIA BORDER. American, 1900–20, machine print. 13″ wide,
18¾″ repeat. Adaptation: bottom motif added. Document in Brunschwig Archives. No.14037.06 (bisque).

ॐ BOTANICA BORDER. French, 1909–20, block print. 4½″ wide,   *below left*
20¼″ repeat. Document at Musée des Arts Décoratifs. No.13437.06   NOUVEAU FLEUR and
(red on mauve).   border, 1910–30.

ॐ BOTANICA CORNER. French, 1909–20, block print. 13⅞″ wide   Victorian Collecti-
each side. Document at Musée des Arts Décoratifs. No.13427.06 (red bles Limited.
on mauve).

ॐ MOTHER GOOSE BORDER ON VINYL. English, 1913, roller print. De-   *below right*
signed by Mabel Lucy Attwell; originally printed by C. and J. G. Pot- URN and border,
ter. Greysmith, fig. 131, p. 174; Oman and Hamilton, no. 753, p. 277. 1900–20. Victorian
8″ wide, 18″ repeat. Adaptation: document colors not reproduced   Collectibles Limited.

AURELIA BORDER, 1900–20. Brunschwig & Fils.

BOTANICA BORDER and corner, 1909. Brunschwig & Fils.

MOTHER GOOSE BORDER, 1913. Brunschwig & Fils.

below
LOTUS FRIEZE, 1900–10. Classic Revivals (St. James Collection).

and pattern reduced. Document in Brunschwig Archives. Period coloring: No.13630.06 (multi on white).

CLASSIC REVIVALS

Authentic Interiors Collection
&❧ BOBBIN BORDER. English, 1925–30, machine print. 8¼″ wide, 1½″ repeat. Archival Collection. No.B-196-8A (orange and yellow).
&❧ MAPLE LEAF BORDER. English, 1920–30, machine print. 4″ wide, 18″ repeat. Archival Collection. No.B-210-10A (red, black, and green).
&❧ ROSE TANA BORDER. English, 1925–30, machine print. 4″ wide, 10½″ repeat. No.F-177-8A (black and red).

Mauny Collection
&❧ CHAMPS ELYSEES. French, 1900–20, block print. 2⅞″ wide. No.2612. Block print.
&❧ CORDE. French, 1920–30, block print. 1⅞″ wide. No.5001 (series). Block print.
&❧ SAINT CYR. French, 1910–20, block print. 2¾″ wide. No.5006B (blue on pink); No.5006E (orange on yellow). Block print.
&❧ SERPENTINE. French, 1920–30, block print. 1″ wide. No.5000 (series). Block print.

St. James Collection
&❧ LOTUS FRIEZE. English, 1900–10, machine print. 10½″ wide. No.LZ13 (turquoise).

top
RALAHYNE FRIEZE, 1900–10. Classic Revivals (St. James Collection).

above
ROSE AND RIBBON FRIEZE, 1900–10. Classic Revivals (St. James Collection).

❧ RALAHYNE FRIEZE. English, 1900–10, machine print. 18" wide. Adaptation: embossing not reproduced. No.HZ16 (drab olive).

❧ ROSE AND RIBBON FRIEZE. English, 1900–10, block print. 20" wide. No.RZ7 (pink).

CHRISTOPHER HYLAND INCORPORATED

❧ PARIS, 1930, BORDER. French, 1930, block print. 20$^1/_4$" wide, 22" repeat, 11 yds. per s/r. No.AB157/1A (plum and pearl). Can be used as either a dado or a sidewall.

❧ PARIS, 1930, BORDER. English or French, 1920–30, machine print. 6$^1/_4$" wide, 20$^1/_2$" repeat. No.AB146/4A (plum and pearl).

COWTAN & TOUT

❧ ROSEDALE BORDER. English, 1900–20, block print. 4" wide, 21" repeat. No.300 (multi on blue). Block print.

LEE JOFA

❧ ROSALIE BORDER. French, 1915–20, block print. 7" wide, 17$^1/_4$" repeat. Adaptation: document color not reproduced. Period coloring: No.P902250 (multi on yellow).

RICHARD E. THIBAUT

❧ ACCOMACK BORDER. American, 1904–20, machine print. 9" wide, 13$^1/_2$" repeat. Historic Homes of America Collection, produced in collaboration with National Preservation Institute. Document at Harmonson House, Onancock, Va. No.839-T-790076 (rust and ochre on ivory).

ARTHUR SANDERSON & SONS

❧ VILLE DE LYONS FRIEZE. English, 1911, block print. 18" wide, 20$^1/_4$" repeat. Adaptation. Document in Sanderson Archives. Period coloring: No.S/B WR 76043-1.

SCALAMANDRE

❧ STANROD LIBRARY STRIPE PANEL. American, 1900–20, machine print. 27" wide, 8' panel, 2 panels per s/r. Reproduced for Stanrod Mansion, Pocatello, Idaho. No.WP81073 (green on white). Special order.

❧ WISTERIA BORDER. English, 1900–25, block print. 21$^1/_4$" wide, 26$^3/_4$" repeat. Historic representation. Reproduced for Leixlip Castle, Kildare, Ireland, in cooperation with Irish Georgian Society. Document color, no. WB81313-99a, is a special order. Period coloring: No.WB81313-001 (coral and spruce on ivory).

SCHUMACHER

❧ STUPA BORDER. American, c. 1905, machine print. 13$^5/_8$" wide,

ROSEDALE BORDER, 1900–20. Cowtan & Tout.

Original document for "Rosalie Border," a paper of 1915–20 reproduced by Lee Jofa.

13⅞" repeat. Document in Schumacher Archive. No.513010 (document green).

VICTORIAN COLLECTIBLES LIMITED

WISTERIA BORDER, 1900–25. Scalamandré.

All documents are in the Brillion Collection. Samples from the same collection are at the Cooper-Hewitt Museum, and selected

TIFFANY BORDER,
1900–20.
Zina Studios.

samples are also at the Victoria and Albert Museum.

ॐ POPPY BORDER. American, 1900–20, machine print. Originally printed by William H. Mairs & Company. 18″ wide, 16″ repeat. No.32-051 (melon, terra cotta, and green on burgundy).

ॐ POPPY BORDER (narrow). American, 1900–20, machine print. 18″ wide, 16″ repeat. Half-scale adaptation of preceding pattern. No.32-061 (melon, terra cotta, and green on burgundy).

ZINA STUDIOS

Order by pattern name.

ॐ TIFFANY BORDER. American, 1900–20, machine print. 9¼″ wide, 5″ repeat. Green and yellow on gray.

CEILING PAPERS

SCALAMANDRE

ॐ BARTON HOUSE RESTORATION BEDROOM CEILING. American, 1900–10, machine print. 48″ wide, 12½″ repeat, 3 yds. per s/r. Reproduced for Barton House, Lubbock, Tex. No.WP81136-001 (pinks, greens, white, and mica). Special order.

ॐ BARTON HOUSE RESTORATION HALL CEILING. American, 1890–1900, machine print. 48″ wide, 1½″ repeat, 3 yds. per s/r. Reproduced for Barton House, Lubbock, Tex. No.WP81110-1 (beige and gold). Special order.

ॐ HIRSHFELD HOUSE DOWNSTAIRS MAIN HALL CEILING. American, 1900–20, machine print. 20″ wide, 6″ repeat, 7 yds. per s/r. Reproduced for Hirshfeld House, Austin, Tex. No.WP81193-001 (metallic silver). Special order.

ᵹ NATHANIEL ORR HOUSE PARLOR. American, 1900–20, machine print. 18" wide, 18⅝" repeat, 8 yds. per s/r. Reproduced for Steilacoom Historical Museum, Steilacoom, Wash. No.WP 81243-001 (ivory, pale greens, pearl, and apricot).

VICTORIAN COLLECTIBLES LIMITED

All documents are in the Brillion Collection. Samples from the same collection are at the Cooper-Hewitt Museum, and selected samples are at the Victoria and Albert Museum.

ᵹ CRACKED ICE. American, 1900–30, machine print. Originally printed by Janeway & Company. 27" wide, 31½" repeat, 5 yds. per s/r. No.47-001 (white mica on white). Period coloring: No.47-005 (white mica on filigree cream).

Anaglypta comes in two weights: Anaglypta Supadurable is the thickness and weight of period Anaglypta, while Anaglypta Original is thinner and was invented in the 1960s to replace the thicker and heavier period product. All Anaglypta patterns listed below were embossed from period rollers. The products come unfinished and must be painted.

RELIEF
DECORATIONS—
ANAGLYPTA

CROWN DECORATIVE PRODUCTS

Crown Decorative Products are available through Bentley Brothers, Classic Ceilings, and Mile Hi Crown.

ᵹ ANAGLYPTA SUPADURABLE. English, 1938, machine embossed. 20½" wide, 24" repeat, 11 yds. per roll. No.RD 108.

ᵹ ANAGLYPTA SUPADURABLE. English, 1935, machine embossed. 20½" wide, 21" repeat, 11 yds. per roll. No.RD 117.

ᵹ ANAGLYPTA ORIGINAL. English, 1900–20, machine embossed. 20½" wide, 3½" repeat, 11 yards per roll. No.RD 124.

ᵹ ANAGLYPTA ORIGINAL. English, 1933, machine embossed. 20½" wide, 5½" repeat, 11 yards per roll. No.RD 125.

ᵹ ANAGLYPTA SUPADURABLE. English, 1900–30, machine embossed. 20½" wide, 21" repeat, 11 yds. per roll. No.RD 137.

ᵹ ANAGLYPTA SUPADURABLE. English, 1900–30, machine embossed. 20½" wide, 5¼" repeat, 11 yds. per roll. No.RD 148.

ᵹ ANAGLYPTA SUPADURABLE. English, 1900–30, machine embossed. 20½" wide, 5¼" repeat, 11 yds. per roll. No.RD 151.

ᵹ ANAGLYPTA SUPADURABLE. English, 1900–30, machine embossed. 20½" wide, 10½" repeat, 11 yds. per roll. No.RD 160.

ᵹ ANAGLYPTA SUPADURABLE. English, 1900–20, machine embossed. 20½" wide, 10½" repeat, 11 yds. per roll. No.RD 648.

DIANA FRIEZE (top) and ADELPHI FRIEZE, 1900–30. Crown Decorative Products.

☙ ANAGLYPTA SUPADURABLE. English, 1920–30, machine embossed. 20$^{1}/_{2}$" wide, 10$^{1}/_{2}$" repeat, 11 yds. per roll. No.RD 650.

The following patterns were created in the 1960s but have a distinct period look.

☙ ANAGLYPTA ORIGINAL. English, machine embossed. 20$^{1}/_{2}$" wide, 10$^{1}/_{2}$" repeat, 11 yards per roll. No.RD 199.

☙ ANAGLYPTA ORIGINAL. English, machine embossed. 20$^{1}/_{2}$" wide, 7" repeat, 11 yards per roll. No.RD 326.

☙ ANAGLYPTA ORIGINAL. English, machine embossed. 20$^{1}/_{2}$" wide, 7" repeat, 11 yards per roll. No.RD 335.

RELIEF DECORATIONS— LINCRUSTA

CROWN DECORATIVE PRODUCTS

Crown Decorative Products are available through Bentley Brothers, Classic Ceilings, and Mile Hi Crown. The products come unfinished and must be painted.

☙ ADAM FRIEZE. English, 1900–30, impressed composition. 20$^{7}/_{8}$" wide, 21" repeat. No.RD 1955.

☙ ADELPHI FRIEZE. English, 1900–30, impressed composition. 10$^{5}/_{8}$" wide, 21$^{1}/_{8}$" repeat. No.RD 1949.

☙ ART NOUVEAU DADO. English, 1906–20, impressed composition. Panel size: 21$^{1}/_{4}$" wide, 36" high, 5 panels per box. No.RD 1951.

☙ CAMEO FRIEZE. English, 1900–30, impressed composition. 11" wide, 21$^{1}/_{8}$" repeat. No.RD 1948.

ART NOUVEAU DADO,
1906. Crown
Decorative Products.

EDWARDIAN DADO,
1906. Crown
Decorative Products.

ॐ DIANA FRIEZE. English, 1900–30, impressed composition. 11 1/16" wide, 20 1/4" repeat. No.RD 1958.

ॐ EDWARDIAN DADO. English, 1906–20, impressed composition. Panel size: 24" wide, 40" high, 5 panels per box. No.RD 1950.

ZUBER

ॐ LES COTES DE VILLEFRANCHE (THE COAST OF VILLEFRANCHE). French, 1929, block print. Designed by Madame Ehney-Vogler. Total width: 21' 7"; total height: 12' 10"; 18 1/2" per panel; 14 panels per set. Block printed in 8 shades of gray from 157 wood blocks or in 48 colors from 264 blocks.

ॐ PAYSAGE ITALIAN (ITALIAN LANDSCAPE). French, 1912, block print. Designed by Arnold Stutz in the style of Antoine Pierre Mongin. Total width: 15'5"; total height: 12' 10"; 18 1/2" per panel; 10 panels per set. Block printed in 10 colors from 240 wood blocks.

Zuber also prints a wide variety of wallpapers and borders. The company prefers that inquiries concerning these additional patterns be made directly to its New York showroom.

BRADBURY & BRADBURY

ॐ SWEET BRIAR. English, 1911, block print. Designed by J. H. Dearle. Oman and Hamilton, no. 1076, p. 385. 27" wide, 13 1/2" repeat, 5 yds. per s/r. Document at Victoria and Albert Museum. Code SRW. Period colorings: No.110 (ashes of roses); No.210 (terracotta); No.410 (aesthetic green); No.550 (eucalyptus).

ARTHUR SANDERSON & SONS

Morris & Company's wallpapers were originally printed by Jeffrey & Company. The original wood blocks are now owned by Arthur Sanderson & Sons, and the following patterns are printed from them.

ॐ ARBUTUS. English, 1903 or 1913, block print. Designed by Kathleen Kersey. Oman and Hamilton, no. 1076, p. 386. 21" wide, 15" repeat, 11 yds. per roll. Document in Sanderson Archives. No.493 (green). Block print.

ॐ LILY BORDER AND CORNER. English, 1917, block print. Designer unknown. Oman and Hamilton, no. 1076, p. 384. 3 1/8" wide, 8 3/4" repeat. Document in Sanderson Archives. Border: No.533 (sage); No.535 (red); No.537 (blue); No.539 (light). Corner: No.534 (sage); No.536 (red); No.538 (blue); No.540 (light). Block print.

SCENIC WALLPAPERS

WALLPAPERS AND BORDERS BY MORRIS & COMPANY

ঌ ORANGE BORDER AND CORNER. English, 1917, block print. Designer unknown. Oman and Hamilton, no. 1076, p. 385. 3¹/₄" wide, 7¹/₂" repeat. Document in Sanderson Archives. Border: No.541 (green); No.543 (red); No.545 (bronze); No.547 (light). Corner: No.542 (green); No.544 (red); No.546 (bronze); No.548 (light). Block print.

ঌ SWEET BRIAR. English, 1911, block print. Designed by John Henry Dearle. Oman and Hamilton, no. 1076, p. 385. 21" wide, 10¹/₂" repeat, 11 yds. per roll. Document in Sanderson Archives. No.482 (green). Block print.

ঌ TULIP FRIEZE. English, 1903, block print. Designed by Kathleen Kersey. Oman and Hamilton, no. 1076, p. 388. Document in Sanderson Archives. No.385 (green). Block print.

The following designs by Morris & Company have been transferred to rollers and are printed by machine.

ঌ BLACKBERRY. English, 1903, block print. Designed by John Henry Dearle. Oman and Hamilton, no. 1076, p. 386. 21" wide, 18" repeat, 11 yds. per roll. Document in Sanderson Archives. Period coloring: No.WM 7425-1 (rose and green on ivory).

ঌ MICHAELMAS DAISY. English, 1912, block print. Designed by John Henry Dearle. Oman and Hamilton, no. 1076, p. 385. 21" wide, 21¹/₂" repeat, 11 yds. per roll. Document in Sanderson Archives. No.WM 7313 (series).

ঌ SWEET BRIAR. English, 1911, block print. Designed by John Henry Dearle. Oman and Hamilton, no. 1076, p. 385. 21" wide, 10¹/₂" repeat, 11 yds. per roll. Document in Sanderson Archives. Period coloring: No.WM 7421-3 (green and apricot on parchment).

CUSTOM PATTERNS FROM MUSEUMS

SOCIETY FOR THE PRESERVATION OF NEW ENGLAND ANTIQUITIES

ঌ HAMILTON HOUSE—RECEPTION ROOM. French, c. 1925, block print. 18¹/₂" wide, 22¹/₂" repeat, 7 yds. per roll. Reproduced for Hamilton House, South Berwick, Maine. Document at Society for Preservation of New England Antiquities. Green on gray.

ঌ HAMILTON HOUSE—TWIN ROOM. American, 1920–30, machine print. 18¹/₂" wide, 3¹/₄" repeat, 7 yds. per roll. Reproduced for Hamilton House, South Berwick, Maine. Document at Society for the Preservation of New England Antiquities. Gray and white.

ঌ HAMILTON HOUSE—YELLOW ROOM. American, 1920–30, machine print. 19" wide, 2¹/₄" repeat, 7 yds. per roll. Reproduced for Hamilton House, South Berwick, Maine. Document at Society for the Preservation of New England Antiquities. White on yellow.

SWEET BRIAR, 1911.
Arthur Sanderson &
Sons.

OTHER WALLCOVERINGS

Grasscloth became a popular wallcovering in the 20th century. Many firms, including Gracie and Scalamandré, can supply grasscloth in a variety of colors and weaves that are appropriate for restoration work.

GRASSCLOTH

Like grasscloth, metallic leaf and tea papers were used extensively in the early 20th century, especially in dining rooms. Most modern metallic papers are distressed or antiqued and therefore only approximate the appearance of the originals. Modern leaf papers are available from Louis W. Bowen, Gracie, Schumacher, and other specialty firms.

LEAF AND TEA PAPERS

Nonrepeating Chinese panels similar in style to those popular in the 18th through the early 20th centuries are available from the following companies: Louis W. Bowen, A. L. Diament & Company, Gracie, and Albert Van Luit and Company (Winterthur Museum Collection). Some of these panels are hand painted.

NONREPEATING CHINESE DESIGNS

Solid stripes were popular from the 1840s to the 1930s. Most firms carry a wide variety of striped wallpapers. Those listed below are only representative examples.

SOLID STRIPES

BRUNSCHWIG & FILS

◈ POMPEIAN STRIPE. English or French, 1850–1910. 27" wide, 5 yds. per s/r. No.13220.06 (series).

COWTAN & TOUT

◈ BALMORAL STRIPE. English, 1880–1900, block print. 21" wide, 2½" stripe, 11 yds. per roll. No.30390 (gray); No.30391 (aqua); No.30395 (blue). Block print.
◈ CLIVEDEN STRIPE. English, 1890–1920, block print. 21" wide, 3½" stripe, 11 yds. per roll. No.29081 (gold and aqua); No.29085 (gold and light rose). Block print.

Wallpaper printing machine at the Centennial Exhibition in Philadelphia, as illustrated in *Harper's Weekly*, December 23, 1876. (Society for the Preservation of New England Antiquities)

❧ MARLBOROUGH STRIPE. English, 1880–1900, machine print. 21" wide, 2¹/₂" stripe, 11 yds. per roll. Period colorings: No.29068 (green); No.29071 (red); No.29077 (dark yellow). Block print.

CHRISTOPHER HYLAND INCORPORATED

❧ CLARENDON. English, 1880–90, block print. 20¹/₂" wide, 11 yds. per roll. No.ZZBL01 (red); No.ZZBL02 (yellow); ZZBL04 (blue and white); ZZBL12 (gray and white).

❧ RAYURE. English, 1870–90. 21" wide, 11 yds. per s/r. No.ZZ2303 (magenta and red).

ARTHUR SANDERSON & SONS

❧ CUMBERLAND. English, 1850–1910, machine print. 20¹/₄" wide, 3¹/₄" stripe, 11 yds. per roll. Document in Sanderson Archives. Period colorings: No.WR 7511-1 (Chinese yellow); No.WR 7511-2 (claret); No.WR 7511-5 (bottle).

❧ MONTPELIER. English, 1840–60, block print. Originally printed by William Woollams & Company. 20¹/₄" wide, 1¹/₂" stripe, 11 yds. per roll. Document in Sanderson Archives. Period colorings: No.WH 7365-1 (blue and white); No.WH 7365-2 (red and white).

❧ SUSSEX. English, 1913–30, machine print. 20¹/₄" wide, 1" stripe, 11 yds. per roll. Document in Sanderson Archives. Period colorings: No.WR 7519-1 (regency red); No.WR 7519-2 (empire green).

THE TWIGS

❧ MRS. KEPPLE STRIPE. French, 1850–90, block print. 26³/₄" wide, alternating wide and narrow stripes, 5 yds. per s/r. No.97100/03 (light beige and dark gray); No.97100/005 (green and gray); No.97100/008 (maize and sage); No.97100/009 (bone and yellow).

WATERHOUSE WALLHANGINGS

❧ TOWNHOUSE STRIPE. Probably American, 1890–1910, machine print. 20¹/₂" wide, 2¹/₂" stripe, 7 yds. per s/r. Document in Waterhouse Archives. Period colorings: No.189518 (yellow and white); No.189488 (beige and white); No.189484 (light and dark blue); No.189635 (brown and white); No.189613 (gray and white); no. 189540 (maroon).

TOILES

In the late 19th and early 20th centuries, many wallpaper patterns were inspired by late 18th-century toiles or plate-printed fabrics. Specific patterns are not listed here because most of the toile patterns available today are direct copies of textiles. These patterns should be reviewed for consideration if a toile-patterned wallpaper is discovered in the course of a restoration project.

SUPPLIERS

Many of the firms listed are wholesale houses whose products are available to the trade only. This means that their wallpapers are sold only through interior designers, architects, and the decorating departments of fine retail and furniture stores. Some of these papers are also available through large wallpaper stores. In some cases, the firms will sell wallpapers directly to nonprofit institutions such as museums, historical societies, preservation organizations, and state-owned historic properties; in other cases, they may refer interested people to their local representative. Arrangements for custom reproductions should always be made through the manufacturer's main office.

LOUIS W. BOWEN. 200 Garden City Plaza, Garden City, NY 11530, (516) 741-9440

BRADBURY & BRADBURY ART WALLPAPERS. P.O. Box 155, Benicia, CA 94510, (707) 746-1900

BRUNSCHWIG & FILS. 979 Third Avenue, New York, NY 10022-1234, (212) 838-7878.

J. R. BURROWS & COMPANY. P.O. Box 522, Rockland, MA 02370, (617) 982-1812

CLARENCE HOUSE. 211 East 58th Street, New York, NY 10022, (212) 752-2890

CLASSIC REVIVALS INC. One Design Center Place, Boston, MA 02210, (617) 574-9030

COLE & SON LTD. P.O. Box 4 BU, 18 Mortimer Street, London W1A 4BU, England (available in the United States exclusively through Clarence House)

COLEFAX & FOWLER. Available through Cowtan & Tout

COWTAN & TOUT. 979 Third Avenue, New York, NY 10022, (212) 753-4488

CROWN DECORATIVE PRODUCTS
East Coast distributor: Bentley Brothers, 2709 South Park Road, Louisville, KY 40219, (800) 824-4777

West Coast distributor: Classic Ceilings, 902 East Commonwealth Avenue, Fullerton, CA 92631, (800) 922-8700

Mile Hi Crown. 1925 Blake Street, Suite 100, Denver, CO 80202

A. L. DIAMENT & COMPANY. P.O. Box 230, Exton, PA 19341, (215) 363-5660

GALACAR & COMPANY. 144 Main Street, Essex, MA 01929, (508) 768-6118

GRACIE. 979 Third Avenue, New York, NY 10022, (212) 753-5350

CHRISTOPHER HYLAND INCORPORATED. 979 Third Avenue, New York, NY 10022, (212) 688-6121

LEE JOFA INC. Headquarters: 800 Central Boulevard, Carlstadt, NJ 07072, (201) 438-8444. Showroom: 979 Third Avenue, New York, NY 10022

KATZENBACH & WARREN. 23645 Mercantile Road, Cleveland, OH 44122, (216) 464-3700

MT. DIABLO HANDPRINTS, INC. 473 E. Channel Road, Benicia, CA 94510, (707) 745-3388

ARTHUR SANDERSON & SONS. 979 Third Avenue, New York, NY 10022, (212) 319-7220

SCALAMANDRE. Showroom: 950 Third Avenue, New York, NY 10022, (212) 980-3888. Mill: Executive offices: 37-24 24th Street, Long Island City, NY 11101, (718) 361-8500

F. SCHUMACHER & COMPANY. Showroom: 939 Third Avenue, New York, NY 10022, (212) 415-3900. Main office: 79 Madison Avenue, New York, NY 10016, (212) 213-7900

RICHARD E. THIBAUT, INC. 706 South 21st Street, Irvington, NJ 07111, (201) 399-7888

THE TWIGS. 5700 Third Avenue, San Francisco, CA 94124-2609, (415) 822-1626

VICTORIAN COLLECTIBLES LIMITED. 845 East Glenbrook Road, Milwaukee, WI 53217, (414) 352-7290

ALBERT VAN LUIT & COMPANY. 23645 Mercantile Road, Cleveland, OH 44122, (216) 464-3700

WATERHOUSE WALLHANGINGS. 99 Paul Sullivan Way, Boston, MA 02118, (617) 423-7688

ZINA STUDIOS, INC. 85 Purdy Avenue, Port Chester, NY 10573, (914) 937-5661

ZUBER & CIE. 979 Third Avenue, New York, NY 10022, (212) 486-9226

CUSTOM ORDERS THROUGH MUSEUMS

ESSEX INSTITUTE. Museum Shop, Essex Institute, 132 Essex Street, Salem, MA 01970, (508) 744-3390

GUNSTON HALL. Gift Shop, Gunston Hall, Lorton, VA 22079, (703) 550-9220

HISTORIC DEERFIELD, INC. J. G. Pratt Museum Store, Historic Deerfield, Inc., Box 321, Deerfield, MA 01342, (413) 774-5581

POCUMTUCK VALLEY MEMORIAL ASSOCIATION. Curator, Memorial Hall Museum, Memorial Street, Deerfield, MA 01342, (413) 774-7476

SOCIETY FOR THE PRESERVATION OF NEW ENGLAND ANTIQUITIES. Reproductions Coordinator, Society for the Preservation of New England Antiquities, 141 Cambridge Street, Boston, MA 02114, (617) 227-3956

STRAWBERY BANKE MUSEUM. Museum Shop, Strawbery Banke Museum, P.O. Box 300, Portsmouth, NH 03802, (603) 433-1114

GLOSSARY

ADAPTATION. A modern wallpaper that retains the overall appearance of the original document although certain changes have been made in the design. The term may apply also to a modern wallpaper produced as a companion to a reproduction fabric.

ANAGLYPTA. A patented embossed wallcovering made from paper and cotton. The color is applied after the paper is hung.

BLOCK PRINTING. A process in which color is transferred to paper by means of a carved wood block.

BLOTCH. A term for a silk screen that prints a solid color. Blotch screens are often used to print the ground color of a reproduction wallpaper.

COLORWAY. A manufacturing term for identifying the predominant color or colors of a wallpaper design. Reproduction wallpapers are often available in several colorways. The document colorway copies the colors of the original wallpaper. The other colorways in which the reproduction design is available are created by the manufacturer to be compatible with modern decorating needs. Colorways that have a distinct period look are listed in this book as period colorings.

DADO. The lower portion of the wall of a room, between the baseboard and the chair rail, often decorated differently from the upper section.

DOCUMENT. The original wallpaper whose design and color are copied for a reproduction wallpaper.

DOCUMENT COLORWAY. See colorway.

FILL. An alternative name for a wallpaper when it is used in combination with a frieze or dado paper; also called a sidewall.

FRIEZE. An alternative name for a wide border.

FLOCKING. A textured surface created by adding chopped textile fibers that adhere to the paper.

GROUND. The background color of a wallpaper design.

HISTORIC REPRESENTATION. A term used by Scalamandré for a reproduction wallpaper in which the scale or composition has been altered slightly because of modern technological limitations.

INGRAIN PAPER. See oatmeal paper.

INTERPRETATION. A modern wallpaper in which one or more motifs from a document wallpaper are reworked into a new design.

LINCRUSTA. A patented composition in which the raised design is impressed with rollers. Color is applied after installation.

MACHINE PRINTING. See roller printing.

MULTI. A modern manufacturing term for a colorway containing many colors.

OATMEAL PAPER. A textured paper made from pulp consisting of colored cotton or wool rags.

PAINTED PAPER. An 18th-century term for wallpaper.

PIECE. An 18th-century term for a roll of wallpaper.

PLAIN PAPER. A wallpaper decorated only with the ground color.

REPEAT. The dimension of one complete design element in a wallpaper.

REPRODUCTION WALLPAPER. A modern wallpaper that faithfully copies the design, color, and scale of an original wallpaper document.

ROLLER PRINTING. A process in which color is transferred to a moving roll of paper by the raised surface of a metal cylinder.

ROOMSET. A modern term for a complete decorative wallpaper scheme that includes coordinated wall and ceiling patterns.

SANDWICH. Layers of wallpaper applied over a period of time. These are studied during historical research to determine the chronological sequence of application and the previous decorative styles of a historic building.

SCREEN PRINTING. A process, similar to stenciling, in which color is deposited on paper through a design cut into a fabric screen.

SERIES. A term for all the colorways of a particular pattern.

SIDEWALL. A term used to differentiate the wallpaper used on the wall from a border or dado paper; also called field or fill.

BIBLIOGRAPHY

This bibliography cites books and articles that will be useful for inquiry into the history and use of wallpapers as well as the history of interior decoration. Both Oman and Hamilton's *Wallpapers* and Lynn's *Wallpapers in America* include extensive bibliographies. *Wallpapers in Historic Preservation* contains an excellent list of 19th-century publications that discuss contemporary attitudes toward wallpaper. The first edition of *Wallpapers for Historic Buildings* contains photographs of many reproduction wallpapers that are not illustrated in this edition.

Ackerman, Phyllis. *Wallpaper: Its History, Design, and Use.* 2d ed. New York: Tudor Publishing Co., 1938.

Adams, Stephen. *The Arts and Crafts Movement.* London: Quintet Publishing, 1987.

Alswang, Hope, and Donald C. Pierce. *American Interiors: New England and the South: Period Rooms at the Brooklyn Museum.* Brooklyn, N.Y.: Brooklyn Museum, 1983.

Aslin, Elizabeth. *The Aesthetic Movement: Prelude to Art Nouveau.* New York: Frederick A. Praeger, 1969.

Ayers, James. *The Shell Book of the Home in Britain: Decoration, Design, and Construction of Vernacular Interiors, 1500–1850.* London: Faber and Faber, 1981.

Banham, Joanna, Sally Macdonald, and Julia Porter. *Victorian Interior Design.* New York: Crescent Books, 1991.

Barnes, Joanna. *A Decorative Art: 19th-Century Wallpapers in the Whitworth Art Gallery.* Manchester, England: The Whitworth Art Gallery, 1985.

Bulletin de la Société Industrielle de Mulhouse, Special issue, "Musée du Papier Peint," no. 793 (1984).

Clark, Fiona. *William Morris: Wallpapers and Chintzes.* London: Academy, 1973.

Clouzot, Henri, and Charles Follot. *Histoire du Papier Peint en France.* Paris: Editions D'Art Charles Moreau, 1935.

"Conservation of Historic Wallpaper," Special issue of the *Journal of the American Institute for Conservation of Historic and Artistic Works*, Spring 1981.

Cooke, Clarence. *The House Beautiful*. New York: Scribner, Armstrong, and Company, 1878.

Cooper-Hewitt Museum. *Wallpapers in the Collection of the Cooper-Hewitt Museum*. Washington, D.C.: Smithsonian Institution Press, 1981.

Cooper, Nicholas. *The Opulant Eye: Late Victorian and Edwardian Taste in Interior Design*. London: Architectural Press, 1976.

Cornforth, John. *English Interiors 1790–1848: The Quest for Comfort*. London: Barrie and Jenkins, 1978.

———. *The Inspiration of the Past: Country House Taste in the Twentieth Century*. New York: Viking, 1985.

———. *The Search for Style: Country Life and Architecture 1897–1935*. London: Andre Deutsch, 1988.

———. "Vitality and Variety: The Musée du Papier Peint at Rixheim, near Mulhouse, France," *Country Life*, April 9, 1987, pp. 138–42.

———. "The Vitality of Papier Peint," *Country Life*, July 11, 1985, pp. 103–6.

Davidson, Caroline. *Women's Worlds: The Art and Life of Mary Ellen Best 1809–1891*. New York: Crown Publishers, 1985.

Dornsife, Samuel A. "Wallpaper." In *The Encyclopaedia of Victoriana*, edited by Harriet Bridgeman and Elizabeth Drury. New York: Macmillan, 1975.

Downing, A. J. *The Architecture of Country Houses, with Remarks on Interiors, Furniture*. New York, 1850. Reprint. New York: Dover, 1969.

Dresser, Christopher. *Studies in Design*. London, 1876. Reprinted as *The Language of Ornament*. New York: Portland House, 1988.

Eastlake, Charles L. *Hints on Household Taste*. London, 1868. 4th ed., 1878. Reprint. New York: Dover, 1969.

Entwisle, Eric A. *The Book of Wallpaper*. London: Arthur Barker, 1954.

———. *French Scenic Wallpapers 1800–1860*. Leigh-on-Sea, England: F. Lewis, 1972.

———. *A Literary History of Wallpaper*. London: B. T. Batsford, 1960.

———. *Wallpapers of the Victorian Era*. Leigh-on-Sea, England: F. Lewis, 1964.

Forge, Suzanne. *Victorian Splendor: Australian Interior Decoration 1837–1901*. Melbourne: Oxford University Press, 1981.

Fowler, John, and John Cornforth. *English Decoration in the 18th Century*. Princeton, N.J.: Pyne Press, 1974.

257

Frangiamore, Catherine Lynn. *Wallpapers in Historic Preservation.* Washington, D.C.: National Park Service, U.S. Department of the Interior, 1977.

————. "Wallpaper: Technological Innovation and Changes in Design and Use." In *Technological Innovation and the Decorative Arts: Winterthur Conference Report 1973,* pp. 277–305. Charlottesville: University Press of Virginia, 1974.

————. "Wallpapers Used in Nineteenth Century America," *The Magazine Antiques,* December 1972, pp. 1042–51.

Garrett, Elisabeth Donaghy. *At Home: The American Family 1750–1870.* New York: Harry N. Abrams, 1990.

Gere, Charlotte. *Nineteenth-Century Interiors: The Art of the Interior.* New York: Harry N. Abrams, 1989.

Giouard, Mark. *Life in the English Country House: A Social and Architectural History.* New Haven: Yale University Press, 1978.

————. *Sweetness and Light: The "Queen Anne" Movement 1860–1900.* New Haven and London: Yale University Press, 1977.

————. *The Victorian Country House.* Rev. ed. New Haven and London: Yale University Press, 1979.

Gordon-Clark, Jane. *Paper Magic.* London: Frances Lincoln Limited, 1991.

Greysmith, Brenda. *Wallpaper.* New York: Macmillan, 1976.

Guibert, Mireille. *Papiers Peints, 1800–1875.* Paris: Société des Amis de la Bibliothèque Forney, 1980.

Halen, Wildar. "Christopher Dresser and the Aesthetic Interior," *The Magazine Antiques,* January 1991, pp. 256–67.

Hamilton, Jean. *An Introduction to Wallpaper.* London: Her Majesty's Stationary Office, 1983.

Hotchkiss, Horace. "Wallpaper Used in America, 1700–1850." In *The Concise Encyclopedia of American Antiques,* edited by Helen Comstock, vol. 2, pp. 488ff. New York: Hawthorne Books, 1958.

Hunter, George Leland. *Home Furnishing.* New York: John Lane Company, 1913.

In Pursuit of Beauty: Americans and the Aesthetic Movement. New York: The Metropolitan Museum of Art, 1986. See particularly Catherine Lynn, "Decorating Surfaces: Aesthetic Delight, Theoretical Dilemma" and "Surface Ornament: Wallpapers, Carpets, Textiles, and Embroidery."

Jackson-Stops, Gervase, and James Pipkin. *The English Country House: A Grand Tour.* Boston: Little, Brown, 1985.

Jacqué, Bernard, and Odile Nouvel-Kammerer. *Le Papier Peint Décor d'Illusion.* Schirmeck: Editions Jean-Pierre Gyss, 1986.

Jones, Chester. *Colefax & Fowler: The Best in English Decoration.* Boston: Little, Brown, 1989.

Jones, Owen. *The Grammar of Ornament.* 1856. Reprint. London: Bernard Quantritch, 1910.

Katzenbach, Lois, and William Katzenbach. *The Practical Book of American Wallpaper.* Philadelphia: J. B. Lippincott Company, 1951.

Kelly, Robert, ed. *Wallpaper Reproduction News.* Published four times a year. Lee, Mass.

Kaplan, Wendy. *"The Art That Is Life": The Arts and Crafts Movement in America, 1875–1920.* Boston: Museum of Fine Arts, 1987.

Lancaster, Clay, ed. *New York Interiors at the Turn of the Century.* New York: Dover, 1976.

Landsun, Susan. *Victorians at Home.* New York: Viking, 1981.

Leopold, Alison Kyle. *Victorian Splendor: Re-creating America's 19th Century Interiors.* New York: Stewart, Tabori, and Chang, 1986.

Loudon, J. C. *An Encyclopaedia of Cottage, Farm, and Villa Architecture and Furniture.* London: Longman, Brown, Green, and Longmans, 1833.

Lynn, Catherine. *Wallpaper in America from the Seventeenth Century to World War I.* New York: W. W. Norton & Co., 1980.

Mayhew, Edgar de N., and Minor Myers, Jr. *A Documentary History of American Interiors from the Colonial Era to 1915.* New York: Charles Scribner's Sons, 1980.

McClelland, Nancy V. *Historic Wall-Papers from Their Inception to the Introduction of Machinery.* Philadelphia and London: J. B. Lippincott, 1924.

———. *The Practical Book of Decorative Wall Treatments.* Philadelphia and London: J. B. Lippincott, 1926.

Murphy, Phyllis, comp. *The Decorated Wall: Eighty Years of Wallpaper in Australia, c. 1850–1930.* Elizabeth Bay: Historic Houses Trust of New South Wales, 1981.

Musée des Arts Décoratifs. *Trois Siècles de Papiers Peints.* Paris: Musée des Arts Décoratifs, 1967.

Naylor, Gillian, ed. *William Morris by Himself: Designs and Writings.* Boston: Little, Brown, and Company, 1988.

Nouvel, Odile. *Wallpapers of France 1800–1850.* New York: Rizzoli, 1981.

Nouvel-Kammerer, Odile, ed. *Papier Peints Panoramiques.* Paris: Flammarion, 1990.

Nylander, Richard C. "Elegant Late Nineteenth-Century Wallpapers," *The Magazine Antiques,* August 1982, pp. 284–87.

———. "English Wallpaper in New England," *Country Life,* April 26, 1979, pp. 1304–7.

———. "Wallpaper and the Historic House." Slide tape. Nashville, Tenn.: American Association for State and Local History, 1977.

———. "Wallpaper Before 1830," *Early American Life,* February 1980, pp. 40–43.

———. *Wallpapers for Historic Buildings: A Guide to Selecting Repro-duction Wallpapers.* 1st ed. Washington, D. C.: Preservation Press, 1983.

Nylander, Richard C., Elizabeth Redmond, and Penny J. Sander. *Wallpaper in New England.* Boston: Society for the Preservation of New England Antiquities, 1986.

Olligs, Heinrich, ed. *Tapeten: Ihre Geschichte bix zur Gegenvart.* 3 vols. Brunswick: Klinkhardt & Breimaun, 1970.

Oman, Charles C. *Catalogue of Wallpapers, Victoria and Albert Mu-seum.* London: 1929.

Oman, Charles C., and Jean Hamilton. *Wallpapers: An International History and Illustrated Survey from the Victoria and Albert Museum.* New York: Abrams, 1982.

Parry, Linda. *William Morris and The Arts and Crafts Movement: A De-sign Source Book.* New York: Portland House, 1989.

Peterson, Harold L. *Americans at Home.* New York: Scribner's, 1971. Reissued as *American Interiors: From Colonial Times to the Late Victorians.* New York: Scribner's, 1979.

Praz, Mario. *An Illustrated History of Furnishing from the Renaissance to the Twentieth Century.* New York: Braziller, 1964. Reissued as *An Illustrated History of Interior Decorating from Pompeii to Art Nou-veau.* New York: Thames on Hudson, 1982.

Reichlin, Ellie, Jean Caslin, and Dan Younger. *A Photographic Inti-macy: The Portraiture of Rooms, 1865–1900. Nineteenth-Century Photographs of Domestic Interiors from the Collections of the Society for the Preservation of New England Antiquities.* Boston: SPNEA and the Photographic Resource Center, 1984.

Sanborn, Kate. *Old Time Wall Papers.* Greenwich, Conn.: Literary Collector Press, 1905.

Saunders, Gil. *Ornate Wallpapers.* Exeter, England: Webb & Bower with the Victoria and Albert Museum, 1985.

Seale, William. *Recreating the Historic House Interior.* Nashville, Tenn.: American Association for State and Local History, 1979.

———. *The Tasteful Interlude: American Interiors Through the Cam-era's Eye, 1860–1917.* New York: Praeger, 1975. Nashville, Tenn.: American Association for State and Local History, 1981.

Stickley, Gustav. *Craftsman Homes.* New York: Craftsman Publishing Company, 1909.

Sugden, Alan V, and J. L. Edmondson. *A History of English Wallpaper, 1509–1914.* New York: Scribner's, 1925; London: B. T. Batsford, 1926.

Teynac, Françoise, Pierre Nolot, and Jean-Denis Vivian. *Wallpaper: A History.* New York: Rizzoli, 1982.

Thornton, Peter. *Authentic Decor. The Domestic Interior: 1620–1920.* New York: Viking Penguin, 1982.

Tunander, Ingemar. *Tapeter i Sverige.* Vasteras, Sweden: ICA Bokfor-log, 1984.

Watkins, Walter Kendell. "The Early Use and Manufacture of Paper-Hangings in Boston," *Old-Time New England,* January 1922, pp. 109–19.

Wells-Cole, Anthony. *Historic Paper Hangings from Temple Newsam Collection and from Other English Houses.* Leeds, England: Leeds City Art Galleries, 1983.

Wheeler, Candace. *Principles of Home Decoration.* New York: Double-day, Page, and Company, 1908.

Whitworth Art Gallery. *Historic Wallpapers in the Whitworth Art Gallery.* Manchester, England: Whitworth Art Gallery, 1972.

Winkler, Gail Caskey, and Roger W. Moss. *Victorian Interior Decoration: American Interiors 1830–1900.* New York: Henry Holt, 1987.

Woods, Christine, ed. *Sanderson, 1860–1985.* London: Arthur Sanderson & Sons, 1985.

SOURCES OF INFORMATION

AMERICAN SOCIETY OF INTERIOR DESIGNERS. 608 Massachusetts Avenue, N.E., Washington, D. C. 20002, (202) 546-3480

THE ANTIQUARIAN AND LANDMARKS SOCIETY, INC. 394 Main Street, Hartford, CT 06103, (203) 247-8996

COLONIAL WILLIAMSBURG FOUNDATION. P.O. Box C, Williamsburg, VA 23187, (804) 229-1000

COOPER-HEWITT MUSEUM. Smithsonian Institution, 2 East 91st Street, New York, NY 10028, (212) 860-6898

ESSEX INSTITUTE. 132 Essex Street, Salem, MA 01970, (508) 744-3390

HISTORIC CHARLESTON FOUNDATION. 51 Meeting Street, Charleston, SC 29401, (803) 723-1623

HISTORIC DEERFIELD. Deerfield, MA 01342, (413) 774-5581

HISTORIC SAVANNAH FOUNDATION. P.O. Box 1733, Savannah, GA 31402, (912) 233-7787

METROPOLITAN MUSEUM OF ART. 82nd Street and Fifth Avenue, New York, NY 10028, (212) 879-5500

MUSEE DES ARTS DECORATIFS. Palais du Louvre, Pavillon de Marsan, 107 rue de Rivoli, 75001 Paris, France

MUSEE DU PAPIER PEINT. 28 rue Zuber, 68170 Rixheim, France

MUSEUM OF ART, RHODE ISLAND SCHOOL OF DESIGN. 2 College Street, Providence, RI 02903, (401) 331-3511

MUSEUM OF EARLY SOUTHERN DECORATIVE ARTS. P.O. Box 10310, Winston-Salem, NC 27108, (919) 721-7360

NATIONAL PRESERVATION INSTITUTE. National Building Museum, Judiciary Square, N.W., Washington, DC 20001, (202) 272-3606

OLD STURBRIDGE VILLAGE. One Old Sturbridge Road, Sturbridge, MA 01566, (508) 347-3362

SOCIETY FOR THE PRESERVATION OF NEW ENGLAND ANTIQUITIES. 141 Cambridge Street, Boston, MA 02114, (617) 227-3956

STRAWBERY BANKE MUSEUM. P.O. Box 300, Portsmouth, NH 03802, (603) 433-1100

VICTORIA AND ALBERT MUSEUM. Exhibition and Cromwell Roads, London, England SW7 2RL

THE VICTORIAN SOCIETY IN AMERICA. 219 East Sixth Street, Philadelphia, PA 19106, (215) 627-4252

WHITWORTH ART GALLERY. Oxford Road, Manchester, England M15 6ER

WILLIAM MORRIS SOCIETY. 420 Riverside Drive, 7D, New York, NY 10025

WINTERTHUR MUSEUM AND GARDENS. Route 52, Kennett Pike, Winterthur, DE 19735, (302) 888-4600

AUTHOR

Richard C. Nylander is curator of collections for the Society for the Preservation of New England Antiquities in Boston, Massachusetts. Coauthor of *Wallpaper in New England*, he lectures extensively and has published numerous articles on historic wallpapers and period interiors in both popular and scholarly journals. He has served as a consultant for many historic house restorations and is a member of the Committee for the Preservation of the White House.